MTEL
47
Middle School
Mathematics
Teacher Certification Exam

By: Sharon Wynne, M.S.
Southern Connecticut State University

"And, while there's no reason yet to panic, I think it's only prudent that we make preparations to panic."

XAMonline, INC.
Boston

To obtain permission(s) to use the material from this work for any purpose including workshops or seminars, please submit a written request to:

XAMonline, Inc.
21 Orient Ave.
Melrose, MA 02176
Toll Free 1-800-509-4128
Email: info@xamonline.com
Web www.xamonline.com
Fax: 1-781-662-9268

Library of Congress Cataloging-in-Publication Data

Wynne, Sharon A.
    Middle School Mathematics 47: Teacher Certification / Sharon A. Wynne. -2nd ed.
    ISBN 978-1-58197-889-6
    1. Middle School Mathematics 47.   2. Study Guides.   3. MTEL
    4. Teachers' Certification & Licensure.   5. Careers

Disclaimer:
The opinions expressed in this publication are the sole works of XAMonline and were created independently from the National Education Association, Educational Testing Service, or any State Department of Education, National Evaluation Systems or other testing affiliates.

Between the time of publication and printing, state specific standards as well as testing formats and website information may change that is not included in part or in whole within this product. Sample test questions are developed by XAMonline and reflect similar content as on real tests; however, they are not former tests. XAMonline assembles content that aligns with state standards but makes no claims nor guarantees teacher candidates a passing score. Numerical scores are determined by testing companies such as NES or ETS and then are compared with individual state standards. A passing score varies from state to state.

Printed in the United States of America   œ-1

MTEL: Middle School Mathematics 47
ISBN: 978-1-58197-889-6

About the Subject Assessments

MTEL™: Subject Assessment in the Middle School Mathematics examination

Purpose: The assessments are designed to test the knowledge and competencies of prospective secondary level teachers. The question bank from which the assessment is drawn is undergoing constant revision. As a result, your test may include questions that will not count towards your score.

Test Version: There are two versions of subject assessment for Mathematics tests in Massachusetts. Mathematics (09) emphasizes comprehension in Number Sense and Operations; Patterns, Relations, and Algebra; Geometry and Measurement; Data Analysis, Statistics, and Probability; Trigonometry, Calculus, and Discrete Mathematics; Integration of Knowledge and Understanding. Middle School Mathematics (047) emphasizes comprehension in Number Sense and Operations; Patterns, Relations, and Algebra; Geometry and Measurement; Data Analysis, Statistics, and Probability; Trigonometry, Calculus, and Discrete Mathematics; Integration of Knowledge and Understanding. The Mathematics examination guide is based on a typical knowledge level of persons who have completed a *bachelor's degree program* in Mathematics.

Time Allowance, Scoring, and Format: You will have 4 hours to finish Middle School Mathematics (0047). There are approximately 100 multiple-choice ―3 HRS questions and 2 constructed-response questions on the exam. For each ― 1 HR constructed-response question you will have 30 minutes to respond. Multiple-choice questions count towards 80% of your total score; constructed-response questions count towards the remaining 20% of your score.

Weighting: In the Middle School Mathematics (047) exam there are approximately 18-20 multiple-choice questions in Number Sense and Operations; 30-32 multiple-choice questions in Patterns, Relations, and Algebra making 5 multiple-choice questions in Geometry making 10% of the total content in the exam; 21-23 multiple-choice questions in Geometry and Measurement; 14-16 multiple-choice questions in Data Analysis, Statistics, and Probability; 12-14 multiple-choice questions in Trigonometry, Calculus, and Discrete Mathematics; 2 constructed-response questions in Integration of Knowledge and Understanding.

Additional Information about the MTEL Assessments: The MTEL series subject assessments are developed *National Evaluation Systems.* They provide additional information on the MTEL series assessments, including registration, preparation and testing procedures, study materials such as topical guides that have about 26 pages of information including approximately 11 additional sample questions.

<u>TABLE OF CONTENTS</u>   PG

Great Study and Testing Tips!

What to study in order to prepare for the subject assessments is the focus of this study guide but equally important is *how* you study.

You can increase your chances of truly mastering the information by taking some simple, but effective steps.

Study Tips:

1. <u>**Some foods aid the learning process.**</u> Foods such as milk, nuts, seeds, rice, and oats help your study efforts by releasing natural memory enhancers called CCKs (*cholecystokinin*) composed of *tryptopha*n, *choline*, and *phenylalanine*. All of these chemicals enhance the neurotransmitters associated with memory. Before studying, try a light, protein-rich meal of eggs, turkey, and fish. All of these foods release the memory enhancing chemicals. The better the connections, the more you comprehend.

Likewise, before you take a test, stick to a light snack of energy boosting and relaxing foods. A glass of milk, a piece of fruit, or some peanuts all release various memory-boosting chemicals and help you to relax and focus on the subject at hand.

2. <u>**Learn to take great notes.**</u> A by-product of our modern culture is that we have grown accustomed to getting our information in short doses (i.e. TV news sound bites or USA Today style newspaper articles.)

Consequently, we've subconsciously trained ourselves to assimilate information better in <u>neat little packages</u>. If your notes are scrawled all over the paper, it fragments the flow of the information. Strive for clarity. Newspapers use a standard format to achieve clarity. Your notes can be much clearer through use of proper formatting. A very effective format is called the *"Cornell Method."*

> Take a sheet of loose-leaf lined notebook paper and draw a line all the way down the paper about 1-2" from the left-hand edge.
>
> Draw another line across the width of the paper about 1-2" up from the bottom. Repeat this process on the reverse side of the page.

Look at the highly effective result. You have ample room for notes, a left hand margin for special emphasis items or inserting supplementary data from the textbook, a large area at the bottom for a brief summary, and a little rectangular space for just about anything you want.

3. <u>Get the concept then the details</u>. Too often we focus on the details and don't gather an understanding of the concept. However, if you simply memorize only dates, places, or names, you may well miss the whole point of the subject.

A key way to understand things is to put them in your own words. If you are working from a textbook, automatically summarize each paragraph in your mind. If you are outlining text, don't simply copy the author's words.

Rephrase them in your own words. You remember your own thoughts and words much better than someone else's, and subconsciously tend to associate the important details to the core concepts.

4. <u>Ask Why?</u> Pull apart written material paragraph by paragraph and don't forget the captions under the illustrations.

Example: If the heading is "Stream Erosion", flip it around to read "Why do streams erode?" Then answer the questions.

If you train your mind to think in a series of questions and answers, not only will you learn more, but it also helps to lessen the test anxiety because you are used to answering questions.

5. <u>Read for reinforcement and future needs</u>. Even if you only have 10 minutes, put your notes or a book in your hand. Your mind is similar to a computer; you have to input data in order to have it processed. *By reading, you are creating the neural connections for future retrieval.* The more times you read something, the more you reinforce the learning of ideas.

Even if you don't fully understand something on the first pass, *your mind stores much of the material for later recall.*

6. <u>Relax to learn so go into exile</u>. Our bodies respond to an inner clock called biorhythms. Burning the midnight oil works well for some people, but not everyone.

If possible, set aside a particular place to study that is free of distractions. Shut off the television, cell phone, pager and exile your friends and family during your study period.

If you really are bothered by silence, try background music. Light classical music at a low volume has been shown to aid in concentration over other types. Music that evokes pleasant emotions without lyrics are highly suggested. Try just about anything by Mozart. It relaxes you.

7. <u>**Use arrows not highlighters.**</u> At best, it's difficult to read a page full of yellow, pink, blue, and green streaks. Try staring at a neon sign for a while and you'll soon see that the horde of colors obscure the message.

A quick note, a brief dash of color, an underline, and an arrow pointing to a particular passage is much clearer than a horde of highlighted words.

8. <u>**Budget your study time.**</u> Although you shouldn't ignore any of the material, *allocate your available study time in the same ratio that topics may appear on the test.*

Testing Tips:

1. Get smart, play dumb. Don't read anything into the question. Don't make an assumption that the test writer is looking for something else than what is asked. Stick to the question as written and don't read extra things into it.

2. Read the question and all the choices _twice_ before answering the question. You may miss something by not carefully reading, and then re-reading both the question and the answers.

If you really don't have a clue as to the right answer, leave it blank on the first time through. Go on to the other questions, as they may provide a clue as to how to answer the skipped questions.

If later on, you still can't answer the skipped ones . . . **_Guess._** The only penalty for guessing is that you _might_ get it wrong. Only one thing is certain; if you don't put anything down, you will get it wrong!

3. Turn the question into a statement. Look at the way the questions are worded. The syntax of the question usually provides a clue. Does it seem more familiar as a statement rather than as a question? Does it sound strange?

By turning a question into a statement, you may be able to spot if an answer sounds right, and it may also trigger memories of material you have read.

4. Look for hidden clues. It's actually very difficult to compose multiple-foil (choice) questions without giving away part of the answer in the options presented.

In most multiple-choice questions you can often readily eliminate one or two of the potential answers. This leaves you with only two real possibilities and automatically your odds go to Fifty-Fifty for very little work.

5. Trust your instincts. For every fact that you have read, you subconsciously retain something of that knowledge. On questions that you aren't really certain about, go with your basic instincts. **Your first impression on how to answer a question is usually correct.**

6. Mark your answers directly on the test booklet. Don't bother trying to fill in the optical scan sheet on the first pass through the test.

Just be very careful not to miss-mark your answers when you eventually transcribe them to the scan sheet.

7. Watch the clock! You have a set amount of time to answer the questions. Don't get bogged down trying to answer a single question at the expense of 10 questions you can more readily answer.

THIS PAGE BLANK

SUBAREA I.   NUMBER SENSE AND OPERATIONS

Competency 0001 Understand the structure of numeration systems and multiple representations of numbers.

1A.   Place Value and Face Value

In a number, every digit has a face value and a place value. For example, in 3467, the digits used are 3, 4, 6 and 7. The face values are respectively 3, 4, 6 and 7. The place value of a digit depends on its position in the number.

Whole Number Place Values are where the digits fall to the left of the decimal point. Consider the number 792. Reading from left to right, the first digit (7) represents the hundreds' place. Thus, there are 7 sets of one hundred in the number 792. The second digit (9) represents the tens' place. The last digit (2) represents the ones' place.

Decimal Place Value is where the digits fall to the right of the decimal point. Consider the number 4.873. Reading from left to right, the first digit, 4, is in the ones' place and tells us the number contains 4 ones. After the decimal, (8) is in the tenths' place and tells us the number contains 8 tenths. (7) is in the hundredths' place and tells us the number contains 7 hundredths. The fourth digit (3) is in the thousandths' place and tells us the number contains 3 sets of one thousandth. Each digit to the left of the decimal point increases progressively in powers of ten. Each digit to the right of the decimal point decreases progressively in powers of ten.

Example: 12345.6789 occupies the following powers of ten positions:

10^4	10^3	10^2	10^1	10^0	0	10^{-1}	10^{-2}	10^{-3}	10^{-4}
1	2	3	4	5	.	6	7	8	9

The usual way of writing a number is known as the **standard form**. The **expanded form** is an alternative method of writing a number. To write a number in expanded form, each digit is multiplied by the power of ten that represents its place value.

Example: Write 73169.00537 in expanded form.

We start by listing all the powers of ten positions.

$$10^4 \quad 10^3 \quad 10^2 \quad 10^1 \quad 10^0 \quad .10^{-1} \quad 10^{-2} \quad 10^{-3} \quad 10^{-4} \quad 10^{-5}$$

Multiply each digit by its power of ten. Add all the results.

Thus $73169.00537 = (7 \times 10^4) + (3 \times 10^3) + (1 \times 10^2) + (6 \times 10^1)$

$$+ (9 \times 10^0) + (0 \times 10^{-1}) + (0 \times 10^{-2}) + (5 \times 10^{-3}) + (3 \times 10^{-4}) + (7 \times 10^{-5})$$

1B. Number bases (e.g. base 2, base 10)

The standard form of writing numbers is the decimal or base 10 system where the digits represent powers of 10. Other bases may also be used to represent a number. The base 2 or binary system, for instance, uses the powers of 2 (2^0, 2^1, 2^2... etc.) to represent a number. Base 2 only uses the digits 0 and 1.

Decimal Binary Conversion		
Decimal	Binary	Place Value
1	1	2^0
2	10	2^1
4	100	2^2
8	1000	2^3

Thus 9 in Base 10 becomes 1001 in Base 2. 9+4 = 13 (Base 10) becomes 1001 + 100 = 1101 (Base 2). Fractions, ratios and other functions alter in the same way.

Number Systems and Bases

Base	Number System
2	Binary
3	Ternary
4	Quarternary
5	Quinary
6	Senary
8	Octal
16	Hexadecimal

Computers use a base of 2 but combine it into 4 units called a byte to function in base 16 (hexadecimal). Older computers also used a base of 8 (octal).

1C. Order relations

Orders are a type of binary relations defined on a set. If K is a set where $\le$ is a relation on K, then $\le$ is a partial order if it is either reflexive, antisymmetrical or transitive, in that for every a, b and c within set K, it follows that:

$a \le a$ (reflexive)

if $a \le b$ and $b \le a$ then $a = b$ (antisymmetrical)

if $a \le b$ and $b \le c$ then $a \le c$ (transitive)

(Note: Here the symbol $\le$ stands not only for "less than or equal to" but also for other relations that satisfy the above three conditions.)

There are many known relations on all real numbers, including natural numbers, integer numbers and rational numbers that are orders in the way defined above. Examples of partial orders are the relation of divisibility applied to the set of natural numbers or the relation of inclusion applied to the set of subsets of a given set.

Orders also have the property of being total, if for every a, b and c within set K, it follows that:

$a \le b$ or $b \le a$ (totality)

Total orders can also be called chains or linear orders. "Less than or equal to" is a total order. The equal sign $=$, is the only relation that is both a partial order and an equivalence relation.

1D. Relationships between operations (e.g. multiplication as repeated additions)

Multiplication is simply repeated addition.

Examples:

$3 \times 4 = 4 + 4 + 4 = 12$

$4 \times 3 = 3 + 3 + 3 + 3$

This relationship also explains the concept of variable addition. We can show that the expression $4x + 3x = 7x$ is true by rewriting 4 times x and 3 times x as repeated addition, yielding the expression $(x + x + x + x) + (x + x + x)$. Thus, because of the relationship between multiplication and addition, variable addition is accomplished by coefficient addition.

Addition and subtraction are really the same operation acting in opposite directions on the number line. Division is the opposite of multiplication just as subtraction and addition are opposite operations.

Some algebraic expressions showing the relationships between operations are:

$$a^2 - b^2 = (a+b)(a-b)$$
$$(a+b)^2 = a^2 + 2ab + b^2$$
$$(a+b)(a-b) = a^2 - ab + ba - b^2 = a^2 - b^2$$

1E.   Number factors and divisibility

GCF is the abbreviation for the **Greatest Common Factor**. The GCF is the largest number that is a factor of all the numbers given in a problem. The GCF can be no larger than the smallest number given in the problem. If no other number is a common factor, then the GCF will be the number 1. To find the GCF, list all possible factors of the smallest number given (include the number itself). Starting with the largest factor (which is the number itself), determine if it is also a factor of all the other given numbers. If so, that is the GCF. If that factor does not work, try the same method on the next smaller factor. Continue until a common factor is found. That is the GCF. (Note: There can be other common factors besides the GCF.)

Example: Find the GCF of 12, 20, and 36.

The smallest number in the problem is 12. The factors of 12 are 1, 2, 3, 4, 6 and 12. 12 is the largest factor, but it does not divide evenly into 20. Neither does 6, but 4 will divide into both 20 and 36 evenly. Therefore, 4 is the GCF.

Example: Find the GCF of 14 and 15.

Factors of 14 are 1, 2, 7 and 14. 14 is the largest factor, but it does not divide evenly into 15. Neither does 7 nor 2. Therefore, the only factor common to both 14 and 15 is the number 1, the GCF.

LCM is the abbreviation for **Least Common Multiple**. The least common multiple of a group of numbers is the smallest number that all of the given numbers will divide into. The least common multiple will always be the largest of the given numbers or a multiple of the largest number.

Example: Find the LCM of 20, 30 and 40.

The largest number given is 40, but 30 will not divide evenly into 40. The next multiple of 40 is 80 (2 x 40), but 30 will not divide evenly into 80 either. The next multiple of 40 is 120. 120 is divisible by both 20 and 30, so 120 is the LCM (least common multiple).

Example: Find the LCM of 96, 16 and 24.

The largest number is 96. 96 is divisible by both 16 and 24, so 96 is the LCM.

Divisibility Tests

a) A number is divisible by 3 if the sum of its digits is evenly divisible by 3.
    The sum of the digits of 964 is 9+6+4 = 19. Since 19 is not divisible by 3, neither is 964. The sum of the digits of 86,514 is 8+6+5+1+4 = 24. Since 24 is divisible by 3, 86,514 is also divisible by 3.

b) A number is divisible by 4 if the number in its last 2 digits is evenly divisible by 4.
    The number 113,336 ends with the number 36 in the last 2 columns. Since 36 is divisible by 4, then 113,336 is also divisible by 4. The number 135,627 ends with the number 27 in the last 2 columns. Since 27 is not evenly divisible by 4, then 135,627 is also not divisible by 4.

c) A number is divisible by 6 if the number is even and the sum of its digits is evenly divisible by 3 or 6.
    4,950 is an even number and its digits add to 18. (4+9+5+0 = 18). Since the number is even and the sum of its digits is 18 (which is divisible by 3 and/or 6), 4950 is divisible by 6. 326 is an even number, but its digits add up to 11. Since 11 is not divisible by 3 or 6, then 326 is not divisible by 6.

d) A number is divisible by 8 if the number in its last 3 digits is evenly divisible by 8. The number 113,336 ends with the 3-digit number 336 in the last 3 columns. Since 336 is divisible by 8, then 113,336 is also divisible by 8. The number 465,627 ends with the number 627 in the last 3 columns. Since 627 is not evenly divisible by 8, then 465,627 is not divisible by 8.

e) A number is divisible by 9 if the sum of its digits is evenly divisible by 9.
The sum of the digits of 874 is 8+7+4 = 19. Since 19 is not divisible by 9, neither is 874. The sum of the digits of 116,514 is 1+1+6+5+1+4 = 18. Since 18 is divisible by 9, 116,514 is also divisible by 9.

1F. Prime and composite numbers

In number theory, the fundamental theorem of arithmetic states that every natural number either is itself a prime number, or can be written as a unique product of prime numbers. Factors are whole numbers that can be multiplied together to get another whole number. Prime numbers are whole numbers greater than 1 that have only 2 factors, 1 and the number itself. When factoring into prime factors, all the factors must be numbers that cannot be factored again (without using 1). Examples of prime numbers are 2, 3, 5, 7, 11, 13, 17, and 19. Note that 2 is the only even prime number. The number 1 is neither prime nor composite.
Composite numbers are whole numbers that have factors other than 1 and the number itself. For example, 9 is composite because 3 is a factor in addition to 1 and 9. 70 is also composite because, besides the factors of 1 and 70, the numbers 2, 5, 7, 10, 14, and 35 are also all factors.

Prime factorization

Through prime factorization, composite numbers are factored repeatedly until only prime numbers remain. First, factor the composite number into any 2 factors. Check each resulting factor to see if it can be factored again. Continue factoring until all remaining factors are prime. This is the list of prime factors. Regardless of the initial 2 factors, the final list of prime factors will always be the same.

<u>Example:</u> Factor 30 into prime factors.

One possible strategy is to divide by 2 as many times as you can, then by 3, then by other successive primes as required.

Factor 30 into any 2 factors.

5 · 6	Now factor the 6.
5 · 2 · 3	These are all prime factors.

Alternatively, factor 30 into two other factors.

3 · 10	Now factor the 10.
3 · 2 · 5	These are the same prime factors even though the original factors were different.

<u>Example:</u> Factor 240 into prime factors.

Factor 240 into any 2 factors.

24 · 10	Now factor both 24 and 10.
4 · 6 · 2 · 5	Now factor both 4 and 6.
2 · 2 · 2 · 3 · 2 · 5	These are prime factors.

This can also be written as $2^4 \cdot 3 \cdot 5$

1G. Multiple representations of numbers (e.g. physical models, diagrams, numerals)

Visual representations of numbers sometimes make it easier for students to grasp new concepts.
The following visual makes it easy to see why 3/4 is less than 5/6:

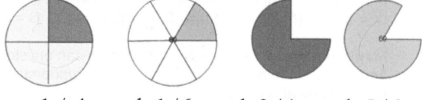

1 / 4 a n d 1 / 6 a n d 3 / 4 a n d 5 / 6

Number Lines are a common way to represent positive and negative numbers:

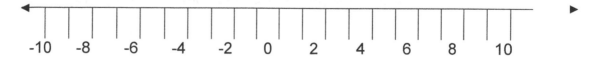

Diagrams can also be used to represent numbers and concepts:

4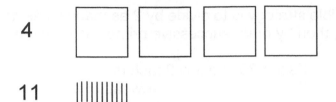

11 |||||||||||

3*3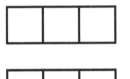

You can also show the geometric foundation of algebra by using Algebra tiles:

▫ a 1 unit by 1 unit square

x unit by x unit square   a 1 unit by x unit rectangle

Finally, numbers can be represented as Roman numerals:
I=1   II = 2   III = 3   IV = 4   V = 5   VI = 6   VII = 7, VIII = 8
IX = 9, X = 10, XI = 11, XII = 12, L =50, C = 100, D = 500, M = 1000

Manipulatives are materials that students can physically handle and move. Manipulatives allow students to understand mathematic concepts by allowing them to see concrete examples of abstract processes. Manipulatives are attractive to students because they appeal to the students' visual and tactile senses. Available for all levels of math, manipulatives are useful tools for reinforcing operations and concepts. They are not, however, a substitute for the development of sound computational skills.

<u>Example</u>: Using 12 tiles, build rectangles of equal area but different perimeters.

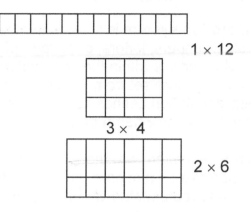

1×12

3×4

2×6

The shaded region below represents 46 out of 100 or 0.46 or $\frac{46}{100}$ or 46%.

Fraction Strips:

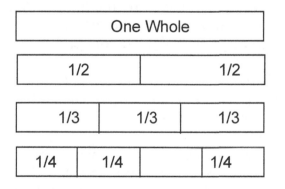

1H. **Properties of early numerations systems (e.g. Mayan, Mesopotamian, Egyptian).**

A **numeration system** is a set of numbers represented by a set of symbols (numbers, letters, or pictographs). Sets can have different bases of numerals within the set. Instead of our base 10, a system may use any base set from 2 on up. The position of the number in that representation defines its exact value. Thus, the numeral 1 has a value of ten when represented as "10."

The *Mesopotamians* are thought to have originated math as they developed tokens that date back to 8000 B.C. They were simply shaped and represented various agricultural items. As cities evolved and grew more complex, tokens began to become more complex as well. They developed tokens that are more complex and two ways of storing them: by punching a hole in complex tokens and stringing them and marking them with a cylinder that had the impression or seal to identify the persons involved in the transaction. The type and number of tokens could not be altered without breaking this seal. The other method was used for the more simple tokens and involved sealing them in a clay envelope. To get around the problem of identifying what was inside, the envelopes were impressed on the outside before the tokens were sealed inside. Finally, there was a merging of these two systems: simple tokens were impressed to make marks on a clay tablet, then the tokens destroyed and the tablets were kept. Eventually, this new method was also used for the more complex tokens but the images did not transfer well onto clay tablets, so an image of the token was actually drawn onto the clay tablet. This system was in place around 3000 B.C. and made it easier to store and use. This was the beginning of a type of numbering system.

The *Babylonians* used position in relation to other numerals or column position for this purpose since they lacked a zero to represent an empty position. They developed problem-text tablets and table-text tablets. The table text tablets were simple in structure and easy to understand even if you had no understanding of the symbols. They used a positional system with a base of 60. They could represent any number using only two symbols, ⊤ and ⟨. The ⊤ represented the number 1; so the number 3 would be ⊤ ⊤ ⊤ until you got to the number 10, which was represented by the symbol ⟨. They would keep putting together these 2 symbols until they reached 60 at which point they would move over a column and start over with the symbol for 1, ⊤.

The *Mayan* number system goes back to the 4th century and used a combination of 3 symbols: the dot (.) for numbers 1-4 and the line (_____) for the number 5. The Mayans were the only ancient civilization to understand the concept of zero, which enabled them to write very large numbers. There numbering system was based on the number 20, not 10 like ours.

The number zero was represented by 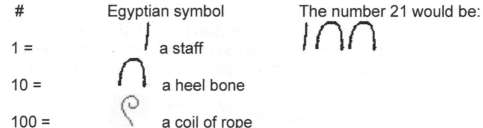 .and in the Maya system, the number 20 was represented by a one and a zero:

The number 6 would be written: ‗. and the number 3: ...
The number 8 would be ‗... and 10 would be = or 2 lines.

The *Egyptians* used hieroglyphics to write numbers and used a base 10 like those that we do:

#	Egyptian symbol	
1 =	❘ a staff	The number 21 would be:
10 =	⌒ a heel bone	
100 =	ℓ a coil of rope	

They were probably the most advance of the ancient civilizations, practicing medicine and applied mathematics. They were able to represent fractions, knew how to make right-angled triangles and had some idea of square roots.

Competency 0002 Understand principles and operations related to integers, fractions, decimals, percents, ratios, and proportions.

2A.   Order of Operations

The Order of Operations are to be followed when evaluating algebraic expressions. Remember the mnemonic **PEMDAS** (Please Excuse My Dear Aunt Sally) to follow these steps in order:

1. Simplify inside grouping characters such as parentheses, brackets, radicals, fraction bars, etc.
2. Multiply out expressions with exponents.
3. Do multiplication or division from left to right.

Note: Multiplication and division are equivalent even though multiplication is mentioned before division in the mnemonic PEMDAS.

4. Do addition or subtraction from left to right
Note: Addition and subtraction are equivalent even though addition is mentioned before subtraction in the mnemonic PEMDAS.

Example: Evaluate $\dfrac{12(9-7)+4\times5}{3^4+2^3}$

$$\dfrac{12(9-7)+4\times5}{3^4+2^3}$$

$$=\dfrac{12(2)+4\times5}{3^4+2^3} \quad \text{Simplify within parenthesis}$$

$$=\dfrac{12(2)+4\times5}{81+8} \quad \text{Multiply out exponent expressions}$$

$$=\dfrac{24+20}{81+8} \quad \text{Do multiplication and division}$$

$$=\dfrac{44}{89} \quad \text{Do addition and subtraction}$$

Example: Evaluate $13(-10)^2+45\div(-5)$

$$13(-10)^2+45\div(-5)$$
$$=13(100)+45\div(-5)$$
$$=1300-9$$
$$=1291$$

Example: Evaluate $\dfrac{(-5)^2 - 4 \times 5}{3^2 + 4 \times 2(-1)^5}$

$$\frac{(-5)^2 - 4 \times 5}{3^2 + 4 \times 2(-1)^5}$$

$$= \frac{25 - 4 \times 5}{9 - 4 \times 2}$$

$$= \frac{25 - 20}{9 - 8}$$

$$= 5$$

2B.   Identity and Inverse Elements

Identity: The number is unchanged by the operation.

Additive Identity
For addition, "the identity" is zero, because adding zero to a number does not change the number. The sum of any number and zero is that number.
$a + 0 = a$
Example: $17 + 0 = 17$

Multiplicative Identity
For multiplication, "the identity" is one, because multiplying by one does not change anything. The product of any number and one is that number.
$a \cdot 1 = a$
Example: $-34 \times 1 = -34$

Inverse: The operation results in 0 or 1.

Additive Inverse
The additive inverse is the same number, but with the opposite sign. $(-a)$ is the additive inverse of a therefore, $a + (-a) = 0$
Example: $25 + -25 = 0$

Multiplicative Inverse
The multiplicative inverse of a number is the reciprocal of the number. $(1/a)$ is the multiplicative inverse of a.
$a \cdot (1/a) = 1$
Example: $5 \times \dfrac{1}{5} = 1$

2C. Associative, commutative and distributive properties

Properties are rules that apply for addition, subtraction, multiplication, or division of real numbers.

Commutative Property
The order of the terms or factors can be changed without changing the result.

Commutative Property of Addition: $a + b = b + a$
Example: $5 + (-8) = -8 + 5 = -3$

Commutative Property of Multiplication: $ab = ba$
Example: $-2 \times 6 = 6 \times (-2) = -12$

The commutative property does not apply to subtraction or division because changing the order of the terms changes the result $(4 - 3 \neq 3 - 4)$.

Associative Property
Terms can be regrouped without changing the result.

Associative Property of Addition: $a + (b + c) = (a + b) + c$
Example: $(-2 + 7) + 5 = -2 + (7 + 5)$
$5 + 5 = -2 + 12 = 10$

Associative Property of Multiplication: $a(bc) = (ab)c$
Example: $(3 \times -7) \times 5 = 3 \times (-7 \times 5)$
$-21 \times 5 = 3 \times -35 = -105$

This rule does not apply for division and subtraction.

Distributive Property
The terms within parentheses can be multiplied by another term individually without first performing operations within the parentheses. This is useful when terms within the parentheses cannot be combined.

Multiplication distributes over addition:
$a (b + c) = ab + ac$

Example:
$6 \times (-4 + 9) = (6 \times -4) + (6 \times 9) = -24 + 54 = 30$

Example:
$$10(2x - y) = 20x - 10y$$

The Property of Equality
You also know (if you have done any equation solving) that you can do anything you want to an equation, as long as you do the same thing to both sides. This is the "property of equality."

Zero Product Property
The basic fact that you need for solving many equations, especially quadratics, is that, if $x \times y = 0$, then either $x = 0$ or else $y = 0$. This is the "zero-product property."

2D. Absolute value

The absolute value of a real number is the positive value of that number. It represents the distance (positive distance) between the number and zero as shown on a number line. Because distances are always positive, the absolute value will also always be the positive

$\qquad |x| = x$ when $x \geq 0$ and

$\qquad |x| = -x$ when $x < 0$

Examples:
$$|7| = 7; \quad |-13| = 13$$

See Competency 0006 for absolute value equations and **Competency 0010** for absolute value functions.

2E. Operations with signed numbers

Addition and subtraction with signed numbers

When adding and subtracting numbers with the same sign, the result will also have the same sign. When adding numbers that have different signs, subtract the smaller number from the larger number (ignoring the sign) and then use the sign of larger number. When subtracting a negative number, change the sign of the number to a positive sign and then add it (i.e. replace the two negative signs by a positive sign).

<u>Examples:</u>

$$(3)+(4)=7$$
$$(-8)+(-4)=-12$$
$$(6)-(5)=1$$
$$(3)-(6)=-3$$
$$(-4)-(2)=-6$$
$$(-6)-(-10)=4$$

Multiplication and division of signed numbers

When we multiply two numbers with the same sign, the result is positive. If the two numbers have different signs, the result is negative. The same rule follows for division.

<u>Examples:</u>

$$(5)(5)=25$$
$$(5)(-6)=-30$$
$$(-19)(-2)=38$$
$$16 \div 4 = 4$$
$$(-34) \div 2 = -17$$
$$(-18) \div (-2) = 9$$
$$27 \div (-3) = -9$$

2F.   Multiple representations of number operations (e.g. area models for multiplication)

Number operations may be represented in different ways to make it easier for students to understand them. Multiplication of two numbers, for instance, may be represented as the area of a rectangle with length and breadth equal to the two numbers.

<u>Example</u>: Evaluate 12 x 11 – 7 x 4.

This expression may be represented as the difference in the areas of two rectangles shown below.

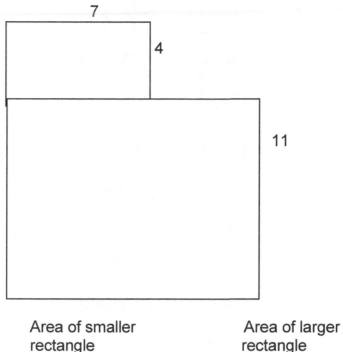

Area of smaller   Area of larger
rectangle   rectangle
    = (7)(4)   = (12)(11)
    = 28 units^2 = 132 units^2

The change in area is 132 – 28 = 104 units^2.

2G.   **Analyzing standard algorithms for addition, subtraction, multiplication and division of integers and rational numbers**

An algorithm is simply a systematic operation used to find an answer.

Standard Addition algorithm

We took for granted a basic property of integers when learning to add as children: adding any 3 single-digit numbers yields a sum that is at most 2 digits long: 9 + 9 + 9 = 27. There are 2 main procedures used in addition: adding single digits and "carrying." We can look at the carrying algorithm visually in 3 different ways.

Example: Find the sum of 258 +121 using Place Value

100	10	1
2	5	8
1	2	1
3	7	9

Standard Algorithm for Addition check:

```
  2 5 8
+ 1 2 1
  3 7 9
```

Example: Find the sum of 346+225 using Place Value

100	10	1
3	4	6
2	2	5
5	6	11
5	7	1

Standard Algorithm for Addition check:

```
  3 ¹4 6
+ 2 2 5
  5 7 1
```

Standard Subtraction algorithm
Example: Find the difference 356 – 145 using Place Value

100	10	1
3	5	6
1	4	5
2	1	1

Standard Algorithm for Subtraction check:

```
  3 5 6
- 1 4 5
  2 1 1
```

<u>Example</u>: Find the difference 234 – 46 using Place Value

100	10	1
2̷1̷	3̷ 13	4
	4	6

100	10	1
1	1̷1̷ 1̷2̷ 12	14
	4	6
1	**8**	**8**

Standard Algorithm for Subtraction check:

```
  2 3 4
−   4 6
  1 8 8
```

Multiplication algorithms

Multiplication algorithms involve multiplication facts, a complete understanding of place value and an understanding of the concept of distributivity. Multiply ones, tens, hundreds, etc. and perform the final sum using a horizontal format. Standard algorithms involve the easiest problems like the product of 2 and 8. We will not review the Lattice Method here. Intermediate algorithms are complicated:

<u>Example</u>: Find the product of 13 and 23.

```
      1 3
    x 2 3
        9
      3 0
      6 0
   +2 0 0
    2 9 9
```

Division Algorithms
Division algorithms are the most complicated of all algorithms and can be done using the Standard Algorithm or Intermediate Algorithm.

Example:
Solve 4209 divided by 6 using the Standard Algorithm

```
        701
   6 ) 4209          4209 divided by 6 = 701 R 3
     -42
       00            Check: 6(701) + 3 = 4209
      - 0                   4206 + 3 = 4209
        09                     4209 = 4209
      -  6
         3
```

Example: Solve 4209 divided by 6 using the Intermediate Algorithm.

```
         2
        33
       666
   6 ) 4209    How many 6's in 4000?  666
     -3996
       213    How many 6's in 200?     33
     -198
        15    How many 6's in 15?    2
     - 12
         3  R        4209 divided by 6 = 666+33+2 =701 R 3
                     Check: 6(701) + 3 = 4209
                     4206 + 3 = 4209
                     4209 = 4209
```

2H. Number operations and their inverses

In mathematics, most operations have an inverse. Inverse operations are operations that "undo" each other.
Addition and subtraction are inverses:

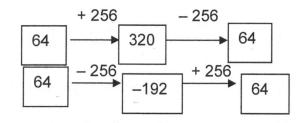

Multiplication and division are inverses as well, except that division by zero is not allowed:

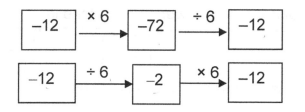

Multiplication and multiplication by the reciprocal are also inverses to each other, as division and multiplication by the reciprocal are equivalent operations.

Squaring a number and taking its square root are also inverse operations:

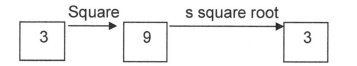

Raising to a power and taking the root are inverse operations:

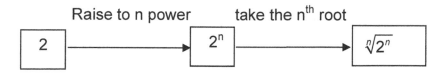

Finally, raising a base to a power and then getting the logarithm to that base are also inverse operations. The expression

$y = 5^x$ means y is equal to 5 raised to the power of x where

x is the exponent and 5 is the base. This is written as $x = \log_5 y$

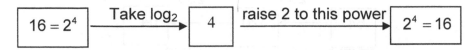

A common pair in logarithms is the natural logarithm, *ln* and the exponent *e*:

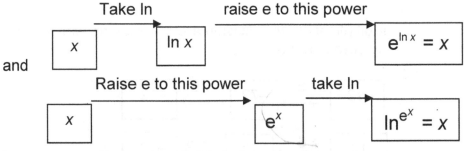

Inverse operations are used to solve equations.

Example: $x + 12 = 17$
Subtract 12 from each side of the equation, since the inverse of addition is subtraction:

$$x + 12 = 17$$
$$-12 \quad -12$$
$$x = 5$$

Example: $4x = -20$
Divide both sides of the equation by 4, since the inverse of multiplication is division.

$$\frac{4x}{4} = \frac{-20}{4}$$
$$x = -5$$

2I.   **The origins and development of standard computational algorithms**

Much calculation in today's world is done by calculators and computers but the standard computational algorithms are still taught early during schooling. The basic mathematics that we learn in elementary school actually came about long before the use of writing as a way to deal with different economic necessities. Ancient civilizations used various methods to calculate such as knotted strings, pebbles and beads on an abacus frame which is still in use today in some countries. Over the centuries, numerous algorithms have been developed for basic arithmetic. The origin of the standard computational algorithm arose out of a need in early civilizations to deal with the problems of trade and sharing. There are various evidences of this need such as a clay tablet, which was found in Baghdad around 2500BC, which demonstrates an algorithm designed to solve a problem of sharing. Around 1600BC, Babylonians developed algorithms for finding square roots and factoring. Euclid's algorithm was devised to determine the greatest common divisor of 2 numbers around 3BC. Al-Khwarizmi, a Persian mathematician, lived around 10BC and it is from the Latin translation of his name, "Algoritmi" that the word "algorithm" is derived. He developed algorithms for solving quadratic equations and linear equations. He introduced algebraic numbers and concepts to India and is thought by some to be the father of algebra. Around 1025BC, Alhazen developed an algorithm that was crucial to the development of integral calculus. There were many important developments not mentioned here before the 1940's and there has been an explosion of development with regard to algorithms since the 1940's that are too numerous to mention.

Standard paper and pencil algorithms are still taught today. There are mental algorithms that are also being taught in many schools for quick calculations. Multiplication tables are not required when using an old Russian algorithm that only requires an ability to add, double and halve numbers. Lattice multiplication is considered to be more efficient than the standard multiplication algorithm for more complex multiple digit problems as it requires only an ability to add single digit numbers and a very basic knowledge of multiplication.

Competency 0003 Understand and solve problems involving integers, fractions, decimals, percents, ratios, and proportions.

3A. **Solving a variety of problems involving integers, fractions, decimals, percents (including percent increase and decrease), ratios, proportions, and average rate of change**

Integers
The following problems involving integers have been solved using algebraic methods.

<u>Example:</u> The sum of two consecutive integers is 51, find the integers.

Let the consecutive integers be x and $(x+1)$.

Given that $x+(x+1)=51$

$2x+1=51$
Subtracting 1 on both sides, $2x=50$
Dividing both sides by 2 $x=25$
Thus the numbers are 25, 26

<u>Example:</u> The product of two consecutive integers is 56. Find the integers.

Let the integers be x and $(x+1)$.

Given that $x(x+1)=56$

$x^2+x=56$
$x^2+x-56=0$, is a quadratic equation.
Factorizing this equation we get
$(x+8)(x-7)=0$
$x=-8$ or $x=7$
So, if $x=7$, $(x+1)=8$, we get $x(x+1)=7\times8=56$, this is our solution.
So if $x=-8,(x+1)=-7$, we get $x(x+1)=(-8)\times(-7)=56$, which is also our solution.
Therefore, we have two sets of solutions, $(7,8)$ and $(-8,-7)$.

Fractions
The unit rate for purchasing an item is its price divided by the number of pounds/ounces, etc. in the item. The item with the lower unit rate has the lower price.

Example: Find the item with the best unit price:

$1.79 for 10 ounces

$1.89 for 12 ounces

$5.49 for 32 ounces

$$\frac{1.79}{10} = 0.179 \text{ per ounce} \qquad \frac{1.89}{12} = 0.1575 \text{ per ounce}$$

$$\frac{5.49}{32} = 0.172 \text{ per ounce}$$

$1.89 for 12 ounces is the best price.

A second way to find the better buy is to set up a proportion equation with the price over the number of ounces, etc.

Example: Find the better buy:
$8.19 for 40 pounds or $4.89 for 22 pounds

Find the unit price.

$$\frac{40}{8.19} \times \frac{1}{x} \qquad\qquad \frac{22}{4.89} \times \frac{1}{x}$$
$$40x = 8.19 \qquad\qquad 22x = 4.89$$
$$x = 0.20475 \qquad\qquad x = 0.22\overline{227}$$

Since $0.20475 < 0.22\overline{227}$, $8.19 for 40 pounds is a better buy.

Decimals
Example: The total snowfall was 27.3 inches in January, 31.5 inches in February, and 18.2 inches in March. What was the average monthly snowfall during these three months?

By definition, to find the average we add up all three numbers and divide by 3.

$$\begin{array}{r} 27.3 \\ 31.5 \\ +\ 18.2 \\ \hline 77.0 \end{array}$$

Dividing 77 by 3 we get $25.666.. \approx 25.67$
Therefore, the average monthly snowfall from January through March was 25.67 inches.

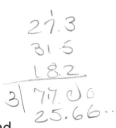

<u>Example</u>: You make $10.75 per hour at your job for regular work and time and a half for work over 40 hours. If you work 48 hours this week, how much will you earn?

First find the amount for the first 40 hours

```
    10.75
  x   40
        0
  43000
$430.00
```

Now compute the overtime wages

```
    10.75
  x   1.5
    5375
  10750
$16.125
```

Now find the earnings for 8 hour of overtime by multiplying
```
    16.125
  x      8
  129.000
```

Now add the regular wages and the overtime wages
     430+129 = 559, you made $559.00 that week

Percentages (including percent increase and decrease)

To find the amount of sales tax on an item, change the percent of sales tax into an equivalent decimal number. Then multiply the decimal number times the price of the object to find the sales tax. The total cost of an item will be the price of the item plus the sales tax.

<u>Example</u>: A guitar costs $120 plus 7% sales tax. How much are the sales tax and the total bill?

     7% = .07 as a decimal
     (.07)(120) = $8.40 sales tax
     Total cost, $120 + $8.40 = $128.40

An alternative method to find the total cost is to multiply the price times the factor 1.07 (price + sales tax):
     $120 \times 1.07 = $128.40

Example: An item that is on sale costs $18. The sale is 10% off of the original price. What was the original price?

Percentages are always based on something. 10% of $18 is not the same as 10% of $20. You can't solve this problem by calculating 10% of $18 and adding it to $18.

To solve this problem, we use an unknown "x" that represents the original price. We know that x minus 10% (.10) of x is equal to $18: $x - .10x = 18$. Simplify and solve:

$.9x = 18$ $1x - .1x = .9x$

$\dfrac{.9x}{.9} = \dfrac{18}{.9} = 20$ Divide both sides by .9

The answer is $20, the original price of the item.

Example: The population of a certain town increased by 3% in one year to 10,000. What was the population the year before the increase?

Let x equal the population before the increase. Since it increased by 3%, the amount it increased by can be obtained by figuring out what 3% (.03) of x is and adding it to x:

$x + .03x = 10,000$

$1.03x = 10,000$

$\dfrac{1.03x}{1.03} = \dfrac{10,000}{1.03} = 9708.74$, rounded to the nearest person

means that the year before the 3% increase, the population was 9709.

Ratios and proportions
A **ratio** is a comparison of 2 numbers. If a class had 11 boys and 14 girls, the ratio of boys to girls could be written one of 3 ways:

11:14   or   11 to 14   or $\dfrac{11}{14}$

The ratio of girls to boys is: 14:11, 14 to 11 or $\dfrac{14}{11}$

Ratios can be reduced to its simplest form by canceling common factors. A ratio of 12 cats to 18 dogs would reduce to 2:3, 2 to 3 or $2/3$.

A **proportion** is an equation in which a fraction is set equal to another. To solve the proportion, multiply each numerator times the other fraction's denominator. Set these two products equal to each other and solve the resulting equation. This is called cross-multiplying the proportion.

<u>Example</u>: Solve the proportion $\dfrac{4}{15} = \dfrac{x}{60}$.

To solve this, cross multiply.

$(4)(60) = (15)(x)$

$240 = 15x$

$16 = x$

<u>Example</u>: Two numbers have a ratio of 3:5. Find the numbers if the difference between their squares is 144.

Let the numbers be x and y.

$\dfrac{y}{x} = \dfrac{3}{5}$ and $x^2 - y^2 = 144$

Substituting $y = \dfrac{3}{5}x$ in the second equation, we get

$x^2 - \dfrac{9}{25}x^2 = 144$

$\dfrac{16}{25}x^2 = 144$

Thus, we get $x = 15, -15$ and $y = 9, -9$

Fractions, decimals, and percents can be used interchangeably within problems.

→ To change a percent into a decimal, move the decimal point two places to the left and drop off the percent sign.

→ To change a decimal into a percent, move the decimal two places to the right and add on a percent sign.

→ To change a fraction into a decimal, divide the numerator by the denominator.

→ To change a decimal number into an equivalent fraction, write the decimal part of the number as the fraction's numerator. As the fraction's denominator use the place value of the last column of the decimal. Reduce the resulting fraction as far as possible.

Example: J.C. Nickels has Hunch jeans 1/4 off the usual price of $36.00. Shears and Roadkill have the same jeans 30% off their regular price of $40. Find the cheaper price.

1/4 = .25 so .25(36) = $9.00 off $36 - 9 = $27 sale price

30% = .30 so .30(40) = $12 off $40 - 12 = $28 sale price

The price at J.C Nickels is actually lower.

Average rate of change

The average rate of change is the amount of change divided by the time it takes to change (e.g. average monthly rainfall, average speed, growth rate of population, etc.). We have had a few examples of rate change problems above; below is an example of a rate, time and distance problem.

Example: On a 500 mile, 4 hour plane trip, the plane was flown at 2 different speeds. For the first part of the trip, the average speed was 100mph. For the remainder of the trip, the plane was flying with the wind and its average speed was 130 mph. For how long did the plane fly at each speed?

The distance equation, $d = rt$ should always come to mind when you hear "for how long" or "how far" or "how fast." In the distance equation, d stands for distance, r stands for rate and t stands for time. First set up a table:

	D	r	t
First part of trip	d =	100	t
Second part of trip	500–d	130	4–t
Total trip	500		4

Using our formula, $d = rt$, the first row is $d = 100t$.

The second row is

$500 - d = 130(4 - t)$, since the 2 distances add up to 500,

add the 2 distances together:

$500 = 100t + 130(4 - t) = 100t + 520 - 130t$

$500 - 520 = -30t$

$-20 = -30t$

$t = \dfrac{2}{3} \text{hr} = 40 \text{ min}$

Since t is the time spent on the first part of the trip, then the second part of the trip is 4-t = 3 hrs 20 min; therefore, the plane flew at 100mph for 40 min and 130mph for another 3 hrs 20 min.

3B.   **Estimation to judge the reasonableness of solutions to problems**

Estimation and approximation may be used to check the reasonableness of answers. This is particularly important when calculators are used. Students need to be able to verify that the answer they are getting by punching in numbers is in the correct range and makes sense in the given context. Estimation requires good mental math skills. There are several different ways of estimating.

A simple check for reasonableness is to ask whether the answer expected is more or less than a given number. It is astonishing how many errors of computation can be avoided using this method. For instance, when converting 20 Km to meters, ask whether you are expecting a number greater or less than 20. That will tell you whether to multiply or divide by 1000 (a common point of confusion in conversion problems).

The most common estimation strategies taught in schools involve replacing numbers with ones that are simpler to compute with. These methods include rounding off, front-end digit estimation and compensation. While rounding off is done to a specific place value (e.g. nearest ten or hundred), front-end estimation involves rounding off or truncating to whatever place value the first digit in a number represents. The following example uses front-end estimation.

Example: Estimate the answer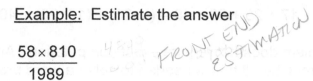

$$\frac{58 \times 810}{1989}$$

58 becomes 60, 810 becomes 800 and 1989 becomes 2000.

$$\frac{60 \times 800}{2000} = 24$$

Compensation involves replacing different numbers in different ways so that one change can more or less compensate for the other.

Example: 32 + 53 = 30 + 55 = 85

Here both numbers are replaced in a way that minimizes the change; one number is increased and the other is decreased.

Another estimation strategy is to estimate a range for the correct answer.

Example: 458+873 > 400 + 800 and 458+873 < 500 + 900.

One can estimate that the sum of 458 and 873 lies in the range 1200 to 1400.

Converting to an equivalent fraction, decimal or percentage can often be helpful.

Example: To calculate 25% of 520, realize that 25% = 1/4 and simply divide 520 by 4 to get 130.

Clustering is a useful strategy when dealing with a set of numbers. Similar numbers can be clubbed together to simplify computation.

Example: 1210 + 655 + 1178 + 683 + 628 + 1223 + 599 = 600 + 600 + 600 + 600 + 1200 + 1200 + 1200.

Clubbing together compatible numbers is a variant of clustering. Here, instead of similar numbers, numbers that together produce easy to compute numbers are clubbed together.

Example: 5 + 17 + 25 + 23 + 40 = (5+25) + (17+23) + 40

Often a problem does not require exact computation. An estimate may sometimes be all that is needed to solve a word problem as in the example below. Therefore, assessing what level of precision is needed in a particular situation is an important skill that must be taught to all students.

Example: Janet goes into a store to purchase a CD on sale for $13.95. While shopping, she sees two pairs of shoes, prices $19.95 and $14.50. She only has $50. Can she purchase everything? (Assume there is no sales tax.)

Solve by rounding up to the nearest dollar:

$19.95→$20.00

$14.50→$15.00

$13.95→$14.00

$49.00   Yes, she can purchase the CD and both pairs of shoes.

Competency 0004 Understand the properties of real numbers and the real number system.

4A. Rational and irrational numbers

Real Numbers

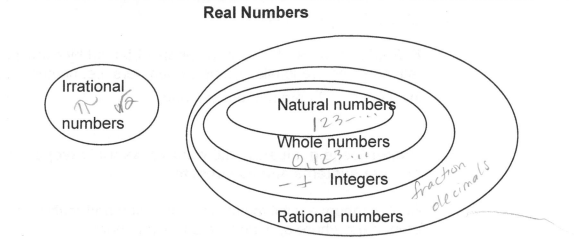

A. **Natural numbers**--the counting numbers, 1,2,3,...

B. **Whole numbers**--the counting numbers along with zero, 0,1,2...

C. **Integers**--the counting numbers, their opposites, and zero...–1, 0, 1 ...

D. **Rationals**—all integers and fractions that can be formed from the whole numbers. Zero cannot be the denominator. In decimal form, these numbers will be either terminating or repeating decimals. Simplify square roots to determine if the number can be written as a fraction.

The fraction $\frac{4}{5}$ is a rational number because it is of the form $\frac{a}{b}$ where "a" and "b" are integers and "b" is not zero.

The rational number $\frac{4}{5}$ can be written as 0.8, a terminating decimal by dividing the denominator into the numerator.

The rational number $\frac{7}{11}$ can be written as 0.636363... a non-terminating repeating decimal.

E. Irrationals--real numbers that cannot be written as a fraction. The decimal forms of these numbers are neither terminating nor repeating. The set of rational numbers and the set of irrational numbers have no elements in common and are mutually exclusive.

Examples: $\pi, e, \sqrt{2}$, etc.

F. Real numbers--the set of numbers obtained by combining the rationals and irrationals. Complex numbers, i.e. numbers that involve i or $\sqrt{-1}$, are not real numbers.

4B.   Properties (e.g. closure, distributive, associative) of the real number systems and its subsets

Real numbers exhibit the following addition and multiplication properties, where *a, b*, and *c* are real numbers.

Note: Multiplication is implied when there is no symbol between two variables. Thus, $a \times b$ can be written *ab*. Multiplication can also be indicated by a raised dot (•).

Closure
For any set of numbers to be closed under an operation, the result of the operation on two numbers in the set must also be included within that set.

The Closure Property for Whole-Number Addition states that the sum of any two whole numbers is a whole number.

Example: Since 2 and 5 are both whole numbers, 7 is also a whole number.

The Closure Property for Whole-Number Multiplication states that the product of any two whole numbers is a whole number.

Example: Since 3 and 4 are both whole numbers, 12 is also a whole number.

Property of Denseness
Between any pair of rational numbers, there is at least one rational number. The set of natural numbers is not dense because between two consecutive natural numbers, another natural number does not exist.

Example: Between 7.6 and 7.7, there is the rational number 7.65. Between 3 and 4, there exists no other natural number.

Summary of other Properties of Real Numbers

Name	Addition	Multiplication
Commutative	$a + b = b + a$	$ab = ba$
Associative	$(a+b)+c = a+(b+c)$	$(ab)c = a(bc)$
Distributive	$a(b+c) = ab+bc$	$(a+b)c = ac+bc$
Identity	$a+0 = a = 0+a$	$a \cdot 1 = a = 1 \cdot a$
Inverses	$a+(-a) = 0 = (-a)+a$	$a(a^{-1}) = 1 = a^{-1}$ if $a \neq 0$

For a detailed discussion of the properties listed in the above table, see **Competency 0002**.

4C. Operations and their inverses

For a discussion of operations and their inverses, see **Competency 0002**.

4D. The Real Number Line

The real number line represents all real numbers (both positive and negative) as a series of points and the magnitude of each number is the distance of the corresponding number from zero.

The real number line is useful for the addition and subtraction of numbers and to show the relations between numbers.

The real number line extends in both the directions infinitely. It extends from a special point, which is called as the Origin. The origin is the number 0. The positive numbers lie on the right hand side of the origin and the negative numbers lie on the left hand side of the origin.

There is an order of real numbers on the real number line. A bigger number is always to the right of the smaller number.

In the figure below a > b.

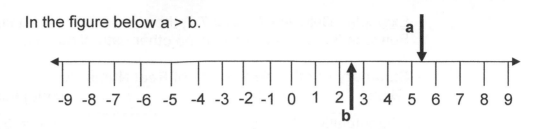

The set of solutions can be marked in the real number line as follows:
A solid circle or dot can be used to include the end point in the solution set whereas an open circle is used to exclude the end point from the solution set.

Example: The set of all real numbers greater than -1 and less than or equal to 4 is marked on the number line as follows:

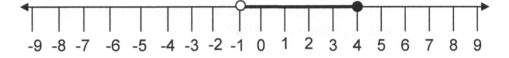

The number –2 is not included in the solution set. Therefore, an "open circle" has been used. The number 4 is included in the solution set, so at 4 there is a solid circle.

Unbounded Set
Example: The set of all numbers greater than or equal to 2 is marked as follows:

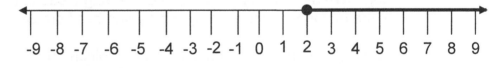

Example: The set of real numbers, which are either greater than 3 or strictly between -2 and 2, is marked in the number line as follows:

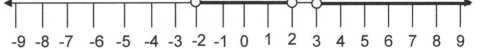

Example: The following is the set of all real numbers with the exception of -2 and 3.

Interval Notation in number lines

Interval notations can also be represented using the real number line. The interval (–3, 4] (set notation: the "bracket" after the "4," designates and endpoint that is part of the set and the parenthesis indicates that –3 is not part of the solution set) can be represented in the real number line as follows:

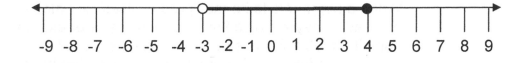

The interval notation $(2, \infty)$ can be represented in the number line as follows:

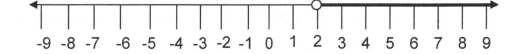

4E. Roots and Powers

Roots and powers are opposites. A power is the same as an exponent: you multiply the number by itself as many times as the power indicates. For example,

$$4^3 = 64 \ (4 \times 4 \times 4).$$
$$7^2 = 49 \ (7 \times 7).$$
$$5^5 = 3125 \ (5 \times 5 \times 5 \times 5 \times 5).$$

The root of a number is the number that needs to be multiplied by itself the number of times indicated by the root to equal the number in question.

For example, the 3rd root of 27 = 3 (3 x 3 x 3 = 27).
the 5th root of 3125 = 5 (5 x 5 x 5 x 5 x 5) = 3125.

Therefore, finding the fifth root of 64 is equivalent to asking 'What number multiplied by itself 5 times equals 64?'

The answer is approximately 2.297. This can be found using calculator: There is no simple way to calculate roots that are more complex by hand. You can see that whole powers, say *n*, of any number, say *x*, are easily calculated by hand: just multiply *x* by itself *n* times. Calculations are much more difficult when you want to find a fractional root or raise a number to a fractional power.

Powers

When a number is to be multiplied by itself repeatedly, powers can be used. They are also known as indices. For example, the quantity $3 \times 3 \times 3 \times 3$ is usually written as 3^4. In this case, the power, or index, is 4. The number 3 is called the base.

Example:

$6^2 = 6 \times 6 = 36$. We say that '6 squared is 36', or '6 to the power 2 is 36'.

$2^5 = 2 \times 2 \times 2 \times 2 \times 2 = 32$. We say that '2 to the power 5 is 32'.

Square roots

A square root is a number that gives the original number when squared.

$\sqrt{a} = x$ means that $x^2 = a$ for $x \geq 0$

x is a non-negative number whose square is "a."

For example, $\sqrt{9} = 3$ since $(3)^2 = 9$.

When 5 is squared, we get 25: $5^2 = 25$.

The reverse of this process is called finding a square root. The square root of 25 is 5. This is written as $\sqrt[2]{25} = 5$ or $\sqrt{25} = 5$.

In addition, when −5 is squared we again obtain 25, i.e. $(-5)^2 = 25$. This means that the number 25 has another square root, −5. Therefore, the two square roots of 25 are +5 and −5.

Any positive number has two square roots, one positive and one negative.

<u>Example:</u> The number 49 has 2 square roots, 7 and –7 because 7^2 = 49 and $(-7)^2$ = 49. The main square root of any real number is the positive root, 7 in the above example.

The square root of a product of two numbers is equal to the product of the square roots of the two numbers. For example

$$\sqrt{9 \times 16} = \sqrt{9} \times \sqrt{16} = 3 \times 4 = 12$$

Properties of Square Roots

1) $\sqrt{ab} = \sqrt{a}\sqrt{b}$ where $a, b \geq 0$

2) $\sqrt{\dfrac{a}{b}} = \dfrac{\sqrt{a}}{\sqrt{b}}$ where $a \geq 0$ and $b > 0$

3) $\sqrt{a^2} = |a|$ for any real number a

4) $\left(\sqrt{a}\right)^2 = a$ for $a \geq 0$

<u>Example:</u>

$$\sqrt{\dfrac{x^2}{49}} = \dfrac{\sqrt{x^2}}{\sqrt{49}} = \dfrac{x}{7}$$

<u>Example:</u>

$$\sqrt{1-\sin x}\sqrt{1+\sin x} = \sqrt{(1-\sin x)(1+\sin x)}$$
$$= \sqrt{1-\sin^2 x}$$
$$= \sqrt{\cos^2 x}$$
$$= |\cos x|$$

In general $\sqrt{a+b} \neq \sqrt{a} + \sqrt{b}$

<u>Example:</u>

$$\sqrt{4+9} \neq \sqrt{4} + \sqrt{9}$$
$$\sqrt{13} \neq 2 + 3$$
$$3.6 \neq 5$$

Cube Roots

The cube root of 8 is 2 because 2 * 2 * 2 = 8. The cube root of –64 is –4 because $(-4)^3 = -64$.

Negative numbers have real cube roots.

Example: Find $\sqrt[3]{27y^3}$

$$\sqrt[3]{27y^3} = \sqrt[3]{3^3 y^3} = \sqrt[3]{(3y)^3} = \left((3y)^3\right)^{\frac{1}{3}} = 3y$$

Other roots or Radicals

The nth root of a number a, denoted $\sqrt[n]{a}$, is defined as follows: (n is a positive integer)

$\sqrt[n]{a} = b$ means $a = b^n$

'n' (the root) is sometimes called the *index* of the radical or root. The expression under the root sign is called the *radicand.*

Simplifying radicals

To simplify a radical, follow these steps:
1. Factor the number or coefficient completely.
2. For **square roots**, group like factors in pairs. For cube roots, arrange like factors in groups of three. For n[th] roots, group like factors in groups of n.
3. For each of these groups, put one of the factors outside the radical. Any factors that cannot be combined in groups should be multiplied together and left inside the radical.

The index number of a radical is the little number on the front of the radical. For a cube root, the index is 3. If no index appears, then the index is 2 and is the square root.

Example: Simplify $\sqrt[3]{432}$

$$\sqrt[3]{432} = \sqrt[3]{3 \times 2 \times 2 \times 2 \times 3 \times 3 \times 2} = \sqrt[3]{3^3 2^4} = 3 \cdot 2 \cdot \sqrt[3]{2} = 6 \cdot \sqrt[3]{2}$$

Note: Remember that the square root of a negative number can be designated by replacing the negative sign inside that square root with an "*i*" in front of the radical (to signify an imaginary number).

Then simplify the remaining positive radical by the normal method. Include the i outside the radical as a part of the answer.
If the index number is an odd number, you can still simplify the radical to get a negative solution.

While adding and subtracting expressions involving radicals, like radicals can be combined.

Example: Simplify $\sqrt{288} + \sqrt{50} + \sqrt{12}$

$$\sqrt{288} + \sqrt{50} + \sqrt{12} = \sqrt{2 \times 144} + \sqrt{25 \times 2} + \sqrt{4 \times 3}$$
$$= 12\sqrt{2} + 5\sqrt{2} + 2\sqrt{3} = 17\sqrt{2} + 2\sqrt{3}$$

When there is a binomial radical expression in the denominator, remove the radical from the denominator by multiplying both the numerator and the denominator by the conjugate (sign between terms reversed) of the radical expression.

Example: Simplify $\dfrac{4}{3 + \sqrt{5}}$

$$\frac{4}{3 + \sqrt{5}} = \frac{4(3 - \sqrt{5})}{(3 + \sqrt{5})(3 - \sqrt{5})} = \frac{4(3 - \sqrt{5})}{9 - 5} = 3 - \sqrt{5}$$

4F. The Laws of Exponents

The **exponent form** is a method to write repeated multiplication. Basic form: b^n, where b is called the base and n is the exponent. b and n are both real numbers. b^n implies that the base b is multiplied by itself n times.

Examples:
1) $3^4 = 3 \times 3 \times 3 \times 3 = 81$

   where 3 is the base and 4 is the exponent.
2) $2^3 = 2 \times 2 \times 2 = 8$
3) $(^-2)^4 = (^-2) \times (^-2) \times (^-2) \times (^-2) = 16$
4) $^-2^4 =^- (2 \times 2 \times 2 \times 2) =^- 16$

The following are basic rules for exponents:

$a^1 = a$ for all values of a; thus $17^1 = 17$

$b^0 = 1$ for all values of b; thus $24^0 = 1$

$10^n = 1$ with n zeros; thus $10^6 = 1,000,000$

Example: $10^7 = 10,000,000$

x^2 *is read,* "x squared"

y^3 *is read,* "y cubed"

For real numbers m and n, and for nonzero 'a',

Product Rule

1) $a^m \cdot a^n = a^{(m+n)}$

Example: $(3^4)(3^5) = 3^9$

2) $a^m \cdot a^m = (ab)^m$

Example: $(4^2)(5^2) = 20^2$

3) $(a^m)^n = a^{mn}$

Example: $(2^3)^2 = 2^6$

Quotient Rule

4) $\dfrac{a^m}{a^n} = a^{(m-n)}$

Example: $2^5 \div 2^3 = 2^2$

5) $a^{-m} = \dfrac{1}{a^m}$

Example: $2^{-2} = \dfrac{1}{2^2}$

Samples of simplifying expressions with exponents:

$(-2)^3 = -8$ $-2^3 = -1 \cdot (2^3) = -8$

$(-2)^4 = 16$ $-2^4 = -1 \cdot (2^4) = -16$ Note change of sign.

$(\frac{2}{3})^3 = \frac{2^3}{3^3} = \frac{8}{27}$

$5^0 = 1$

$4^{-1} = \frac{1}{4}$

Example: Simplify $\dfrac{3^5 \left(3^{-2} + 3^{-3}\right)}{9}$

$\dfrac{3^5 \left(3^{-2} + 3^{-3}\right)}{9} = \dfrac{3^5 \left(3^{-2} + 3^{-3}\right)}{3^2} = 3^3 \left(3^{-2} + 3^{-3}\right)$

$= 3^3 3^{-2} + 3^3 3^{-3} = 3^{3-2} + 3^{3-3} = 3 + 1 = 4$

Example: Simplify $\dfrac{3^2 \cdot 5^{-2} \cdot 2^5}{6^2 \cdot 5}$

$\dfrac{3^2 \cdot 5^{-2} \cdot 2^5}{6^2 \cdot 5} = \dfrac{3^2 \cdot 5^{-2} \cdot 2^5}{3^2 \cdot 2^2 \cdot 5} = 5^{-2-1} \cdot 2^{5-2} = \dfrac{2^3}{5^3} = \dfrac{8}{125}$

Note: Unless the negative sign is inside the parentheses and the exponent is outside the parentheses, the sign is not affected by the exponent.

Example:
$(^-2)^4 = (-2) \times (-2) \times (-2) \times (-2) = 16$
That is, -2 is multiplied by itself 4 times.
$^-2^4 = -(2 \times 2 \times 2 \times 2) = -16$
That is 2 is multiplied by itself 4 times and the answer is negated.
A radical may also be expressed using a rational exponent in the following way:

$$\sqrt[n]{a} = a^{\frac{1}{n}}$$

Example:
$$\sqrt{5} = 5^{\frac{1}{2}}; \quad \sqrt[5]{7} = 7^{\frac{1}{5}}$$

All the exponent laws discussed above also apply to rational exponents.

Example:

$$(\sqrt[5]{6})^3 = (6^{\frac{1}{5}})^3 = 6^{\frac{1}{5} \times 3} = 6^{\frac{3}{5}}$$

Example: Simplify $(-32)^{\frac{3}{5}} + 16^{\frac{3}{4}}$

$$(-32)^{\frac{3}{5}} + 16^{\frac{3}{4}} = (\sqrt[5]{-32})^3 + (\sqrt[4]{16})^3 = (-2)^3 + 2^3 = -8 + 8 = 0$$

4G.   Scientific Notation

Scientific notation is a more convenient method for writing very large and very small numbers. It employs two factors. The first factor is a number between -10 and 10. The second factor is a power of 10. This notation is a shorthand way to express large numbers (like the weight of 100 freight cars in kilograms) or small numbers (like the weight of an atom in grams).

$10^n = (10)^n$ Ten multiplied by itself n times.

$10^6 = 1,000,000$ (mega)

$10^3 = 10 \times 10 \times 10 = 1000$ (kilo)

$10^2 = 10 \times 10 = 100$ (hecto)

$10^1 = 10$ (deca)

$10^0 = 1$ Any nonzero number raised to power of zero is 1.

$10^{-1} = 1/10$ (deci)

$10^{-2} = 1/100$ (centi)

$10^{-3} = 1/1000$ (milli)

$10^{-6} = 1/1,000,000$ (micro)

Scientific Notation Format. Convert a number to a form of $b \times 10^n$ where $-10 < b < 10$ and n is an integer.

Example: 356.73 can be written in various forms.

$356.73 = 3567.3 \times 10^{-1}$ (1)

$= 35673 \times 10^{-2}$ (2)

$= 35.673 \times 10^1$ (3)

$= 3.5673 \times 10^2$ (4)

$= 0.35673 \times 10^3$ (5)

Only (4) is written in proper scientific notation format.

Example: Write 46,368,000 in scientific notation.

1)   Introduce a decimal point. 46,368,000 = 46,368,000.0
2)   Move the decimal place to **left** until only one nonzero digit is in front of it, in this case between the 4 and 6.
3)   Count the number of digits the decimal point moved, in this case 7. This is the nth the power of ten and is **positive** because the decimal point moved **left**.

Therefore, $46,368,000 = 4.6368 \times 10^7$

Example:

Write 0.00397 in scientific notation

1)   Decimal point is already in place.
2)   Move the decimal point to the **right** until there is only one nonzero digit in front of it, in this case between the 3 and 9.
3)   Count the number of digits the decimal point moved, in this case 3. This is the nth the power of ten and is **negative** because the decimal point moved **right**.

Therefore, $0.00397 = 3.97 \times 10^{-3}$.

To add or subtract in scientific notation, the exponents must be the same. Then add the decimal portions, keeping the power of 10 the same. Then move the decimal point and adjust the exponent to keep the number to the left of the decimal point to a single digit.

Example:

6.22×10^3

$+ 7.48 \times 10^3$ Add these as is.

13.70×10^3 Now move decimal 1 more place to the left and

1.37×10^4 add 1 more exponent.

To multiply or divide in scientific notation, multiply or divide the decimal part of the numbers. In multiplication, add the exponents of 10. In division, subtract the exponents of 10. Then move the decimal point and adjust the exponent to keep the number to the left of the decimal point to a single digit.

Example:

$(5.2 \times 10^5)(3.5 \times 10^2)$ Multiply 5.2×3.5

18.2×10^7 Add exponent

1.82×10^8 Move decimal point and increase the
                              exponent by 1.

Example:

$\dfrac{(4.1076 \times 10^3)}{2.8 \times 10^{-4}}$ Divide 4.1076 by 2.8

                       Subtract $3 - (-4)$

1.467×10^7

4H. **Using Number properties to prove theorems (e.g., the product of two even numbers is even)**

Theorem 1: The product of two even numbers is even.

Proof: An even number is in the form of n = 2k, where k is an integer (i.e. even numbers are divisible by 2). Therefore, the even numbers are:

... −10, −8, −6, −4, −2, 0, 2, 4, 6, 8, 10...

Let a and b be even integers where $a = 2k_1$ and $b = 2k_2$, and where k_1 and k_2 are integers.

The product of the two even numbers a and b is

$(a)(b) = (2k_1)(2k_2) = 4k_1k_2$ (by distributive property of numbers)

$$= 4k_3 \text{ where } k_3 \text{ is also an integer}$$

(By the closure property of numbers, integers are closed under multiplication)

Since the product of any two even integers is divisible by 2. Therefore, the product of two even numbers is even.

Theorem 2: The product of two odd numbers is odd.

Proof: Let x and y be two odd integers such that $x = 2s + 1$ and $y = 2t + 1$ where s and t are integers.

$xy = (2s + 1)(2t + 1)$

$\quad = 4st + 2s + 2t + 1$ (by distributive property of numbers)

$\quad = 2(2st + s + t) + 1$

$\quad = 2W + 1$ where W is an integer (since integers are closed under addition)

Therefore, the product of two odd numbers is also odd.

Theorem 3: The sum of any three even numbers is even.

Proof: Let x, y, z be even. By the definition of even, $x = 2k_1,$ $y = 2k_2,$ $z = 2k_3$ where k_1, k_2, k_3 are integers.

The sum of these 3 even numbers can be expressed as

$x + y + z = 2^*k_1 + 2^*k_2 + 2k_3 = 2^*(k_1 + k_2 + k_3) = 2^*k_4$

where $k_4 = k_1 + k_2 + k_3$ (since integers are closed under addition)

Therefore, by definition, the sum $x + y + z$ is an even integer.

Theorem 4: The nth power of an even number is divisible by 2^n

Proof: Let x be an even number. By definition of even, x can be written as $x = 2\,k$, where k is an integer

The nth power of x is $x^n = (2\,k)^n = 2^n \times k^n$

Dividing by 2^n,

$\dfrac{x^n}{2^n} = \dfrac{2^n \times k^n}{2^n} = k^n$, where k^n is an integer. (Since integers closed under multiplication)

Since $\dfrac{x^n}{2^n}$ is an integer, by definition x^n is divisible by 2^n

4I.   **Problems involving real numbers and their operations**

Competency 0003 contains many examples of problems involving operations on real numbers. Following are several examples of problems using percentages.

Example: The Ski Club has 85 members. Eighty percent of the members are able to attend the meeting. How many members attend the meeting?

Restate the problem.   What is 80% of 85?
Write an equation. $n = 0.8 \times 85$
Solve. $n = 68$

Sixty-eight members attend the meeting.

Example: There are 64 dogs in the kennel. Forty-eight are collies. What percent are collies?

Restate the problem.	48 is what percent of 64?
Write an equation.	$48 = n \times 64$
Solve.	$\dfrac{48}{64} = n$
	$n = \dfrac{3}{4} = 75\%$

75% of the dogs are collies.

Example: The auditorium was filled to 90% capacity. There were 558 seats occupied. What is the capacity of the auditorium?

Restate the problem.	90% of what number is 558?
Write an equation.	$0.9n = 558$
Solve.	$n = \dfrac{558}{.9}$
	$n = 620$

The capacity of the auditorium is 620 people.

The relative size of real numbers expressed as fractions, decimals, percents and scientific notation

Compare the relative size of real numbers expressed in a variety of forms, including fractions, decimals, percents, and scientific notation:

To convert a **fraction** to a **decimal**, simply divide the numerator (top) by the denominator (bottom). Use long division if necessary.

Example: Find the decimal equivalent of $\dfrac{7}{10}$.

$$
\begin{array}{r}
0.7 \\
10\overline{)7.0} \\
\underline{70} \\
00
\end{array}
$$

Since 10 cannot divide into 7 evenly, put a decimal point in the answer row on top; put a zero behind 7 to make it 70. Continue the division process. If a remainder occurs, put a zero by the last digit of the remainder and continue the division.

$$\text{Thus } \frac{7}{10} = 0.7$$

It is a good idea to write a zero before the decimal point so that the decimal point is emphasized.

<u>Example:</u> Find the decimal equivalent of $\dfrac{7}{125}$.

$$
\begin{array}{r}
0.056 \\
125{\overline{\smash{\big)}\,7.000}} \\
\underline{625} \\
750 \\
\underline{750} \\
0
\end{array}
$$

If a decimal has a fixed number of digits, the decimal is said to be terminating. A terminating **decimal** can be converted into a **fraction** by multiplying by 1 in the form of a fraction (e.g. $\dfrac{10}{10}, \dfrac{100}{100}, \dfrac{1000}{1000}$) to get rid of the decimal point.

<u>Example:</u> Convert 0.056 to a fraction.

Multiplying 0.056 by $\dfrac{1000}{1000}$ to get rid of the decimal point

$$0.056 \times \frac{1000}{1000} = \frac{56}{1000} = \frac{7}{125}$$

If a decimal continues forever by repeating a string of digits, the decimal is said to be repeating. To write a repeating decimal as a fraction, follow these steps:

1. Let x = the repeating decimal

    (e.g., $x = 0.716716716...$)

2. Multiply x by the multiple of ten that will move the decimal just to the right of the repeating block of digits.

    (e.g. $1000x = 716.716716...$)

3. Subtract the first equation from the second.

    (e.g. $1000x - x = 716.716.716... - 0.716716...$)

4. Simplify and solve this equation. The repeating block of digits will subtract out.

$$(\text{e.g. } 999x = 716 \text{ so } x = \frac{716}{999})$$

The solution will be the fraction for the repeating decimal.

A **decimal** can be converted to a **percent** by multiplying by 100%, or merely moving the decimal point two places to the right. A **percent** can be converted to a **decimal** by dividing by 100%, or moving the decimal point two places to the left.

Examples: Convert the following decimals into percents.

0.375 = 37.5%

0.7 = 70%

0.04 = 4 %

3.15 = 315 %

Examples: Convert the following percents into decimals.

84% = 0.84

3% = 0.03

60% = 0.6

110% = 1.1

$\frac{1}{2}$% = 0.5% = 0.005

A **percent** can be converted to a **fraction** by placing it over 100 and reducing to simplest terms.

Examples: Convert the following percents into fractions.

$32\% = \frac{32}{100} = \frac{8}{25}$

$6\% = \frac{6}{100} = \frac{3}{50}$

$111\% = \frac{111}{100} = 1\frac{11}{100}$

$= \frac{10}{100} = \frac{1}{10}$

The **percentage** of a number can be found by converting the percentage into decimal form and then multiplying the decimal by the number.

Example: Find 23% of 1000.

$$23\% = 0.23$$
$$0.23 \times 1000 = 230$$

SUBAREA II.   PATTERNS, RELATIONS, AND ALGEBRA

Competency 0005 Understand and use patterns to model and solve problems.

5A.   Making conjectures about patterns presented in numeric, geometric or tabular form

A numerical sequence is a pattern of numbers arranged in a particular order. Thus, given part of the sequence, one can use a prescribed rule to find the numbers that follow or precede that part. Even though arithmetic and geometric sequences are the most common patterns, one can have series based on other rules as well. In some problems, the student will not be given the rule that governs a pattern but will have to inspect the pattern to find out what the rule is. For instance, 1, 4, 9, 16... is a series that consists of the squares of the natural numbers. Using this rule, the next term in the series 25 can be found by squaring the next natural number 5.

Example: Find the next term in the series 1, 1, 2, 3, 5, 8,.....

Inspecting the terms in the series, one finds that this pattern is neither arithmetic nor geometric. Every term in the series is a sum of the previous two terms.

Thus, the next term = 5 + 8 = 13.

This particular sequence is a well-known series named the Fibonacci sequence.

Example: Kepler discovered a relationship between the average distance of a planet from the sun and the time it takes the planet to orbit the sun.

The following table shows the data for the six planets closest to the sun:

	Mercury	Venus	Earth	Mars	Jupiter	Saturn
Average distance, x	0.387	0.723	1	1.523	5.203	9.541
x^3	0.058	0.378	1	3.533	140.852	868.524
Time, y	0.241	0.615	1	1.881	11.861	29.457
y^2	0.058	0.378	1	3.538	140.683	867.715

Looking at the data in the table, we can assume that $x^3 = y^2$
We can conjecture the following function for Kepler's relationship:
$$y = \sqrt{x^3}$$

5B.   Representing patterns and relations using symbolic notation

Other patterns can be created using algebraic variables. Patterns may also be pictorial. In each case, one can predict subsequent terms or find a missing term by first discovering the rule that governs the pattern.

<u>Example:</u> Find the next term in the sequence $ax^2y, ax^4y^2, ax^6y^3, \ldots$

Inspecting the pattern we see that this is a geometric sequence with common ratio x^2y .

Thus, the next term = $ax^6y^3 \times x^2y = ax^8y^4$.

<u>Example:</u> Find the next term in the pattern:

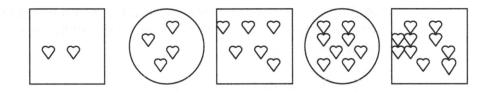

Inspecting the pattern one observes that it has alternating squares and circles that include a number of hearts that increases by two for each subsequent term.

Hence, the next term in the pattern will be as follows:

Use a Diagram or Model

Sometimes a diagram makes it easier to see the next number in a series. Take the following:

1 3 6 10 15

Organizing the diagram gives:

	1st term	2nd term	3rd term	4th term	5th term	6th term	nth term
	*	**	***	****	* ** *** **** *****		
Total	1	3	6	10	15		
# Added:	1	2	3	4	5		

The 6th term will be $1 + 2 + 3 + 4 + 5 + 6 = 21$
The 10th term will be $1 + 2 + 3 + 4 + 5 + 6 + 7 + 8 + 9 + 10 = 55$
The nth terms will be $1 + 2 + 3 + 4 + ... + n$

5C. Identifying patterns of change created by functions (e.g. linear, quadratic, exponential)

Patterns of change created by linear functions: A linear function is a function defined by the equation $y = mx + b$. With linear functions, the **difference** between successive y's for a constant change in x, is **constant**. It is determined by m, the coefficient of x and the slope of the line, otherwise known as the rate of change. . The slope of the linear function measures rise over run, or how much y, the output changes for every change of 1 in x, the input. The slope is constant everywhere on the line.

Example: Suppose we have an equation $y = 2x + 1$. We construct a table of values in order to graph the equation to see if we can find a pattern.

x	y
-2	-3
-1	-1
0	1
1	3
2	5

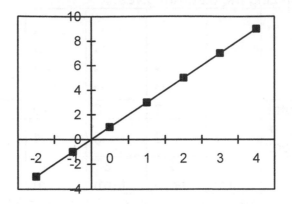

The pattern formed by the points is that they all lie on a straight line and the difference between successive y's is constant. We, therefore, can determine any solution of y by picking an x-coordinate and finding the corresponding point on the line. For example, if we want to know the solution of y when x is equal to 4, we find the corresponding point and see that y is equal to 9.

Example: What patterns appear in a table for the equation y = 2x + 4 ?

x	y	Differences between outputs are **constant**
0	4	$\lvert 4-6 \rvert = 2$
1	6	$\lvert 6-8 \rvert = 2$
2	8	$\lvert 8-10 \rvert = 2$
3	10	$\lvert 12-10 \rvert = 2$
4	12	

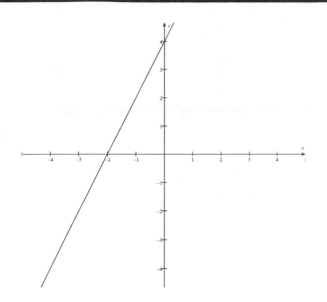

Patterns of change created by quadratic functions: The standard form of a quadratic function is $f(x) = ax^2 + bx + c$ where the highest exponent is 2. With quadratic functions, the successive output **differences** are **linear** and the **second differences** are **constant**. This is the pattern for all quadratic functions.

Example:
What patterns appear in a table for $y = x^2 - 5x + 6$?

x	y	Difference between outputs are linear	Second differences are constant
1	6	$\lvert 6-2 \rvert = 4$	
1	2	$\lvert 2-0 \rvert = 2$	$\lvert 4-2 \rvert = 2$
2	0	$\lvert 0-0 \rvert = 0$	$\lvert 2-0 \rvert = 2$
3	0	$\lvert 0-2 \rvert = 2$	$\lvert 0-2 \rvert = 2$
4	2	$\lvert 2-6 \rvert = 4$	$\lvert 2-4 \rvert = 2$

Also note that the values for *y* are symmetrically arranged.

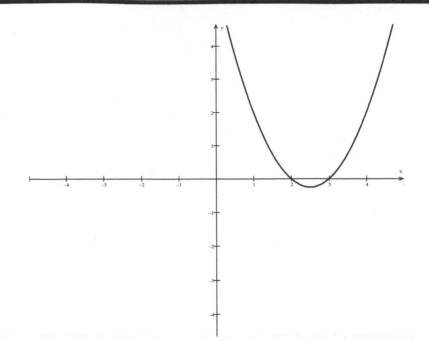

Patterns of change created by exponential functions: An exponential function is a function defined by the equation $y = ab^x$, where a is the starting value, b is the growth factor, and x tells how many times to multiply by the growth factor. For exponential functions, the **ratio** between successive y's or outputs are **constant**. In other words, each y or output, is a constant multiple of the previous y.

If $a > 0$ and b is between 0 and 1 the graph of the exponential function will be decreasing or decaying.

If $a > 0$ and b is greater than 1, the graph will be increasing or growing.

<u>Example</u>: Identify the pattern represented by $y = 100(0.5)^x$

x	y	ratio of change is a constant 50% increase indicated by multiplying by 1.5:
0	100	
1	150	$1.5(100) = 150$
2	225	$1.5(150) = 225$
3	337.5	$1.5(225) = 337.5$
4	506.25	$1.5(337.51) = 506.25$

5D. **Using finite and infinite series and sequences (e.g. Fibonacci, arithmetic, geometric) to model and solve problems.**

Sequences can be **finite** or **infinite**. An example of a finite sequence is a sequence whose domain consists of the set {1, 2, 3 ... n} or the first n positive integers. An example of an infinite sequence is a sequence whose domain consists of the set {1, 2, 3 ...}; which is, in other words, all positive integers.

The most common **numerical patterns** are arithmetic sequences and geometric sequences. In an arithmetic sequence, each term is separated from the next by a fixed number (e.g. 3, 6, 9, 12, 15...). In a geometric sequence, each term in the series is multiplied by a fixed number to get the next term (e.g. 3, 6, 12, 24, 28...)

Arithmetic Sequences

An arithmetic sequence is a set of numbers with a common difference between the terms. Terms and the distance between terms can be calculated using use the following formula:
$a_n = a_1 + (n-1)d$ where
a_1 = the first term
a_n = the nth term (general term)
n = the number of the term in the sequence
d = the common difference

The formula essentially expresses the arithmetic sequence as an **algebraic pattern** a_1, a_1+d, a_1+2d, a_1+3d .... And so on where any numbers can be substituted for a_1 and d to derive different numerical sequences.

Example: Find the 8th term of the arithmetic sequence 5, 8, 11, 14...

$a_n = a_1 + (n-1)d$
$a_1 = 5$ identify the 1st term
$d = 8 - 5 = 3$ find d
$a_8 = 5 + (8-1)3$ substitute
$a_8 = 26$

Example: Given two terms of an arithmetic sequence, find a_1 and d

$a_4 = 21$	$a_6 = 32$
$a_n = a_1 + (n-1)d$	$a_4 = 21, n = 4$
$21 = a_1 + (4-1)d$	$a_6 = 32, n = 6$
$32 = a_1 + (6-1)d$	

$21 = a_1 + 3d$ solve the system of equations
$32 = a_1 + 5d$

$32 = \quad a_1 + 5d$
$\underline{-21 = -a_1 - 3d}$ multiply by -1
$11 = \qquad\quad 2d$ add the equations

$5.5 = d$

$21 = a_1 + 3(5.5)$ substitute d = 5.5 into either equation
$21 = a_1 + 16.5$
$a_1 = 4.5$

The sequence begins with 4.5 and has a common difference of 5.5 between numbers.

Geometric Sequences

A geometric sequence is a series of numbers in which a common ratio can be multiplied by a term to yield the next term. The common ratio can be calculated using the formula:

$$r = \frac{a_{n+1}}{a_n}$$ where r = common ratio and a_n = the nth term

The ratio is then used in the geometric sequence formula:

$$a_n = a_1 r^{n-1}$$

The formula essentially expresses the geometric sequence as an algebraic pattern $a_1, a_1 r, a_1 r^2, a_1 r^3, a_1 r^4$.... and so on where any numbers can be substituted for a1 and r to derive different numerical sequences.

<u>Example:</u> Find the 8th term of the geometric sequence 2, 8, 32, 128...

$r = \dfrac{a_{n+1}}{a_n}$ use common ratio formula to find the ratio

$r = \dfrac{8}{2}$ $\qquad\qquad$ substitute $a_n = 2$, $a_{n+1} = 8$

$r = 4$

$a_n = a_1 \bullet r^{n-1}$ $\qquad$ use $r = 4$ to solve for the 8th term

$a_8 = 2 \bullet 4^{8-1}$

$a_8 = 32{,}768$

<u>Example:</u> The seventh and fourth terms of a geometric sequence are $\dfrac{1}{64}$ and $\dfrac{1}{8}$ respectively. Find the first term and the common ratio.

$a_7 = \dfrac{1}{64}$ and $a_4 = \dfrac{1}{8}$

Dividing we get $\dfrac{a_7}{a_4} = \dfrac{\frac{1}{64}}{\frac{1}{8}} = \dfrac{1}{8}$

$a_n = a_1\, r^{n-1}$

But $\dfrac{a_7}{a_4} = \dfrac{a_1 r^6}{a_1 r^3} = r^3$

Therefore, $r^3 = \dfrac{1}{8}$ and $r = \dfrac{1}{2}$

Now $a_4 = a_1 r^3 = \dfrac{1}{8}$

That is $a_1\left(\dfrac{1}{8}\right) = \dfrac{1}{8}$

So $a_1 = 1$

First term = 1 and the common ratio is 1/2

For the Fibonacci sequence and other recursive patterns, see **Competency 0020B.**

Competency 0006   Understand how to manipulate and simplify algebraic expressions and translate problems into algebraic notation.

6A.   The nature of a variable

An entity that can take different values is a variable. For example, height can be considered a variable because height can take different values for different people. Similarly, a city can be considered a variable because a person's city can be assigned a value. Letters represent variables in algebraic equations and expressions

There are two types of variables, **independent** and **dependent** variables. This is the relationship between cause and effect. The independent variable is who is manipulated, a treatment, intervention or cause. The variable which is affected by the independent variable is dependent variable, which is the effect or outcome. For example, in the ordered pair, x-coordinates are independent variables as it can be selected in random and y-coordinates are dependent variables which depend on the x-coordinates. Similarly, in the study of effects on achievement of a new educational intervention, the intervention is the independent variable and the measure of achievement is the dependent variable.

6B.   Evaluating algebraic expressions for a given value of a variable

An algebraic expression consists of one or more algebraic terms in a phrase. It includes constants, variables and operating symbols such as plus and minus signs.

Example: $5x^2 - 2y + 3xy + 2$

The above example has four terms: $5x^2$, $2y$, $3xy$ and 2. The terms may be variables with coefficients, and constants.

When evaluating algebraic expressions, the Order of Operations (see **Competency 0002A**) needs to be followed.

Example: Evaluate the algebraic expression $x^2 - 6$ for the given value of $x = 2$.

Let $f(x) = x^2 - 6$. To find $f(2)$, substitute 2 for x.

Therefore, $f(2) = 2^2 - 6 = 4 - 6 = -2$

<u>Example</u>: Evaluate the expression $y^2 + 4x - 9$ for $y = 3$

Let $f(y) = y^2 + 4x - 9$. To find $f(3)$, substitute 3 for y.

So, $f(3) = 3^2 + 4(3) - 9 = 9 + 12 - 9 = 12$

6C. The relationship between standard computational algorithms and algebraic processes

An **algorithm** is an ordered sequence of steps that yields the solutions to a problem. In math, they are operations such as addition, multiplication, division, etc.

Algebraic processes follow the same logic used in numerical computations. For instance, the polynomial multiplication problem $(2x - 1)(x + 5)$ can be represented as an integer multiplication problem 54*26. Collecting like terms of polynomials and adding them is like adding multi-digit integers considering the place value.

An algorithm must be formulated as a sequence of logical or mathematical steps in order to describe exactly the way to find out the solution to every problem for a particular operation, rather than demonstrating the procedure for *some* examples. A procedure which solves only some of the problems in a given operation is not an algorithm.

Practicing with arithmetic algorithms is the first step with the formal manipulation of mathematical symbols. Polynomial division can be done using the standard division algorithm for integers, and so on.

All algorithms should be both reliable and efficient. Reliable means without errors (i.e. the steps in the algorithm will give the correct answer to every problem within the given operation). Efficient means there should be as few as possible arithmetic steps in the algorithm.

<u>Example</u>: 856 divided by 14

10 14's are 140
20 14's are 140 +140 = 280
30 14's are 280 + 140 = 420
40 14's are 420 + 140 = 560
50 14's are 560 + 140 = 700
60 14's are 700 + 140 = 840

Subtract 840 from the dividend 856, which gives 16

1 14 is 14

Subtract 14 from 16, which leaves 2.

Therefore, quotient is 60 + 1 = 61 and the remainder is 2.

Standard Division Algorithm
The two numbers used are "current dividend" and "current quotients." Each of them will be updated any number of times during the execution of the algorithm. To start with, let the current dividend be the dividend and the current quotient is 0. Continue performing the following steps until Step 1 tells you to stop.

Step 1: If the current dividend is less than the divisor, stop. The quotient is the current quotient and the remainder is the current dividend. Otherwise, continue with Step 2.

Step 2: From among the multiples of the divisor by the following multipliers:

1, 2, 3, 4, 5, 6, 7, 8, 9,
10, 20, 30, 40, 50, 60, 70, 80, 90,
100, 200, 300, 400, 500, 600, 700, 800, 900,

Select the largest multiple that is less than or equal to the current dividend.

Step 3: Subtract that multiple from the current dividend to update the current dividend

Step 4: Add the current quotient and the selected multiplier to update the current quotient

Step 5: Go to Step 1

This loop continues until the current dividend is less than the divisor.

6D. Expressing direct and inverse relationships algebraically

Two or more quantities can vary directly or inversely with each other. If two variables vary directly, as one gets larger, the other also gets larger. If one gets smaller, then the other gets smaller too. If two variables vary inversely, as one gets larger, the other one gets smaller. To express the relationship as an equation, we introduce another constant quantity called the constant of proportionality.

Direct Variation

A **direct variation** can be expressed by the formula

$y = kx$ where k is a constant, $k \neq 0$.

k is the slope of the straight line that represents this relationship graphically.

.

Example: If y varies directly as x and $y = -8$ when $x = 4$, find y when $x = 11$

First find the **constant of variation**, k.

$$k = \frac{y}{x} = \frac{-8}{4} = -2$$

Thus $y = kx = -2x$

For $x = 11$, $y = -2(11) = -22$

Example: If \$30 is paid for 5 hours work, how much would be paid for 19 hours work?

Since pay is varies directly with work:
\$30 = c(5 hours) where c is the constant of proportionality.
Solving for c which is the hourly pay rate in this case, we find that
c = \$6/hour.

Thus, pay for 19 hours of work = ($6/hour) (19 hours) = $114.
This could also be done

as a proportion: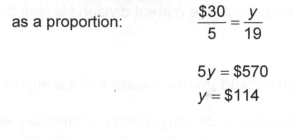

$$\frac{\$30}{5} = \frac{y}{19}$$

$$5y = \$570$$
$$y = \$114$$

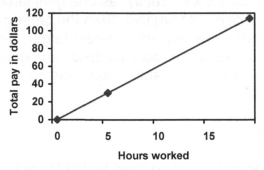

Inverse Variation

An **inverse variation** can be expressed by the formula

$xy = k$, where k is a constant, $k \neq 0$.

The graph of the relationship is not a straight line in this case.

<u>Example</u>: If y varies inversely as x and $y = 20$ when $x = -4$, find y when $x = 14$

$$k = 20(-4) = -80$$
Thus xy = -80
For x = 14, $y = \frac{-80}{14} = -5\frac{5}{7}$

<u>Example</u>: On a 546 mile trip from Miami to Charlotte, one car drove 65 mph while another car drove 70 mph. How does this affect the driving time for the trip?

This is an inverse variation, since increasing your speed should decrease your driving time. Use the equation

$t = \dfrac{d}{r}$ where t=driving time, r = speed and d = distance traveled.

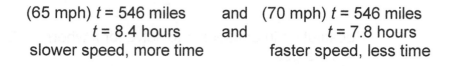

(65 mph) t = 546 miles   and   (70 mph) t = 546 miles
t = 8.4 hours   and t = 7.8 hours
slower speed, more time   faster speed, less time

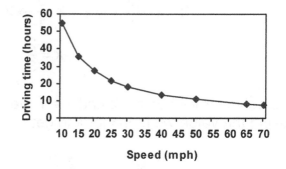

A quantity may also vary with different exponents of another quantity as shown in the examples below.

<u>Example</u>: A varies inversely as the square of R. When A = 2, R = 4. Find A if R = 10.

Since A varies inversely as the square of R,

$$A = \dfrac{k}{R^2} \text{ (equation 1), } k \text{ is a constant.}$$

Use equation 1 to find k when A = 2 and R = 4.

$$2 = \dfrac{k}{4^2} \rightarrow 2 = \dfrac{k}{16} \rightarrow k = 32 .$$

Substituting k = 32 into equation 1 with R =10, we get:

$$A = \dfrac{32}{10^2} \rightarrow A = \dfrac{32}{100} \rightarrow A = 0.32$$

Example: x varies directly as the cube root of y and inversely as the square of z. When $x = 2$, $y = 27$ and $z = 1$. Find y when $z = 2$ and $x = 1$.

Since x varies directly as the cube root of y and inversely as the square of z.

$$x = k \cdot \frac{\sqrt[3]{y}}{z^2} \quad \text{(equation 1)}, \ k \text{ is constant.}$$

Substituting in equation 1 to solve for k when $x = 2$, $y = 27$ and $z = 1$ we get:

$$2 = k \cdot \frac{\sqrt[3]{27}}{1^2} \rightarrow 2 = k \cdot \frac{3}{1} \rightarrow 2 = 3k$$

$$k = \frac{2}{3}$$

To solve for y when $z = 2$ and $x = 1$, we substitute in equation 1 using the value we found for k to get:

$$1 = \frac{2}{3} \cdot \frac{\sqrt[3]{y}}{2^2} \rightarrow 1 = \frac{2 \cdot \sqrt[3]{y}}{3(4)} \rightarrow 1 = \frac{2 \cdot \sqrt[3]{y}}{12}$$

$$1 = \frac{\sqrt[3]{y}}{6} \rightarrow 6 = \sqrt[3]{y} \qquad \text{Cube both sides.}$$

$$6^3 = \left(\sqrt[3]{y} \right)^3$$

$$y = 216$$

6E.   Expressing one variable in terms of another

The steps to solve for one variable in a multivariate equation are:

1. Combining like terms
2. Isolating the terms that contain the variable you wish to solve for
3. Isolating the variable (removing the coefficients)
4. Substituting the answer into the original equation and verify

<u>Example:</u> Given the equation $2(5x + z) = 30x + 3y + 10$, find the value of x in terms of y and z.

1. Combining like terms
   Expanding the equation by removing the parentheses using associative property
   $10x + 2z = 30x + 3y + 10$
   $10x - 10x + 2z = 30x - 10x + 3y + 10$ subtract 10x from both sides
   $2z = 20x + 3y + 10$

2. Isolate the terms that contain the variable x
   $2z - 3y - 10 = 20x + 3y - 3y + 10 - 10$ subtract 3y and 10 from both sides
   $2z - 3y - 10 = 20x$

3. Isolate the variable (remove the coefficients)
   Here the coefficient of x is 20. Therefore, divide both sides of
   The equation by 20 to isolate x:

$$2z - 3y - 10 = 20x$$

$$\frac{2z - 3y - 10}{20} = x$$

<u>Example:</u> Solve $A = p + prt$ for t.

$$A - p = prt$$

$$\frac{A - p}{pr} = \frac{prt}{pr}$$

$$\frac{A - p}{pr} = t$$

<u>Example:</u>

Solve $A = 1/2\ h(b_1 + b_2)$ for b_2

$A = 1/2\ hb_1 + 1/2\ hb_2$ ← step a

$2A = hb_1 + hb_2$ ← step b

$2A - hb_1 = hb_2$ ← step c

$\dfrac{2A - hb_1}{h} = \dfrac{hb_2}{h}$ ← step d

$\dfrac{2A - hb_1}{h} = b_2$ ← will not reduce

6F. Manipulating and simplifying algebraic expressions

The following properties of real numbers (where *a, b, c, d* are any real numbers) are useful for manipulation of algebraic expressions.

$a=a$	Reflexive property
$a + b$ is a unique real number	Closure property of addition
ab is a unique real number	Closure property of multiplication
If $a = b$, then $b = a$	Symmetric property
If $a = b$ and $b = c$, then $a = c$	Transitive property
If $a+b=c$ and $b=d$, then $a+d = c$	Substitution property
If $a=b$, then ac $= b - c$	Substitution property
If $a=b$, then $ac = bc$	Multiplication property
If $a=b$ and $c \neq 0$, then $\dfrac{a}{c} = \dfrac{b}{c}$	Division property
$a + b = b + a$	Property of addition
$ab = ba$	Property of multiplication
$a+(b+c) = (a+b)+c$	Associative property of addition
$a(bc) = (ab)c$	Associative property of multiplication
$a+0=0+a=a$	Additive identity; the number 0 is called the additive identity
$a(1)=1(a)=a$	Associative identity; the number 1 is called the multiplicative identity
$a(b+c)=a(b)+a(c)$ and $(b+c)a=b(a)+c(a)$	Distributive Property

Example: Simplify. $3^3 - 5(b + 2)$

$$= 3^3 - 5b - 10$$

$$27 - 5b - 10 = 17 - 5b$$

Add or subtract rational expressions

In order to add or subtract rational expressions, they must have a common denominator. If they don't have a common denominator, then factor the denominators to determine what factors are missing from each denominator to make the LCD. Multiply both numerator and denominator by the missing factor(s). Once the fractions have a common denominator, add or subtract their numerators, but keep the common denominator the same. Factor the numerator if possible and reduce if there are any factors that can be cancelled.

Find the least common denominator for $6a^3b^2$ and $4ab^3$.

These factors into $2 \cdot 3 \cdot a^3 \cdot b^2$ and $2 \cdot 2 \cdot a \cdot b^3$.
The first expression needs to be multiplied by another 2 and b.

The other expression needs to be multiplied by 3 and a^2.
Then both expressions would be $2 \cdot 2 \cdot 3 \cdot a^3 \cdot b^3 = 12a^3b^3 = \text{LCD}$

Add, subtract and multiply polynomials

Addition of polynomials
Find the sum of two polynomials by grouping the like powers, retaining their signs and adding the coefficients of like powers.

Example: Add $\left(2x^2 - 4\right)$ and $\left(x^2 + 3x - 3\right)$

Remove parenthesis, identify like terms. Group the like terms together. Add the like terms.

$$\left(2x^2 - 4\right) + \left(x^2 + 3x - 3\right) = 2x^2 + x^2 + 3x - 4 - 3$$
$$= 3x^2 + 3x - 7$$

Example: Add $\left(5x - 1\right) + \left(10x^2 + 7x\right)$
$$\left(5x - 1\right) + \left(10x^2 + 7x\right) = 10x^2 + 5x + 7x - 1$$
$$= 10x^2 + 12x - 1$$

Subtraction of polynomials
Subtract like terms, by changing the signs of the terms being subtracted and following the rules for addition of polynomials.

Example: Subtract $\left(y^4 + 4y^2 + 5y - 4\right)$ from $\left(3y^5 + y^4 - 3y^3 - 2y + 1\right)$
First, change the sign of each term of the polynomial being subtracted. So the polynomial $y^4 + 4y^2 + 5y - 4$
becomes $-y^4 - 4y^2 - 5y + 4$.

$$\left(3y^5 + y^4 - 3y^3 - 2y + 1\right) - \left(y^4 + 4y^2 + 5y - 4\right)$$
$$= \left(3y^5 + y^4 - 3y^3 - 2y + 1\right) + \left(-y^4 - 4y^2 - 5y + 4\right)$$
$$= 3y^5 + 0y^4 - 3y^3 - 7y + 5$$
$$= 3y^5 - 3y^3 - 7y + 5$$

Example: Subtract $\left(p^3 + 4p^2 - 5p - 6\right)$ from $\left(7p^3 - 3p + 5\right)$
$$\left(7p^3 - 3p + 5\right) - \left(p^3 + 4p^2 - 5p - 6\right) = 7p^3 - p^3 - 4p^2 - 3p + 5p + 5 + 6$$

Multiplication of polynomials
All the terms of the second polynomial are to be multiplied by each term of the first polynomial to get the product.

Example: Simplify $(-3x)\left(4x^2 - x + 10\right)$
$$(-3x)\left(4x^2 - x + 10\right) = \left(-3x \times 4x^2\right) - \left(-3x \times x\right) + \left(-3x \times 10\right)$$
$$= -12x^3 - \left(-3x^2\right) + -30x$$
$$= -12x^3 + 3x^2 - 30x$$

Example: Find the product of $(2p + 6)(2p - 6)$
$$(2p + 6)(2p - 6) = (2p \times 2p) - (2p \times 6) + (6 \times 2p) - (6 \times 6)$$
$$= 4p^2 - 12p + 12p - 36$$
$$= 4p^2 - 36$$

Example: Find the LCD for $x^2 - 4$, $x^2 + 5x + 6$, and $x^2 + x - 6$.

$$x^2 - 4 \qquad \text{factors into } (x - 2)(x + 2)$$
$$x^2 + 5x + 6 \quad \text{factors into } (x + 3)(x + 2)$$
$$x^2 + x - 6 \quad \text{factors into } (x + 3)(x - 2)$$

To make these lists of factors the same, they must all be $(x + 3)(x + 2)(x - 2)$. This is the LCD.

Add subtract, multiply and divide algebraic fractions

To **add** algebraic fractions, first express them in terms of their lowest common denominator (LCD) and then add their numerators to obtain the numerator that is divided by the LCD to arrive the answer.

Example: Add $\left(\dfrac{3a}{2}\right)$ and $\left(\dfrac{5a}{3}\right)$

$$\left(\dfrac{3a}{2}\right)+\left(\dfrac{5a}{3}\right)=\left(\dfrac{3a\times3}{6}\right)+\left(\dfrac{5a\times2}{6}\right)$$

$$=\dfrac{9a}{6}+\dfrac{10a}{6}$$

$$=\dfrac{19a}{6}=3\dfrac{1}{6}a$$

Example: Find the sum of $\left(\dfrac{5}{x+y}\right)$ and $\left(\dfrac{4}{x-y}\right)$

$$\left(\dfrac{5}{x+y}\right)+\left(\dfrac{4}{x-y}\right)=\left(\dfrac{5(x-y)}{(x+y)(x-y)}\right)+\left(\dfrac{4(x+y)}{(x+y)(x-y)}\right)$$

$$=\dfrac{5(x-y)+4(x+y)}{(x+y)(x-y)}$$

$$=\dfrac{5x-5y+4x+4y}{x^2-y^2}$$

$$=\dfrac{9x-y}{x^2-y^2}$$

Subtraction of algebraic fractions

To subtract algebraic fractions, first express them in terms of their LCD and then subtract their numerator to obtain the numerator that is divided by the LCD to arrive the answer.

Example: Simplify $\left(\dfrac{3y}{5}\right) - \left(\dfrac{y}{10}\right)$

$$\left(\dfrac{3y}{5}\right) - \left(\dfrac{y}{10}\right) = \left(\dfrac{3y \times 2}{5 \times 2}\right) - \left(\dfrac{y \times 1}{10 \times 1}\right)$$

$$= \dfrac{6y}{10} - \dfrac{y}{10}$$

$$= \dfrac{6y - y}{10}$$

$$= \dfrac{5y}{10} = \dfrac{y}{2}$$

Example: $\left(\dfrac{5}{x+y}\right) - \left(\dfrac{4}{x-y}\right)$

$$\left(\dfrac{5}{x+y}\right) - \left(\dfrac{4}{x-y}\right) = \left(\dfrac{5(x-y)}{(x-y)(x+y)}\right) - \left(\dfrac{4(x+y)}{(x-y)(x+y)}\right)$$

$$= \dfrac{5(x-y) - 4(x+y)}{(x+y)(x-y)}$$

$$= \dfrac{5x - 5y - 4x - 4y}{x^2 - y^2} = \dfrac{x - 9y}{x^2 - y^2}$$

Multiplication of algebraic fractions
Factorize the numerators and denominators. Then cancel the factors common to the numerator and denominator before applying multiplication to obtain the answer

Example: Find the product of $\left(\dfrac{a}{3}\right)$ and $\left(\dfrac{b}{4}\right)$

$$\left(\dfrac{a}{3}\right) \cdot \left(\dfrac{b}{4}\right) = \dfrac{a \cdot b}{3 \cdot 4} = \dfrac{ab}{12}$$

Example: Simplify $\left(\dfrac{5x^2}{2x^2-2x}\right)\left(\dfrac{x^2-1}{x^2+x}\right)$

$\left(\dfrac{5x^2}{2x^2-2x}\right)\left(\dfrac{x^2-1}{x^2+x}\right)=\left(\dfrac{5x^2}{2x(x-1)}\right)\left(\dfrac{(x+1)(x-1)}{x(x+1)}\right)=\dfrac{5}{2}$, since all the

common factors from the numerator and the denominator are cancelled

Example: Multiply $\left(\dfrac{4x^2}{x-2}\right)\left(\dfrac{x^2-4}{12}\right)$

$\left(\dfrac{4x^2}{x-2}\right)\left(\dfrac{x^2-4}{12}\right)=\left(\dfrac{4x^2}{x-2}\right)\left(\dfrac{(x-2)(x+2)}{4\times3}\right)$

$=\dfrac{x^2(x+2)}{3}$

Division of algebraic fractions
To divide the algebraic fractions, invert the second fraction and multiply it by the first fraction. That is we have to multiply both the fractions after taking the reciprocal of the divisor. Then factorize the numerator and denominator and cancel all the common factors.

Example: Simplify $\left(\dfrac{x-3}{4}\right)\div\left(\dfrac{x+3}{8}\right)$

$\left(\dfrac{x-3}{4}\right)\div\left(\dfrac{x+3}{8}\right)=\left(\dfrac{x-3}{4}\right)\left(\dfrac{8}{x+3}\right)$

$=\dfrac{2(x-3)}{x+3}$

Example: Simplify $\left(\dfrac{m^2+2m}{3m^3}\right)\div\left(\dfrac{5m+10}{6}\right)$

$\left(\dfrac{m^2+2m}{3m^3}\right)\div\left(\dfrac{5m+10}{6}\right)=\left(\dfrac{m(m+2)}{3m^3}\right)\div\left(\dfrac{5(m+2)}{6}\right)$

$=\left(\dfrac{m(m+2)}{3m^3}\right)\left(\dfrac{6}{5(m+2)}\right)$

$=\dfrac{2}{5m^2}$

6G. Solving Equations

The procedure for solving algebraic equations is demonstrated using the example below.

<u>Example</u>: $3(x+3) = -2x+4$ Solve for x.

1)   Expand to eliminate all parentheses

$3x+9 = -2x+4$

2)   Multiply each term by the LCD to eliminate all denominators (there are none here)

3)   Combine like terms on each side when possible (there is no need to do that here)

4)   Use real number properties to put all variables on one side and all constants on the other

$\rightarrow 3x+9-9 = -2x+4-9$ (Subtract 9 from both sides)

$\rightarrow 3x = -2x-5$

$\rightarrow 3x+2x = -2x+2x-5$ (add 2x to both sides)

$\rightarrow 5x = -5$

$\rightarrow \dfrac{5x}{5} = \dfrac{-5}{5}$ (divide both sides by 5)

$\rightarrow x = -1$

<u>Example:</u> Solve $3(2x+5) - 4x = 5(x+9)$

$6x+15-4x = 5x+45$
$2x+15 = 5x+45$
$-3x+15 = 45$
$-3x = 30$
$x = -10$

Example:

$2a + 4 = a - 2$

$2a + 4 - a = a - 2 - a$ Subtract a from both sides

$a + 4 = -2$

$a + 4 - 4 = -2 - 4$ Subtract 4 from both sides

$a = -6$

Check the solution by substitution

$2(-6) + 4 = -6 - 2$

$-12 + 4 = -8$

$-8 = -8$

Absolute value equations

To solve linear equations involving the absolute value of a variable, derive two equations.

If $|x| = n$, then $x = n$ or $x = -n$

Example: Find the values of y that satisfy $|y - 7| = 2$.

$$y - 7 = 2 \quad or \quad y - 7 = -2$$
$$y = 9 \quad or \quad y = 5$$

The solutions must be checked.

$\|y - 7\| = 2$	$\|y - 7\| = 2$
$\|9 - 7\| = 2$	$\|5 - 7\| = 2$
$\|2\| = 2$	$\|-2\| = 2$
$2 = 2$	$2 = 2$
true ✓	true ✓

Example: Find the values of x that satisfy $|3x|+4=x$.

$$|3x|+4=x$$
$$|3x|=x-4$$

$3x = x-4$ or $3x=-(x-4)$
$2x = -4$ $3x = -x+4$
                    $4x = 4$

$x = -2$ or $x = 1$

The solutions must be checked.

$|3x|+4=-2$ $|3x|+4=1$

$|3(-2)|+4=-2$ $|3(1)|+4=1$

$|-6|+4=-2$ $|3|+4=1$

$6+4=-2$ $3+4=1$

$10 \neq -2$ $7 \neq 1$

Since no solution is true, the solution set is empty.

If a and b are real numbers, and k is a non-negative real number, the solution of $|ax+b|=k$ is $ax+b=k$ or $ax+b=-k$

Example: $|2x+3|=9$ solve for x.

$2x+3=9$ or $2x+3={}^-9$

$2x+3-3=9-3$ or $2x+3-3={}^-9-3$

$2x=6$ or $2x={}^-12$

$\dfrac{2x}{2}=\dfrac{6}{2}$ or $\dfrac{2x}{2}=\dfrac{{}^-12}{2}$

$x=3$ or $x={}^-6$

Therefore, the solution is $x=\{3,{}^-6\}$

Example: Solve and check:

$$|2x - 5| + 1 = 12$$
$$|2x - 5| = 11 \quad \text{Get absolute value alone.}$$

Rewrite as 2 equations and solve separately.

right hand side positive   right hand side negative

$$2x - 5 = 11 \qquad\qquad 2x - 5 = -11$$
$$2x = 16 \qquad \text{and} \qquad 2x = -6$$
$$x = 8 \qquad\qquad\qquad x = -3$$

Checks: $|2x - 5| + 1 = 12 \qquad |2x - 5| + 1 = 12$

$$|2(8) - 5| + 1 = 12 \qquad |2(-3) - 5| + 1 = 12$$
$$|11| + 1 = 12 \qquad\qquad |-11| + 1 = 12$$
$$12 = 12 \qquad\qquad\qquad 12 = 12$$

This time both 8 and -3 check

An **inequality with absolute value** can be solved in a similar manner to an equation. Further, for $r > 0$ (where r is a positive real number)

$$\text{If } |x| < r \text{ then } -r < x < r$$
$$\text{and if } |x| > r \text{ then } x < -r \text{ or } x > r$$

Example: $|x - 1| < 4$

$$x - 1 < 4 \quad \text{and} \quad x - 1 > -4$$
$$x < 5 \quad \text{and} \quad x > -3$$

Thus, the solution set is all real numbers between −3 and 5.

Example: $|4+x|-3 \geq 0$

$\qquad |4+x| \geq 3$

$\qquad 4+x \geq 3 \quad$ or $\quad 4+x \leq -3$

$\qquad x \geq -1 \qquad\qquad x \leq -7$

The solution set is all real number less than or equal to –7, or greater than or equal to –1.

Example: Solve and check:

$\qquad 2|x-7|-13 \geq 11$

$\qquad 2|x-7| \geq 24 \qquad$ Get absolute value alone

$\qquad |x-7| \geq 12$

Rewrite as 2 inequalities and solve separately.

right hand side positive   right hand side negative

$\qquad x-7 \geq 12 \qquad$ or $\qquad x-7 \leq -12$

$\qquad x \geq 19 \qquad\qquad\qquad x \leq -5$

6H. Using algebraic expressions to model situations

Many word problems do not give explicit equations or relationships in mathematical or algebraic form. As a result, it is necessary to be able to convert plain language into algebraic relationships that can be used to model situations described in a particular problem. For instance, basic arithmetic operations can involve terms such as the following:

Addition: plus, sum, total, add
Subtraction: less, difference, take away, minus, subtract
Multiplication: product, times, multiply
Division: fraction, over, divide

Furthermore, it is necessary not only to identify the operations involved in a particular verbal expression, but the variables or parameters involved in those operations as well.

Example: Write the following statement as an algebraic equation: "The height of the rocket is the product of the speed and the amount of time in flight, plus the starting height."

$$h = vt + h_0$$

First, define the variables involved in the problem. Express the height of the rocket h, in terms of the speed v, the time in flight t, and the initial height s. If ambiguity arises, such as might take place were the above statement spoken instead of written (the lack of a comma might lead to the question as to whether the second term in the product is t or $(t + s)$), choose the interpretation that makes the most sense according to the situation.

Next, write the equation using the defined variables:

$$h = vt + s$$

Example: Mark and Mike are twins. Three times Mark's age plus four equals four times Mike's age minus 14. How old are the boys?

$$3 \cdot m + 4 = 4 \cdot M_2 - 14$$

Since the boys are twins, their ages are the same. "Translate" the English into Algebra.

Let x = their age
$3x + 4 = 4x - 14$
$18 = x$

$$3m + 4 = 4m - 14$$
$$-3m + 14 \quad -3m + 14$$
$$18 = m$$

The boys are each 18 years old.

Example: The Simpsons went out for dinner. All 4 of them ordered the Aardvark steak dinner. Bert paid for the 4 meals and included a tip of $12 for a total of $84.60. How much was an Aardvark steak dinner?

Let x = the price of one Aardvark dinner
So $4x$ = the price of 4 Aardavark dinners
$4x = 84.60 - 12$
$4x = 72.60$
$x = \dfrac{72.60}{4} = \$18.15$ The price of one Aardvark dinner.

$$4m + 12 = 84.60$$
$$4m = 84.60 - 12$$
$$4m = 72.60$$
$$\frac{4m}{4} \quad \frac{72.60}{4}$$
$$m = \$18.15$$

Proportions can be used to solve word problems whenever relationships are compared. Some situations include scale drawings and maps, similar polygons, speed, time and distance, cost, and comparison shopping.

Example: A car travels 125 miles in 2.5 hours. How far will it go in 6 hours?

Write a proportion comparing the distance and time.

$$\frac{\text{miles}}{\text{hours}} = \frac{125}{2.5} = \frac{x}{6}$$
$$2.5x = 750$$
$$x = 300$$

Thus, the car can travel 300 miles in 6 hours.

Example: The scale on a map is $\frac{3}{4}$ inch = 6 miles. What is the actual distance between two cities if they are $1\frac{1}{2}$ inches apart on the map?

Write a proportion comparing the scale to the actual distance.

$$\begin{array}{cc} \text{scale} & \text{actual} \end{array}$$
$$\frac{\frac{3}{4}}{1\frac{1}{2}} = \frac{6}{x}$$
$$\frac{3}{4}x = 1\frac{1}{2} \times 6$$
$$\frac{3}{4}x = 9$$
$$x = 12$$

Thus, the actual distance between the cities is 12 miles.

Competency 0007 Understand properties of functions and relations.

7A. The difference between functions and relations

A **relation** is a set of ordered pairs.({ } is the symbol for a set.) Functions are a special kind of relation such as {(1,2), (4,39), (33,8)}. The main **difference** between functions and relations is that **each x-value in a function has one and only one y-value**. A function has a **domain** and a **range**, which are the x and y values of ordered pairs.
<u>Example:</u>

Relation 1: {(0, 1), (1, 2), (2, 4)}

Relation 2: {(0, 1), (1, 2), (1, 4)}

Comparing the two relations above, we see that they differ just by one number. Since relation #1 has only one y value for each x value, this relation is a function. On the other hand, relation #2 has two distinct y values '2' and '4' for the same x value of '1'. Therefore, relation #2 does not satisfy the definition of a mathematical function.

7B. The generation and interpretation of graphs that model real-world situations

Identification of the properties of a graph can be helpful in determining the corresponding function that is being plotted (either exactly or approximately), or can provide information about the behavior of functions over certain intervals. For instance, the **slope** of the graph is the rate of increase in the vertical direction for a given increase in the horizontal direction. The slope is defined as positive when the plot of the function increases when going from left to right, and it is defined as negative when the function decreases when going from left to right.

Only straight lines have a constant slope; other functions generally have a slope that varies continuously over the domain of the function. For instance, the function shown below has a varying slope that is positive for positive x values and negative for negative x values.

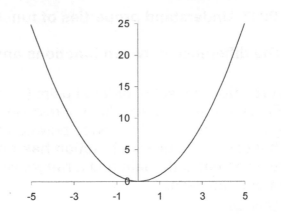

The **intervals of increase or decrease** for a function are those respective portions of the domain for which the function is increasing monotonically or decreasing monotonically. In the example graph above, the function has an interval of decrease over $(-\infty, 0)$ and an interval of increase over $(0, \infty)$.

Furthermore, the function graphed above has an **axis of symmetry** at $x = 0$. An axis of symmetry is simply a line that divides two symmetric portions of a function. The function displays a mirror image across such a line, with the axis of symmetry acting as the hypothetical mirror.

The **intercepts** of a function are those points at which the function crosses one or both of the axes. Since a function has only one value in the range corresponding to each value in the domain, a function can have only one y-intercept. Nevertheless, a function can have infinitely many x-intercepts. Consider the graph of the cosine function, as shown below.

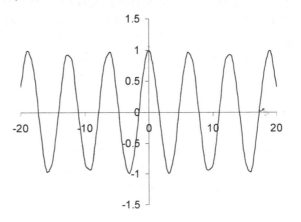

The cosine function has a *y*-intercept at *y* = 1 and numerous *x*-intercepts (the total number of *x*-intercepts is infinite, but only 12 are shown here). The *x*-intercepts are at $x = \dfrac{n\pi}{2}$, where *n* = ±1, ±2, ±3 and so on.

<u>Example:</u> Identify the critical properties of the following graph.

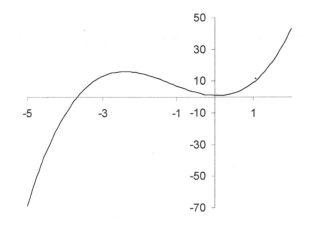

The function depicted above has no apparent axes of symmetry. It has a *y*-intercept at about *y* = 2 and an *x*-intercept at about *x* = 3.7. The intervals of increase are (extrapolating from the given information) approximately $(-\infty, -2.6)$ and $(0, \infty)$. If only the information in the visible graph is used, and no assumptions about the function outside the limits of the graph are made, then the intervals of increase are about $(-5, -2.6)$ and $(0, 2)$. The lone interval of decrease is about $(-2.6, 0)$.

The slope of the graph can be approximated, if necessary, on a point by point basis. It is noteworthy that the slope of the graph is zero at about *x* = –2.6 and *x* = 0.

7C.   Multiple ways of representing functions (e.g. tabular, graphic, verbal, symbolic)

A relationship between two quantities can be shown using a table, graph, written description or symbolic rule. In the following example, the rule y= 9x describes the relationship between the total amount earned, y, and the total amount of $9 sunglasses sold, x.

A table using this data would appear as:

number of sunglasses sold	1	5	10	
total dollars earned	9	45	90	

Each *(x,y)* relationship between a pair of values is called the coordinate pair and can be plotted on a graph. The coordinate pairs *(1,9)*, *(5,45)*, *(10,90)*, and *(15,135)*, are plotted on the graph below.

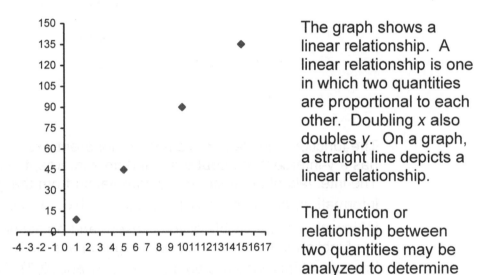

The graph shows a linear relationship. A linear relationship is one in which two quantities are proportional to each other. Doubling *x* also doubles *y*. On a graph, a straight line depicts a linear relationship.

The function or relationship between two quantities may be analyzed to determine how one quantity depends on the other.

For example, the function below shows a linear relationship between *y* and *x*: $y=2x+1$. The function, $y=2x+1$, is written as a symbolic rule. The same relationship is also shown in the table below:

x	0	2	3	6	
y	1	5	7	13	

A relationship could be written in words by saying "The value of y is equal to two times the value of x, plus one." This relationship could be shown on a graph by plotting given points such as the ones shown in the table above.

Another way to describe a function is as a process in which one or more numbers are input into an imaginary machine that produces another number as the output. If 5 is input (x) into a machine with a process of x +1, the output (y) will equal 6.

In real situations, relationships can be described mathematically. The function, y=x+1, can be used to describe the idea that people age one year on their birthday. To describe the relationship in which a person's monthly medical costs are 6 times a person's age, we could write y=6x. The monthly cost of medical care could be predicted using this function. A 20 year-old person would spend $120 per month (120=20*6). An 80 year-old person would spend $480 per month (480=80*6). Therefore, one could analyze the relationship to say: as you get older, medical costs increase $6.00 per month each year.

It is important to notice that the particular symbols used in function notation are not important, as long as they are used consistently. Thus, the following are all the same functions, but simply use different symbols to represent the erstwhile x and y notation.

$$f(\alpha) = \alpha^2$$
$$\beta(r) = r^2$$
$$\Pi(W) = W^2$$

The fundamental principle for this function notation is to represent that for each x (or, generally, variable) value, the function (be it f, β, or any other symbol) has only one value.

7D. Properties of functions and relations (e.g. domain, range, continuity)

The **domain** of a relation is the set made of all the first coordinates of the ordered pairs, i.e. the x-values. The **range** of a relation is the set of all the second coordinates or **y-values**.

A **function** is a relation in which different ordered pairs have different first coordinates. On a graph, use the **vertical line test** to look for a function. If any vertical line intersects the graph of a relation in more than one point, then the relation is not a function.

Example: Determine whether the following graph depicts a function.

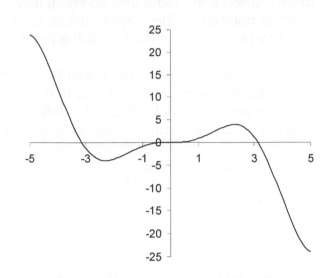

Use the vertical line test on the graph, as shown below. For every location of the vertical line, the plotted curve crosses the line only once. Therefore, the graph depicts a function.

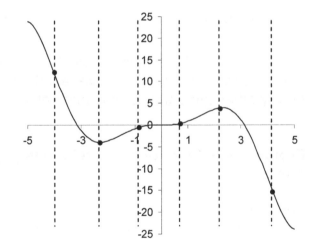

<u>Example:</u> Determine whether the following graph depicts a function.

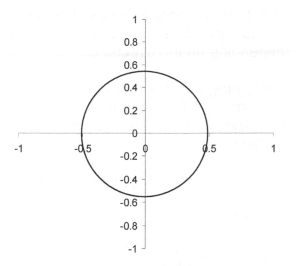

It is clear that a vertical line drawn on the graph would intersect the curve in more than one place, thus indicating there can be multiple y values for some x values. As a result, this graph does not meet the definition of a function.

<u>Example:</u> Determine the domain of the function depicted in the following graph.

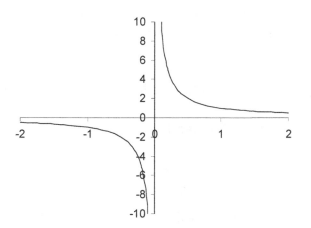

Note that this function is not **continuous**. It has two asymptotes: one for $y = 0$ and one for $x = 0$. It is apparent that the function is not defined for $x = 0$, but that it has finite values everywhere else. Thus, the domain of the function is all real numbers except 0.

The function plotted here is $y = \dfrac{1}{x}$; thus, by way of the function, it is clear that the range includes all real values except 0, for which the function goes to either positive or negative infinity in the limit (depending on the direction).

A **mapping** is a diagram with arrows drawn from each element of the domain to the corresponding elements of the range. If 2 arrows are drawn from the same element of the domain, then it is not a function.

<u>Example:</u> Are the mappings shown below true functions?

f 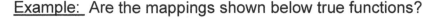 h

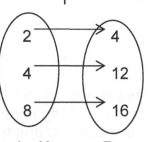 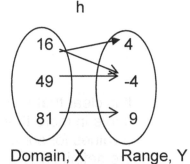

Domain, X   Range, Y   Domain, X   Range, Y

This is a "true" function.   This is not a "true" function.

A relation may also be described algebraically. An equation such as $y = 3x + 5$ describes a relation between the independent variable x and the dependent variable y. Thus, y is written as $f(x)$ "function of x."

<u>Example:</u> Given a function $f(x) = 3x + 5$, find $f(2)$; $f(0)$; $f(-10)$

$f(2)$ denotes the value of the function $f(x)$ at $x = 2$.

$f(2) = 3(2) + 5 = 6 + 5 = 11$

$f(0) = 3(0) + 5 = 0 + 5 = 5$ Substitute for x.

$f(-10) = 3(-10) + 5 = -30 + 5 = -25$

<u>Example:</u> Which set illustrates a function?

A)   { (0,1) (0,2) (0,3) (0,4) }
B)   { (3,9) (−3,9) (4,16) (− 4,16)}
C)   {(1,2) (2,3) (3,4) (1,4) }
D)   { (2,4) (3,6) (4,8) (4,16) }

Each number in the domain can only be matched with one number in the range. A is not a function because 0 is mapped to 4 different numbers in the range. In C, 1 is mapped to two different numbers. In D, 4 is also mapped to two different numbers. So answer is B.

<u>Example:</u> Give the domain for the function over the set of real numbers: $y = \dfrac{3x + 2}{2x^2 - 3}$

Solve the denominator for 0. These values will be excluded from the domain.

$$2x^2 - 3 = 0$$
$$2x^2 = 3$$
$$x^2 = 3/2$$

$$x = \sqrt{\frac{3}{2}} = \sqrt{\frac{3}{2}} \cdot \sqrt{\frac{2}{2}} = \frac{\pm\sqrt{6}}{2}$$

<u>Example:</u> Determine the domain and range of the following graph:

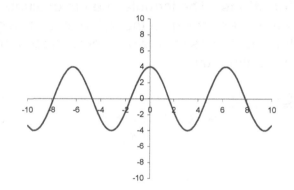

The domain of the function shown in the graph $= -\infty, \infty$.

Since the function is periodic and the y values vary between +4 and -4, the range of the function is -4 to +4.

<u>Example:</u> Determine the domain and range of this mapping.

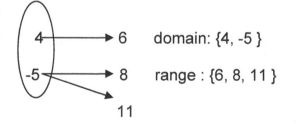

domain: {4, -5 }

range : {6, 8, 11 }

Example: Decide if the following condition determines a function: If a is a positive real number, then output the value of x for $a = x^2$.

In this case, the domain of the condition is the set of real numbers expressed as a. The relation yields the value of x for the equation $a = x^2$. Graphing the results is possible, but it is sufficient to solve for x. This yields $x = \pm\sqrt{a}$. Note that both positive and negative values of x can satisfy the equation $a = x^2$. As a result, each a value corresponds to two distinct x values (for instance, $(-2)^2 = (2)^2 = 4$ where $a = 4$).

This condition, then, does not determine a function.

7E. Piecewise-defined Functions

Functions defined by two or more formulas are **piecewise functions**. The formula used to evaluate piecewise functions varies depending on the value of x. The graphs of piecewise functions consist of two or more pieces, or intervals, and are often discontinuous.

Example:
$$f(x) = \begin{array}{ll} x + 1 & \text{if } x > 2 \\ x - 2 & \text{if } x \leq 2 \end{array}$$

Example:
$$f(x) = \begin{array}{ll} x & \text{if } x \geq 1 \\ x^2 & \text{if } x < 1 \end{array}$$

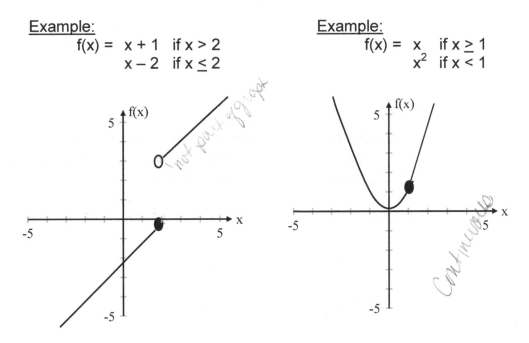

When graphing or interpreting the graph of piecewise functions it is important to note the points at the beginning and end of each interval because the graph must clearly indicate what happens at the end of each interval. Note that in the graph of Example 1, point (2, 3) is not part of the graph and is represented by an empty circle. On the other hand, point (2, 0) is part of the graph and is represented as a solid circle. Note also that the graph of Example 2 is continuous despite representing a piecewise function.

The Greatest Integer Function or **Step Function** has the equation: $f(x) = j[rx - h] + k$ or $y = j[rx - h] + k$. (h, k) is the location of the left endpoint of one step. j is the vertical jump from step to step. r is the reciprocal of the length of each step. If (x, y) is a point of the function, then when x is an integer, its y value is the same integer. If (x, y) is a point of the function, then when x is not an integer, its y value is the first integer less than x. Points on $y = [x]$ would include:

(3,3), ($^-$2,$^-$2), (0,0), (1.5,1), (2.83,2), ($^-$3.2,$^-$4), ($^-$.4,$^-$1).

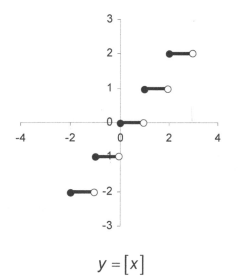

$$y = [x]$$

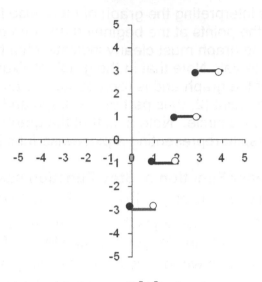

$$y = 2[x] - 3$$

Practice: Graph the following piecewise equations.

1. $f(x) = x^2$ if x > 0
        $= x + 4$ if x ≤ 0

2. $f(x) = x^2 - 1$ if x > 2
        $= x^2 + 2$ if x ≤ 2

7F.   **Addition, Subtraction and Composition of Functions**

Addition of Functions
(f + g)(x) = f (x) + g(x)

To add two functions, add together the solution for each.
For example, if
$f(x) = x^2 + 1$ and $g(x) = 6x - 1$, then

$(f + g)(1) = f(1) + g(1) = 2 + 5 = 7$

$(f + g)(x) = f(x) + g(x) = (x^2 + 1) + (6x - 1) = x^2 + 6x.$

$y = f(x)$, $y = g(x)$, and
$y = (f + g)(x):$

Subtraction of Functions
$(f - g)(x) = f(x) - g(x)$

To subtract two functions, subtract the solution of each.
For example, if $f(x) = 3x - 4$ and $g(x) = 5x + 2$,

then $(f - g)(2) = f(2) - g(2) = 2 - 12 = -10$.

$(f - g)(x) = f(x) - g(x) = (3x - 4) - (5x + 2) = -2x - 6$.

Example: Given $f(x) = 3x + 1$ and $g(x) = 4 + 3x$,

Find $(f + g)(x)$, $(f - g)(x)$, $(f \times g)(x)$, and $(f / g)(x)$.
To find the answers, just apply the operations (plus, minus, times, and divide)

$$(f + g)(x) = f(x) + g(x) = [3x + 1] + [4 + 3x]$$
$$= 3x + 3x + 1 + 4$$
$$= 6x + 5$$

$$(f - g)(x) = f(x) - g(x) = [3x + 1] - [4 + 3x]$$
$$= 3x - 3x + 1 - 4$$
$$= -3$$

$$(f \times g)(x) = [f(x)][g(x)] = (3x + 1)(4 + 3x)$$
$$= 12x + 4 + 9x^2 + 3x$$

$$= 9x^2 + 15x + 4$$

$$\left(\frac{f}{g}\right)x = \frac{f(x)}{g(x)} = \frac{3x + 1}{4 + 3x}$$

Example: Given $f(x) = 2x$, $g(x) = x + 4$, and $h(x) = 5 - x^3$,

find $(f + g)(2)$, $(h - g)(2)$, $(f \times h)(2)$, and $(h / g)(2)$.

$f(2) = 2(2) = 4$
$g(2) = (2) + 4 = 6$
$h(2) = 5 - (2)^3 = 5 - 8 = -3$
Evaluate the following:
$(f + g)(2) = f(2) + g(2) = 4 + 6 = 10$
$(h - g)(2) = h(2) - g(2) = -3 - 6 = -9$
$(f \times h)(2) = f(2) \times h(2) = (4)(-3) = -12$
$(h / g)(2) = h(2) \div g(2) = -3 \div 6 = -0.5$
The addition of *functions* is commutative and associative:
$f + g = g + f$ and $(f + g) + h = f + (g + h)$.

Composition
The process of substituting an entire function into another function to get a new function is called Composition.

The composition of two functions $f(x)$ and $g(x)$ is denoted by $(f \circ g)(x)$ or $f(g(x))$.

The domain of the composed function $f(g(x))$ is the set of all values of x in the domain of g that produce a value for $g(x)$ which is in the domain
of f.
Example: If $f(x) = x + 1$ and $g(x) = x^3$, find the composition functions $f \circ g$ and $g \circ f$ and state their domains.

$(f \circ g)(x) = f(g(x)) = f(x^3) = x^3 + 1$
$(g \circ f)(x) = g(f(x)) = g(x + 1) = (x + 1)^3$

The domain of both composite functions is the set of all real numbers.
Note that $f(g(x))$ and $g(f(x))$ are not the same. In general, unlike multiplication and addition, composition is *not* reversible.
Therefore, the order of composition is important.

Example: If $f(x) = \sqrt{x}$ and $g(x) = x + 2$, find the composition functions $f \circ g$ and $g \circ f$ and state their domains.

$(f \circ g)(x) = f(g(x)) = f(x + 2) = \sqrt{x + 2}$
$(g \circ f)(x) = g(f(x)) = g(\sqrt{x}) = \sqrt{x} + 2\sqrt{x + 2}$

The domain of $f(g(x))$ is $x \geq -2$ because $x + 2$ must be non-negative in order to take the square root.
The domain of $g(f(x))$ is $x \geq 0$ because x must be non-negative in order to take the square root. Note that defining the domain of composite functions is important when square roots are involved.

7G. Graphs of functions and their transformations (e.g., the relationships among $f(x)$, $f(x + k)$, and $f(x) + k$)

Transformations of functions follow the rules given below:

- $f(x) + a$ means $f(x)$ shifted upward by "a" units

- $f(x) - a$ means $f(x)$ shifted downward by "a" units

- $f(x + a)$ means $f(x)$ shifted left by "a" units

- f(x – a) means f(x) shifted right by "a" units
- –f(x) means f(x) flipped upside down ("reflected about the x-axis")
- f(–x) means f(x) flipped left to right ("reflected about the y-axis")

f(x) = x²

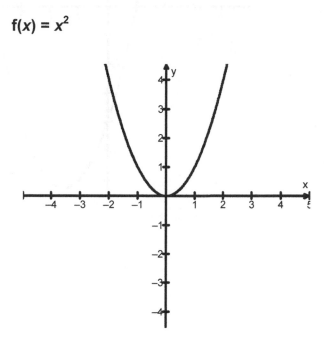

Transformation 1:

f(x) = –x²–4x+5

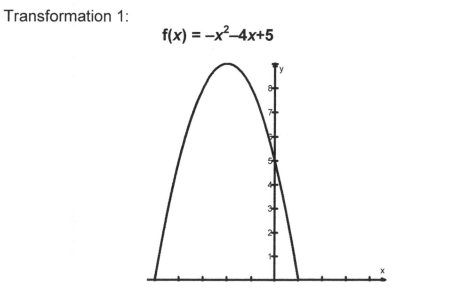

Transformation 2:

$$f(x) = x^2 - 3x - 4$$

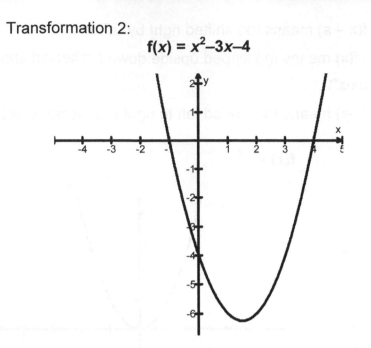

Transformation 3:

$$f(x) = (x+4)^2$$

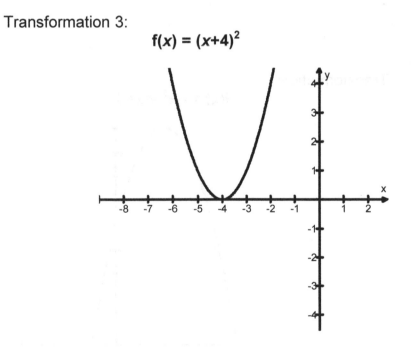

Transformation 4:

$$f(x) = x^2 + 3$$

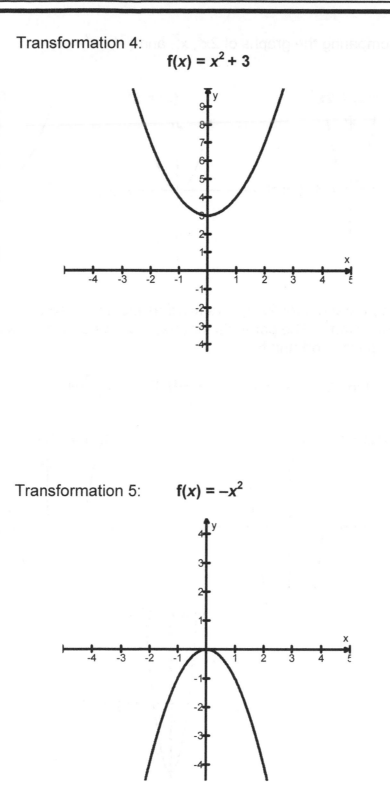

Transformation 5: $f(x) = -x^2$

The above graph is just f(x) flipped upside down. The points on the x-axis remain the same but the points off the axis switch sides. Therefore, − f(x) is just f(x) flipped upside down.

Comparing the graphs of $2x^2$, x^2, and $(\frac{1}{2})x^2$

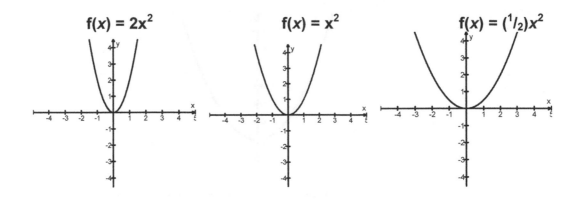

f(x) = 2x²   f(x) = x²   f(x) = (¹/₂)x²

The parabola for $2x^2$ grows twice as fast as x^2, so the graph is tall and skinny. The parabola for $(1/2)x^2$ grows only half as fast, so its graph is short and fat.

Comparing the graphs of $2(x^2-4)$, x^2-4, $(2x)^2-4$

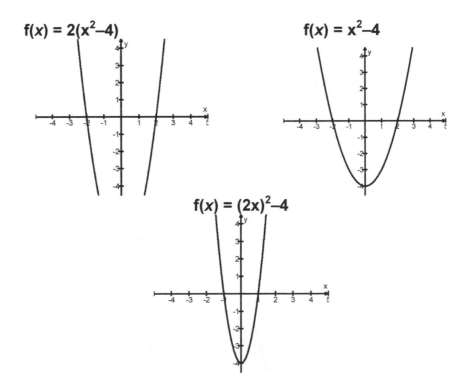

f(x) = 2(x²–4)   f(x) = x²–4

f(x) = (2x)²–4

The various transformations are "left", "right", "up", "down", "flip", "mirror", "stretching" and "squeezing". Multiplying inside the function (i.e. inside the argument of the function), makes the graph become thin.

Competency 0008 Understand properties and applications of linear relations and functions.

8 A. The relationship between linear models and rate of change

A **linear function** is a function defined by the equation $f(x) = mx + b$. Many real world situations involve linear relationships. One example is the relationship between distance and time traveled when a car is moving at a constant speed. The relationship between the price and quantity of a bulk item bought at a store is also linear assuming that the unit price remains constant. These relationships can be expressed using the equation of a straight line and the slope is often used to describe a constant or average rate of change. These problems usually involve units of measure such as miles per hour or dollars per year. Where the line intercepts the x- and y- axis indicates a starting point or a point at which values change from positive to negative or negative to positive.

Example: A man drives a car at a speed of 30 mph along a straight road. Express the distance d traveled by the man as a function of the time t assuming the man's initial position is d_0. The equation relating d and t is given by:

$$d = 30t + d_0$$

Notice that this equation is in the familiar slope-intercept form $y = mx + b$. In this case, time t (in hours) is the independent variable, the distance d (in miles) is the dependent variable. The **slope** is the **rate of change** of distance with time, i.e. the speed (in mph). The **y-intercept** or intercept on the distance axis d_0 represents the **initial position** of the car at the start time $t = 0$.

The above equation is plotted below with $d_0 = 15$ miles (the point on the graph where the line crosses the y-axis).

$$d = 30t + 15$$

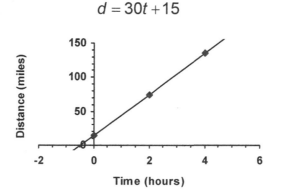

The **x-intercept** or intercept on the time axis represents the time at which the car would have been at $d = 0$ assuming it was traveling with the same speed before $t = 0$. This value can be found by setting d=0 in the equation:

$$0 = 30t + 15$$
$$30t = -15$$
$$t = \frac{-15}{30} = -\frac{1}{2}\text{hr}$$

This simply means that if the car was at $d = 15$ miles when we started measuring the time ($t = 0$), it was at $d = 0$ miles half an hour before that.

Example: A model for the distance traveled by a migrating monarch butterfly looks like $f(t) = 80t$, where t represents time in days.

We interpret this to mean that the average speed of the butterfly is 80 miles per day and distance traveled may be computed by substituting the number of days traveled for t. In a linear function, there is a **constant** rate of change.

Example: The town of Verdant Slopes has been experiencing a boom in population growth. By the year 2000, the population had grown to 45,000, and by 2005, the population had reached 60,000. Using the formula for slope as a model, find the average rate of change in population growth, expressing your answer in people per year. Then using the average rate of change determined, predict the population of Verdant Slopes in the year 2010.

Let t represent the time and p represent population growth. The two observances are represented by (t_1, p_1) and (t_2, p_2)

1st observance = (t_1, p_1) = (2000, 45000)
2nd observance = (t_2, p_2) = (2005, 60000)

Use the formula for slope to find the average rate of change.

$$\text{Rate of change} = \frac{p_2 - p_1}{t_2 - t_1}$$

$$= \frac{60000 - 45000}{2005 - 2000}$$

$$= \frac{15000}{5} = 3000 \text{ people / year}$$

The average rate of change in population growth for Verdant Slopes between the years 2000 and 2005 was 3000 people/year.

The population of Verdant Slopes can be predicted using the following:

3000 people/year x 5 years = 15,000 people
60000 people + 15000 people = 75,000 people

At a continuing average rate of growth of 3000 people/year, the population of Verdant Slopes could be expected to reach 75,000 by the year 2010.

8 B.   Direct variation

See **Competency 0006** for a detailed discussion of direct variation.

8 C.   Graphs of linear equations

First degree equations have exponents no greater than one and are also known as **linear equations** because their graphs are straight lines.

To graph a first degree equation, find both one point on the line and the slope of the line. The best way to find a point and the slope is to solve the equation for y. A linear equation that has been solved for y is in **slope intercept form, y = mx+b**. The point (0,**b**) is where the line intersects with the y-axis, **b is the y-intercept** and **m is the slope of the line**.

Another way to graph a linear equation is to find any two points on the line and connect them. To find points on the line, substitute any number for x, solve for y, then repeat with another number for x. Often the two easiest points to find are the intercepts. To find the intercepts, substitute 0 for x and solve for y, then substitute 0 for y and solve for x. Note that this method will only work when the slope is a nonzero and defined. It will not work for vertical and horizontal lines as defined below.

Remember that graphs will go up as they go to the right when the slope is positive. Negative slopes make the lines go down as they go to the right.
If the equation solves to **x = any number**, then the graph is a **vertical line**. It only has an x intercept. Its slope is **undefined**.

If the equation solves to **y = any number**, then the graph is a **horizontal line**. It only has an y intercept. Its slope is 0 (zero).

To graph **an inequality**, solve the inequality for y. This gets the inequality in the **slope intercept form**, (for example: $y < mx + b$). The point (0,b) is the y -intercept and m is the line's slope.

- If the inequality solves to $x >, \geq, < $ or $ \leq $ **any number**, then the graph includes a **vertical line**.

- If the inequality solves to $y >, \geq, < $ or $ \leq $ **any number**, then the graph includes a **horizontal line**.

When graphing a linear inequality, the line will be dotted if the inequality sign is $<$ or $>$. If the inequality signs are either $\geq$ or $\leq$, the line on the graph will be a solid line. Shade above the line when the inequality sign is $\geq$ or $>$. Shade below the line when the inequality sign is $<$ or $\leq$. Inequalities of the form $x >, x \leq, x <,$ or $x \geq$ number, draw a vertical line (solid or dotted). Shade to the right for $>$ or $\geq$. Shade to the left for $<$ or $\leq$. Remember: **Dividing or multiplying by a negative number will reverse the direction of the inequality sign.**

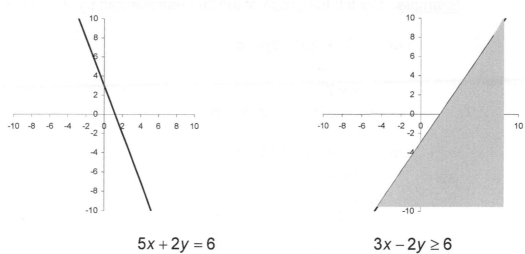

$$5x + 2y = 6$$
$$y = -5/2\,x + 3$$

$$3x - 2y \geq 6$$
$$y \leq 3/2\,x - 3$$

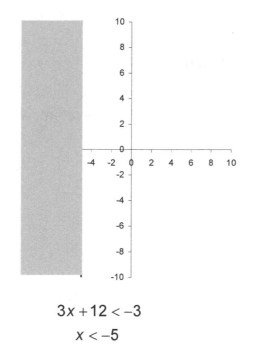

$$3x + 12 < -3$$
$$x < -5$$

Example: Sketch the graph of the line represented by $2x + 3y = 6$.

$$\text{Let } x = 0 \rightarrow 2(0) + 3y = 6$$
$$\rightarrow 3y = 6$$
$$\rightarrow y = 2$$
$$\rightarrow (0,2) \text{ is the } y \text{ intercept.}$$

$$\text{Let } y = 0 \rightarrow 2x + 3(0) = 6$$
$$\rightarrow 2x = 6$$
$$\rightarrow x = 3$$
$$\rightarrow (3,0) \text{ is the } x \text{ intercept.}$$

$$\text{Let } x = 1 \rightarrow 2(1) + 3y = 6$$
$$\rightarrow 2 + 3y = 6$$
$$\rightarrow 3y = 4$$
$$\rightarrow y = \frac{4}{3}$$
$$\rightarrow \left(1, \frac{4}{3}\right) \text{ is the third point.}$$

Plotting the three points on the coordinate system, we get the following:

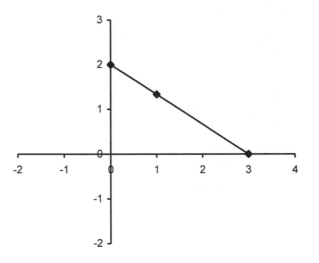

8 D.   Slope and intercepts of lines

The **slope** of a line is the "slant" of the line. A line slanting downward from left to right has a negative slope. An line slanting upward from left to right has a positive slope. Slope is also defined as the rate of change. The formula for calculating the slope of a line that includes points (x_1, y_1) and (x_2, y_2) is:

$$slope = \frac{y_2 - y_1}{x_2 - x_1}$$

The top of the fraction represents the change in the **y**-coordinates; it is called the **rise**.

The bottom of the fraction represents the change in the **x**-coordinates; it is called the **run.**

<u>Example:</u> Find the slope of a line with points at (2, 2) and (7, 8).

$$\frac{(8) - (2)}{(7) - (2)}$$ plug the values into the formula

$$\frac{6}{5}$$ solve the rise over run

$$= 1.2$$ solve for the slope

The y-intercept is the y-coordinate of the point where a line crosses the y-axis. The equation of a straight line can be written in slope-intercept form, $y = mx + b$, where m is the slope and b is the y-intercept. To rewrite the equation into another form, multiply each term by the common denominator of all the fractions. Then rearrange terms as necessary.

To find the y-intercept, substitute 0 for x and solve for y. This is the y-intercept. The y intercept is also the value of b in $y = mx + b$.

The x-intercept is the x-coordinate of the point where a line crosses the x-axis. To find the x-intercept, substitute 0 for y and solve for x.

Example: Find the x and y intercepts of the following graph.

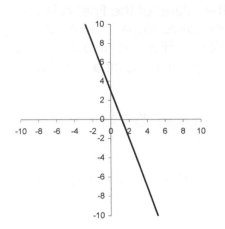

The graph above represents the following equation
$5x + 2y = 6$

Changing the equation to slope-intercept form,

$y = -5/2 x + 3$

The y-intercept = b = 3. The x-intercept is the x value for which y = 0.

Substituting y = 0,

$y = -\frac{5}{2} x + 3$

$0 = -\frac{5}{2} x + 3$

$-\frac{5}{2} x = 3$

$x = 3\left(\frac{-2}{5}\right) = -\frac{6}{5}$

So the x-intercept is –6/5.

Example: Find the slope and intercepts of $3x + 2y = 14$.

$$3x + 2y = 14$$
$$2y = {}^-3x + 14$$
$$y = {}^-2/3 \; x + 7$$

The slope of the line is $^-2/3$, the value of m.
The y intercept of the line is 7.

The intercepts can also be found by substituting 0 in place of the other variable in the equation.

To find the y intercept:

let $x = 0$; $3(0) + 2y = 14$

$0 + 2y = 14$

$2y = 14$

$y = 7$

$(0,7)$ is the y intercept.

To find the x intercept:

let $y = 0$; $3x + 2(0) = 14$

$3x + 0 = 14$

$3x = 14$

$x = 14/3$

$(14/3, 0)$ is the x intercept.

Find the slope and the intercepts (if they exist) for these equations:

1. $5x + 7y = {}^-70$
2. $x - 2y = 14$
3. $5x + 3y = 3(5 + y)$
4. $2x + 5y = 15$

8 E. Finding an equation for a line

The equation of a line can be found from its graph by finding its slope and y-intercept and substituting them in the slope-intercept form $y = mx + b$ (m is the slope, b is the y-intercept).

An alternate form of a linear equation is the point-slope form given below. Given the slope of a line and any one point (x_a, y_a) the line passes through, its equation may be written as

$$y - y_a = m\left(x - x_a\right)$$

Example: Find the equation of a line that has a slope of -1.5 and passes through the point (3,2).

Substituting the values of the slope m and the point (x_a, y_a) in the point-slope form of the equation we get

$$y - 2 = -1.5(x - 3) \quad \text{(point-slope form)}$$

Rearranging the terms,

$$y = -1.5x + 6.5 \quad \text{(slope-intercept form)}$$

or, multiplying by 2 and moving the x-term to the left hand side,

$$3x + 2y = 13 \quad \text{(standard form)}$$

The equation of a line may be expressed in any one of the above forms. All of them are equally valid.

Equation of a line that passes through two points
Given two points on a line, the first thing to do is to find the slope of the line. If 2 points on the graph are (x_1, y_1) and (x_2, y_2), then the slope is found using the formula:

$$\text{slope} = \frac{y_2 - y_1}{x_2 - x_1}$$

The slope will now be denoted by the letter **m**. To write the equation of a line, choose either point. Substitute them into the formula:

$$Y - y_a = m(X - x_a)$$

Remember (x_a, y_a) can be (x_1, y_1) or (x_2, y_2) If **m**, the value of the slope, is distributed through the parentheses, the equation can be rewritten into other forms of the equation of a line.

If the graph is a **vertical line**, then the equation solves to **x = the x co-ordinate of any point on the line**.

If the graph is a **horizontal line**, then the equation solves to **y = the y coordinate of any point on the line**.

<u>Example</u>: Find the equation of a line that passes through the points (9,–6) and (–1, 2).

$$\text{slope} = \frac{y_2 - y_1}{x_2 - x_1} = \frac{2 - (-6)}{-1 - 9} = \frac{8}{-10} = -\frac{4}{5}$$

The y-intercept may be found by substituting the slope (m) and the coordinates (x, y) for one of the data points in the slope-intercept form of the equation y = mx+b giving

$$-6 = -\frac{4}{5} \times 9 + b \quad \text{where b is the y-intercept}$$

$$b = \frac{6}{5}$$

Thus the slope-intercept form of the equation is:
$$y = -\frac{4}{5}x + \frac{6}{5}$$
Multiplying by 5 to eliminate fractions, it is:

$$5y = -4x + 6 \rightarrow 4x + 5y = 6 \quad \text{Standard form}$$

Practice Problems:
Write the equation of a line through these two points:

1. (5,8) and (⁻3,2)

2. (11,10) and (11,⁻3)

3. (⁻4,6) and (6,12)

4. (7,5) and (⁻3,5)

Equation of a line that is perpendicular or parallel to a given line

Lines that are equidistant from each other and never intersect are **parallel**. Parallel lines, therefore, must have they have the same slope. Note that vertical lines are parallel to other vertical lines despite having undefined slopes.

Perpendicular lines form 90° angles at their intersection. The slopes of perpendicular lines are the negative reciprocals of each other. In other words, if a line has a slope of -2, a perpendicular line would have a slope of ½. Note that the product of these slopes is −1.

<u>Example:</u> One line passes through the points (–4, –6) and (4, 6); another line passes through the points (–5, –4) and (3, 8). Are these lines parallel, perpendicular or neither?

Find the slopes.

$$m = \frac{y_2 - y_1}{x_2 - x_1}$$

$$m_1 = \frac{6-(-6)}{4-(-4)} = \frac{6+6}{4+4} = \frac{12}{8} = \frac{3}{2}$$

$$m_2 = \frac{8-(-4)}{3-(-5)} = \frac{8+4}{3+5} = \frac{12}{8} = \frac{3}{2}$$

Since the slopes are equal, the lines are parallel.

<u>Example:</u> One line passes through the points (1, –3) and (0, –6); another line passes through the points (4, 1) and (–2, 3). Are these lines parallel, perpendicular or neither?

Find the slopes.

$$m = \frac{y_2 - y_1}{x_2 - x_1}$$

$$m_1 = \frac{-6-(-3)}{0-1} = \frac{-6+3}{-1} = \frac{-3}{-1} = 3$$

$$m_2 = \frac{3-1}{-2-4} = \frac{2}{-6} = -\frac{1}{3}$$

The slopes are negative reciprocals, so the lines are perpendicular.

Example: One line passes through the points (–2, 4) and (2, 5); another line passes through the points (–1, 0) and (5, 4). Are these lines parallel, perpendicular or neither?

Find the slopes.

$$m = \frac{y_2 - y_1}{x_2 - x_1}$$

$$m_1 = \frac{5-4}{2-(-2)} = \frac{1}{2+2} = \frac{1}{4}$$

$$m_2 = \frac{4-0}{5-(-1)} = \frac{4}{5+1} = \frac{4}{6} = \frac{2}{3}$$

Since the slopes are not equal, the lines are not parallel. Since they are not negative reciprocals, they are not perpendicular either. Therefore, the answer is "neither."

Example: The equation of a line is $x + 3y = 0$. Determine whether it is parallel or perpendicular to the following straight lines.
(a) $y - 3x = 5$ (b) $y + x - 5 = 0$ (c) $2x + 6y = 7$

Putting the given equation in the slope-intercept form, we get

$$x + 3y = 0$$
$$\Rightarrow 3y = -x$$
$$\Rightarrow y = -\frac{1}{3}x$$

Therefore, the slope of the given line is $-\frac{1}{3}$.

We can find the slopes of the lines (a), (b) and (c) to determine whether they are parallel or perpendicular to the given line.

(a)
$$y - 3x = 5$$
$$\Rightarrow y = 3x + 5$$

The slope of this line is 3, the negative reciprocal of $-\frac{1}{3}$. Thus, this line is perpendicular to the given line.

(b)
$$y + x - 5 = 0$$
$$\Rightarrow y = -x + 5$$

The slope of this line is -1. Therefore, it is neither parallel nor perpendicular to the given line.

$$2x + 6y = 7$$

$$(c) \Rightarrow 6y = -2x + 7$$

$$\Rightarrow y = -\frac{1}{3}x + \frac{7}{6}$$

The slope of this line is $-\frac{1}{3}$. Thus, it is parallel to the given line.

8 F. Methods of solving systems of linear equations and inequalities (e.g. graphing and substitution)

Solving a system of linear equations

A system of linear equations is collection of linear equations with same set of variables. The solution of a system of linear equations should satisfy all the equations of the system.

$$\left.\begin{array}{l} 5x + 3y = 2 \\ 2x - 4y = 1 \end{array}\right\} \qquad \left.\begin{array}{l} x - 4y = -2 \\ 2x + 3y = 6 \end{array}\right\} \qquad \left.\begin{array}{l} 5x + 6y = 0 \\ 2x - 5y = 8 \end{array}\right\}$$

Each pair of equations shown above is a system of linear equations with two variables.

A solution is the value which satisfies each of the equations of the system. The set of all possible solutions is called the solution set. There are three possible kinds of solutions to a system of linear equations: infinitely many solutions, a single unique solution, no solutions.

A system of linear equations may be solved using one of the following methods:
1) Substitution Method
2) Elimination / Addition Method
3) Solving by graphing

Example: Solve the system of linear equations using the substitution method.

$x + 2y = 4$

$2x - y = 3$

$x + 2y = 4 ----(1)$

$2x - y = 3 ----(2)$

from equation (1), $x = 4 - 2y$

substitute $x = 4 - 2y$ in equation (2), we get

$2(4 - 2y) - y = 3$

$8 - 4y - y = 3$

$8 - 5y = 3$

$-5y = -5$

$y = 1$

So $x = 4 - 2(1) = 4 - 2 = 2$

So the solution is $x = 2$ and $y = 1$

Example: Solve the system of linear equations using the elimination method.

$x + 3y = 1$

$2x - y = 4$

$x + 3y = 2 ------(1)$

$2x - y = 4 ------(2)$

Multiply equation (2) by 3 and add to (1)

$6x - 3y = 12$

$x + 3y = 2$

_____

$7x = 14$

$x = 2$

substitute $x = 2$ in equation (1), we get,

$2 + 3y = 2$

$-2 + 2 + 3y = -2 + 2$

$3y = 0$

$y = 0$

Therefore, the solution is $x = 2$ and $y = 0$

Example: Solve by graphing the system of linear equations

$$x + y = 4$$
$$2x - y = 5$$

We have to graph the lines separately and see whether the lines intersect each other. The point of intersection is the solution to the given system of linear equations.

First, we have to solve the equations for $"y ="$, so we can graph them easily.

$$y = 4 - x$$
$$y = 2x - 5$$

Taking some random values for x and finding the corresponding y values

x	$y = 4 - x$	$y = 2x - 5$
1	3	-3
2	2	-1
3	1	1

Graphing the lines:

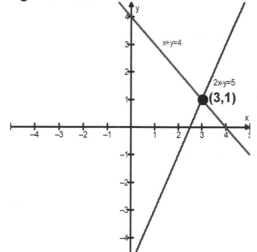

From the graph, we can see that (3, 1) is the point of intersection of the two lines. So, (3, 1) is the solution for the given system of linear equations.

Solving linear inequalities
Linear inequalities are solved following a procedure similar to that used for solving linear equations. There is however one important point that must be noted while solving inequalities: dividing or multiplying by a negative number will reverse the direction of the inequality sign.

First-degree inequalities involving one variable on a number line
The solution to an inequality with one variable is represented in graphical form on the number line or in interval form. When graphing a linear inequality, the dot on the number line will be hollow if the inequality sign is < or > and solid if the inequality sign is ≥ or ≤. The arrow goes to the right for ≥ or > and to the left for ≤ or <.

Example: Solve $2(3x-7)>10x-2$ for x.

$$2(3x-7) > 10x-2$$

$$6x-14 > 10x-2$$

$$-4x > 12$$

$$x < -3$$

Note the change of inequality symbol when dividing by a negative number.

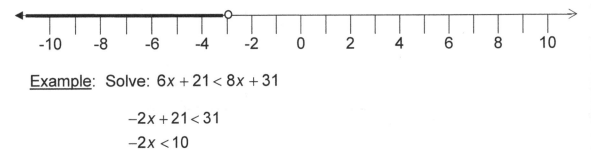

Example: Solve: $6x+21 < 8x+31$

$$-2x+21 < 31$$

$$-2x < 10$$

$$x > -5$$

Note that the inequality sign has changed.

Example: Solve the inequality, show its solution using interval form, and graph the solution on the number line.

$$\frac{5x}{8} + 3 \geq 2x - 5$$

$$8\left(\frac{5x}{8}\right) + 8(3) \geq 8(2x) - 5(8) \quad \text{Multiply by LCD = 8.}$$

$$5x + 24 \geq 16x - 40$$
$$5x + 24 - 24 - 16x \geq 16x - 16x - 40 - 24$$

Subtract 16x and 24 from both sides of the equation.

$$^-11x \geq\ ^- 64$$

$$x \leq \frac{64}{11} \ ; \ x \leq 5\frac{9}{11}$$

Note the change in direction of the equality with division by a negative number.

Solution in interval form: $\left(^-\infty, 5\frac{9}{11}\right]$

Note: "] " means $5\frac{9}{11}$ is included in the solution.

Example: Solve the following inequality and express your answer in both interval and graphical form.

$$3x - 8 < 2(3x - 1)$$

$$3x - 8 < 6x - 2 \qquad \text{Distributive property.}$$

$$3x - 6x - 8 + 8 < 6x - 6x - 2 + 8$$

Add 8 and subtract 6x from both sides of the equation.

$$-3x < 6$$

$$\frac{-3x}{-3} > \frac{6}{-3} \qquad\qquad x > -2$$

Graphical form:

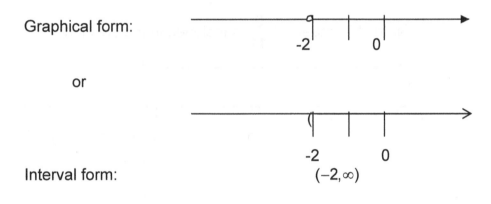

or

Interval form: $(-2, \infty)$

Recall: a) Using a parentheses or an open circle implies the point in not included in the answer

b) Using a bracket or a closed circle implies the point is included in the answer.

System of Linear Inequalities in two variables
A system of linear inequalities may be solved by graphing and finding the intersections of the solution regions. The solution consists of the part of the graph where the shaded areas for all the inequalities in the system overlap. For instance, if the graph of one inequality was shaded with red, and the graph of another inequality was shaded with blue, then the overlapping area would be shaded purple. The points in the purple area would be the solution set of this system.

<u>Example</u>: Solve by graphing:

$$x + y \leq 6$$
$$x - 2y \leq 6$$

Solving the inequalities for y, they become:

$$y \leq -x + 6 \quad (y\text{-intercept of 6 and slope} = -1)$$
$$y \geq 1/2\,x - 3 \quad (y \text{ intercept of } -3 \text{ and slope} = 1/2)$$

A graph with the solution area shaded is shown below. It is the area where the solution to $y \leq -x + 6$ (area below the line) overlaps with the solution to $y \geq 1/2\,x - 3$ (area above the line).

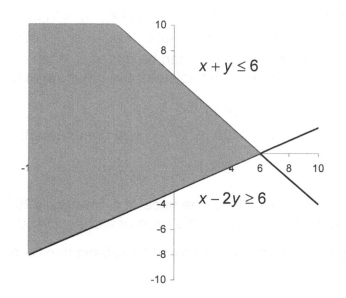

Practice Problems:

1. $5x - 1 > 14$
2. $7(2x - 3) + 5x = 19 - x$
3. $3x + 42 \geq 12x - 12$
4. $5 - 4(x + 3) = 9$

8 G. Modeling and solving problems using linear functions and systems

Many word problems may be modeled and solved using linear systems of equations and inequalities. Some examples are given below.

<u>Example</u>: Farmer Greenjeans bought 4 cows and 6 sheep for $1700. Mr. Ziffel bought 3 cows and 12 sheep for $2400. If all the cows were the same price and all the sheep were another price, find the price charged for a cow or for a sheep.

> Let x = price of a cow
> Let y = price of a sheep

Then Farmer Greenjeans' equation would be: $4x + 6y = 1700$
Mr. Ziffel's equation would be: $3x + 12y = 2400$

To solve by **addition-subtraction**:

Multiply the first equation by $^-2$: $^-2(4x + 6y = 1700)$
Keep the other equation the same : $(3x + 12y = 2400)$
By doing this, the equations can be added to each other to eliminate one variable and solve for the other variable.

$$^-8x - 12y = {}^-3400$$
$$\underline{3x + 12y = 2400} \qquad \text{Add these equations.}$$
$$^-5x \qquad = {}^-1000$$

$x = 200 \leftarrow$ the price of a cow was $200.
Solving for y, $y = 150 \leftarrow$ the price of a sheep, $150.

(This problem can also be solved by substitution or determinants.)

Example: Mrs. Allison bought 1 pound of potato chips, a 2-pound beef roast, and 3 pounds of apples for a total of $8.19. Mr. Bromberg bought a 3-pound beef roast and 2 pounds of apples for $9.05. Kathleen Kaufman bought 2 pounds of potato chips, a 3-pound beef roast, and 5 pounds of apples for $13.25. Find the per pound price of each item.

To solve by **substitution**:

Let x = price of a pound of potato chips
Let y = price of a pound of roast beef
Let z = price of a pound of apples

Mrs. Allison's equation would be: $1x + 2y + 3z = 8.19$
Mr. Bromberg's equation would be: $3y + 2z = 9.05$
K. Kaufman's equation would be: $2x + 3y + 5z = 13.25$

Take the first equation and solve it for x. (This was chosen because x is the easiest variable to get alone in this set of equations). This equation would become:

$$x = 8.19 - 2y - 3z$$

Substitute this expression into the other equations in place of the letter x:

$$3y + 2z = 9.05 \leftarrow \text{ equation 2}$$
$$2(8.19 - 2y - 3z) + 3y + 5z = 13.25 \leftarrow \text{ equation 3}$$

Simplify the equation by combining like terms:

$$3y + 2z = 9.05 \leftarrow \text{ equation 2}$$
$$-1y - 1z = -3.13 \leftarrow \text{equation 3}$$

Solve equation 3 for either y or z:

* $y = 3.13 - z$ Substitute this into equation 2 for y:

$$3(3.13 - z) + 2z = 9.05 \leftarrow \text{ equation 2}$$
$$-1y - 1z = -3.13 \leftarrow \text{ equation 3}$$

Combine like terms in equation 2:

$$9.39 - 3z + 2z = 9.05$$
$$z = \$0.34 \quad \text{per pound price of apples}$$

Substitute .34 for z in the * equation above to solve for y:
$$y = 3.13 - z \text{ becomes } y = 3.13 - .34, \text{ so}$$
$$y = \$2.79 = \text{per pound price of roast beef}$$

Substituting .34 for z and 2.79 for y in one of the original equations, solve for x:

$$1x + 2y + 3z = 8.19$$
$$1x + 2(2.79) + 3(.34) = 8.19$$
$$x + 5.58 + 1.02 = 8.19$$
$$x + 6.60 = 8.19$$
$$x = \$1.59 \text{ per pound of potato chips}$$

$$(x, y, z) = (\$1.59, \$2.79, \$0.34)$$

Example: Aardvark Taxi charges $4 initially plus $1 for every mile traveled. Baboon Taxi charges $6 initially plus $.75 for every mile traveled. Determine the mileage at which it becomes cheaper to ride with Baboon Taxi than it is to ride Aardvark Taxi.

Aardvark Taxi's equation:	$y = 1x + 4$
Baboon Taxi's equation :	$y = .75x + 6$
Use substitution:	$.75x + 6 = x + 4$
Multiply both sides by 4:	$3x + 24 = 4x + 16$
Solve for x :	$8 = x$

This tells you that, at 8 miles, the total charge for the two companies is the same. If you compare the charge for 1 mile, Aardvark charges $5 and Baboon charges $6.75. Therefore, Aardvark Taxi is cheaper for distances up to 8 miles, but Baboon is cheaper for distances greater than 8 miles.

This problem can also be solved by graphing the 2 equations.

$$y = 1x + 4 \qquad y = .75x + 6$$

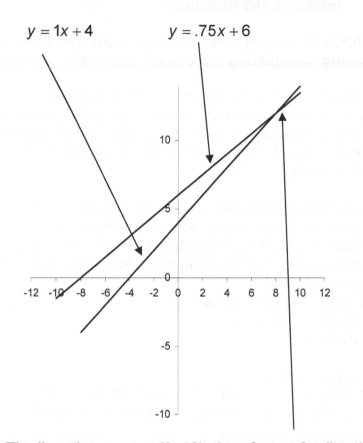

The lines intersect at (8, 12), therefore at 8 miles, both companies charge $12. For distances less than 8 miles, Aardvark Taxi charges less (the graph is below Baboon). For distances greater than 8 miles, Aardvark charges more (the graph is above Baboon).

For examples of problems using systems of linear inequalities, see **Competency 0020 E**.

Competency 0009 Understand properties and applications of quadratic relations and functions.

9A.   **Methods of solving quadratic equations and inequalities (e.g. factoring, completing the square, quadratic formula, graphing)**

A quadratic equation is expressed in the form $ax^2 + bx + c = 0$, where a, b, and c are real numbers and $a \neq 0$. The degree of a quadratic equation (i.e. the highest exponent of the unknown variable x) is 2. Examples of quadratic equations are $5x^2 + 6x + 7 = 0$, $9x^2 - 4 = 0$, $2x^7 - 3x = 0$.

If $p(x) = 0$ is a quadratic equation, then the zeros of the polynomial $p(x)$ are called the roots or solutions of equation $p(x) = 0$. Finding the roots of a quadratic equation is known as solving for "x".
There are several different methods for solving quadratic equations:
Factoring Method
1) Completing the Square
2) Quadratic Formula
3) Graphing

Factoring method
This method is only applicable for quadratic equations where the polynomial can be expressed as a product of linear factors.

If a quadratic polynomial $ax^2 + bx + c = 0$ is expressible as a product of two linear factors, say (px + q) and (rx + s), where p, q, r, s are real numbers, then $ax^2 + bx + c = 0$ may be rewritten as

$$(px + q)\ (rx + s) = 0$$

This implies that either of the two factors must be equal to zero:

$$(px + q) = 0 \text{ or } (rx + s) = 0$$

Solving these linear equations, we get the possible roots of the given quadratic equation as:

$$x = -\frac{p}{q} \text{ and } x = -\frac{s}{r}$$

<u>Example</u>: Solve the following equation.

$x^2 + 10x - 24 = 0$

$(x + 12)(x - 2) = 0$ Factor.

$x + 12 = 0$ or $x - 2 = 0$ Set each factor equal to 0.

$x = -12$ $x = 2$ Solve.

Check:

$x^2 + 10x - 24 = 0$

$(-12)^2 + 10(-12) - 24 = 0$ $(2)^2 + 10(2) - 24 = 0$

$144 - 120 - 24 = 0$ $4 + 20 - 24 = 0$

$0 = 0$ $0 = 0$

Completing the square method

A quadratic equation may be solved by **completing the square**. To complete the square, the coefficient of the x^2 term must be 1.

To solve a quadratic equation using this method:
1. Isolate the x^2 and x terms.
2. Add half of the coefficient of the x term squared to both sides of the equation.
3. Finally take the square root of both sides and solve for x.

<u>Example</u>: Solve the following equation:

$x^2 - 6x + 8 = 0$

$x^2 - 6x = -8$ Move the constant to the right side.

$x^2 - 6x + 9 = -8 + 9$ Add the square of half the coefficient
                            of x to both sides.

$(x - 3)^2 = 1$ Write the left side as a perfect square.

$x - 3 = \pm\sqrt{1}$ Take the square root of both sides.

$x - 3 = 1$ $x - 3 = -1$ Solve.

$x = 4$ $x = 2$

Check:

$x^2 - 6x + 8 = 0$

$4^2 - 6(4) + 8 = 0$ $2^2 - 6(2) + 8 = 0$

$16 - 24 + 8 = 0$ $4 - 12 + 8 = 0$

$0 = 0$ $0 = 0$

Quadratic formula

To solve a quadratic equation using the **quadratic formula**, be sure that your equation is in the form $ax^2 + bx + c = 0$. Substitute the values of a, b and c into the formula:

$$x = \frac{-b \pm \sqrt{b^2 - 4ac}}{2a}$$

Simplify the result to find the answers. (Remember, there could be 2 real answers, one real answer, or 2 complex answers that include "i").

<u>Example:</u> Solve the following equation using the quadratic formula:

$$3x^2 = 7 + 2x \rightarrow 3x^2 - 2x - 7 = 0$$

$$a = 3 \quad b = {}^-2 \quad c = {}^-7$$

$$x = \frac{-({}^-2) \pm \sqrt{({}^-2)^2 - 4(3)({}^-7)}}{2(3)}$$

$$x = \frac{2 \pm \sqrt{4 + 84}}{6}$$

$$x = \frac{2 \pm \sqrt{88}}{6}$$

$$x = \frac{2 \pm 2\sqrt{22}}{6}$$

$$x = \frac{1 \pm \sqrt{22}}{3}$$

Solving by graphing

See section **9C.** for information on graphing quadratic functions and solving quadratic equations by graphing.

9B. **Real and complex roots of quadratic equations**

The **discriminant** is the portion of the quadratic formula which is found under the square root sign; that is $b^2 - 4ac$.

$$x = \frac{-b \pm \sqrt{b^2 - 4ac}}{2a}$$

Note that the radical sign is **not** part of the discriminant. Determine the value of the discriminant by substituting the values of a, b and c from $ax^2 + bx + c = 0$.

The discriminant can be used to determine the nature of the solution of a quadratic equation.

1)   If $b^2 - 4ac < 0$, there are **no real roots** and **two complex roots** that include the imaginary number I (square root of -1).

2)   If $b^2 - 4ac = 0$, there is only **one real rational root**.

3)   If $b^2 - 4ac > 0$ and also a perfect square, there are **two real rational roots**. (There are no longer any radical signs.)

4)   If $b^2 - 4ac > 0$ and not a perfect square, then there are **two real irrational roots**. (There are still unsimplified radical signs.)

Example: Find the value of the discriminant for the equation $2x^2 - 5x + 6 = 0$. Then determine the number and nature of the solutions of that quadratic equation.
$a = 2$, $b = {}^-5$, $c = 6$ so $b^2 - 4ac = ({}^-5)^2 - 4(2)(6) = 25 - 48 = {}^-23$.

Since ${}^-23$ is a negative number, there are **no real roots** and **two complex roots** .

$$x = \frac{5}{4} + \frac{i\sqrt{23}}{4}, \quad x = \frac{5}{4} - \frac{i\sqrt{23}}{4}$$

Example: Find the value of the discriminant for the equation $3x^2 - 12x + 12 = 0$. Then determine the number and nature of the solutions of the quadratic equation.

$a = 3$, $b = {}^-12$, $c = 12$ so $b^2 - 4ac = ({}^-12)^2 - 4(3)(12) = 144 - 144 = 0$

Since 0 is the value of the discriminant, there is only
1 real rational root $x=2$.

To write a quadratic equation from its roots:
1. Add the roots together. The answer is their **sum**. Multiply the roots together. The answer is their **product**.
2. A quadratic equation can be written using the sum and product like this:

$$x^2 + (\text{opposite of the sum})x + \text{product} = 0$$

3. If there are any fractions in the equation, multiply every term by the common denominator to eliminate the fractions.
4. If a quadratic equation has only 1 root, use it twice and follow the first 3 steps above.

<u>Example</u>: Find a quadratic equation with roots of 4 and $^-9$.

The sum of 4 and $^-9$ is $^-5$. The product of 4 and $^-9$ is $^-36$.
The equation would be:

$$x^2 + (\text{opposite of the sum})x + \text{product} = 0$$
$$x^2 + 5x - 36 = 0$$

<u>Example</u>: Find a quadratic equation with roots of $5 + 2i$ and $5 - 2i$.

The sum of $5 + 2i$ and $5 - 2i$ is 10. The product of $5 + 2i$ and $5 - 2i$
is $25 - 4i^2 = 25 + 4 = 29$

The equation would be:

$$x^2 + (\text{opposite of the sum})x + \text{product} = 0$$
$$x^2 - 10x + 29 = 0$$

$$12(x^2 + 1/12\,x - 1/2) = 0$$
$$12x^2 + 1x - 6 = 0$$
$$12x^2 + x - 6 = 0$$

9C. Graphs of quadratic functions

The general technique for graphing quadratics is the same as for graphing linear equations. Graphing a quadratic equation, however, results in a parabola instead of a straight line.

The general form of a quadratic function is $y = ax^2 + bx + c$. Once a function is identified as quadratic, it is helpful to recognize several features that can indicate the form of the graph. The parabola has an axis of symmetry along $x = -\dfrac{b}{2a}$ which is the x-coordinate of the vertex (turning point) of the graph.

This can be understood more clearly if we consider an alternate form of a quadratic equation, the standard form for a parabola

$$y = a(x - h)^2 + k$$

where (h, k) denote the coordinates of the vertex of the parabola.
Transforming the general form $y = ax^2 + bx + c$ into the above form,

$$y = ax^2 + bx + c$$

$$\Rightarrow y = a(x^2 + \frac{b}{a}x) + c$$

$$\Rightarrow y = a(x^2 + 2 \cdot \frac{b}{2a}x + (\frac{b}{2a})^2) - \frac{b^2}{4a} + c$$

$$\Rightarrow y = a(x + \frac{b}{2a})^2 - \frac{b^2}{4a} + c$$

Thus the coordinates of the vertex are given by $(-\dfrac{b}{2a}, -\dfrac{b^2}{4a} + c)$.

<u>Example</u>: Graph $y = 3x^2 + x - 2$

Expressing this function in standard form we get

$$y = 3(x + \frac{1}{6})^2 - \frac{25}{12}$$

Thus, the graph is a parabola with an axis of symmetry $x = -\frac{1}{6}$

and the vertex is located at the point $(-\frac{1}{6}, -\frac{25}{12})$.

x	$y = 3x^2 + x - 2$
-2	8
-1	0
0	-2
1	2
2	12

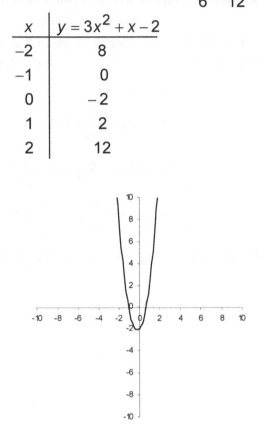

If the quadratic term is positive, then the parabola is concave up; if the quadratic term is negative, then the parabola is concave down. The function $-x^2 - 2x - 3$ is one such example and is shown below.

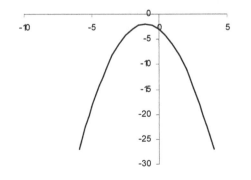

In addition, it is helpful to find the number of roots. A quadratic function with two real roots (see example problems) will have two crossings of the x-axis. A quadratic function with one real root will graph as a parabola that is tangent to the x-axis. An example of such a quadratic function is shown in the example below for the function $x^2 + 2x + 1$. The function has a single real root at $x = -1$.

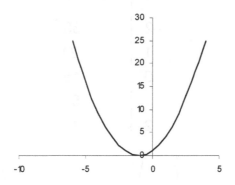

A quadratic function with no real roots will not cross the axis at any point. An example is the function $x^2 + 2x + 2$, which is plotted below.

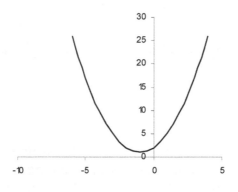

Example: Solve by graphing $x^2 - 8x + 15 = 0$

The roots of the polynomial $x^2 - 8x + 15$ are the x values for which the graph intersects the x-axis.

x	$y = x^2 - 8x + 15$
−2	35
−1	24
0	15
1	8
2	3

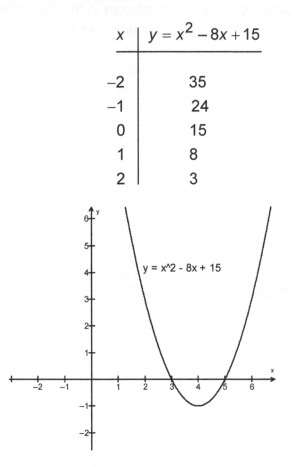

y = x^2 - 8x + 15

From the above graph, the *x*-intercepts or zeroes are 3 and 5. So the solutions of the given quadratic equation are 3 and 5.

To **graph a quadratic inequality**, graph the quadratic as if it were an equation; however, if the inequality has just a > or < sign, then make the curve dotted. Shade above the curve for > or ≥. Shade below the curve for < or ≤.

Example: $y < -x^2 + x - 2$

The quadratic function $-x^2 + x - 2$ is plotted with a dotted line since the inequality sign is $<$ and not $\leq$. Since y is "less than" this function, the shading is done below the curve.

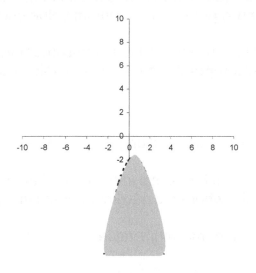

Example: $y \geq x^2 - 2x - 9$

The quadratic function $x^2 - 2x - 9$ is plotted with a solid line since the inequality sign is $\geq$. Since y is "greater than or equal to" this function, the shading is done above the curve.

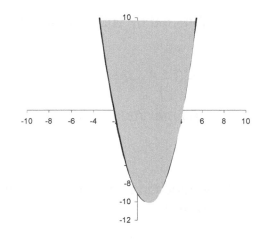

9D. Quadratic minimum and maximum problems

As discussed in the previous section, the graph of a quadratic function $f(x) = ax^2 + bx + c$ has a vertex at (h, k) where

$$h = -b/2a \quad \text{and} \quad k = c - b^2/4a$$

If **a > 0**, the quadratic function will have a minimum value and the vertex is the **minimum point.** The minimum value occurs at $x = h = -b/2a$.

If **a < 0**, the quadratic function will have a maximum value and the vertex is the **maximum point**. The maximum value occurs at $x = h = -b/2a$.

<u>Example:</u> For the quadratic function $y = 3x^2 + 5x - 7$

a) Determine whether it has a maximum or minimum value
b) Find the value of x where the maximum or minimum value occurs
c) Find the maximum or minimum value

a) The quadratic function is $y = 3x^2 + 6x - 7$

Here a = 3   b = 6   c = –7

a = 3 > 0, so the given quadratic equation has a minimum value

b) The minimum value occurs at $x = -b/2a = -6/2(3) = -6/6 = -1$

c) The minimum value is obtained by substituting $x = -1$ in the given function

$$y = 3(-1)^2 + 6(-1) - 7 = 3 - 6 - 7 = -10$$

<u>Example:</u> Find the vertex and maximum value of the function

$f(x) = -2x^2 + 7x - 9$.

The vertex of the quadratic function is given by (h, k) where
$h = -b/2a$ and $k = c - (b^2/4a)$

Here a = –2   b = 7   c = –9

Substituting the values of a, b and c,

h = (−7) / (2(−2)) = 7/4

k = −9 − [49/ (−8)] = −9 + (49/8) = (−72 + 49)/8 = −23/8

So the vertex is (7/4, −23/8)

The maximum value is at x = 7/4

Substituting x = 7/4 in the given function,

f (7/4) = -2(7/4)^2 + 7(7/4) − 9 = −98/16 + 49/4 − 9 = −46/16 = −23/8

So the maximum value of the given function is −23/8.

9E. Modeling and solving problems using quadratic relations, functions and systems

Some word problems may be modeled using a quadratic equation. Examples of this type of problem follow.

Example: A family is planning to add a new room to their house. They would like the room to have a length that is 10 ft more than the width and a total area of 375 sq. feet. Find the length and width of the room.

Let x be the width of the room.
Length of the room = x+10

Thus,
$$x(x+10) = 375$$
$$x^2 + 10x - 375 = 0$$

Factor the quadratic expression to solve the equation:
$x^2 + 25x - 15x - 375 = 0$ Break up the middle
$x(x+25) - 15(x+25) = 0$ term using factors of 375
$(x+25)(x-15) = 0$
$x = -25$ or $x = 15$

Since the dimension of a room cannot be negative, we choose the positive solution x=15. Thus, the width of the room is 15 ft and the length of the room is 25ft.

Example: A family wants to enclose 3 sides of a rectangular garden with 200 feet of fence. A wall borders the fourth side of the garden. In order to have a garden with an area of **at least** 4800 square feet, find the dimensions the garden should be.

Existing Wall

Solution:
Let x = distance
from the wall

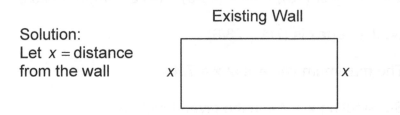

Then 2x feet of fence is used for these 2 sides. The side opposite the existing wall would use the remainder of the 200 feet of fence, that is, $200 - 2x$ feet of fence. Therefore the width (w) of the garden is x feet and the length (l) is $200 - 2x$ feet.

The area is calculated using the formula
$a = lw = x(200-2x) = 200x - 2x^2$, and needs to be greater than or equal to 4800 sq. ft., yielding the inequality $4800 \leq 200x - 2x^2$. Subtract 4800 from each side and the inequality becomes

$$200x - 2x^2 \geq 4800$$
$$-2x^2 + 200x - 4800 \geq 0$$
$$2\left(-x^2 + 100x - 2400\right) \geq 0$$
$$-x^2 + 100x - 2400 \geq 0$$
$$(-x + 60)(x - 40) \geq 0$$
$$-x + 60 \geq 0$$
$$-x \geq -60$$
$$x \leq 60$$
$$x - 40 \geq 0$$
$$x \geq 40$$

solved for x.

The area will be at least 4800 square feet if the width of the garden is from 40 up to 60 feet. (The length of the rectangle would vary from 120 feet to 80 feet depending on the width of the garden.)

Example: The height of a projectile fired upward at a velocity of v meters per second from an original height of h meters is $y = h + vx - 4.9x^2$. If a rocket is fired from an original height of 250 meters with an original velocity of 4800 meters per second, find the approximate time the rocket would drop to sea level (a height of 0).

Substituting the height and velocity into the equation yields: $y = 250 + 4800x - 4.9x^2$. If the height at sea level is zero, then $y = 0$ so $0 = 250 + 4800x - 4.9x^2$. Solving for x could be done by using the quadratic formula.

$$x = \frac{-4800 \pm \sqrt{4800^2 - 4(-4.9)(250)}}{2(-4.9)}$$

$x \approx 979.53$ or $x \approx -0.05$ seconds

Since the time has to be positive, it will be approximately 980 seconds until the rocket reaches sea level.

Competency 0010 **Understand properties and applications of exponential, polynomial, rational, and absolute value functions and relations.**

10A. **Problems involving exponential growth (e.g., population growth, compound interest) and decay (e.g., half-life)**

Exponential growth

A quantity which grows by a fixed percent at regular intervals, i.e. in proportion to the existing amount, demonstrates exponential growth (see **Competency 0005, section C** for a discussion of exponential functions). If a population has a constant birth rate through the years and is not affected by food or disease, it has exponential growth. The birth rate alone controls how fast the population grows exponentially.

<u>Example</u>: A population of a city is 20,000 and it increases at an annual rate of 20%. What will be the population of the city after 10 years?

The formula for the growth is $y = a(1 + r)^t$
where a is the initial amount, r is the growth rate, and t is the number of time intervals

Here a = 20000 r = 20% = 0.2 t = 10

Substituting the values,
Population Growth = y = 20000$(1 + 0.2)^{10}$

$$= 20000(1 + 0.2)^{10}$$

$$= 20000(1.2)^{10}$$

$$= 20000(6.19)$$

$$= 123800$$

So the population of the city after 10 years is 123,800.

What will be the population of the city after 50 years?

In 50 years, population = 20000$(1 + 0.2)^{50}$

$$= 20000(1 + 0.2)^{50}$$

$$= 20000(1.2)^{50}$$

$$= 20000(9100.44)$$

$$= 182008800$$

The population after 50 years will be 182,008,800.

Another example of exponential growth is the growth of money through compound-interest.

Example: How long will it take $2,000 to triple if it is invested at 15% compounded continuously?

Exponential growth formula for continuously compounding interest is

$$A = Pe^{rt}$$

where A is the amount of money in the account, P is Principal amount invested, r stands for rate of interest, t is the period in years, and e is the base of the natural log (an irrational number with value 2.71828...).

Substituting the given values in the formula:

$$A = Pe^{rt}$$

$$6000 = 2000e^{0.15t}$$

$$3 = e^{0.15t}$$

taking natural log of both sides,

$$\ln 3 = \ln e^{0.15t}$$

using the property of logarithm $\ln x^r = r \ln x$,

$$\ln 3 = 0.15t \,(\ln e)$$

$$\ln 3 = 0.15t \,(\text{since } \ln e = 1)$$

using the calculator to find the value of $\ln 3$,

$$1.098 = 0.15t$$

$$t = \frac{1.098}{0.15} = 7.3$$

Therefore, the amount of $2,000 is tripled in 7.3 years.

Exponential Decay

Exponential decay is decrease by a fixed percent at regular intervals of time. Radioactive decay is an example of this.

<u>Example</u>: If 40 grams of Iodine has reduced to 20 grams in 6 days, what is the rate of decay?

The formula for exponential decay is $Q = ae^{rt}$ where Q is the amount of material at time t, a is the initial amount, r is the decay rate and t is the time period in days.

$Q = ae^{rt}$

$20 = 40e^{r(6)}$ Isolate e

$0.5 = e^{6r}$ Take ln of both sides

$\ln 0.5 = 6r$ Solve for r

$\dfrac{\ln 0.5}{6} = r$

$r = -0.1155$ Note : r is negative because it is decay

rate of decay is $0.1155 = 11.55\%$

10B. Inverse variation

For a discussion of inverse variation see **Competency 0006, section D.**

10C. Modeling problems using rational functions

Some problems can be solved using equations with rational expressions. First write the equation. To solve it, multiply each term by the LCD of all fractions. This will cancel out all of the denominators and give an equivalent algebraic equation that can be solved.

<u>Example:</u> The denominator of a fraction is two less than three times the numerator. If 3 is added to both the numerator and denominator, the new fraction equals 1/2 .

original fraction: $\dfrac{x}{3x-2}$ revised fraction: $\dfrac{x+3}{3x+1}$

$$\dfrac{x+3}{3x+1} = \dfrac{1}{2} \qquad\qquad 2x+6 = 3x+1$$

$$x = 5$$

original fraction: $\dfrac{5}{13}$

Example: Elly Mae can feed the animals in 15 minutes. Jethro can feed them in 10 minutes. How long will it take them if they work together?

If Elly Mae can feed the animals in 15 minutes, then she could feed 1/15 of them in 1 minute, 2/15 of them in 2 minutes, $x/15$ of them in x minutes. In the same fashion Jethro could feed $x/10$ of them in x minutes. Together they complete 1 job. The equation is:

$$\frac{x}{15} + \frac{x}{10} = 1$$

Multiply each term by the LCD of 30:

$$2x + 3x = 30$$
$$x = 6 \text{ minutes}$$

Example: A salesman drove 480 miles from Pittsburgh to Hartford. The next day he returned the same distance to Pittsburgh in half an hour less time than his original trip took, because he increased his average speed by 4 mph. Find his original speed.

Since distance = rate x time then time = $\dfrac{\text{distance}}{\text{rate}}$

original time $-$ 1/2 hour = shorter return time

$$\frac{480}{x} - \frac{1}{2} = \frac{480}{x+4}$$

Multiplying by the LCD of $2x(x + 4)$, the equation becomes:

$$480\big[2(x+4)\big] - 1\big[x(x+4)\big] = 480(2x)$$

$$960x + 3840 - x^2 - 4x = 960x$$

$$x^2 + 4x - 3840 = 0$$

$(x+64)(x-60) = 0$ Either (x-60=0) or (x+64=0) or both=0

$x = 60$ 60 mph is the original speed.

                     This is the solution since the time

$x + 4 = 64$ cannot be negative. Check your answer

$$\frac{480}{60} - \frac{1}{2} = \frac{480}{64}$$

$$8 - \frac{1}{2} = 7\frac{1}{2}$$

$$7\frac{1}{2} = 7\frac{1}{2}$$

Try these practice problems:

1. Working together, Larry, Moe, and Curly can paint an elephant in 3 minutes. Working alone, it would take Larry 10 minutes or Moe 6 minutes to paint the elephant. How long would it take Curly to paint the elephant if he worked alone?

2. The denominator of a fraction is 5 more than twice the numerator. If the numerator is doubled, and the denominator is increased by 5, the new fraction is equal to 1/2. Find the original number.

3. The distance from Augusta, Maine to Galveston, Texas is 2108 miles. If a car drove 6 mph faster than a truck and got to Galveston 3 hours before the truck, find the speeds of the car and the truck.

10D. Properties and graphs of polynomial, rational and absolute value functions

Polynomial functions

The degree of a polynomial in a single variable is the exponent of the highest power to which the variable is raised. $5x^2 - 4x - 6$, for instance, is a second degree polynomial whereas $2x^3 - 5x^2 + x$ is a polynomial of degree 3. If a term has more than one variable (e.g. $2xy$) it is necessary to add the exponents of the variables within the term to get the degree of the polynomial. Since $1 + 1 = 2$, $2xy = 6$ is of the second degree.

The following points are points on the graph:

X	Y
⁻3	⁻5
⁻2	8
⁻1	9
0	4
1	⁻1
2	0
3	13

Note the change in sign of the y value between $x = {}^-3$ and $x = {}^-2$. This indicates there is a zero between $x = {}^-3$ and $x = {}^-2$. Since there is another change in sign of the y value between $x = 0$ and $x = {}^-1$, there is a second root there. When $x = 2$, $y = 0$ so $x = 2$ is an exact root of this polynomial.

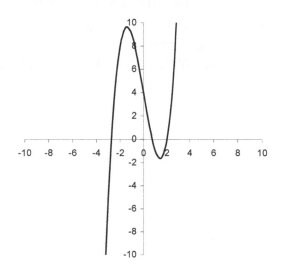

Rational functions and expressions: a rational expression can be written as the ration of 2 polynomial expressions and a rational function is simply a function that gets its value from the rational expression. Examples of rational functions (and their associated expressions) are:

$$r(x) = \frac{x^2 + 2x + 4}{x - 3} \text{ and } r(x) = \frac{x}{x - 3}$$ which is clearly the ratio of 2 polynomials. The following is a rational expression:

$$\frac{1}{x + \dfrac{2}{x}}$$

(it is not in standard form but can be converted to standard

form by multplying by $\dfrac{x}{x}$) $= \dfrac{x}{2x + 1}$

A rational function is given in the form $f(x) = p(x)/q(x)$. In the equation, $p(x)$ and $q(x)$ both represent polynomial functions where $q(x)$ does not equal zero. The branches of rational functions approach asymptotes. Setting the denominator equal to zero and solving will give the value(s) of the vertical asymptotes(s) since the function will be undefined at this point. If the value of $f(x)$ approaches b as the $|x|$ increases, the equation $y = b$ is a horizontal asymptote. To find the horizontal asymptote it is necessary to make a table of values for x that are to the right and left of the vertical asymptotes. The pattern for the horizontal asymptotes will become apparent as the $|x|$ increases.

If there are more than one vertical asymptotes, remember to choose numbers to the right and left of each one in order to find the horizontal asymptotes and have sufficient points to graph the function.

Example: Graph $f(x) = \dfrac{3x+1}{x-2}$.

$x - 2 = 0$
$x = 2$

1. Set denominator $= 0$ to find the vertical asymptote.

x	$f(x)$
3	10
10	3.875
100	3.07
1000	3.007
1	$^{-}4$
$^{-}10$	2.417
$^{-}100$	2.93
$^{-}1000$	2.99

2. Make a table choosing numbers to the right and left of the vertical asymptote.

3. The pattern shows that as the $|x|$ increases f(x) approaches the value 3, therefore a horizontal asymptote exists at $y = 3$

Absolute Value Functions

The **absolute value function** for a 1st degree equation is of the form: $y = m(x - h) + k$. Its graph is in the shape of a $\vee$. The point (h,k) is the location of the maximum/minimum point on the graph. "$\pm$ m" are the slopes of the 2 sides of the $\vee$. The graph opens up if m is positive and down if m is negative.

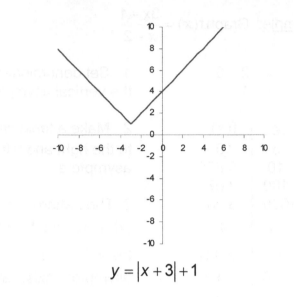

$$y = |x + 3| + 1$$

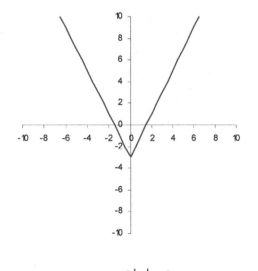

$$y = 2|x| - 3$$

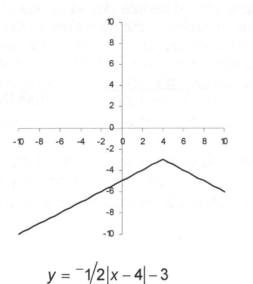

$$y = {}^-1/2|x - 4| - 3$$

Note that on the first graph, the graph opens up since m is positive 1. It has ($^-$3,1) as its minimum point. The slopes of the 2 upward rays are $\pm$ 1.

The second graph also opens up since m is positive. (0, $^-$3) is its minimum point. The slopes of the 2 upward rays are $\pm$ 2.

The third graph is a downward $\wedge$ because m is $^-$1/2. The maximum point on the graph is at (4, $^-$3). The slopes of the 2 downward rays are $\pm$ 1/2.

The **identity function** is the linear equation $y = x$. Its graph is a line going through the origin (0, 0) and through the first and third quadrants at a 45° degree angle.

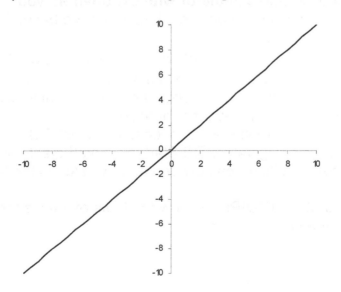

Note that both graphs should denote closed circles at the left side of each step, and open circles at the right side. In the graph of the first equation, the steps are going up as they move to the right. Each step is one space wide (inverse of r) with a solid dot on the left and a hollow dot on the right where the jump to the next step occurs. Each step is one square higher (j = 1) than the previous step. One step of the graph starts at (0,0) ← values of (h,k).

-In the second graph, the graph goes up to the right. One step starts at the point (0,3) ← values of (h,k). Each step is one square wide (r = 1) and each step is 2 squares higher than the previous step (j = 2).

Practice problems:

Graph the following equations:

1. $f(x) = x$
2. $y = ^-|x-3|+5$
3. $y = 3[x]$
4. $y = \frac{2}{5}|x-5|-2$

10 E. The use of graphing calculators and computers to find numerical solutions to problems involving exponential, polynomial, rational and absolute value functions

Using a graphing calculator with exponents: you can use the caret key ^ to evaluate powers. First enter the base, then ^ and then the exponent.

To use a table to evaluate 10^x and 10^{-x} for $x = 2,3,4,5,6,$ by

1. Press "Y=" and enter "10^X" for Y1 and "10^(−)X" for Y2. Please note that the calculator key for a negative sign (−) is different from the key for subtraction -.
2. Press "2nd" "WINDOW" to choose the TABLE SETUP menu. Set the starting value, TBLStart to 0 and the set value, ΔTbl to 1 so that the difference between each x-value in the table will be 1.
3. Press "2nd" "GRAPH" to view the table of values for 10^x and 10^{-x}.

Using a graphing calculator with polynomial functions:

Solve $x^2 + 2x - 8$ for its roots by graphing on a calculator:

1. Press "Y=" and enter X^2+2X-8 for Y1.
2. Press "GRAPH".
3. Identify the x-intercepts of the parabola. The x-intercepts are -4 and 2.
4. Notice the parabola at x= -1- this is the line of the axis of symmetry and the vertex is at the bottom of the line; it is located halfway between the 2 x-intercepts.

Using a graphing calculator with rational functions:

Graph the functions f, g, $f+g$ for x for the interval $[-p, p]$

1. Press the GRAPH key and then choose $y(x)=$ by pressing the F1 key.
2. If needed, press the F4 key until only $y1=$ appears on the screen.
3. Type in X^2, then press the ENTER key.
4. Type in COSX and press the ENTER key.
5. Type in y1+y2 and press the ENTER key. NOTE: Both y's must be lower case.
6. The range settings for the graph above are $[-p, p] \times [-1, 10]$.
7. Note that the graphs of the functions are plotted in the order in which they are entered above. You can plot only one or two of the graphs by using the SELCT key on the **y(x)=** screen.

Using a graphing calculator with absolute value functions:

Solve $2|x - 3| = 4$ using a table on the graphing calculator.

1. Enter the left side of the equation in the "Y=" editor. Press the "MATH" key and use the NUM menu for ABS(.
2. Use the defaults for "2nd" "WINDOW" (TBLSET) and then press "2nd" "GRAPH" TABLE to see the values of the equation above when $x = 0, 1, 2, 3, 4...$
3. Note that Y1=4 when $x = 1$ and when $x = 5$.

SUBAREA III.   GEOMETRY AND MEASUREMENT

Competency 0011 Understand principles, concepts, and procedures related to measurement.

11A.   Using appropriate units of measurement

Systems of units

Customary or Imperial units are the familiar everyday units used in the United States. Inch, foot, yard and the mile are commonly used units of **length.**
1 yard = 3 feet = 36 inches
1 mile = 1,760 yards

The basic unit of **weight** is pound (lb).
1 pound = 16 ounces (oz)
1 ounce = 16 drams
Short ton (U.S.) = 2,000 lb
Long ton (British) = 2,240 lb

The basic unit of **liquid measure** or liquid capacity is the gallon.
1 gallon = 4 quarts = 8 pints = 16 cups = 128 ounces

The basic unit of **dry measure** or dry capacity is the bushel.
1 bushel = 4 pecks = 32 dry quarts = 64 dry pints = 2,150.42 cubic inches.

The **metric or SI system** is commonly used in many countries around the world for making everyday measurements. It is also the standard system used in scientific measurements. The metric system is convenient to use since units at different scales are related by multiples of ten.

The metric unit for **length** is the meter (m). The basic metric unit for **weight** or mass is the gram (g). The basic metric unit for **volume** is the liter (L).

These are the most commonly used units:
Appropriate units and equivalents

1 cm = 10 mm		
1 m = 1000 mm	1000 mL= 1 L	1000 mg = 1 g
1 m = 100 cm	1 kL = 1000 L	1 kg =1000 g
1000 m = 1 km		

Different units within the same system of measurement are selected based on the scale at which the measurement is being made. For example, the height of a person is measured in feet whereas the distances between cities are measured in miles. To estimate measurements of familiar objects, it is necessary to first determine the units to be used.

Examples:

Length
1. The coastline of Florida miles or kilometers
2. The width of a ribbon inches or millimeters
3. The thickness of a book inches or centimeters
4. The length of a football field yards or meters
5. The depth of water in a pool feet or meters

Weight or mass
1. A bag of sugar pounds or grams
2. A school bus tons or kilograms
3. A dime ounces or grams

Capacity
1. Paint to paint a bedroom gallons or liters
2. Glass of milk cups or liters
3. Bottle of soda quarts or liters
4. Medicine for child ounces or milliliters

In order to estimate measurements, it is helpful to have a familiar reference with a known measurement. For instance, you can use the knowledge that a dollar bill is about six inches long or that a nickel weighs about 5 grams to make estimates of weight and length without actually measuring with a ruler or a balance.

Some common equivalents include:

ITEM	APPROXIMATELY EQUAL TO	
	METRIC	IMPERIAL
large paper clip	1 gram	1 ounce
	1 liter	1 quart
average sized man	75 kilograms	170 pounds
	1 meter	1 yard
math textbook	1 kilogram	2 pounds
	1 kilometer	1 mile
	30 centimeters	1 foot
thickness of a dime	1 millimeter	0.1 inches
1 football field		6400 sq. yd.
temperature of boiling water	100°C	212°F
temperature of ice	0°C	32°F
1 cup of liquid	240 ml	8 fl. oz.
1 teaspoon	5 ml	

Estimate the measurement of the following items:

The length of an adult cow = _____meters
The thickness of a compact disc = _____millimeters
Your height = _____meters
length of your nose = _____centimeters
weight of your math textbook = _____kilograms
weight of an automobile = _____kilograms
weight of an aspirin = _____grams

11B. Unit conversions within and among measurement systems

There are many methods for converting measurements to other units within a system or between systems. One method is to multiply the given measurement by a conversion factor. This conversion factor is the ratio of:

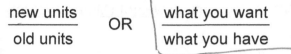

$$\frac{\text{new units}}{\text{old units}} \quad \text{OR} \quad \frac{\text{what you want}}{\text{what you have}}$$

The fundamental feature of **unit analysis** or **dimensional analysis** is that conversion factors may be multiplied together and units cancelled in the same way as numerators and denominators of numerical fractions. The following examples will make this clear.

<u>Example:</u> Convert 3 miles to yards.

Multiply the initial measurement by the conversion factor, cancel the mile units, and solve:

$$\frac{3 \text{ miles}}{1} \times \frac{1{,}760 \text{ yards}}{1 \text{ mile}} = 5280 \text{ yards}$$

<u>Example:</u> It takes Cynthia 45 minutes to get ready each morning. How many hours does she spend getting ready each week?

Multiply the initial measurement by the conversion factors from minutes to hours and from days to weeks, cancel the minute and day units, and solve:

$$\frac{45 \text{ min}}{\text{day}} \times \frac{1 \text{ hour}}{60 \text{ min}} \times \frac{7 \text{ days}}{\text{week}} = 5.25 \frac{\text{hours}}{\text{week}}$$

Conversion factors for different types of units are listed below:

<u>Measurements of length (English system)</u>

12 inches (in)	=	1 foot (ft)
3 feet (ft)	=	1 yard (yd)
1760 yards (yd)	=	1 mile (mi)

<u>Measurements of length (Metric system)</u>

Kilometer (km)	=	1000 meters (m)
Hectometer (hm)	=	100 meters (m)
Decameter (dam)	=	10 meters (m)
Meter (m)	=	1 meter (m)
Decimeter (dm)	=	1/10 meter (m)
Centimeter (cm)	=	1/100 meter (m)
Millimeter (mm)	=	1/1000 meter (m)

Conversion of length from English to Metric

1 inch	=	2.54 centimeters
1 foot	≈	30.48 centimeters
1 yard	≈	0.91 meters
1 mile	≈	1.61 kilometers

Measurements of weight (Metric system)

kilogram (kg)	=	1000 grams (g)
gram (g)	=	1 gram (g)
milligram (mg)	=	1/1000 gram (g)

Conversion of weight from Metric to English

28.35 grams (g)	=	1 ounce (oz)
16 ounces (oz)	=	1 pound (lb)
2000 pounds (lb)	=	1 ton (t) (short ton)
1.1 ton (t)	=	1 metric ton (t)

Conversion of weight from English to metric

1 ounce	≈	28.35 grams
1 pound	≈	0.454 kilogram
1.1 ton	=	1 metric ton

Measurement of volume (English system)

8 fluid ounces (oz)	=	1 cup (c)
2 cups (c)	=	1 pint (pt)
2 pints (pt)	=	1 quart (qt)
4 quarts (qt)	=	1 gallon (gal)

Measurement of volume (Metric system)

Kiloliter (kl)	=	1000 liters (l)
Liter (l)	=	1 liter (l)
Milliliter (ml)	=	1/1000 liter (ml)

Conversion of volume from English to metric

1 teaspoon (tsp)	≈	5 milliliters
1 fluid ounce	≈	29.57 milliliters
1 cup	≈	0.24 liters
1 pint	≈	0.47 liters
1 quart	≈	0.95 liters
1 gallon	≈	3.8 liters

Note: (') represents feet and (") represents inches.

Conversions within the metric or customary systems

To change from a **larger unit to a smaller unit, multiply**.
To change from a **smaller unit to a larger unit, divide**.

<u>Example:</u> 21 in. = _____ ft.

12 in. = 1 ft.
21 in. ÷ 12 in./ft. = $1\frac{3}{4}$ ft.

<u>Example:</u> $2\frac{3}{4}$ T. = _____ lb.

2000 lb. = 1 T.
$2\frac{3}{4}$ T. × 2000 lb./T. = 5500 lb.

Square units can be derived with knowledge of basic units of length by squaring the equivalent measurements.

1 square foot (sq. ft. or ft²) = 144 sq. in.
1 sq. yd. = 9 sq. ft.
1 sq. yd. = 1296 sq. in.

<u>Example:</u> 14 sq. yd. = _____ sq. ft.

1 sq. yd. = 9 sq. ft.
14 sq. yd. × 9 sq. ft./sq. yd. = 126 sq. ft.

The **metric system** is based on multiples of ten. Conversions are made by simply moving the decimal point to the left or right.

The prefixes are commonly listed from left to right for ease in conversion.

K H D U D C M

<u>Example:</u> 63 km = _____ m

Since there are 3 steps from <u>K</u>ilo to <u>U</u>nit, move the decimal point 3 places to the right.

63 km = 63,000 m

Example: 14 mL = _____ L

Since there are 3 steps from Milli to Unit, move the decimal point 3 places to the left.

14 mL = 0.014 L

11C. Problems involving length, area, volume, mass, capacity, density, time, temperature, angles, and rates of change

Measurements and unit conversions appear in many situations in daily life. The following are some problems of this type.

Length

Length refers to distance or the extent of an object in any direction. In common parlance, however, length is sometimes used to mean the longest dimension of an object.

Example: A car skidded 170 yards on an icy road before coming to a stop. How long is the skid distance in kilometers?

Since 1 yard ≈ 0.9 meters, multiply 170 yards by 0.9 meters/1 yard.

$$170 \text{ yd.} \times \frac{0.9 \text{ m}}{1 \text{ yd.}} = 153 \text{ m}$$

Since 1000 meters = 1 kilometer, multiply 153 meters by 1 kilometer/1000 meters.

$$153 \text{ m} \times \frac{1 \text{ km}}{1000 \text{ m}} = 0.153 \text{ km}$$

Example: The distance around a race course is exactly 1 mile, 17 feet, and $9\frac{1}{4}$ inches. Approximate this distance to the nearest tenth of a foot. Convert the distance to feet.

1 mile = 1760 yards = 1760 × 3 feet = 5280 feet.

$$9\frac{1}{4} \text{ in.} = \frac{37}{4} \text{ in.} \times \frac{1 \text{ ft.}}{12 \text{ in.}} = \frac{37}{48} \text{ ft.} \approx 0.77083 \text{ ft.}$$

So 1 mile, 17 ft. and $9\frac{1}{4}$ in. = 5280 ft. + 17 ft. + 0.77083 ft. ft.

$$= 5297.\underline{77083} \text{ ft.}$$

Now, we need to round to the nearest tenth digit. The underlined 7 is in the tenth place. The digit in the hundredth place, also a 7, is greater than 5, the 7 in the tenths place needs to be rounded up to 8 to get a final answer of 5297.8 feet.

Area and perimeter
See **Competency 0013F & G** for examples.

Volume and Surface Area
See **Competency 0014A** for examples.

Mass, weight and density
People often confuse mass with weight, when they are, in fact, very different. Think of it this way, an astronaut in outer space is weightless, yet still has the same amount of mass and density. Mass is the amount or quantity of matter in an object. Density is the mass per unit volume. The weight of an object is the force of earth's gravity on the mass. The metric system measures mass in Kilograms and force in Newtons but the pound is the unit of both force and mass in America.

Example: A sample of steel has a mass of .95 pounds and a volume of 3.38 cubic inches. Find the density of the steel.

Density is equal to mass divided by volume. Therefore, the density for this problem would be $\dfrac{.95}{3.38} = .28 lb / cubic$" and the density of steel is therefore, .28lb per cubic inch.

Example: Kathy has a bag of potatoes that weighs 5 lbs. 10 oz. She uses one third of the bag to make mashed potatoes. How much does the bag weigh now?
1 lb. = 16 oz.
 5(16 oz.) + 10 oz. = 80 oz + 10 oz = 90 oz.
$90 - (\frac{1}{3})90$ oz. = 90 oz. − 30 oz. = 60 oz.
60 ÷ 16 = 3.75 lbs.

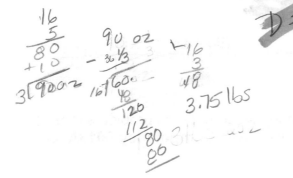

Capacity

Capacity or volume is measured in units such as gallon or liter that are equivalent to length units cubed (e.g. cm^3).

Example: Students in a fourth grade class want to fill a 3-gallon jug using cups of water. How many cups of water are needed?

1 gallon = 16 cups of water

$$3 \text{ gal.} \times \frac{16 \text{ c.}}{1 \text{ gal.}} = 48 \text{ c. water are needed.}$$

Time

Typical time problems in real life involve the calculation of elapsed time.

Example: A race took the winner 1 hr. 58 min. 12 sec. on the first half of the race and 2 hr. 9 min. 57 sec. on the second half of the race. How much time did the entire race take?

```
1 hr.  58 min.  12 sec.
      + 2 hr.    9 min.    57 sec.  Add
        3 hr.  67 min.    69 sec.
              + 1 min.  –60 sec.  Convert 60 sec. to 1 min.
        3 hr.  68 min.     9 sec.
      + 1 hr.–60 min.              Convert 60 min. to 1 hr.
        4 hr.   8 min.     9 sec. ← Final answer
```

Temperature

The Fahrenheit scale is used to measure temperature in the U.S. The Celsius scale is used in many other countries including Canada. Scientists everywhere typically use the Celsius scale.

Example: If the temperature is 90° F, what is it expressed in Celsius units?

To convert between Celsius (C) and Fahrenheit (F), use the formula $\dfrac{C}{5} = \dfrac{F - 32}{9}$

If F = 90, then $C = 5\dfrac{(90 - 32)}{9} = \dfrac{5 \times 58}{9} = 32.2$

Angles

There are many different types problems to be solved in geometry involving angles. See **Competency 0013A** for examples.

Rate of Change

Many situations in real life involve a constant rate of change of a certain quantity.. See **Competencies 0003 & 0008** for problems involving rate of change.

11D. Problems involving similar plane figures and indirect measurement

Similar figures have the same shape but different sizes. The symbol used to denote the similarity is ~. When two figures are similar:
1) The lengths of corresponding sides are proportional
2) The corresponding angles are congruent

Example: Given the following similar quadrilaterals, find the lengths of sides x, y, and z.

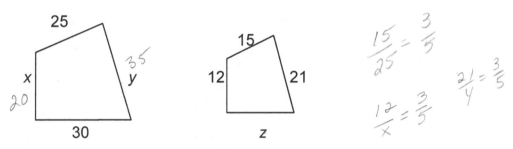

Since corresponding sides are proportional, $15/25 = 3/5$, so the scale factor is 3/5.

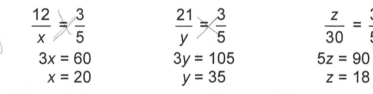

$$\frac{12}{x} = \frac{3}{5}$$
$$3x = 60$$
$$x = 20$$

$$\frac{21}{y} = \frac{3}{5}$$
$$3y = 105$$
$$y = 35$$

$$\frac{z}{30} = \frac{3}{5}$$
$$5z = 90$$
$$z = 18$$

Example: Tommy draws and cuts out 2 triangles for a school project. One of them has sides of 3, 6, and 9 inches. The other triangle has sides
of 2, 4, and 6. Is there a relationship between the two triangles?

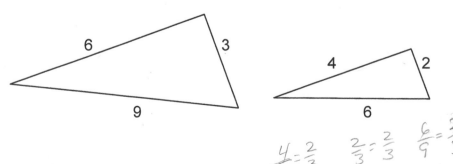

Determine the proportions of the corresponding sides.

$$\frac{2}{3} \qquad \frac{4}{6} = \frac{2}{3} \qquad\qquad \frac{6}{9} = \frac{2}{3}$$

The smaller triangle is 2/3 the size of the large triangle, therefore they are similar triangles.

Indirect measurement is needed when it is difficult or impossible to measure a quantity directly. In this case, the needed measurement can be calculated from other direct measurements when the relationships between the quantities are known.
For instance, proportions may be used to perform indirect measurements. if it is known that two triangles are similar, the fact that their sides are related by the same proportion may be used to derive the measurements of one triangle from the other.
<u>Example</u>: In the diagram below *X* represents the distance between two points with an unknown length. If the two triangles shown are similar, find X.

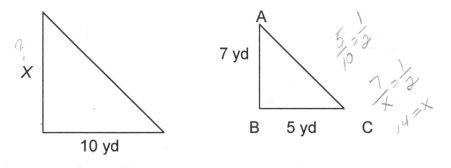

If the dimensions of a similar triangle are known, the problem can be solved by setting up the proportion below and solving for *X*.

$$\frac{X}{10 \text{ yd}} = \frac{7 \text{ yd}}{5 \text{ yd}}$$

After cross-multiplying, the equation can be written as 5*X* = 70; *X* equals 14 yards. Without actually measuring the distance with a measuring tape or other tool, the distance between the points is determined.

Indirect measurement occurs in instances other than measuring length. The area of a room can be measured using a scale drawing. Measuring the mass of the moon is possible using the measurable effects the moon exerts on the earth, such as the changes in tides. Another familiar indirect measurement is the Body Mass Index (BMI), which indicates body composition. The body composition uses height and weight measurements to measure health risks.

11E. The effect of changing linear dimensions on measures of length, area or volume

Determining how a change in a dimension affects other measurements depends upon the role of the dimension in the formula. If the dimension changed is raised to a power in the formula, the measurement will change by the multiple of the dimension raised to the same power. For example, if the radius of a circle is doubled, the circumference of the circle, $2\pi r$, will be doubled, but the area (which has r^2 in the formula) will be increased by a factor of 2^2.

Example: The side of a cube is 9 ft in length. If each side of the cube is reduced to one-third of its initial length, by what factor will the volume of the cube change?

Volume of a cube = a^3 where a is the side of the cube.

Initial volume of cube = 9 x 9 x 9 = 729 cu. ft
Changed volume of cube = 3 x 3 x 3 = 27 cu. ft.

When the side of the cube was reduced to one-third of its initial length, the volume of the cube was reduced by a factor of 3^3 or 27.

Example: If the radius of a cylinder is doubled, by what factor will its volume change?

The volume of a cylinder is given by $V = \pi r^2 h$ where r is the radius of the cylinder and h is its height.

If the radius of the cylinder is doubled, the ratio of the new and old volumes will be

$$\frac{V_{new}}{V_{old}} = \frac{\pi(2r)^2 h}{\pi r^2 h} = 4$$

Notice that the volume changes by a factor of 4 since the radius r is squared in the formula for the volume. The other length dimension h remains unchanged.

<u>Example</u>: The length, width and height of a rectangular pyramid is given by 2, 5 and 7 respectively. Find the volume of the pyramid. Also if the height is doubled, width is tripled and length is quadrupled, what will be the new volume?

The volume of a rectangular pyramid is given by $V = l \times w \times h$ where l is the length, w is the height and h is its height.

Volume = 2 x 5 x 7 = 70

New Length = 2 x 4 = 8
New Width = 5 x 3 = 15
New Height = 7 x 2 = 14

New volume = 8 x 15 x 14 = 1680
    = 2 (3) (4) (70) = 2(3)(4)(Old Volume)

So the volume will change by the factor 24.

11F. The effects of measurement error and rounding on computed quantities (e.g., area, density, speed)

Measurement error and rounding

Most numbers in mathematics are "exact" or "counted". Measurements are "approximate". They usually involve interpolation or figuring out which mark on the ruler is closest. Any measurement you get with a measuring device is approximate. Variations in measurement are called precision and accuracy. The error in a measurement is essentially the uncertainty in the measurement.

Precision is a measurement of how exactly a measurement is made, without reference to a true or real value. The precision of a measuring device is the smallest fractional or decimal division on the instrument. **Accuracy** is a measure of how close the result of measurement comes to the "true" value. If you are throwing darts, the true value is the bull's eye. If the three darts land on the bull's eye, the dart thrower is both precise (all land near the same spot) and accurate (the darts all land on the "true" value).

Error in measurement may also be expressed by a **percentage of error**. For example, a measurement of 12 feet may be said to be off by 2%. This means that the actual measurement could be between
12 - (2% of 12) and 12 + (2% of 12)
12 - (.02)12 and 12 + (.02)12
11.76 ft. and 12.24 feet

To determine the percent error between our measurement of a value and the actual value, use the formula:

$$\text{Percent Error} = \frac{|\text{Measured} - \text{Actual}|}{\text{Actual}} \times 100$$

Error in measurement may also be indicated by the terms "rounded" or "to the nearest". For example, the length of a side of a square to the nearest inch is 10 inches. This means that the actual length of the side could be between 9.5 inches and 10.4 inches (since all of these values round to 10).

Effect of measurement error on computed quantities

When a quantity such as area or density is computed based on measurements, the uncertainty in the calculated quantity is greater than the errors in the original measurements since the original errors are combined together in the calculation. This is known as **propagation of error**.

A measured value is typically expressed in the form $x \pm \Delta x$, where Δx is the uncertainty or margin of error. What this means is that the value of the measured quantity lies somewhere between $x - \Delta x$ and $x + \Delta x$, but our measurement techniques do not allow us any more precision. If several measurements are required to ultimately decide a value, we must use formulas to determine the total uncertainty that results from all the measurement errors. A few of these formulas for simple functions are listed below:

Formula	Uncertainty
$X = A \pm B$	$(\Delta X)^2 = (\Delta A)^2 + (\Delta B)^2$
$X = cA$	$\Delta X = c\Delta A$
$X = c(A \cdot B)$	$\left(\frac{\Delta X}{X}\right)^2 = \left(\frac{\Delta A}{A}\right)^2 + \left(\frac{\Delta B}{B}\right)^2$
$X = c\left(\frac{A}{B}\right)$	$\left(\frac{\Delta X}{X}\right)^2 = \left(\frac{\Delta A}{A}\right)^2 + \left(\frac{\Delta B}{B}\right)^2$

For example, if we wanted to determine the density of a small piece of metal, we would have to measure its weight on a scale and then determine its volume by measuring the amount of water it displaces in a graduated cylinder. There will be error associated with measurements made by both the scale and the graduated cylinder. Let's suppose we took the following measurements:

Mass: 57± 0.5 grams

Volume: 23 ± 3 mm^3

Since density is simply mass divided by the volume, we can determine its value to be:

$$\rho = \frac{m}{V} = \frac{57g}{23mm^3} = 2.5\frac{g}{mm^3}$$

Now we must calculate the uncertainty on this measurement, using the formula above:

$$\left(\frac{\Delta x}{x}\right)^2 = \left(\frac{\Delta A}{A}\right)^2 + \left(\frac{\Delta B}{B}\right)^2$$

$$\Delta x = \left(\sqrt{\left(\frac{\Delta A}{A}\right)^2 + \left(\frac{\Delta B}{B}\right)^2}\right) x = \left(\sqrt{\left(\frac{0.5g}{57g}\right)^2 + \left(\frac{3mm^3}{23mm^3}\right)^2}\right) \times 2.5\frac{g}{mm^3} = 0.3\frac{g}{mm^3}$$

Thus, the final value for the density of this object is 2.5 ± 0.3 g/mm^3.

Competency 0012 Understand the principles of Euclidean geometry and use them to prove theorems.

12A. Nature of axiomatic systems

Plane or Euclidean geometry is a classic example of an axiomatic system. An axiomatic system is composed of terms (or concepts) and axioms, also called postulates, which embody assumptions about the relationships between the terms. From these, theorems are logically derived. A simple example of an axiom is "the sun will rise tomorrow." It is a statement that we cannot prove, but accept as true.

An axiomatic system must be consistent in that there are no contradictions, i.e. there is no statement that you can prove both true and false. Otherwise, it has no mathematical value as it has no basis in truth. An axiomatic system is said to be complete if a statement and its negation are derivable within that system; therefore, an axiomatic system cannot be both complete and consistent. An example is the relative consistency of absolute geometry with respect to the real number system.

Within an axiomatic system, an axiom is considered independent if it is not derived from other axioms. The system itself is independent when each of its axioms is independent. **Logical axioms are universally true whereas non-logical axioms are defined for specific theory.**

The axiomatic system of plane geometry consists of the following:

Undefined terms: For example, points, lines and planes are intuitively understood but do not have specific, universally accepted definitions

⇓

Defined terms: Ray, angle and triangle are defined using undefined terms.

⇓

Axioms / Postulates: These are assumed statements that we accept without proof, similar to undefined terms. For example, the parallel postulate states: Given a line and a point not on that line, precisely one line can be drawn that contains the point *and* is parallel to the original line.

⇓

Theorems: These are proven statements. With a few axioms given as true, we can prove a multitude of theorems such as the faimilar Pythagorean Theorem.

12B. Undefined terms and postulates of Euclidean geometry

The three basic undefined terms of geometry are point, line, and plane.

A **point** indicates place or position. It has no length, width or thickness.

•   point A
A

A **line** is considered a set of points. Lines may be straight or curved, but the term line commonly denotes a straight line. Lines extend indefinitely. A line is defined by any two points that fall on the line; therefore a line may have multiple names.

$\longleftrightarrow$
G   H   I

This line can be named by any two points on the line.

It could be named $\overleftrightarrow{GH}$, $\overleftrightarrow{HI}$, $\overleftrightarrow{GI}$, $\overleftrightarrow{IG}$, $\overleftrightarrow{IH}$, or $\overleftrightarrow{HG}$. Any 2 points (letters) on the line can be used and their order is not important in naming a line.

A **line segment** is a portion of a line. It is the shortest distance between two endpoints and is named using those end points. Line segments therefore have exactly two names (i.e. $\overline{AB}$ or $\overline{BA}$). Because line segments have two endpoints, they have a defined length or distance.

•————————————•
A   B

segment $\overline{AB}$

A **ray** has exactly one endpoint and extends indefinitely in one direction. Rays are named using the endpoint as the first point and any other point on the ray as the second.

•————————•———————→
A   B

ray $\overrightarrow{AB}$

<u>Example:</u> Using the diagram below, name the line, line segments, and rays.

$\longleftrightarrow$
A   B   C

Line: $\overleftrightarrow{AB}$, $\overleftrightarrow{BA}$, $\overleftrightarrow{BC}$, $\overleftrightarrow{CB}$, $\overleftrightarrow{AC}$, or $\overleftrightarrow{CA}$ all name the line above.

Line Segments: $\overline{AB}$ or $\overline{BA}$, $\overline{BC}$ or $\overline{CB}$ and $\overline{AC}$ or $\overline{CA}$ name the three line segments.

Ray: $\overrightarrow{AB}$ or $\overrightarrow{AC}$, $\overrightarrow{BC}$, $\overrightarrow{CB}$ or $\overrightarrow{CA}$ and $\overrightarrow{BA}$ name the rays.

Note that the symbol for a line includes two arrows (indicating infinite extent in both directions), the symbol for a ray includes one arrow (indicating that it has one end point) and the symbol for a line segment has no arrows (indicating two end points).

Example: Use the diagram below, calculate the length of $\overline{AB}$ given $\overline{AC}$ is 6 cm and $\overline{BC}$ is twice as long as $\overline{AB}$.

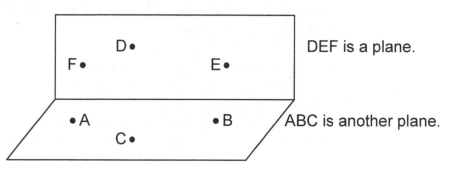

$$\overline{AB} + \overline{BC} = \overline{AC}$$

Let $x = \overline{AB}$

$x + 2x = 6 \text{ cm}$

$3x = 6 \text{ cm}$

$x = 2 \text{ cm}$

A **plane** is a flat surface that extends forever in two dimensions. It has no ends or edges. It has no thickness. It is usually drawn as a parallelogram that can be named either by 3 non-collinear points (3 points that are not on the same line) on the plane or by placing a letter in the corner of the plane that is not used elsewhere in the diagram.

DEF is a plane.

ABC is another plane.

Definitions are explanations of all mathematical terms except those that are undefined.

Postulates are mathematical statements that are accepted as true statements without providing a proof.

accepted as true

The following algebraic postulates are frequently used as reasons for statements in 2 column geometric proofs:

Addition Property: If $a = b$ and $c = d$, then $a + c = b + d$.
Subtraction Property: If $a = b$ and $c = d$, then $a - c = b - d$.
Multiplication Property: If $a = b$ and $c \neq 0$, then $ac = bc$.
Division Property: If $a = b$ and $c \neq 0$, then $a/c = b/c$.
Reflexive Property: $a = a$
Symmetric Property: If $a = b$, then $b = a$.
Transitive Property: If $a = b$ and $b = c$, then $a = c$.
Distributive Property: $a(b + c) = ab + ac$
Substitution Property: If $a = b$, then b may be substituted for a in any other expression (a may also be substituted for b).

Basic Postulates of Euclidean Geometry

The following are the five basic postulates:
1. Through any two points, exactly one line can be drawn.
2. A line segment can be extended indefinitely along a straight line.
3. A circle can be drawn with a radius and a center point.
4. All right angles are congruent.
5. If two lines are parallel and are cut by a transversal, corresponding angles have the same measure. This is called the parallel lines postulate.

Other Postulates of Euclidean Geometry

1. Two lines can intersect at only one point.
2. There is only one midpoint for a line segment.
3. The intersection of two planes is a line.
4. There is a unique distance between two points.
5. Exactly one plane can be drawn using 3 non-collinear points.
6. If two points lie on a plane, the line joining them also lies on the same plane.
7. The sum of the lengths of two sides of any triangle is greater than the length of the third side of that triangle. This is called the triangle inequality postulate.
8. The sum of the lengths of three sides of any quadrilateral is greater than the length of the fourth side. This is called the quadrilateral inequality postulate.

A + B > C

A + B + C > D

12C.   Relationships among points, lines, angles, and planes

An **angle** is formed by the intersection of two rays.

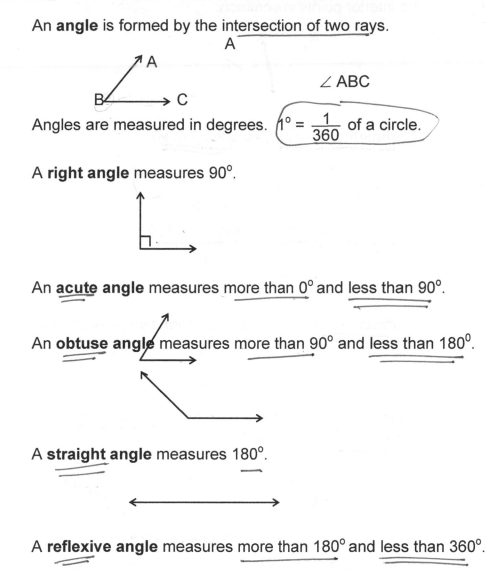

Angles are measured in degrees. $1° = \frac{1}{360}$ of a circle.

∠ ABC

A **right angle** measures 90°.

An **acute angle** measures more than 0° and less than 90°.

An **obtuse angle** measures more than 90° and less than 180°.

A **straight angle** measures 180°.

A **reflexive angle** measures more than 180° and less than 360°.

Angles can be classified in a number of ways. Some classifications are outlined here.

Adjacent angles have a common vertex and one common side but no interior points in common.

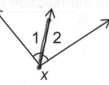

Complementary angles add up to 90°.

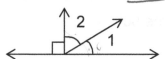

Supplementary angles add up to 180°.

Vertical angles have sides that form two pairs of opposite rays.

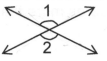

Corresponding angles are in the same corresponding position on two parallel lines cut by a transversal.

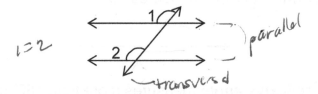

Parallel Lines Postulate: If two lines are parallel and are cut by a transversal, corresponding angles have the same measure.

Alternate interior angles are diagonal angles on the inside of two parallel lines cut by a transversal.

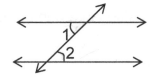

Alternate exterior angles are diagonal on the outside of two parallel lines cut by a transversal.

Alternate Interior Angles Theorem: If two parallel lines are cut by a transversal, the alternate interior angles are congruent.

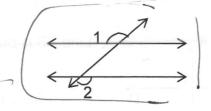

An infinite number of lines can be drawn through any point.

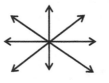

Exactly one line can be drawn through two points.

Just as intersecting lines share a common point, **intersecting planes** share a common set of points or line.

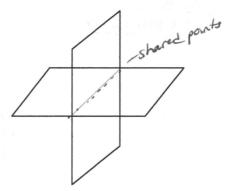

Skew lines do not intersect because they do not lie on the same plane.

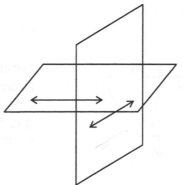

Perpendicular lines or planes form a 90° angle to each other. Perpendicular lines have slopes that are the negative reciprocals of each other.

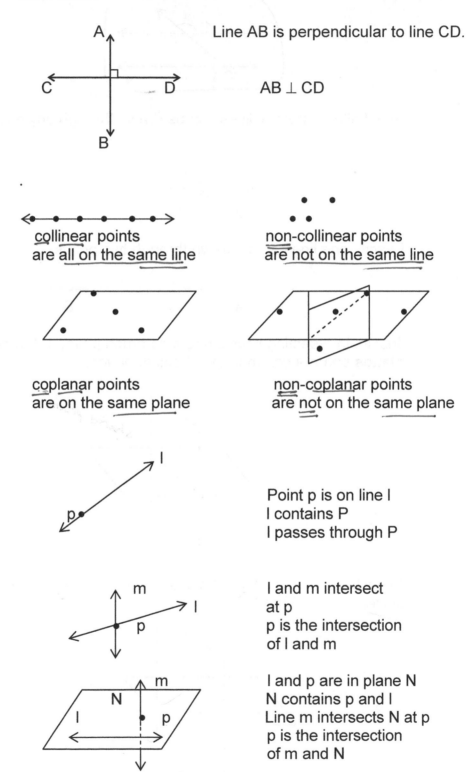

Line AB is perpendicular to line CD.

AB ⊥ CD

collinear points
are all on the same line

non-collinear points
are not on the same line

coplanar points
are on the same plane

non-coplanar points
are not on the same plane

Point p is on line l
l contains P
l passes through P

l and m intersect
at p
p is the intersection
of l and m

l and p are in plane N
N contains p and l
Line m intersects N at p
p is the intersection
of m and N

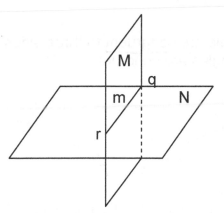

Planes M and N intersect at rq
rq is the intersection
of M and N
rq is in M and N
M and N contain rq

12D.   **Methods for proving triangles congruent**

Congruent figures have the same size and shape. If one is placed above the other, it will fit exactly. Congruent lines have the same length. Congruent angles have equal measures.
The symbol for congruent is (≅)

Polygons (pentagons) *ABCDE* and *VWXYZ* are congruent. They are exactly the same size and shape.

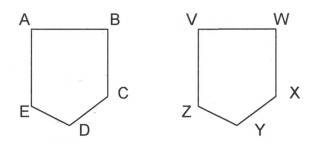

$$ABCDE \cong VWXYZ$$

Corresponding parts are those congruent angles and congruent sides, that is:

corresponding angles

$\angle A \leftrightarrow \angle V$
$\angle B \leftrightarrow \angle W$
$\angle C \leftrightarrow \angle X$
$\angle D \leftrightarrow \angle Y$
$\angle E \leftrightarrow \angle Z$

corresponding sides

$AB \leftrightarrow VW$
$BC \leftrightarrow WX$
$CD \leftrightarrow XY$
$DE \leftrightarrow YZ$
$AE \leftrightarrow VZ$

Two triangles can be proven congruent by comparing pairs of appropriate congruent corresponding parts.

SSS postulate

If three sides of one triangle are congruent to three sides of another triangle, then the two triangles are congruent.

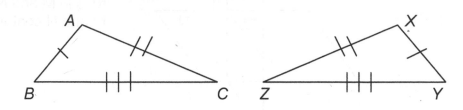

Since $AB \cong XY$, $BC \cong YZ$ and $AC \cong XZ$, then $\triangle ABC \cong \triangle XYZ$.

<u>Example</u>: Given isosceles triangle ABC with D the midpoint of base AC, prove the two triangles formed by BD are congruent.

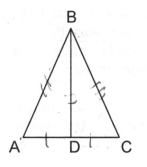

Proof:
1. Isosceles triangle ABC,
   D midpoint of base AC Given
2. $AB \cong BC$ An isosceles $\triangle$ has two congruent sides
3. $AD \cong DC$ Midpoint divides a line into two equal parts
4. $BD \cong BD$ Reflexive property
5. $\triangle ABD \cong \triangle BCD$ SSS

SAS postulate

If two sides and the included angle of one triangle are congruent to two sides and the included angle of another triangle, then the two triangles are congruent.

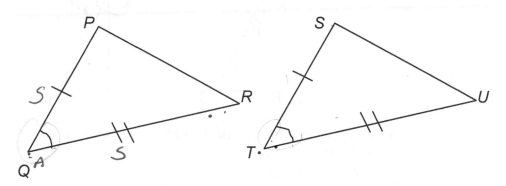

$PQ \cong ST$, $\angle Q \cong \angle T$, $QR \cong TU$ then $\triangle PQR \cong \triangle STU$ by SAS

Example:

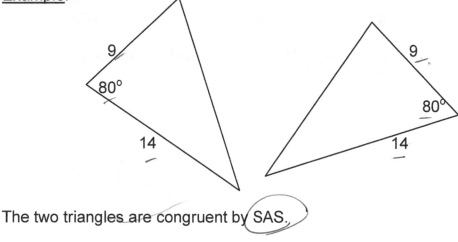

The two triangles are congruent by SAS.

ASA postulate

If two angles and the included side of one triangle are congruent to two angles and the included side of another triangle, the triangles are congruent.

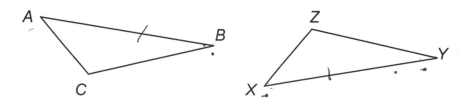

$\angle A \cong \angle X$, $\angle B \cong \angle Y$, $AB \cong XY$ then $\triangle ABC \cong \triangle XYZ$ by ASA

<u>Example:</u> Given two right triangles with one leg of each measuring 6 cm and the adjacent angle 37°, prove the triangles are congruent.

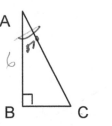
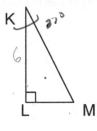

1. Right triangles *ABC* and *KLM*   Given
    $AB = KL = 6$ cm
    $\angle A = \angle K = 37°$

2. $AB \cong KL$ Figures with the same
    $\angle A \cong \angle K$ measure are congruent

3. $\angle B \cong \angle L$ All right angles are
                                               congruent.

4. $\triangle ABC \cong \triangle KLM$ ASA

<u>Example:</u> What method would you use to prove the triangles congruent?

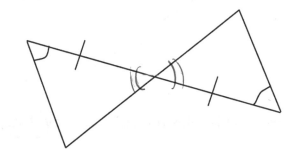

ASA because the vertical angles are congruent.

AAS theorem

If two angles and a non-included side of one triangle are congruent to the corresponding parts of another triangle, then the triangles are congruent.

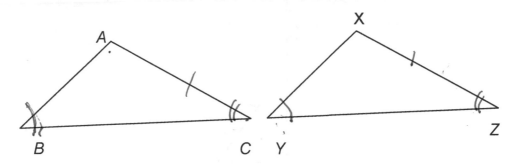

$\angle B \cong \angle Y$, $\angle C \cong \angle Z$, $AC \cong XZ$, then $\triangle ABC \cong \triangle XYZ$ by AAS.
We can derive this theorem because if two angles of the triangles are congruent, then the third angle must also be congruent. Therefore, we can use the ASA postulate.

HL theorem

If the hypotenuse and a leg of one right triangle are congruent to the corresponding parts of another right triangle, the triangles are congruent.

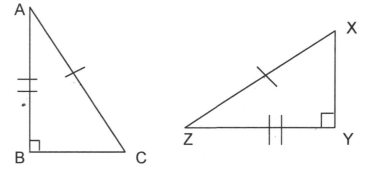

Since $\angle B$ and $\angle Y$ are right angles and $AC \cong XZ$ (hypotenuse of each triangle), $AB \cong YZ$ (corresponding leg of each triangle), then $\triangle ABC \cong \triangle XYZ$ by HL.

Example: What method would you use to prove the triangles congruent?

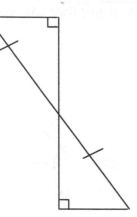

AAS

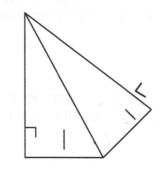

HL

Overlapping Triangles
Two triangles are overlapping if a portion of the interior region of one triangle is shared in common with all or a part of the interior region of the second triangle.

The most effective method for proving two overlapping triangles congruent is to draw the two triangles separated. Separate the two triangles and label all of the vertices using the labels from the original overlapping figures. Once the separation is complete, apply one of the congruence shortcuts: SSS, ASA, SAS, AAS, or HL.

12E. Properties of similar triangles

For a definition of similarity see **Competency 0011D.**

AA Similarity Postulate

If two angles of one triangle are congruent to two angles of another triangle, then the triangles are similar.

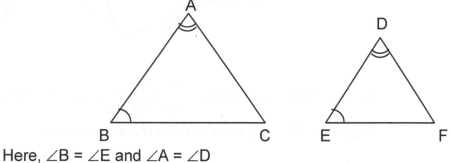

Here, $\angle B = \angle E$ and $\angle A = \angle D$

SAS Similarity Theorem

If an angle of one triangle is congruent to an angle of another triangle and the sides adjacent to those angles are in proportion, then the triangles are similar.

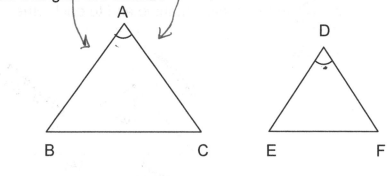

$$\frac{AB}{DE} = \frac{AC}{DF} \quad \text{and} \quad \angle A = \angle D$$

SSS Similarity Theorem

If the sides of two triangles are in proportion, then the triangles are similar.

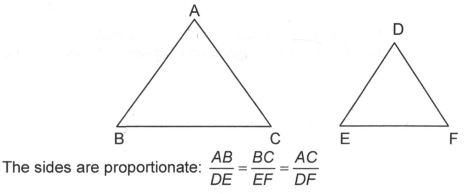

The sides are proportionate: $\dfrac{AB}{DE} = \dfrac{BC}{EF} = \dfrac{AC}{DF}$

Example: A graphic artist is designing a logo containing two triangles. The artist wants the triangles to be similar. Determine whether the artist has created similar triangles.

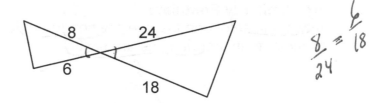

The sides are proportional $\left(\dfrac{8}{24} = \dfrac{6}{18} = \dfrac{1}{3}\right)$ and vertical angles are congruent. The two triangles are therefore similar.

A **right triangle** is a triangle with one right angle. The side opposite the right angle is called the **hypotenuse**. The other two sides are the **legs**. An **altitude** is a line drawn from one vertex, perpendicular to the opposite side. When an altitude is drawn to the hypotenuse of a right triangle, then the two triangles formed are similar to the original triangle and to each other.

Example:

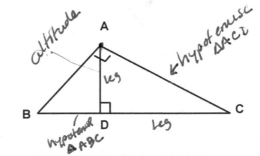

Given right triangle ABC with right angle at A, altitude AD drawn to hypotenuse BC at D.

$\triangle ABC \sim \triangle ABD \sim \triangle ACD$ The triangles formed are similar to each other and to the original right triangle.

$$\frac{a}{b} = \frac{b}{c}$$

If a, b and c are positive numbers so that $\dfrac{a}{b} = \dfrac{b}{c}$ then b is called the **geometric mean** between a and c.

Example: Find the geometric mean between 6 and 30.

$$\frac{6}{x} = \frac{x}{30}$$
$$x^2 = 180$$
$$x = \sqrt{180} = \sqrt{36 \cdot 5} = 6\sqrt{5}$$

The geometric mean is significant when the altitude is drawn to the hypotenuse of a right triangle. The length of the altitude is the ~~BD~~ geometric mean between each segment of the hypotenuse, and each leg is the geometric mean between the hypotenuse and the segment of the hypotenuse that is adjacent to the leg.

Example:

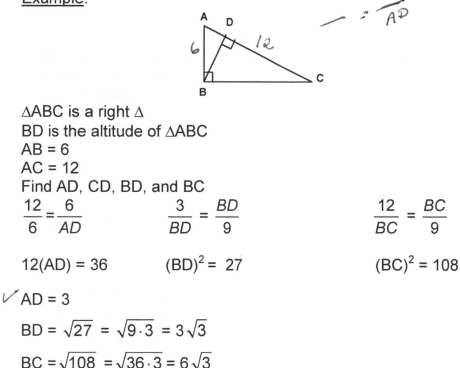

$\triangle ABC$ is a right $\triangle$
BD is the altitude of $\triangle ABC$
AB = 6
AC = 12
Find AD, CD, BD, and BC

$$\frac{12}{6} = \frac{6}{AD}$$

$$\frac{3}{BD} = \frac{BD}{9}$$

$$\frac{12}{BC} = \frac{BC}{9}$$

$12(AD) = 36$ $\qquad$ $(BD)^2 = 27$ $\qquad\qquad$ $(BC)^2 = 108$

✓ AD = 3

$BD = \sqrt{27} = \sqrt{9 \cdot 3} = 3\sqrt{3}$

$BC = \sqrt{108} = \sqrt{36 \cdot 3} = 6\sqrt{3}$

✓ CD = 12 - 3 = 9

12F.   **Geometric constructions**

Classical construction refers to the use of a straightedge and compass for creating geometrical figures that match certain criteria. A construction consists of only segments, arcs, and points. Typical constructions includes the replication of line segments, angles or shapes, bisection of angles and lines, drawing lines that are parallel or perpendicular to a given line, as well as drawing different kinds of polygons and circles.

Duplication of line segments and angles

. The easiest construction to make is to **duplicate a given line segment**. Given segment AB, construct a segment equal in length to segment AB by following these steps.

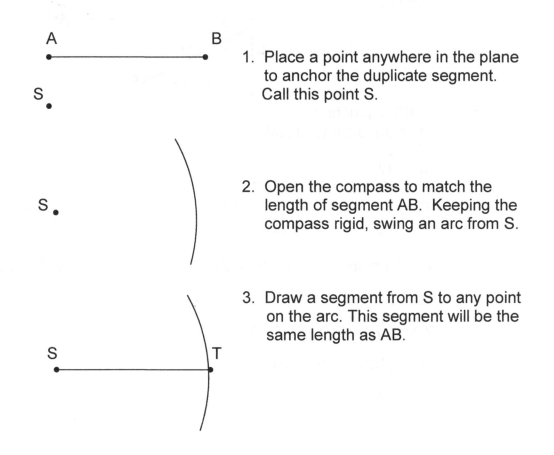

1. Place a point anywhere in the plane to anchor the duplicate segment. Call this point S.

2. Open the compass to match the length of segment AB. Keeping the compass rigid, swing an arc from S.

3. Draw a segment from S to any point on the arc. This segment will be the same length as AB.

To construct an angle congruent to a given angle:

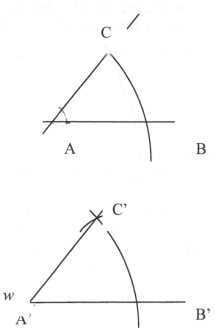

1. Given the angle A, draw an arc with any radius such that it intersects the sides of the angle at B and C.

2. On a working line *w*, select a point A' as the vertex of the angle to be drawn. With A' as the center and the same radius as the previous arc, draw an arc that intersects the line *w* in B'.

3. With B' as the center and radius equal to BC (measured off by placing ends of compass on B and C), draw a second arc that intersects the first arc at C'.

4. Join points A' and C'. The angle A' is congruent to the given angle A.

Construction of perpendicular lines and bisectors

Given a line segment with two endpoints such as A and B, follow these steps to **construct the line that both bisects and is perpendicular** to the line given segment.

1. Swing an arc of any radius from point A. Swing another arc of the same radius from B. The arcs will intersect at two points. Label these points C and D.

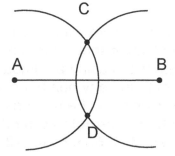

2. Connect C and D to form the perpendicular bisector of segment

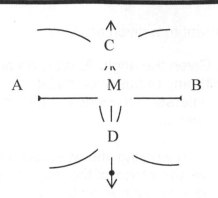

3. The point M where line CD and segment AB intersect is the midpoint of segment AB.

Construction of angle bisectors
To **bisect a given angle** such as angle *FUZ*, follow these steps.

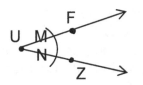

1. Swing an arc of any length with its center at point U. This arc will intersect rays *UF* and *UZ* at M and N.

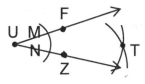

2. Open the compass to any length and swing one arc from point M and another arc of the same radius from point N. These arcs will intersect in the interior or angle *FUZ* at point T.

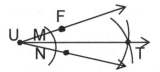

3. Connect U and T for the ray which bisects angle *FUZ*. Ray *UT* is the angle bisector of angle *FUZ*

Construction of regular polygons
Not all regular polygons can be constructed with a compass and straightedge. The mathematician Gauss showed that a regular polygon with n sides can be constructed using a compass and ruler only if n is a product of a power of 2 and any number of distinct Fermat primes. Since the only known small Fermat primes are 3, 5, and 27, **a regular polygon can be constructed only if it has one of the following number of sides: 3, 4, 5, 6, 8, 10, 12, 15, 16, 17, 20, 24,.. and so on.**

We have already constructed an **equilateral triangle** and **square** in replicating a shape. Constructing a regular hexagon and **regular** octagon within a circle is also relatively simple. For construction of a **regular hexagon**, draw a diameter (AB in the figure below) in a circle. Then using the end points of the diameter A and B as centers, draw arcs with radius equal to the radius of the circle to intersect the circle in four points (C&D from A, E&F from B) that are the other vertices of the hexagon.

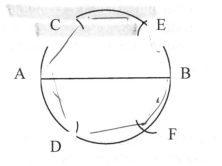

A **regular octagon** may be constructed by drawing two perpendicular diameters within a circle followed by lines that bisect the angles formed by the diameters. The points where all these lines intersect the circle are the vertices of a regular octagon.

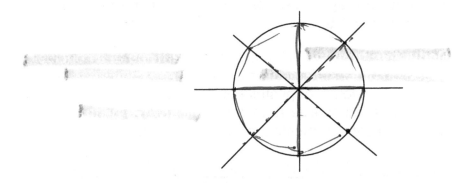

Construction of a **regular pentagon** is a little more involved.

12G. **Proving theorems within the axiomatic structure of Euclidean geometry**

Theorems are mathematical statements that can be proven to be true based on postulates, definitions, algebraic properties, given information, and previously proven theorems.

Inductive thinking is the process of finding a pattern from a group of examples. That pattern is the conclusion that this set of examples indicate. It may be a correct conclusion or it may be an incorrect conclusion because other examples may not follow the predicted pattern.

Example:
Suppose:
    On Monday Mr.Peterson eats breakfast at McDonalds.
    On Tuesday Mr.Peterson eats breakfast at McDonalds.
    On Wednesday Mr.Peterson eats breakfast at McDonalds.
    On Thursday Mr.Peterson eats breakfast at McDonalds again.

Conclusion: On Friday Mr. Peterson will eat breakfast at McDonalds again.

This may or may not be true, but it is a conclusion arrived at by inductive thinking.

Deductive thinking is the process of arriving at a conclusion based on other statements that are all known to be true, as theorems, axioms, or postulates. Conclusions found by deductive thinking based on true statements will **always** be true. Valid mathematical arguments are deductive in nature.

A **direct proof** will demonstrate a proposition by beginning with the given information and showing that it leads to the proposition through logical steps. An **indirect proof** of a proposition may be carried out by demonstrating that the opposite of the proposition is untenable.

A proof of a geometrical proposition is typically presented in a format with two columns side by side. In a **two-column proof** of this type, the left column consists of the given information or statements that can be proved by deductive reasoning. The right column consists of the reasons used to justify each statement on the left. The right side should identify given information or state the theorems, postulates, definitions or algebraic properties used to show that particular step is true.

Some basic theorems of Euclidean geometry are proven below.

Theorem 1
Two distinct lines cannot have more than one point in common.

Proof
Let two lines be *l* and *m*. To prove that they have only one point in common, let us suppose that the two lines intersect in two distinct points, *P* and *Q*. So, two lines are passing through two distinct points *P* and *Q*. But this assumption clashes with the axiom that only one line can pass through two distinct points. So, the assumption that we started with, that two lines can pass through two distinct points is invalid.

Therefore, it can be concluded that two distinct lines cannot have more than one point in common.

Theorem 2
If two lines intersect each other, then the vertically opposite angles are equal.

Proof
It is given that 'two lines intersect each other'. So, let AB and CD be the two lines intersecting at O as shown in the figure below:

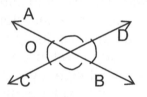

Two pairs of vertically opposite angles are

(i) ∠ AOC and ∠ BOD   (ii) ∠AOD and ∠BOC.
To prove that ∠AOC = ∠BOD and ∠AOD = ∠BOC.
The ray OA intersects the line CD.

Therefore, ∠AOC + ∠AOD = 180° (Linear pair axiom) (1)
∠AOD + ∠BOD = 180°   (2)

From (1) and (2),
∠AOC + ∠AOD = ∠AOD + ∠BOD
∴ ∠AOC = ∠BOD

Similarly, it can be proven that ∠AOD = ∠BOC

12H. **The origins and development of geometry in different cultures (e.g., Greek, Hindu, Chinese)**

Origins and Development of Geometry
The field of *geometry* began as a crude collection of rules for calculating lengths, areas, and volumes. Ancient practitioners of construction, surveying, and navigation used basic geometric principles in performing their trades.

Historians believe that the Egyptians and Babylonians, as well as the Indians and Chinese, used geometry as early as 3000 B.C. The early Hindu cultures of India and Pakistan extensively used weights and measures in construction, circles and triangles in art, and rudimentary compasses for navigation. Later, Hindu cultures formalized geometric concepts with rules and theorems. For example, the *Suba Sutras,* written in India between 800 and 500 B.C., contains geometric proofs and the Pythagorean Theorem. Early Chinese culture also used geometry in construction and measurement. Among the geometric principles used by the early Chinese cultures were area formulas for two-dimensional figures, proportionality constants such as π and the Pythagorean Theorem.

The Greeks took ancient geometric thought and developed it into a true mathematical science. The evolution of Greek geometry began with Thales, who introduced the concept of theorems by proof, the defining characteristic of Greek mathematics. Next, Pythagoras and his disciples created a large body of geometric thought through deduction. Finally, Euclid organized and added to previous knowledge, by writing *Elements*, his thirteen-volume compilation of Greek geometry to number theory in 300 B.C. *Elements* was the first formal system of mathematics in which assumptions, called axioms and postulates, logically led to the formation of various theorems, corollaries, and definitions. Euclidean geometry, the system of geometry based on Euclid's *Elements*, is the traditional form of geometry studied in elementary and secondary schools today.

Though Greek geometry began to decline around 200 B.C., geometry continued to develop in other cultures. The Islamic empire contributed greatly to the development of geometry from 700 to 1500 A.D. For example, the Persian poet and mathematician Omar Khayyam created the field of algebraic geometry in the 11th Century and paved the way for the development of non-Euclidean geometry.

In the 17th Century, Rene Descartes and Pierre de Fermat created analytic geometry, the geometry of coordinates and equations. Analytic geometry is the precursor of calculus. In addition, Girard Desargues created projective geometry, the study of geometry without measurement.

The 18th and 19th centuries saw the development of non-Euclidean geometry or hyperbolic, elliptical and absolute geometry. Non-Euclidean geometry rejects Euclid's fifth postulate of parallel lines. Finally, the advances in technology in the 20th Century sparked the development of computational or digital geometry.

Competency 0013 Apply Euclidean geometry to analyze the properties of two-dimensional figures and to solve problems.

13A. **Using deduction to justify properties of and relationships among triangles, quadrilaterals, and other polygons (e.g., length of sides, angle measure)**

Polygons

A polygon is a simple closed figure composed of line segments. Triangles and quadrilaterals, for instance, are polygons. The number of sides in a polygon is equal to the number of vertices; thus, for instance, a quadrilateral has four sides and four vertices. In a **regular polygon,** all sides are the same length and all angles are the same measure.

Here we will consider only **convex polygons**, i.e. polygons for which the measure of each internal angle is less than 180°. Of the two polygons shown below, the one on the left is a convex polygon.

The sum of the measures of the **interior angles** of a polygon can be determined using the following formula, where n represents the number of sides in the polygon.

Sum of $\angle s = 180(n - 2)$

The measure of each interior angle of a regular polygon can be found by dividing the sum of the measures by the number of angles.

Measure of $\angle = \dfrac{180(n - 2)}{n}$

<u>Example:</u> Find the measure of each angle of a regular octagon.

Since an octagon has eight sides, each angle equals:

$$\frac{180(8 - 2)}{8} = \frac{180(6)}{8} = 135°$$

The sum of the measures of the **exterior angles** of a polygon, taken one angle at each vertex equals 360°. The measure of each exterior angle of a regular polygon can be determined using the following formula, where n represents the number of angles in the polygon.

MIDDLE SCHOOL MATHEMATICS 190

Measure of exterior $\angle$ of regular polygon $= 180 - \dfrac{180(n-2)}{n}$

or, more simply $= \dfrac{360}{n}$

Example: Find the measure of the interior and exterior angles of a regular pentagon.

Since a pentagon has five sides, each exterior angle measures:

$$\frac{360}{5} = 72^0$$

Since each exterior angle is supplementary to its interior angle, the interior angle measures 180 – 72 or 108°.

[handwritten: 180(3), 540/5, INT∠ 108°]

Triangles

A triangle is a polygon with three sides. Triangles can be classified by the types of angles or the lengths of their sides.

An **acute** triangle has exactly three *acute* angles.
A **right** triangle has one *right* angle.
An **obtuse** triangle has one *obtuse* angle.

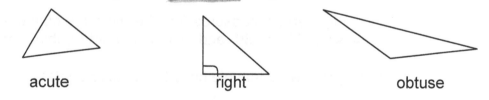

acute   right   obtuse

All *three* sides of an **equilateral** triangle are the same length.
Two sides of an **isosceles** triangle are the same length.
None of the sides of a **scalene** triangle are the same length.

equilateral   isosceles   scalene

<u>Theorem:</u> The sum of the angles of a triangle is 180º.
<u>Proof</u>

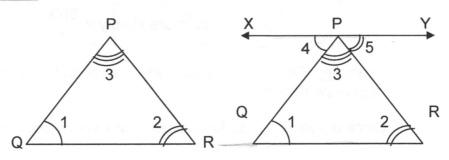

PQR is a triangle and ∠1, ∠2 and ∠3 are the angles of ΔPQR (figure 1).

To prove that ∠1 + ∠2 + ∠3 = 180°, let us draw a line XPY parallel to QR through the opposite vertex P, as shown in Figure 2, so that we can use the properties of parallel lines.

Now, XPY is a line.

Therefore, ∠4 + ∠3 + ∠5 = 180° .... (1)

But XPY || QR and PQ, PR are transversals.

So, ∠4 = ∠1 and ∠5 = ∠2 (Pairs of alternate angles)

Substituting ∠4 and ∠5 in (1),

∠1 + ∠3 + ∠2 = 180°

That is, ∠1 + ∠2 + ∠3 = 180°

<u>Example:</u> Can a triangle have two right angles?

No. Right angle measures 90º, therefore the sum of two right angles would be 180º and there could not be third angle.

<u>Example:</u> Can a triangle have two obtuse angles?

No. Since an obtuse angle measures more than 90º the sum of two obtuse angles would be greater than 180º.

<u>Example:</u> Can a right triangle be obtuse?

No. Once again, the sum of the angles would be more than 180º.

<u>Example:</u> In a triangle, the measure of the second angle is three times the first. The third angle equals the sum of the measures of the first two angles. Find the number of degrees in each angle.

Let x = the number of degrees in the first angle
$3x$ = the number of degrees in the second angle
$x + 3x$ = the measure of the third angle

Since the sum of the measures of all three angles is 180°.

$$x + 3x + (x + 3x) = 180$$
$$8x = 180$$
$$x = 22.5$$
$$3x = 67.5$$
$$x + 3x = 90$$

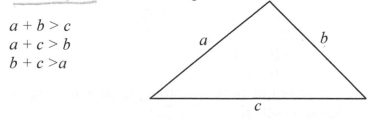

Thus the angles measure 22.5°, 67.5°, and 90°. Additionally, the triangle is a right triangle.

Theorem: The **Triangle Inequality Theorem** states that the sum of the lengths of any two sides of a triangle is greater than the length of the remaining side. In the triangle below,

$a + b > c$
$a + c > b$
$b + c > a$

If a triangle has an unknown side, the Triangle Inequality Theorem can be applied to determine a reasonable range of possible values for the unknown side.

Example: Determine the range of possible values for the unknown side, p.

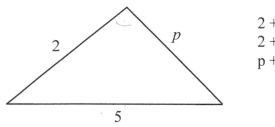

$2 + p > 5$
$2 + 5 > p$
$p + 5 > 2$

The expressions could be arranged to show:
$p > 5–2$ or $p > 3$; $7 > p$; $p > –3$.
Thus p is a value between 3 and 7.

An **angle-side relationship** exists between angles and the sides opposite them. The side of the triangle that is opposite the largest angle is the longest side. The side opposite the smallest angle is the smallest. This rule can be used to determine a reasonable range of measurement for an unknown angle.

<u>Example:</u> Order the sides of the following triangle by length.

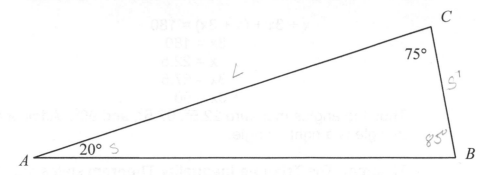

Because the sum of all angles in a triangle is equal to 180°, ∠B can be calculated.

$$\angle A + \angle B + \angle C = 180°$$
$$20° + \angle B + 75° = 180°$$
$$\angle B = 180° - 20° - 75°$$
$$\angle B = 85°$$

To order the sides according to size, the angle-side relationship can be applied: $\overline{BC} < \overline{AB} < \overline{AC}$

Two adjacent angles form a linear pair when they have a common side and their remaining sides form a straight angle. Angles in a linear pair are supplementary. An **exterior angle** of a triangle forms a linear pair with an angle of the triangle.

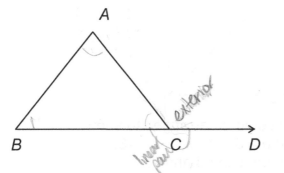

∠ACD is an exterior angle of triangle ABC, forming a linear pair with ∠ACB.

<u>Theorem:</u> The **Exterior Angle Theorem** states that the measure of an exterior angle of a triangle is equal to the sum of the measures of the two non-adjacent interior angles.

<u>Proof:</u> We can easily demonstrate this by taking the above triangle ABC as an example. In this triangle

∠ABC+∠BAC+∠ACB=180° (Sum of interior angles of a triangle)

Also, ∠ACD+∠ACB=180° (Exterior angle and adjacent interior
angle are supplementary)

Therefore, ∠ACD=∠ABC+∠BAC.

Example: In triangle ABC, the measure of ∠A is twice the measure
of ∠B. ∠C is 30° more than their sum. Find the measure of the
exterior angle formed at ∠C.

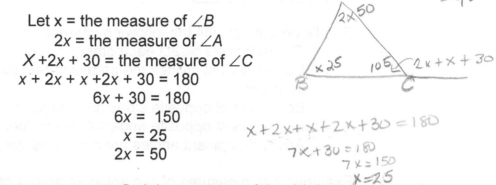

Let x = the measure of ∠B
2x = the measure of ∠A
X +2x + 30 = the measure of ∠C
x + 2x + x +2x + 30 = 180
6x + 30 = 180
6x = 150
x = 25
2x = 50

It is not necessary to find the measure of the third angle, since the
exterior angle equals the sum of the opposite interior angles. Thus
the exterior angle at ∠C measures 75°.

Theorem: The line segment joining the mid-points of two sides of a
triangle is parallel to the third side.

Proof:

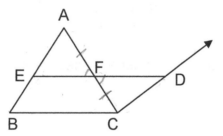

From the figure E and F are mid-points of AB and AC respectively,
and CD ∥ BA.
Δ AEF ≅ Δ CDF (ASA Postulate)
So, EF = DF and AE = DC.
Since AE = BE (E is mid-point of AB), BE = AE = DC.
Since BE is also parallel to DC, BCDE is a parallelogram and EF ∥
BC.

Quadrilaterals

A quadrilateral is a polygon with four sides. The sum of the measures of the angles of a quadrilateral is 360°.

A **parallelogram** is a quadrilateral with <u>two</u> pairs of parallel sides.

Parallelograms exhibit the following characteristics:
- The diagonals bisect each other.
- Each diagonal divides the parallelogram into two congruent triangles.
- Both pairs of opposite sides are congruent.
- Both pairs of opposite angles are congruent.
- Any two adjacent angles are supplementary.

<u>Example:</u> The measures of two adjacent angles of a parallelogram are $3x + 40$ and $x + 70$. Find the measures of each angle.

Since any two adjacent angles of a parallelogram are supplementary,

$$3x + 40 + x + 70 = 180$$
$$4x + 110 = 180$$
$$4x = 70$$
$$x = 17.5$$
$$3x + 40 = 92.5$$
$$x + 70 = 87.5$$

Thus, the pairs of opposite angles measure 92.5° and 87.5° each.

Example: Given parallelogram ABCD with diagonals AC and BD intersecting at E, prove that AE ≅ CE.

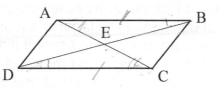

1. Parallelogram ABCD, with diagonals AC and BD intersecting at E	Given
2. AB ‖ DC	Opposite sides of a parallelogram are parallel
3. ∠BDC ≅ ∠ABD	If parallel lines are cut by a transversal, their alternate interior angles are congruent.
4. AB ≅ DC	Opposite sides of a parallelogram are congruent.
5. ∠BAC ≅ ∠ACD	If parallel lines are cut by a transversal, their alternate interior angles are congruent.
6. △ABE ≅ △CDE	ASA
7. AE ≅ CE	Corresponding parts of congruent triangles are congruent.

13B. Identifying plane figures given characteristics of sides, angles, and diagonals

Quadrilaterals include many other special types of four-sided polygons in addition to the familiar squares and rectangles. Some quadrilaterals are included in several different sets; for instance, a square is also a rectangle and rhombus, as well as a parallelogram, and it has all the characteristics of these different figures. The following set diagram shows the relationships of special quadrilaterals.

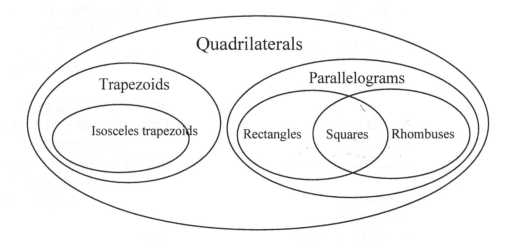

The particular characteristics of each group of special quadrilaterals are summarized below.

A **trapezoid** (shown below) is a quadrilateral with exactly one pair of parallel sides (called bases). The non-parallel sides are called legs. An **altitude** is a line segment drawn from a point on either base, perpendicular to the opposite base. The **median** is a line segment that joins the midpoints of each leg.

In an **isosceles trapezoid**, the non-parallel sides (legs) are congruent.

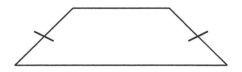

Theorems:
1. The median of a trapezoid is parallel to the bases and equal to one-half the sum of the lengths of the bases.
2. The base angles of an isosceles trapezoid are congruent.
3. The diagonals of an isosceles trapezoid are congruent.

Example: In trapezoid ABCD, AB = 17 and DC = 21. Find the length of the median.

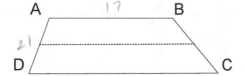

The median is one-half the sum of the bases.

$$\frac{1}{2}(17 + 21) = \frac{1}{2}(38) = 19$$

A **rhombus** is a parallelogram with all sides of equal length. Rhombuses have all the properties of parallelograms. In addition, the following properties also apply:

- All sides are congruent.
- The diagonals are perpendicular.
- The diagonals bisect the angles.

Example: In rhombus ABCD, side AB = 3x − 7 and side CD = x + 15. Find the length of each side.

Since all the sides are the same length, 3x − 7 = x + 15
$$2x = 22$$
$$x = 11$$

Since 3(11) − 7 = 26 and 11 + 15 = 26 each side measures 26 units.

A **rectangle** is a parallelogram in which each interior angle is 90°. Rectangles have all the properties of parallelograms. In addition, rectangles have the following properties:
- All interior angles are right angles.
- The diagonals are congruent.

A **square** is a rectangle with all sides of equal length. Squares have all the properties of rectangles and all the properties of rhombuses.

The following table summarizes the properties of each type of parallelogram.

	Parallel Opposite Sides	Bisecting Diagonals	Equal Opposite Sides	Equal Opposite Angles	Equal Diagonals	All Sides Equal	All Angles Equal	Perpendicular Diagonals
Parallelogram	x	x	x	x				
Rectangle	x	x	x	x	x		x	
Rhombus	x	x	x	x		x		x
Square	x	x	x	x	x	x	x	x

The attributes of particular special quadrilaterals can be the key to solving problems that involve these figures. For instance, a problem might involve determining whether a quadrilateral with some given characteristics is a parallelogram. For such a problem, it is helpful to realize that the quadrilateral is a parallelogram if any <u>one</u> of the following statements is true:

1. One pair of opposite sides is both parallel and congruent.
2. Both pairs of opposite sides are congruent.
3. Both pairs of opposite angles are congruent.
4. The diagonals bisect each other.

<u>Example:</u> Given quadrilateral ABCD with AB ≅ DC and ∠BAC ≅ ∠ACD, prove that ABCD is a parallelogram.

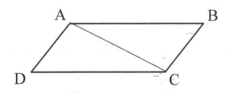

1. Quadrilateral ABCD
   AB ≅ DC
   ∠BAC ≅ ∠ACD

2. AC ≅ AC

3. △ABC ≅ △ADC

4. AD ≅ BC

5. ABCD is a parallelogram

Given

Reflexive

SAS

Corresponding parts of congruent triangles are congruent.

If both pairs of opposite sides of a quadrilateral are congruent, the quadrilateral is a parallelogram.

Problems may also involve the vertices or diagonals of a polygon. For instance, a specific problem might call for the calculation of the area of a triangle formed by a diagonal in a polygon. In such a case, it is helpful to apply the characteristics of the polygon (especially if the problem involves a regular polygon).

<u>Example:</u> Calculate the area of triangle ABC in the regular pentagon with sides of length 2.

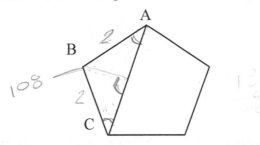

Since the sides of the polygon are all of length 2, triangle ABC is isosceles; angles ∠BAC and ∠BCA are therefore congruent. In addition, the interior angles of a regular pentagon are 108°. First, bisect this angle with an altitude, thereby forming two right triangles.

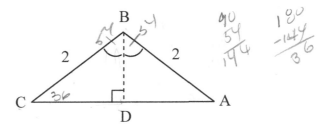

Since the bisected angle yields two 54° angles, angles ∠BAC and ∠BCA are each equal to 36°. Using the trigonometric ratios, the lengths CD and BD can be found. The area of triangle ABC is simply the product of CD and BD (or half the base times the height).

$$\text{Cos } 36° = \frac{CD}{2}$$
$$CD = 2 \cos 36° \approx 1.618$$

$$\text{Sin } 36° = \frac{BD}{2}$$

$$BD = 2 \sin 36° \approx 1.176$$

Thus the area of triangle ABC is (1.618) (1.176) = 1.903 square units.

13C.   **The Pythagorean Theorem**

The **Pythagorean Theorem** states that, in a right triangle, the square of the length of the hypotenuse is equal to the sum of the squares of the lengths of the legs. Symbolically, it is stated as:

$$c^2 = a^2 + b^2$$

Example: Given the right triangle below, find the hypotenuse.

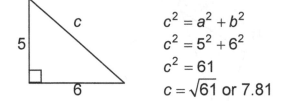

$$c^2 = a^2 + b^2$$
$$c^2 = 5^2 + 6^2$$
$$c^2 = 61$$
$$c = \sqrt{61} \text{ or } 7.81$$

The **converse** of the Pythagorean Theorem states if the square of one side of a triangle is equal to the sum of the squares of the other two sides, then the triangle is a right triangle.

Example: A triangle has sides measuring 12, 16 and 20 cm. Is it a right triangle?

$$c^2 = a^2 + b^2$$
$$20^2 \ \underline{?} \ 12^2 + 16^2$$
$$400 \underline{?} \ 144 + 256$$
$$400 = 400$$

Yes, the triangle is a right triangle.

This theorem can be expanded to determine if triangles are obtuse or acute. If the square of the longest side of a triangle is greater than the sum of the squares of the other two sides, then the triangle is an obtuse triangle. If the square of the longest side of a triangle is less than the sum of the squares of the other two sides, the triangle is an acute triangle.

Example: A triangle has sides measuring 7, 12, and 14 in. Is the triangle right, acute, or obtuse?

$$14^2 \ \underline{?} \ 7^2 + 12^2$$
$$196 \ \underline{?} \ 49 + 144$$
$$196 > 193$$

Therefore, the triangle is obtuse.

Example: An interior quadrangle in an office building has a diagonal pathway going from one corner to another. If the length of the quadrangle is 12m and its width is 9m, what is the length of the pathway?

Draw and label sketch. The diagonal pathway is the hypotenuse of a right triangle with the length and width of the quadrangle as its sides.

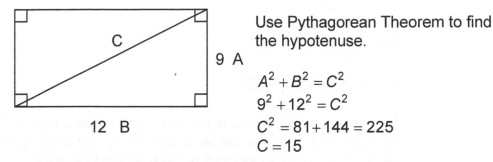

9 A

12 B

Use Pythagorean Theorem to find the hypotenuse.

$$A^2 + B^2 = C^2$$
$$9^2 + 12^2 = C^2$$
$$C^2 = 81 + 144 = 225$$
$$C = 15$$

Thus, the length of the diagonal pathway is 15m.

13D. Special right triangle relationships

Special right triangles have set relationships between the hypotenuse and the legs.

The first of these is a 30°-60°-90° right triangle. In the diagram below the short leg (*sl*) is opposite the 30° angle, the long leg (*ll*) is opposite the 60° angle and *h* is the hypotenuse.

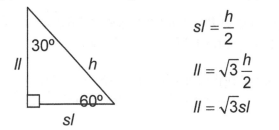

$$sl = \frac{h}{2}$$
$$ll = \sqrt{3}\,\frac{h}{2}$$
$$ll = \sqrt{3}\,sl$$

Example: Find the length of the legs of the 30°-60°-90° right triangle.

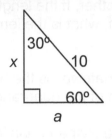

$a = 5$

$x = a\sqrt{3} = 5\sqrt{3}$ or 8.66

Example: A 20 ft ladder is propped up against a wall. If the distance from the bottom of the ladder to the wall is half the length of the ladder, how high up the wall is the top of the ladder?

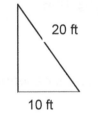

Since the length of the shorter leg of a 30°-60°-90° right triangle is half the length of the hypotenuse, the ladder forms a 30°-60°-90° right triangle with the wall and ground.

Thus, the longer leg of the right triangle = $10\sqrt{3} = 17.3$ ft and the top of the ladder is placed 17.3 ft up the wall.

The second special right triangle is a 45°-45°-90° right triangle. In the diagram below, the legs (*l*) are opposite the 45° angle and *h* is the hypotenuse.

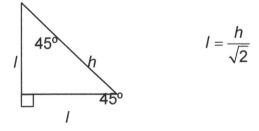

$l = \dfrac{h}{\sqrt{2}}$

Example: A woman is making a scarf in the shape of a right triangle. She wants the two shorter sides to be equal in length and the long side to be 15 inches long. What should the length of each of the shorter sides be?

Since the two shorter sides are equal in length, the scarf is an isosceles right triangle, i.e. a 45°-45°-90° right triangle.

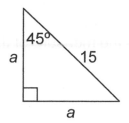

Thus the length of each short side = $\dfrac{15}{\sqrt{2}} = 10.6$ in.

13E   **Arcs, angles, and segments associated with circles**

Circle major and minor arcs

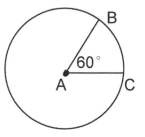

Central angle BAC = 60°
Minor arc BC = 60°
Major arc BDC = 360 − 60 = 300°

If we draw **two radii** in a circle, the angle they form with the center as the vertex is a central angle. The piece of the circle "inside" the angle is an arc. Just like a central angle, an arc can have any degree measure from 0 to 360. The measure of an arc is equal to the measure of the central angle that forms the arc. Since a diameter forms a semicircle and the measure of a straight angle like a diameter is 180°, the measure of a semicircle is also 180°.

Given two points on a circle, the two points form two different arcs. Except in the case of semicircles, one of the two arcs will always be greater than 180° and the other will be less than 180°. The arc less than 180° is a **minor arc** and the arc greater than 180° is a **major arc**.

Example:

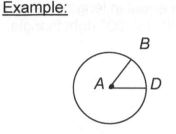

$m\angle BAD = 45°$
What is the measure of the major arc BD?

$\angle BAD = $ minor arc BD

The measure of the central angle 45° = minor arc BD is the same as the measure of the arc it forms.

360 – 45 = major arc BD

A major and minor arc always add to 360°.

315° = major arc BD

Example:

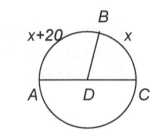

D.

$\overline{AC}$ is a diameter of circle What is the measure of $\angle BDC$?

$m\angle ADB + m\angle BDC = 180°$

$x + 20 + x = 180$

$2x + 20 = 180$

$2x = 160$

$x = 80$

minor arc $BC = 80°$

$m\angle BDC = 80°$

A diameter forms a semicircle that has a measure of 180°.

A central angle has the same measure as the arc it forms.

While an arc has a measure associated to the degree measure of a central angle, it also has a length that is a fraction of the circumference of the circle. For each central angle and its associated arc, there is a sector of the circle that resembles a pie piece. The area of such a sector is a fraction of the area of the circle. The fractions used for the area of a sector and length of its associated arc are both equal to the ratio of the central angle to 360°.

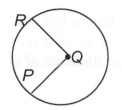

$$\frac{\angle PQR}{360°} = \frac{\text{length of arc } RP}{\text{circumference of } \angle Q} = \frac{\text{area of sector } PQR}{\text{area of } \angle Q}$$

Example:

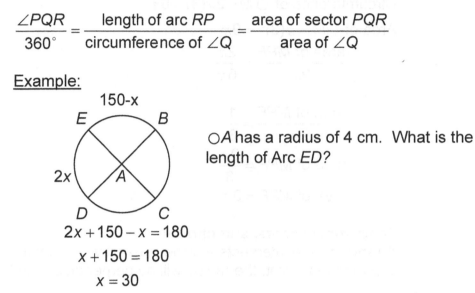

$\bigcirc A$ has a radius of 4 cm. What is the length of Arc *ED*?

$$2x + 150 - x = 180$$
$$x + 150 = 180$$
$$x = 30$$

Arc *BC* and arc *DC* make a semicircle.

Arc $ED = 2(30) = 60°$

The ratio 60° to 360° is equal to the ratio of arch length *ED* to the circumference of $\bigcirc A$.

$$\frac{60}{360} = \frac{\text{arc length } ED}{2\pi 4}$$

Cross multiply and solve for the arc length.

$$\frac{1}{6} = \frac{\text{arc length}}{8\pi}$$

$$\frac{8\pi}{6} = \text{arc length}$$

$$\text{arc length } ED = \frac{4\pi}{3} \text{ cm}$$

Example:

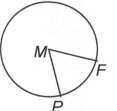

The radius of ○ M is 3 cm. The length of arc *PF* is 2π cm. What is the area *M* of sector *MPF*?

Circumference of ○ $M = 2\pi(3) = 6\pi$

Area of ○$M = \pi(3)^2 = 9\pi$

$$\frac{\text{area of } MPF}{9\pi} = \frac{2\pi}{6\pi}$$

$$\frac{\text{area of } MPF}{9\pi} = \frac{1}{3}$$

$$\text{area of } MPF = \frac{9\pi}{3}$$

$$\text{area of } MPF = 3\pi$$

Tangents, secants, and chords

A **tangent line** intersects a circle in exactly one point. If a radius is drawn to that point, the radius will be perpendicular to the tangent.

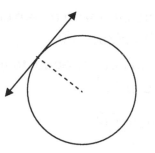

A **secant line** intersects a circle in two points and includes a **chord** which is a segment with endpoints on the circle. If a radius or diameter is perpendicular to a chord, the radius will cut the chord into two equal parts and vice-versa.

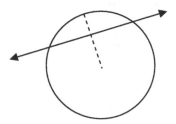

If **two chords** in the same circle have the same length, the two chords will have arcs that are the same length, and the two chords will be equidistant from the center of the circle. Distance from the center to a chord is measured by finding the length of a segment from the center perpendicular to the chord.

Example:

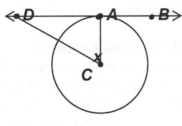

$\overrightarrow{DB}$ is tangent to $\angle C$ at **A**.
$m\angle ADC = 40°$ **Find x.**

$\overline{AC} \perp \overrightarrow{DB}$ A radius is $\perp$ to a tangent at the point of tangency.

$m\angle DAC = 90°$ Two segments that are $\perp$ form a $90°$ angle.

$40 + 90 + x = 180$ The sum of the angles of a triangle is $180°$.

$x = 50°$ Solve for x.

Example:

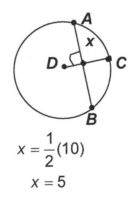

$\overline{CD}$ **is a radius and** $\overline{CD} \perp$ chord $\overline{AB}$.
$\overline{AB} = 10$. Find x.

$x = \dfrac{1}{2}(10)$

$x = 5$ If a radius is $\perp$ to a chord, the radius bisects the chord.

Angles with their vertices on the circle:
An inscribed angle is an angle whose vertex is on the circle. Such an angle could be formed by two chords, two diameters, two secants, or a secant and a tangent. An inscribed angle has one arc of the circle in its interior. The measure of the inscribed angle is one-half the measure of this intercepted arc. If two inscribed angles intercept the same arc, the two angles are congruent (i.e. their measures are equal). If an inscribed angle intercepts an entire semicircle, the angle is a right angle.

Angles with their vertices in a circle's interior:
When two chords intersect inside a circle, two sets of vertical angles are formed. Each set of vertical angles intercepts two arcs that are across from each other. The measure of an angle formed by two chords in a circle is equal to one-half the sum of the angle intercepted by the angle and the arc intercepted by its vertical angle.

Angles with their vertices in a circle's exterior:
If an angle has its vertex outside of the circle and each side of the circle intersects the circle, then the angle contains two different arcs. The measure of the angle is equal to one-half the difference of the two arcs.

Example:

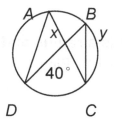

Find x and y.

$$m\angle DAC = \frac{1}{2}(40) = 20°$$

$\angle DAC$ and $\angle DBC$ are both inscribed angles, so each one has a measure equal to one-half the measure of arc DC.

$$m\angle DBC = \frac{1}{2}(40) = 20°$$

$x = 20°$ and $y = 20°$

Intersecting chords:
If two chords intersect inside a circle, each chord is divided into two smaller segments. The product of the lengths of the two segments formed from one chord equals the product of the lengths of the two segments formed from the other chord.

Intersecting tangent segments:
If two tangent segments intersect outside of a circle, the two segments have the same length.

Intersecting secant segments:
If two secant segments intersect outside a circle, a portion of each segment will lie inside the circle and a portion (called the exterior segment) will lie outside the circle. The product of the length of one secant segment and the length of its exterior segment equals the product of the length of the other secant segment and the length of its exterior segment.

Tangent segments intersecting secant segments:
If a tangent segment and a secant segment intersect outside a circle, the square of the length of the tangent segment equals the product of the length of the secant segment and its exterior segment.

Example:

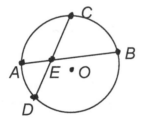

$\overline{AB}$ and $\overline{CD}$ are chords.
$CE=10$, $ED=x$, $AE=5$, $EB=4$

$$(AE)(EB) = (CE)(ED)$$

$$5(4) = 10x$$
$$20 = 10x$$
$$x = 2$$

Since the chords intersect in the circle, the products of the segment pieces are equal.

Solve for x.

2.

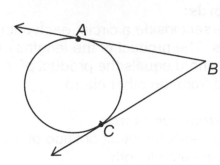

$\overline{AB}$ and $\overline{CD}$ are chords.
$\overline{AB} = x^2 + x - 2$
$\overline{CB} = 5 - 3x - x^2$
find the length of
$\overline{AB}$ and $\overline{BC}$

$\overline{AB} = x^2 + x - 2$

$\overline{BC} = x^2 - 3x + 5$

Given

$\overline{AB} = \overline{BC}$

Intersecting tangents are equal.

$x^2 + x - 2 = x^2 - 3x + 5$

Set the expression equal and solve.

$4x = 7$

Substitute and solve.

$x = 1.75$

$(1.75)^2 + 1.75 - 2 = \overline{AB}$

$\overline{AB} = \overline{BC} = 2.81$

13F. Deriving and applying formulas for the area of composite shapes

The strategy for solving problems of this nature should be to cut the compound shape into smaller, more familiar shapes and then compute the total area by adding or subtracting (in the case of cut out shapes) the areas of the smaller parts.

FIGURE	AREA FORMULA	PERIMETER FORMULA
Rectangle	LW	$2(L + W)$
Triangle	$\frac{1}{2}bh$	$a + b + c$
Parallelogram	bh	sum of lengths of sides
Trapezoid	$\frac{1}{2}h(a + b)$	sum of lengths of sides

<u>Example:</u> Find the area of the given shape.

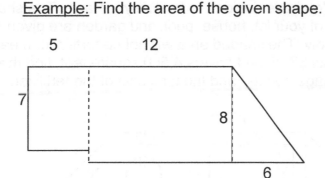

1. Using dotted lines cut the shape into smaller parts that are familiar.

2. Use the appropriate formula for each shape and find the sum of all areas.

Area 1 = LW	Area 2 = LW	Area 3 = ½bh
= (5)(7)	= (12)(8)	= ½(6)(8)
= 35 units²	= 96 units²	= 24 units²

Total area = Area 1 + Area 2 + Area 3
  = 35 + 96 + 24
  = 155 units²

<u>Example:</u> Find the area of one side of the metal in the circular flat washer shown below:

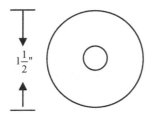

1. the shapes are both circles.

2. use the formula A = πr^2 for both.

    (Inside diameter is $3/8$"**)**

Area of larger circle   Area of smaller circle

A = πr^2 A = πr^2

A = $\pi(.75^2)$ A = $\pi(.1875^2)$

A = 1.76625 in²   A = .1103906 in²

Area of metal washer = larger area - smaller area

  = 1.76625 in² − .1103906 in²

  = 1.6558594 in²

<u>Example:</u> You have decided to fertilize your lawn. The shapes and dimensions of your lot, house, pool, and garden are given in the diagram below. The shaded area will not be fertilized. If each bag of fertilizer costs $7.95 and covers 4,500 square feet, find the total number of bags needed and the total cost of the fertilizer.

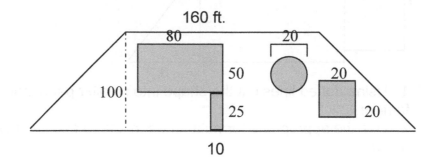

Area of Lot	Area of House	Area of Driveway
$A = \frac{1}{2}\, h(b_1 + b_2)$	$A = LW$	$A = LW$
$A = \frac{1}{2}(100)(180 + 160)$	$A = (80)(50)$	$A = (10)(25)$
$A = 17{,}000$ sq ft	$A = 4{,}000$ sq ft	$A = 250$ sq ft

Area of Pool	Area of Garden
$A = \pi r^2$	$A = s^2$
$A = \pi (10)^2$	$A = (20)^2$
$A = 314.159$ sq. ft.	$A = 400$ sq. ft.

Total area to fertilize = Lot area − (House + Driveway + Pool + Garden)

$$= 17{,}000 - (4{,}000 + 250 + 314.159 + 400)$$
$$= 12{,}035.841 \text{ sq ft}$$

Number of bags needed = $\dfrac{\text{Total area to fertilize}}{4{,}500 \text{ sq.ft. bag}}$

$$= \frac{12{,}035.841}{4{,}500}$$
$$= 2.67 \text{ bags}$$

Since we cannot purchase 2.67 bags we must purchase 3 full bags.

Total cost = Number of bags * $7.95
$$= 3 * \$7.95$$
$$= \$23.85$$

13G. Modeling and solving problems involving two-dimensional figures

In the previous section, we solved some problems evaluating areas of composite shapes. Here we will consider other types of problems involving two-dimensional figures.

Example: Find the cost of fencing a rectangular park of length 170m and width 100m at the rate of $5 per meter.

Perimeter of the rectangle $P = 2l + 2b$
$= 2 \times 170\ m + 2 \times 100\ m = 340\ m + 200\ m = 540\ m$
Cost of fencing 1 m = $ 5
Therefore cost of fencing 540 m = $ 540 × 5 = $ 2700

Example: John brought a plot in the shape of a right triangle for $50,000 at the rate of $200 per sq.m. If the length of one side containing the right angle is 25 m, find the length of the other side containing the right angle.

Total cost of the plot is $50000.
For $200 we get 1 sq.m.
So for $50000 we get 50000 / 200 = 250 sq.m.

The area of the right triangle = $1/2\ bh$ where h is the length of the other side containing the right angle.
$1/2\ bh =$. $1/2 \times 25 \times h = 250$
Therefore $h = 500 / 25 = 20\ m$

Example: The length, width and height of a room are 5m, 4m and 3m respectively. The room has two doors each of dimensions 2m × 1m and five windows each of dimensions 1m × 0.8m. What is the area of the walls to be washed?

Perimeter of the room $p = 2 \times 5\ m + 2 \times 4\ m = 10\ m + 8\ m = 18\ m$
Area of the four walls including doors and windows = 18 m × 3 m = $54m^2$
Area of 2 doors = 2 × 2m × 1m = $4m^2$
Area of 5 windows = 5 × 1m × 0.8m = $4m^2$
Total area of 2 doors + 5 windows = $4m^2 + 4m^2 = 8m^2$
Area of the walls to be washed = (Area of the 4 walls) – (Area occupied by doors and windows) = 54 – 8 = $46m^2$

Competency 0014 Solve problems involving three-dimensional shapes.

14A. Area and volume of and relationship among three-dimensional figures (e.g., prisms, pyramids, cylinders, cones)

Three-dimensional figures in geometry are called **solids**. A solid is the union of all points on a simple closed surface and all points in its interior.

A three-dimensional figure, sometimes called a solid, is composed of surface and plane regions, all within a three-dimensional space. The **faces** are the surface areas of the figure and they are 2-dimensional. The **edges** are one-dimensional lines where the faces of the solid meet. The end-points of the edges are called its **vertices** and are zero-dimensional.

The most common three-dimensional figures have only a few faces, the surfaces are very simple, and there are no "loose ends" - that is, every vertex is the end of at least two edges, and at least two faces meet at every edge.

The surfaces of a three-dimensional figure may be flat or curved. If all the faces are flat, every edge is the intersection of two faces, every vertex is the intersection of at least three edges, and no two faces cross each other, the figure is called a **polyhedron**. The fact that the faces are flat means that every edge is a straight line and every face is a polygon. Polyhedra are classified according to the number of faces (e.g. tetrahedron with 4 faces, octahedron with 8 faces).

Familiar polyhedra include **cubes**, **pyramids** and **rectangular or triangular prisms**. A cube has 6 identical square faces, 12 edges and 8 vertices.

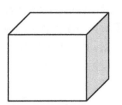

A pyramid is a polyhedron with three or more triangular faces meeting at a common vertex. The base is a polygon. The number of triangular faces is the same as the number of sides of the polygonal base. A pyramid with a triangular base is known as a **tetrahedron**. A square pyramid is shown below.

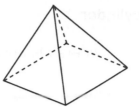

A prism is a polyhedron with two identical parallel faces known as bases. It is named according to the shape of the base and the shape of the base determines how many other faces the prism has. A triangular prism, for instance, has triangular bases and three faces (corresponding to the sides of the triangle) in addition to the bases.

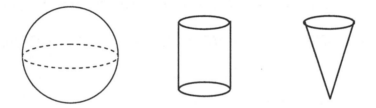

Common three-dimensional figures with **curved surfaces** include **spheres**, **cylinders** and **cones**.

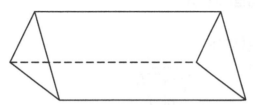

All points on the surface of a sphere are equidistant from its center. A cylinder is similar to a prism in that it has two identical parallel bases. The bases, however, are circles and not polygons.
A cone is similar to a pyramid in that it has a single base and a vertex outside the base joined to every point on the perimeter of the base by a straight line. Here, again, the base is a circle and not a polygon.

The **lateral area** is the area of the faces excluding the bases.

The **surface area** is the total area of all the faces, including the bases.

The **volume** is the number of cubic units in a solid.

Right circular cylinder

$S = 2\pi r(r + h)$ (where r is the radius of the base)
$V = \pi r^2 h$

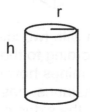

Right circular cone

$V = \frac{1}{3}Bh = \frac{1}{3}(\pi r^2)h$

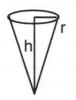

A summary of the **Volume** and **Surface area** formulas:

FIGURE	VOLUME	TOTAL SURFACE AREA	LATERAL AREA
Right Cylinder	$\pi r^2 h$	$2\pi rh + 2\pi r^2$	$2\pi rh$
Right Cone	$\dfrac{\pi r^2 h}{3}$	$\pi r\sqrt{r^2 + h^2} + \pi r^2$	$\pi r\sqrt{r^2 + h^2}$
Sphere	$\dfrac{4}{3}\pi r^3$	$4\pi r^2$	
Rectangular Solid	LWH	$2LW + 2WH + 2LH$	

Note: $\sqrt{r^2 + h^2}$ is equal to the slant height of the cone.

FIGURE	LATERAL AREA	TOTAL AREA	VOLUME
Right prism	Ph	2B+Ph	Bh
Regular Pyramid	1/2Pl	1/2Pl+B	1/3Bh

P = Perimeter; h = height; B = Area of Base; l = slant height

Example: Given the figure below, find the volume and surface area.

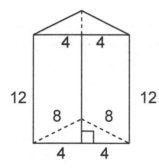

$r = 5\,\text{in}$ $h = 6.2\,\text{in}$

Volume $= \dfrac{\pi r^2 h}{3}$ First write the formula.

$\dfrac{1}{3}\pi(5^2)(6.2)$ Then substitute.

162.23333 cubic inches   Finally solve the problem.

Surface area $= \pi r \sqrt{r^2 + h^2} + \pi r^2$ First write the formula.

$\pi 5\sqrt{5^2 + 6.2^2} + \pi 5^2$ Then substitute.

203.549 square inches   Compute.

Note: volume is always given in cubic units and area is always given in square units.

Example: Find the total area of the given figure:

```
        /\
       /  \
      / 4  \ 4
     |------|
     |      |
  12 |      | 12
     | 8    8
     |\    /|
     | \  / |
     |__\/__|
       4  4
```

1. Since this is a triangular prism, first find the area of the bases.
2. Find the area of each rectangular lateral face.
3. Add the areas together.

$A = \dfrac{1}{2}bh$ $A = LW$ 1. write formula

$8^2 = 4^2 + h^2$ 2. find the height of
$h = 6.928$ the base triangle

$A = \dfrac{1}{2}(8)(6.928)$ $A = (8)(12)$

                                                            3. substitute known values

$A = 27.713$ sq. units $A = 96$ sq. units   4. compute

Total Area $= 2(27.713) + 3(96)$ $= 343.426$ sq. units

14B. Perspective drawings

Perspective drawing is a technique of drawing objects in three dimensions. It is commonly used for building construction.

Perspective is the image of an object which is perceived by the eye approximately. With perspective drawings, the viewer is assumed to be at a certain distance from the drawing. The objects are not scaled correctly. A square may look like a trapezoid and ellipse may look like a circle. This is known as **foreshortening**.

The **horizon** line is directly opposite to a person's view in perspective drawings and represents the position of an object that is very far from the viewer's eye. A **vanishing point** is a point where parallel lines seem to converge.

One-point Perspective
In the case of the one-point perspective drawing, the number of vanishing points is one which is opposite to the viewer's eye and lies on the horizon line. This is used for roads, railroad tracks and buildings. In this case the viewer can see the front view.

Two-Point Perspective
In the case of a two-point perspective drawing, the number of vanishing points is two, representing two different sets of parallel lines. This will be the case when looking at the corner of a house or looking at two forked roads.

Three-point perspective
If there are 3 vanishing points, it is known as three-point perspective. This is used to view the top view or bottom view of buildings. Two vanishing points for two walls and one point will be below the ground. Viewing a tall building is an example of third point perspective. In this case, the vanishing point is high in space.

Zero- point Perspective
If there are no parallel lines, then there are no vanishing points and the perspective is zero-point. An example of this is viewing a mountain range which does not contain any parallel lines.

14C. Cross sections (including conic sections) and nets

Cross Section

If a 3-dimensional object intersects with a plane, it forms a **cross section**. In the picture below, the blue portion is a cross section of a cube.

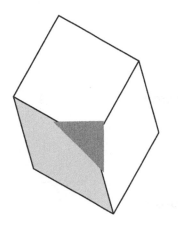

Conic sections

A Conic section, i.e. a circle, ellipse, parabola, or hyperbola is formed by the intersection of a cone with a plane.

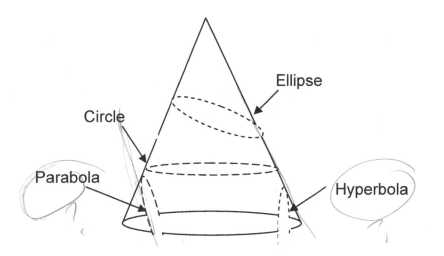

Circles and ellipses are both closed figures. The plane creating the circle cross-section in intersection with the cone is parallel to the base of the cone. Parabolas and hyperbolas are open figures. The plane creating the parabola cross-section in intersection with the cone is parallel to the slant side of the cone.

Nets

A **net** is a two-dimensional figure that can be cut out and folded up to make a three-dimensional solid. Below are models of the examples regular solids with their corresponding face polygons and nets. Nets clearly show the shape and number of faces of a solid.

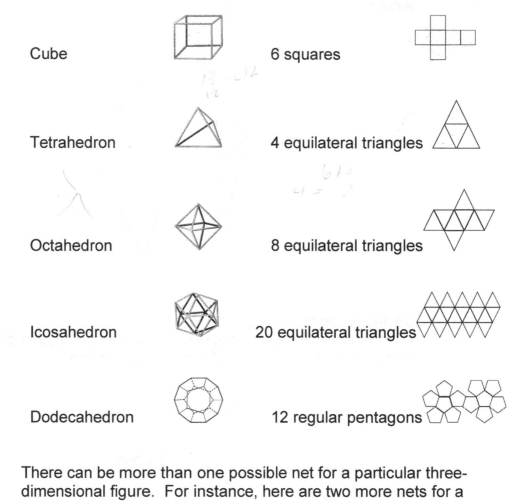

Cube	6 squares	
Tetrahedron	4 equilateral triangles	
Octahedron	8 equilateral triangles	
Icosahedron	20 equilateral triangles	
Dodecahedron	12 regular pentagons	

There can be more than one possible net for a particular three-dimensional figure. For instance, here are two more nets for a tetrahedron.

For a polyhedron, the numbers of vertices (*V*), faces (*F*), and edges (*E*) are related by **Euler's Formula**: $V + F = E + 2$.

Example: We want to create a pentagonal pyramid, and we know it has six vertices and six faces.

Using Euler's Formula, we compute:

$$V + F = E + 2$$

$$6 + 6 = E + 2$$

$$E = 10$$

Thus, we know that our figure should have 10 edges

Example: Draw the net of a triangular prism. Identify the polygons that make up the faces. How many vertices and edges do triangular prisms have?

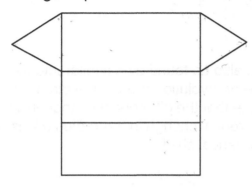

V + F = E + 2
+ 5 = 9 + 2
V = 6

Two triangles and three rectangles are the faces. There are nine edges (three between the rectangle faces and three on each side where the triangle faces meet the rectangle faces). There are six vertices at the vertices of the two triangle faces.

V − 1 = 9 + 2

14D. Deriving properties of three-dimensional figures from two-dimensional shapes

Three-dimensional figures require more complicated mathematical manipulations to derive or apply such properties as surface area and volume. In some instances, two-dimensional concepts can be applied directly.

The volume and surface area of three-dimensional figures can be derived most clearly (in some cases) using integral calculus. For instance, the volume of a **sphere** of radius r can be derived by revolving a semicircular area around the axis defined by its diameter.

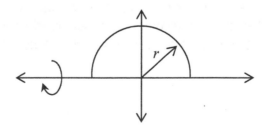

The result of this revolution is a solid sphere of radius r. To perform the integral, use the function $f(x)$ for the semicircle of radius r.

$$f(x) = \sqrt{r^2 - x^2}$$

$$V = \pi \int_{-r}^{r} \left[\sqrt{r^2 - x^2} \right]^2 dx$$

$$V = \pi \int_{-r}^{r} \left(r^2 - x^2 \right) dx$$

$$V = \pi \left[r^2 x - \frac{x^3}{3} \right]_{-r}^{r} = \pi \left[\left(r^3 + r^3 \right) - \left(\frac{r^3}{3} + \frac{r^3}{3} \right) \right]$$

$$V = \pi \left[2r^3 - \frac{2r^3}{3} \right] = \frac{4}{3} \pi r^3$$

The surface area can also be found by a similar integral that calculates the surface of revolution around the diameter, but there is a simpler method. Note that the differential change in volume of a sphere (*dV*) for a differential change in the radius (*dr*) is an infinitesimally thick spherical shell.

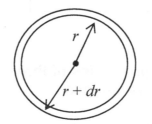

This infinitesimally thick shell is simply a surface with an area, but no volume. Find the derivative of the volume to get the surface area.

$$S = \frac{dV}{dr} = \frac{d}{dr} \frac{4}{3} \pi r^3$$
$$S = 4\pi r^2$$

The volume and surface area of a **right cone**, use an approach similar to that of the sphere. In this case, however, a line segment, rather than a semicircle, is revolved around the horizontal axis. The cone has a height *h* and a base radius *r*.

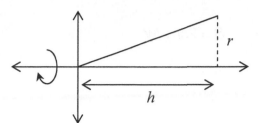

For right circular cylinders, the volume is simply the area of a cross section (a circle of radius r) multiplied by the height h of the cylinder. The **lateral surface area** (the surface area excluding the area on the ends of the figure) is simply the circumference of the circular cross section multiplied by the height h.

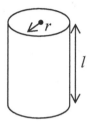

$$V = \pi r^2 h$$
$$S = 2\pi rh$$

For figures such as pyramids and prisms, the volume and surface areas must be derived by breaking the figure into portions for which these values can be calculated easily. For instance, consider the following figure.

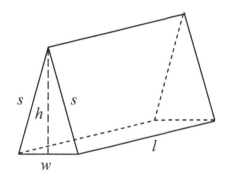

The volume of this figure can be found by calculating the area of the triangular cross section and then multiplying by l.

$$V = \frac{1}{2}hwl$$

The lateral surface area can be found by adding the areas of each side.

$S = 2sl + lw$

14E. Modeling and solving problems involving three-dimensional geometry

Many real life problems may be modeled and solved using the methods of three-dimensional geometry.

Example: A water company is trying to decide whether to use traditional cylindrical paper cups or to offer conical paper cups since both cost the same. The traditional cups are 8 cm wide and 14 cm high. The conical cups are 12 cm wide and 19 cm high. The company will use the cup that holds the most water.

Draw and label a sketch of each.

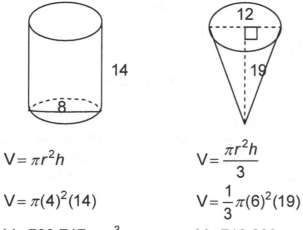

$V = \pi r^2 h$

$V = \pi(4)^2(14)$

$V = 703.717 \text{ cm}^3$

$V = \dfrac{\pi r^2 h}{3}$

$V = \dfrac{1}{3}\pi(6)^2(19)$

$V = 716.283 \text{ cm}^3$

The choice should be the conical cup since its volume is more.

Example: How much material is needed to make a basketball that has a diameter of 15 inches? How much air is needed to fill the basketball?

Draw and label a sketch:

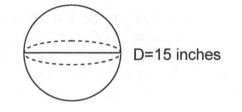 D=15 inches

Total Surface Area

$\text{TSA} = 4\pi r^2$

$= 4\pi(7.5)^2$

$= 706.9 \text{ in}^2$

Volume

$V = \frac{4}{3}\pi r^3$

$= \frac{4}{3}\pi(7.5)^3$

$= 1767.1 \text{ in}^3$

Example: A building shaped like a regular pyramid with a square base needs a fresh coat of paint. The painters will charge $5 per square foot. If the height of the building is 24 ft and each side of the square base is 20 ft, how much will it cost to paint the building?

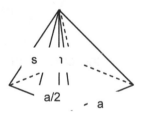

The painters will paint the lateral area of the pyramid. The lateral area is the sum of the areas of the four triangular faces. In order to find the area of the triangle, the height of the triangle, which is the slant height of the pyramid, has to be found.
Note in the figure that the slant height *s* is the hypotenuse of a right-angled triangle that has legs *h* (height of pyramid) and *a*/2 (half the length of the square base).

$$s = \sqrt{24^2 + 10^2} = \sqrt{576 + 100} = \sqrt{676} = 26 \text{ ft}$$

Area of one triangle = base x height/2 = 20 x 26/2=260 sq. ft.
Lateral area of pyramid = 260 x 4 = 1040 sq.ft.
Cost of painting the building = 1040 x 5 = $5200.

Competency 0015 Understand the principles and properties of coordinate and transformational geometry.

15A. Representing geometric figures (e.g. triangles, circles) in the coordinate plane

Coordinate geometry involves the application of algebraic methods to geometry. The locations of points in space are expressed in terms of coordinates on a plane. The horizontal line or axis is labeled "*x*" and the vertical axis is labeled "*y*." In the rectangular coordinate system, the point (*x*, *y*) is an ordered pair that describes the point whose distance along the *x*-axis is "*x*" and whose distance along the *y*-axis is "*y*." In the example below, three points are plotted and connected by line segments to represent a triangle. Point (2, 1), for instance, is 2 units to the right of the origin and 1 unit above the origin.

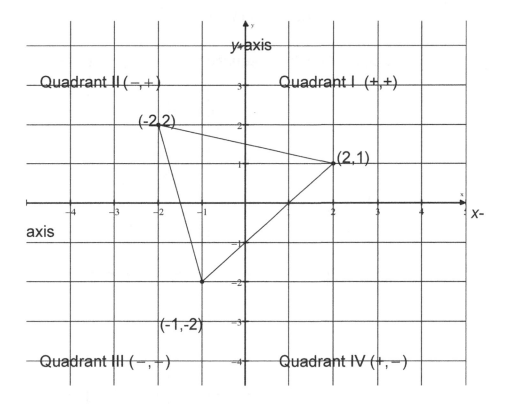

The relationships between the coordinates of different points may be expressed as equations. When a circle is graphed on the coordinate plane and centered at the origin, it may be described by a standard equation of the form $x^2 + y^2 = r^2$.

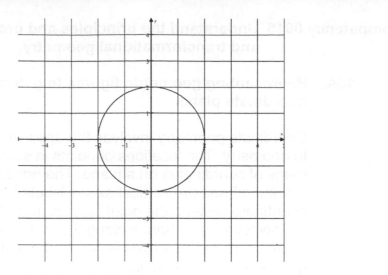

The equation of a circle with its center at (h, k) and a radius r units is:

$$(x - h)^2 + (y - k)^2 = r^2$$

Example: Graph the equation $(x - 1)^2 + (y - 2)^2 = 2^2$

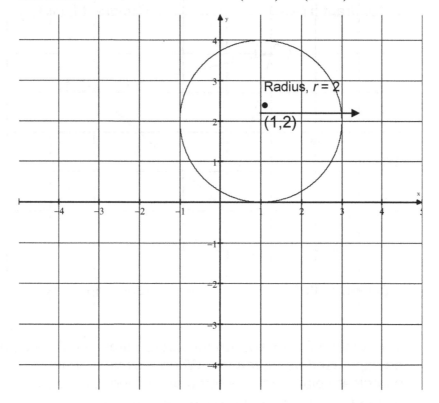

Example: Given the center and radius, write the equation of the circle.

Center ($^{-}1$, 4); radius 11

$(x-h)^2+(y-k)^2=r^2$	1. Write standard equation.
$(x-(-1))^2+(y-4)^2=11^2$	2. Substitute.
$(x+1)^2+(y-4)^2=121$	3. Simplify.

15B. **Using concepts of distance, midpoint, slope and parallel and perpendicular lines to classify and analyze figures (e.g. parallelograms)**

The following concepts and formulae are used to analyze relationships in the coordinate plane:

1. **Midpoint formula**: The midpoint (x, y) of the line joining points (x_1, y_1) and (x_2, y_2) is given by

$$(x, y) = \left(\frac{x_1 + x_2}{2}, \frac{y_1 + y_2}{2} \right)$$

2. **Distance formula:** The distance between points (x_1, y_1) and (x_2, y_2) is given by

$$D = \sqrt{(x_2 - x_1)^2 + (y_2 - y_1)^2}$$

3. **Slope formula:** The slope m of a line passing through the points (x_1, y_1) and (x_2, y_2) is given by

$$m = \frac{y_2 - y_1}{x_2 - x_1}$$

4. **Equation of a line**: The equation of a line is given by $y = mx + b$, where m is the slope of the line and b is the y-intercept, i.e. the y-coordinate at which the line intersects the y-axis.

5. **Parallel and perpendicular lines**: Parallel lines have the same slope. The slope of a line perpendicular to a line with slope m is $-1/m$.

Example: Find the center of a circle with a diameter whose endpoints are (3, 7) and $(-4, -5)$.

$$\text{Midpoint} = \left(\frac{3 + (-4)}{2}, \frac{7 + (-5)}{2} \right)$$

$$\text{Midpoint} = \left(\frac{-1}{2}, 1 \right)$$

Example: Find the midpoint given the two points $\left(5, 8\sqrt{6} \right)$ and $\left(9, -4\sqrt{6} \right)$.

$$\text{Midpoint} = \left(\frac{5 + 9}{2}, \frac{8\sqrt{6} + (-4\sqrt{6})}{2} \right)$$

$$\text{Midpoint} = \left(7, 2\sqrt{6} \right)$$

Example: Find the perimeter of a figure with vertices at (4,5), ($^-$4,6) and ($^-$5, $^-$8).

The figure being described is a triangle. Therefore, the distance for all three sides must be found. Carefully, identify all three sides before beginning.

Side 1 = (4,5) to ($^-$4,6)

Side 2 = ($^-$4,6) to ($^-$5, $^-$8)

Side 3 = ($^-$5, $^-$8) to (4,5)

$$D_1 = \sqrt{(^-4 - 4)^2 + (6 - 5)^2} = \sqrt{65}$$

$$D_2 = \sqrt{((^-5 - (^-4))^2 + (^-8 - 6)^2} = \sqrt{197}$$

$$D_3 = \sqrt{((4 - (^-5))^2 + (5 - (^-8)^2))} = \sqrt{250} \text{ or } 5\sqrt{10}$$

$$\text{Perimeter} = \sqrt{65} + \sqrt{197} + 5\sqrt{10}$$

The **distance from a point to a line** is the distance between the point and the intersection of the line with a perpendicular to the line (shown by the dotted line below) drawn from the point.

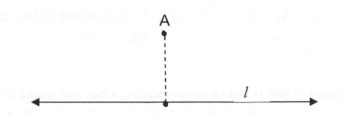

The **distance between two parallel lines**, such as line AB and line CD as shown below is the line segment RS, the perpendicular between the two parallels.

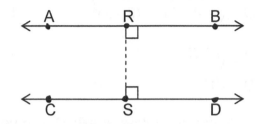

<u>Example</u>: Given the point ($^-4$, 3) and the line $y = 4x + 2$, find the distance from the point to the line.

Since the slope of the line is 4/1, the perpendicular line will have a slope of $^-1/4$.

$y = \left(^-1/4\right)x + b$ 1. Use the new slope and the given point to find the equation of the perpendicular line.

$3 = \left(^-1/4\right)\left(^-4\right) + b$ 2. Substitute ($^-4$,3) into the equation.

$3 = 1 + b$ 3. Solve.

$2 = b$ 4. Given the value for b, write the equation of the perpendicular line.

$y = \left(^-1/4\right)x + 2$ 5. Write in standard form.

$x + 4y = 8$ 6. Use both equations to solve by elimination to get the point of intersection.

$^-4x + y = 2$
$\underline{x + 4y = 8}$ 7. Multiply the bottom row by 4.

$^-4x + y = 2$
$\underline{4x + 16y = 32}$ 8. Solve.

$17y = 34$

$y = 2$

$y = 4x + 2$ 9. Substitute to find the x value.
$2 = 4x + 2$ 10. Solve.
$x = 0$

(0,2) is the point of intersection. Use this point on the original line and the original point to calculate the distance between them.

$$D = \sqrt{(x_2 - x_1)^2 + (y_2 - y_1)^2}$$ where points are (0,2) and (-4,3).

$$D = \sqrt{(^-4 - 0)^2 + (3 - 2)^2}$$ 1. Substitute.

$$D = \sqrt{(16) + (1)}$$ 2. Simplify.
$$D = \sqrt{17}$$

<u>Example:</u> Is the quadrilateral ABCD with vertices A(-3,0), B(−1,0), C(0,3) and D(2,3) a parallelogram?

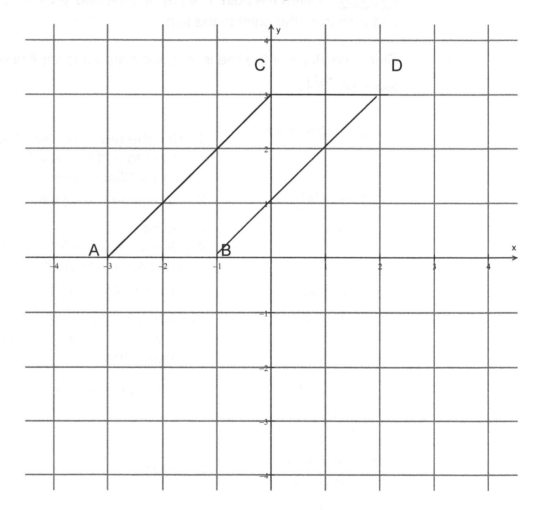

By definition, a parallelogram has diagonals that bisect each other. Using the midpoint formula, $(x, y) = \left(\dfrac{x_1 + x_2}{2}, \dfrac{y_1 + y_2}{2} \right)$, find the midpoints of $\overline{AD}$ and $\overline{BC}$.

The midpoint of $\overline{BC} = \left(\dfrac{-1 + 0}{2}, \dfrac{0 + 3}{2} \right) = \left(\dfrac{-1}{2}, \dfrac{3}{2} \right)$

The midpoint of $\overline{AD} = \left(\dfrac{-3 + 2}{2}, \dfrac{0 + 3}{2} \right) = \left(\dfrac{-1}{2}, \dfrac{3}{2} \right)$

Since the midpoints of the diagonals are the same, the diagonals bisect each other. Hence the polygon is a parallelogram.

15C. Characteristics of dilations, translations, rotations, reflections and glide-reflections

Dilations

Dilations involve an expansion of a figure and a translation of that figure (the translation may be for a distance zero). These two transformations are obtained by first defining a **center of dilation**, C, which is some point that acts like an origin for the dilation. The distance from C to each point in a figure is then altered by a **scale factor** s. If the magnitude of s is greater than zero, the size of the figure is increased; if the magnitude of s is less than zero, the size is decreased. For instance, if $s = 2$, the expanded figure will be twice the size of the original figure.

A dilation maintains the angles and relative proportions of a figure. The translation of a geometric figure depends on the location of the center of dilation, C. If C is located at the center of the figure, for instance, the figure is dilated without translation of its center.

<u>Example:</u> Dilate the figure shown by a scale factor of 2 using the origin of the coordinate system as the center of dilation.

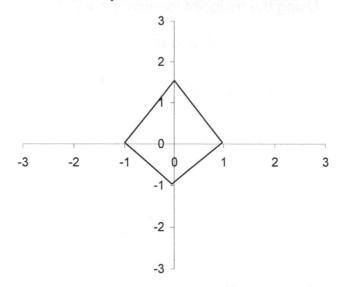

To perform this dilation, the distance between the origin and each point on the figure must be increased by a factor of 2. It is sufficient, however, to simply increase the distance of the vertices of the figure by a factor of 2 and then connect them to form the dilated figure.

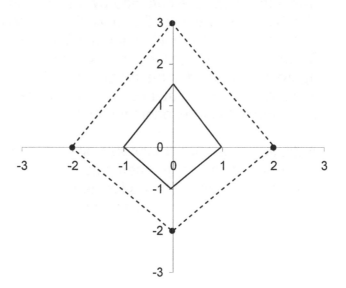

The resulting figure above (dashed line) is the dilation of the original figure.

Translations

A **translation** is a transformation that "slides" an object a fixed distance in a given direction. The original object and its translation have the same shape and size, and they face in the same direction. Multiple translations can be performed in any order.

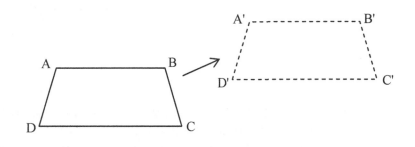

Rotations

A rotation is a transformation that turns a figure about a fixed point, which is called the center of rotation. An object and its rotation are the same shape and size, but the figures may be oriented in different directions. Rotations can occur in either a clockwise or a counterclockwise direction.

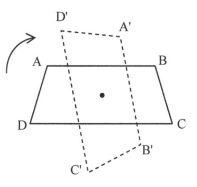

Reflections

An object and its reflection have the same shape and size, but the figures face in opposite directions. The line (where a hypothetical mirror may be placed) is called the **line of reflection**. The distance from a point to the line of reflection is the same as the distance from the point's image to the line of reflection.

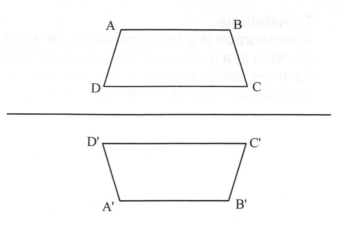

The line (where a mirror may be placed) is called the **line of reflection**. The distance from a point to the line of reflection is the same as the distance from the point's image to the line of reflection.

Glide reflections

A composition of 3 reflections that intersect in more than 1 point is called a glide reflection. It is a glide or translation that is reflected in a line that is parallel to the translation vector.

Example: Find the image of △ABC under a glide reflection where the glide is given by the vector (0, -4) and the reflection is located in x = 0.

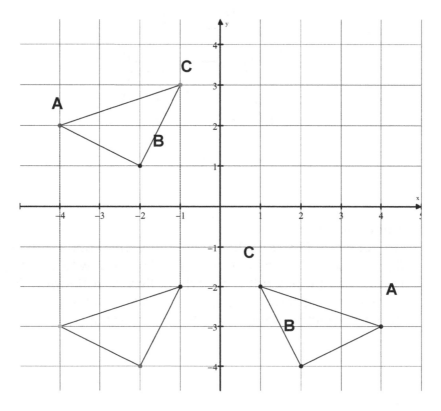

For some problems, there is no need to work with coordinate axes. For instance, the problem may simply require transformations without respect to any absolute positioning.

Example: Rotate the following regular pentagon by 36° about its center and then reflect it about the horizontal line.

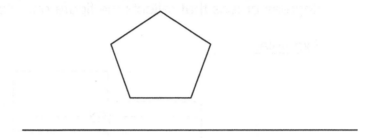

First, perform the rotation. In this case, the direction is not important because the pentagon is symmetric. As it turns out in this case, a rotation of 36° yields the same result as flipping the pentagon vertically (assuming the vertices of the pentagon are indistinguishable).

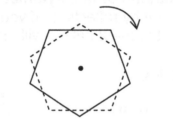

Finally, perform the reflection. Note that the result here is the same as a downward translation (assuming the vertices of the pentagon are indistinguishable).

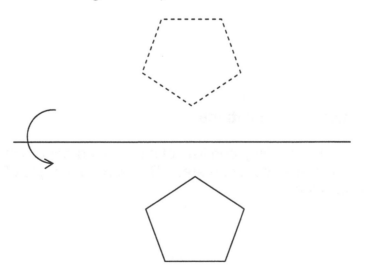

15D. Types of symmetry

A figure has symmetry when there is isometry that maps the figure onto itself. A plane figure has line symmetry or reflectional symmetry, if a line exists where the figure can be reflected onto itself. A figure has **rotational symmetry** if there is a rotation of 180 degrees or less that reflects the figure onto itself.

Example:

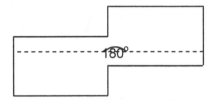

Point symmetry is when a plane figure can be mapped onto itself by a half-turn or a rotation of 180 degrees.

Reflectional or line symmetry is an isometry that maps the figure onto itself by reflection. If you fold a figure along a line of symmetry, the 2 halves will match perfectly.

Examples:

One line of symmetry

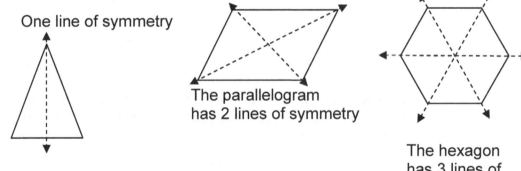

The parallelogram has 2 lines of symmetry

The hexagon has 3 lines of symmetry

15E. Properties of tessellations

A tessellation or tiling, consists of a repeating pattern of figures, which completely cover an area. Below are a couple of example of art tessellations.

A regular tessellation is made by taking a pattern of polygons that are interlocked and can be extended infinitely. There is an example of a tessellation made with hexagons below. It is made by taking congruent, regular polygons and covering a plane with them in a way so that *there are no holes or overlaps*. A semi-regular tessellation is made with polygons arranged exactly the same way at every vertex point. Tessellations occur in frequently in nature. A bee's honeycomb is an example of a tessellation found in nature. The sum of the measures of the angles around any vertex is 360 degrees.

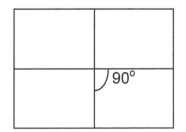

Tessellations can be found everywhere in nature and art.

Tessellations include various types of symmetry, including translational and glide-reflectional symmetry. There are 2 theorems about tessellations:

1.	Every triangle tessellates.

2.	Every quadrilateral tessellates.

A **pure** tessellation is a tessellation that consists of congruent copies of a figure. Only 3 pure tessellations exist made up of regular polygons:

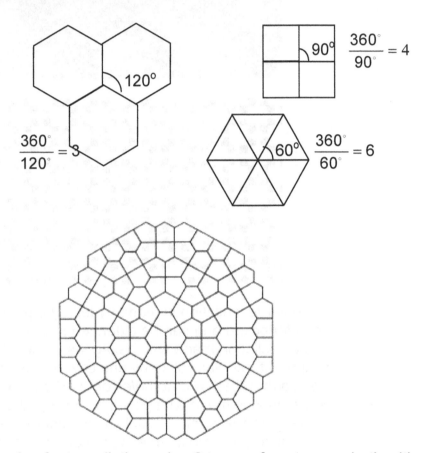

An example of a tessellation using 2 types of pentagons, both with 2, 90° angles.

Tessellations and symmetry

Below is an example of translational symmetry and glide reflectional symmetry.

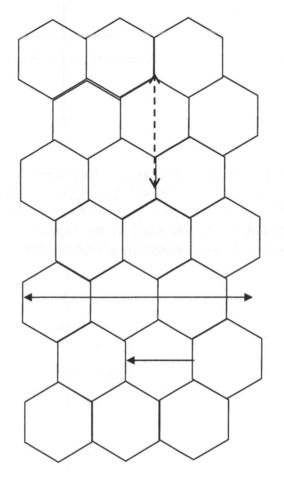

The vertical dashed arrow shows translational symmetry: a translation maps the tessellation onto itself.

The horizontal solid arrows show glide reflection symmetry: a glide reflection that maps the tessellation onto itself.

15 F. Transformations in the coordinate plane

It is crucial that the proper order of transformations (whether determined by the details of the problem or some other consideration) be followed.

Example: Find the final location of a point at (1, 1) that undergoes the following transformations: rotate 90° counter-clockwise about the origin; translate distance 2 in the negative *y* direction; reflect about the *x*-axis.

First, draw a graph of the *x*- and *y*-axes and plot the point at (1, 1).

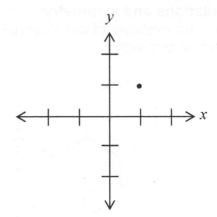

Next, perform the rotation. The center of rotation is the origin and is in the counter-clockwise direction. In this case, the even value of 90° makes the rotation simple to do by inspection. Next, perform a translation of distance 2 in the negative *y* direction (down). The results of these transformations are shown below.

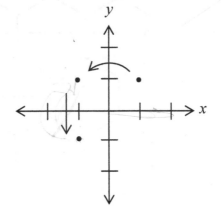

Finally, perform the reflection about the *x*-axis. The final result, shown below, is a point at (1, −1).

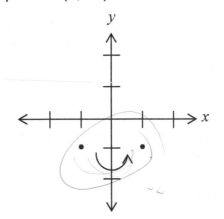

Using this approach, polygons can be transformed on a point-by-point basis.

Rotational transformations in the coordinate plane: rotate △*ABC*, located in Quadrant I, around point A, 180° and note the new location of △*A′B′C′*:

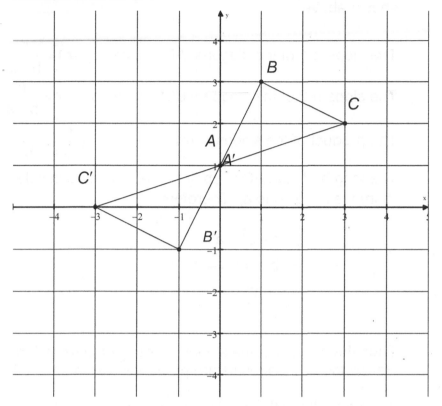

15G. Using coordinate and transformational geometry to prove theorems and solve problems.

Coordinate geometry methods can be used to prove familiar theorems of Euclidean geometry. This is demonstrated in the examples that follow.

<u>Example:</u> Prove that the diagonals of a rhombus are perpendicular to each other.

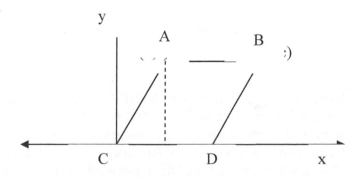

Draw a rhombus ABCD with side of length *a* such that the vertex C is at the origin and the side CD lies along the x-axis. The coordinates of the corners of the rhombus can then be written as shown above.

The slope m1 of the diagonal AD is given by $m1 = \dfrac{c}{b-a}$.

The slope m2 of the diagonal BC is given by $m2 = \dfrac{c}{b+a}$.

The product of the slopes is $m1 \cdot m2 = \dfrac{c}{b-a} \cdot \dfrac{c}{b+a} = \dfrac{c^2}{b^2 - a^2}$.

The length of side AC = $\sqrt{b^2 + c^2} = a$ (since each side of the rhombus is equal to a). Therefore,

$$b^2 + c^2 = a^2$$
$$\Rightarrow b^2 - a^2 = -c^2$$
$$\Rightarrow \dfrac{c^2}{b^2 - a^2} = -1$$

Thus the product of the slopes of the diagonals $m1 \cdot m2 = -1$. Hence the two diagonals are perpendicular to each other.

<u>Example:</u> Prove that the line joining the midpoints of two sides of a triangle is parallel to and half of the third side.

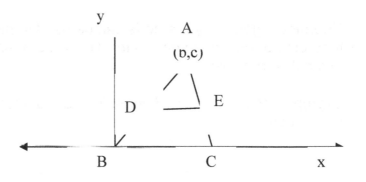

Draw triangle ABC on the coordinate plane in such a way that the vertex B coincides with the origin and the side BC lies along the x-axis. Let point C have coordinates (a,0) and A have coordinates (b,c). D is the midpoint of AB and E is the midpoint of AC.
We need to prove that DE is parallel to BC and is half the length of BC.

Using the midpoint formula,

coordinates of $D = \left(\dfrac{b}{2}, \dfrac{c}{2}\right)$; coordinates of $E = \left(\dfrac{b+a}{2}, \dfrac{c}{2}\right)$.

The slope of the line DE is then given by $\dfrac{\dfrac{c}{2} - \dfrac{c}{2}}{\dfrac{b+a}{2} - \dfrac{b}{2}} = 0$, which is

equal to the slope of the x-axis. Thus DE is parallel to BC.

The length of the line segment DE =

$$\sqrt{\left(\dfrac{b+a}{2} - \dfrac{b}{2}\right)^2 + \left(\dfrac{c}{2} - \dfrac{c}{2}\right)^2} = \sqrt{\left(\dfrac{a}{2}\right)^2} = \dfrac{a}{2}$$

Thus the length of DE is half that of BC.

SUBAREA IV.   DATA ANALYSIS, STATISTICS, AND PROBABILITY

Competency 0016 Understand descriptive statistics and the methods used in collecting, organizing, reporting, and analyzing data.

16A. **Constructing and interpreting tables, charts and graphs (e.g. line plots, stem-and-leaf plots, box plots, scatter plots)**

Bar graphs
Bar graphs are used to compare various quantities. To make a bar graph or a pictograph, determine the scale to be used for the graph. Then determine the length of each bar on the graph or determine the number of pictures needed to represent each item of information. Be sure to include an explanation of the scale in the legend.

	Test 1	Test 2	Test 3	Test 4	Test 5
Evans, Tim	75	66	80	85	97
Miller, Julie	94	93	88	97	98
Thomas, Randy	81	86	88	87	90

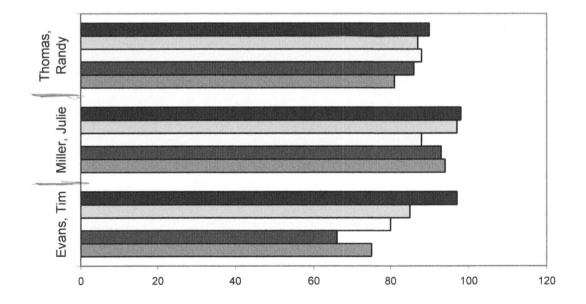

Circle graphs

Circle graphs show the relationship of various parts to each other and the whole. Percents are used to create circle graphs.

<u>Example:</u> Julie spends 8 hours each day in school, 2 hours doing homework, 1 hour eating dinner, 2 hours watching television,10 hours sleeping and the rest of her time doing other activities.

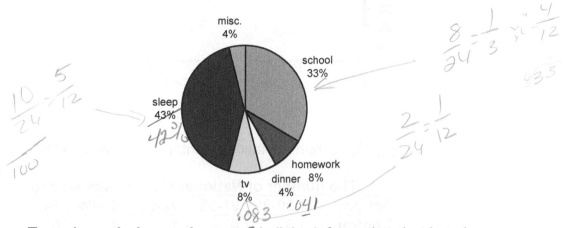

To make a **circle graph**, we total all the information that is to be included on the graph. We then determine the central angle to be used for each sector of the graph using the following formula:

$$\frac{\text{information}}{\text{total information}} \times 360^\circ = \text{degrees in central} \sphericalangle$$

We lay out the central angles to these sizes, label each section, and include its percent.

Line Graph

Line graphs are used to show trends, often over a period of time. To make a line graph, determine appropriate scales for both the vertical and horizontal axes (based on the information to be graphed). Describe what each axis represents and mark the scale periodically on each axis. Graph the individual points of the graph and connect the points on the graph from left to right.

	Test 1	Test 2	Test 3	Test 4	Test 5
Evans, Tim	75	66	80	85	97
Miller, Julie	94	93	88	97	98
Thomas, Randy	81	86	88	87	90

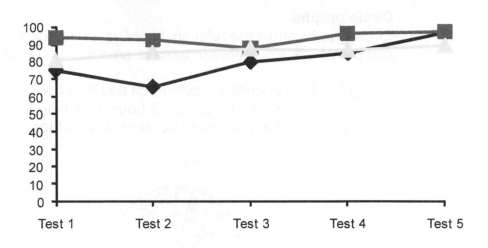

Example: Graph the following information using a line graph.

The number of National Merit finalists/school year

School	90-91	91-92	92-93	93-94	94-95	95-96
Central	3	5	1	4	6	8
Wilson	4	2	3	2	3	2

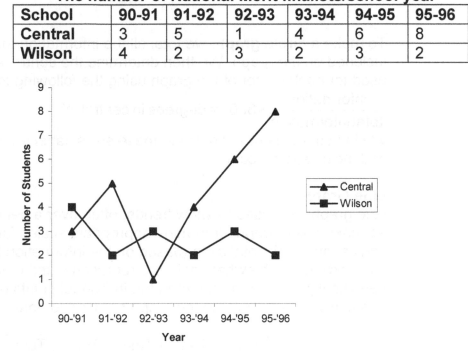

Line plots

Line plots are usually used for one group of data with less than fifty values. A line plot consists of a horizontal line with an *x* marked above a value for each occurrence of that value in the data set.

Example:

Each of 25 workers in a candle shop took a box of 20 candles and counted the number of red candles in the box. The distribution of red candles in their boxes is shown below.

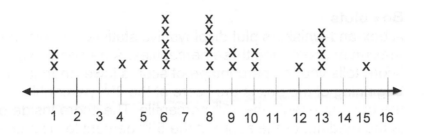

Number of red candles in sample

The line plot indicates that 2 workers had 1 red candle, 1 had 3, 1 had 4, 1 had 5, 5 had 6, 5 had 8, 2 had 9, 2 had 10, 1 had 12, 4 had 13, and 1 had 15.

Stem and leaf plots
Stem and leaf plots are visually similar to line plots. The **stems** are the digits in the greatest place value of the data values, and the **leaves** are the last digits in the data. Stem and leaf plots are best suited for small sets of data and are especially useful for comparing two sets of data.

The first thing to do when creating a stem and leaf plot is to arrange the data from smallest to largest. The second thing to do is to list the range of scores for the stems in a column. Lastly, you take each score, one at a time and put the last digit in a column next to its stem.

The following is an example using test scores:
The test scores are: 49, 54, 59, 61, 62, 63, 64, 66, 67, 68, 68, 70, 73, 74, 76, 76, 76, 77, 77, 77, 77, 78, 78, 78, 78, 83, 85, 85, 87, 88, 90, 90, 93, 94, 95, 100, 100.

Stem	Leaves
4	9
5	4 9
6	1 2 3 4 6 7 8 8
7	0 3 4 6 6 6 7 7 7 7 8 8 8 8
8	3 5 5 7 8
9	0 0 3 4 5
10	0 0

Box plots

A box-and-whiskers plot displays five statistics: a minimum score, a maximum score, and three percentiles. A percentile value for a score tells you the percentage of scores lower than it. The beginning of the box is the score at the 25th percentile. The end of the box represents the 75th percentile. The score inside of the box is the median, or the score at the 50th percentile. The score at the end of the left whisker is the minimum score. The score at the end of the right whisker is the maximum score.

<u>Example:</u>

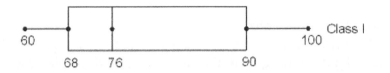

The above box-and-whiskers plot summarizes the scores on a mathematics test for the students in Class I. It indicates that the lowest score is 60, while the highest score is 100. Twenty-five percent of the class scored 68 or lower, 50% scored 76 or lower, and 25% scored 90 or higher.

Scatter plots

Scatter plots compare two characteristics of the same group of things or people and usually consist of a large body of data. They show how much one variable affects another. The relationship between the two variables is their **correlation**. The closer the data points come to making a straight line when plotted, the closer the correlation.

16B. Measures of central tendency (e.g. mean, median, mode) and dispersion (e.g. range, standard deviation)

The mean, median and mode are measures of central tendency (i.e., the average or typical value) in a data set. They can be defined both for discrete and continuous data sets. A **discrete variable** is one that can only take on certain specific values. For instance, the number of students in a class can only be a whole number (e.g., 15 or 16, but not 15.5). A **continuous variable**, such as the weight of an object, can take on a continuous range of values.

Discrete variables

For discrete data, the **mean** is the average of the data items, or the value obtained by adding all the data values and dividing by the total number of data items. For a data set of n items with data values $x_1, x_2, x_3, \ldots, x_n$, the mean is given by

$$\overline{X} = \frac{x_1 + x_2 + x_3 + \ldots + x_n}{n}$$

The **median** is found by putting the data in order from smallest to largest and selecting the item in the middle (or the average of the two values in the middle if the number of data items is even). The **mode** is the most frequently occurring datum. There can be more than one mode in a data set.

Example: Find the mean, median, and mode of the test scores listed below:

85	77	65
92	90	54
88	85	70
75	80	69
85	88	60
72	74	95

Mean: sum of all scores ÷ number of scores = 78 ✓
Median: put numbers in order from smallest to largest. Pick the middle number.

54, 60, 65, 69, 70, 72, 74, 75, 77, 80, 85, 85, 85, 88, 88, 90, 92, 95

Both values are in the middle.
Therefore, median is average of two numbers in the middle, or 78.5

Mode: most frequent number = 85

Range is a measure of variability that is calculated by subtracting the smallest value from the largest value in a set of discrete data.

The **variance** and **standard deviation** are measures of the "spread" of data around the mean. It is noteworthy that descriptive statistics involving such parameters as variance and standard deviation can be applied to a set of data that spans the entire population (parameters, typically represented using Greek symbols) or to a set of data that only constitutes a portion of the population (sample statistics, typically represented by Latin letters).

The mean of a set of data, whether for a population (μ) or for a sample ($\overline{x}$), uses the formula discussed in Skill a, and can be represented as either a set of individual data or as a set of data with associated frequencies. The variance and standard deviation for the population differ slightly from those of a sample. The population variance (σ^2) and the population standard deviation (σ) are as follows:

$$\sigma^2 = \frac{1}{n}\sum(x_i - \mu)^2$$

$$\sigma = \sqrt{\sigma^2}$$

For a sample, the data does not include the entire population. As a result, it should be expected that the sample data might not be perfectly representative of the population. To account for this shortcoming in the sample variance (s^2) and standard deviation (s), the sum of the squared differences between the data and the mean is divided by ($n - 1$) instead of just n. This increases the variance and standard deviation slightly, which in turn increases slightly the data spread to account for the possibility that the sample may not accurately represent the population.

$$s^2 = \frac{1}{n-1}\sum(x_i - \overline{x})^2$$

$$s = \sqrt{s^2}$$

Example: Calculate the range, variance and standard deviation for the following data set: {3, 3, 5, 7, 8, 8, 8, 10, 12, 21}.

The range is simply the largest data value minus the smallest. In this case, the range is 21 − 3 = 18.

To calculate the variance and standard deviation, first calculate the mean. If it is not stated whether a data set constitutes a population or sample, assume it is a population. (In this case, if the data was labeled as "ages of the 10 people in a room," this would be a population. If the data was labeled "ages of males at a crowded circus event," the data would be a sample.)

$$\mu = \frac{3+3+5+7+8+8+8+10+12+21}{10} = 8.5$$

Use this mean to calculate the variance.

$$\sigma^2 = \frac{1}{10}\sum(x_i - 8.5)^2$$

$$\sigma^2 = \frac{1}{10}\left\{(3-8.5)^2 + (3-8.5)^2 + (5-8.5)^2 + \ldots + (21-8.5)^2\right\}$$

$$\sigma^2 = \frac{246.5}{10} = 24.65$$

The standard deviation is

$$\sigma = \sqrt{\sigma^2} = \sqrt{24.65} \approx 4.96$$

Continuous Variables

The range for a continuous data distribution is the same as that for a discrete distribution; the largest value minus the smallest value. Calculation of the mean, variance and standard deviation are similar, but slightly different. Since a continuous distribution does not permit a simple summation, integrals must be used. The mean μ of a distribution function $f(x)$ is expressed below:

$$\mu = \int_{-\infty}^{\infty} xf(x)\,dx$$

The variance σ^2 over also has an integral form, and has a form similar to that of a discrete distribution.

$$\sigma^2 = \int_{-\infty}^{\infty} (x-\mu)^2 f(x)\,dx$$

The standard deviation σ is simply

$$\sigma = \sqrt{\sigma^2}$$

<u>Example:</u> Calculate the standard deviation of a data distribution function $f(x)$ where

$$f(x) = \begin{cases} 0 & x < 1 \\ -2x^2 + 2 & -1 \le x \le 1 \\ 0 & x > 1 \end{cases}$$

First calculate the mean of the function. Since the function is zero except between 1 and –1, the integral can likewise be evaluated from –1 to 1.

$$\mu = \int_{-1}^{1} \left(-2x^2 + 2\right) x\, dx$$

$$\mu = -2 \int_{-1}^{1} \left(x^3 - x\right) dx$$

$$\mu = -2 \left[\frac{x^4}{4} - \frac{x^2}{2} \right]_{x=-1}^{x=1}$$

$$\mu = -2 \left\{ \left[\frac{(1)^4}{4} - \frac{(1)^2}{2} \right] - \left[\frac{(-1)^4}{4} - \frac{(-1)^2}{2} \right] \right\} = 0$$

The mean can also be seen clearly by the fact that the graph of the function $f(x)$ is symmetric about the y-axis, indicating that its center (or mean) is at $x = 0$. Next, calculate the variance of f.

$$\sigma^2 = \int_{-1}^{1} (x-0)^2 \left(-2x^2 + 2\right) dx = -2 \int_{-1}^{1} x^2 \left(x^2 - 1\right) dx$$

$$\sigma^2 = -2 \int_{-1}^{1} \left(x^4 - x^2\right) dx$$

$$\sigma^2 = -2 \left[\frac{x^5}{5} - \frac{x^3}{3} \right]_{x=-1}^{x=1} = -2 \left\{ \left[\frac{(1)^5}{5} - \frac{(1)^3}{3} \right] - \left[\frac{(-1)^5}{5} - \frac{(-1)^3}{3} \right] \right\}$$

$$\sigma^2 = -2 \left\{ \frac{1}{5} - \frac{1}{3} - \left(-\frac{1}{5}\right) + \left(-\frac{1}{3}\right) \right\} = -2 \left(\frac{2}{5} - \frac{2}{3} \right)$$

$$\sigma^2 = \frac{8}{15} \approx 0.533$$

The standard deviation is

$$\sigma = \sqrt{\sigma^2} = \sqrt{\frac{8}{15}} \approx 0.730$$

16C. Frequency distributions

If the data set is large, it may be expressed in compact form as a **frequency distribution**. The number of occurrences of each data point is the **frequency** of that value. The **relative frequency** is defined as the frequency divided by the total number of data points. Since the sum of the frequencies equals the number of data points, the relative frequencies add up to 1. The relative frequency of a data point, therefore, represents the probability of occurrence of that value. Thus, a distribution consisting of relative frequencies is known as a **probability distribution**.

For data expressed as a frequency distribution, the mean is given by

$$\overline{x} = \frac{\sum x_i f_i}{\sum f_i} = \sum x_i f_i'$$

where x_i represents a data value, f_i the corresponding frequency and f_i' the corresponding relative frequency.

The **cumulative frequency** of a data point is the sum of the frequencies from the beginning up to that point. The median of a frequency distribution is the point at which the cumulative frequency reaches half the value of the total number of data points.
The mode is the point at which the frequency distribution reaches a maximum. There can be more than one mode in which case the distribution is **multimodal**.

<u>Example:</u> The frequency distribution below shows the summary of some test results where people scored points ranging from 0 to 45 in increments of 5. One person scored 5 points, 4 people scored 10 points and so on. Find the mean, median and mode of the data set.

Points	Frequency	Cumulative Frequency	Relative Frequency
5	1	1	0.009
10	4	5	0.035
15	12	17	0.105
20	22	39	0.193
25	30	69	0.263
30	25	94	0.219
35	13	107	0.114
40	6	113	0.053
45	1	114	0.009

The mean score is the following:
(5x1+10x4+15x12+20x22+25x30+30x25+35x13+40x6+45x1)/114
= (5+40+180+440+750+750+455+240+45)/114 = 25.5.

The median score (the point at which the cumulative frequency reaches or surpasses the value 57) is 25.

The mode (or value with the highest frequency) is 25.

A **histogram** is used to display a discrete frequency distribution graphically. It shows the counts of data in different ranges, the center of the data set, the spread of the data, and whether there are any outliers. It also shows whether the data has a single mode or more than one.

Example: The histogram below shows the summary of some test results where people scored points ranging from 0 to 45. The total range of points has been divided into bins 0-5, 6-10, 11-15 and so on. The frequency for the first bin (labeled 5) is the number of people who scored points ranging from 0 to 5; the frequency for the second bin (labeled 10) is the number of people who scored points ranging from 6 to 10 and so on.

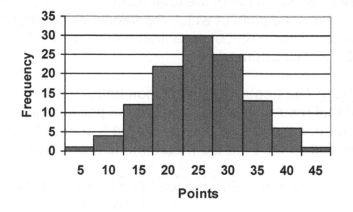

A histogram can be used to represent discrete as well as continuous data (data that can take on a continuous range of values, e.g. height) sorted in bins. A large data set of continuous data may also be represented using a continuous frequency distribution, which is essentially a histogram with very narrow bars. Below, a trend line has been added to the example histogram above. Notice that this approximates the most common continuous distribution, a **normal or bell curve**.

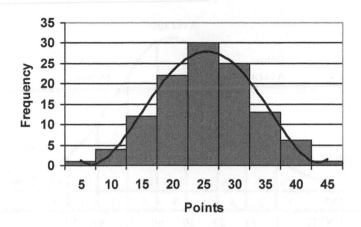

A normal distribution is symmetric with the mean equal to the median. The tails of the curve in both directions fall off rapidly. The spread of data is measured by the standard deviation. For descriptions of other kinds of continuous distributions see the following:
http://mathworld.wolfram.com/ContinuousDistribution.html

16D. Percentile scores

Percentiles divide data into 100 equal parts. A datum that falls in the nth percentile means that this datum exceeds (by whatever measure) n percent of the other data and that $(100 - n)$ percent of the data exceed this datum. For instance, a person whose score on a test falls in the 65th percentile has outperformed 65 percent of all those who took the test. This does not mean that the score was 65 percent out of 100, nor does it mean that 65 percent of the questions answered were correctly. Instead, this score means that the grade was higher than 65 percent of all those who took the test.
Stanine "standard nine" scores combine the understandability of percentages with the properties of the normal curve of probability. Stanines divide the bell curve into nine sections, the largest of which stretches from the 40th to the 60th percentile and is the "Fifth Stanine" (the average of taking into account error possibilities).

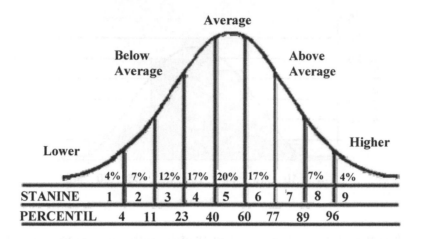

	4%	7%	12%	17%	20%	17%		7%	4%
STANINE	1	2	3	4	5	6	7	8	9
PERCENTIL	4	11	23	40	60	77	89	96	

Quartiles divide the data into four segments. To find the quartile of a particular datum, first determine the median of the data set (which is labeled Q2), then find the median of the upper half (labeled Q3) and the median of the lower half (labeled Q1) of the data set. There is some confusion in determining the upper and lower quartile, and statisticians do not agree on the appropriate method to use. Tukey's method for finding the quartile values is to find the median of the data set, then find the median of the upper and lower halves of the data set. If there is an odd number of values in the data set, include the median value in both halves when finding the quartile values. For example, consider the following data set:

$$\{1, 4, 9, 16, 25, 36, 49, 64, 81\}$$

Quartiles divide the data into 4 parts. First find the median of the data set (Q2), then find the median of the upper (Q3) and lower (Q1) halves of the data set. If there are an odd number of values in the data set, include the median value in both halves when finding quartile values. For example, given the data set: {1, 4, 9, 16, 25, 36, 49, 64, 81} first find the median value, which is 25. This is the second quartile. Since there are an odd number of values in the data set (9), we include the median in both halves.

To find the quartile values, we must find the medians of: {1, 4, 9, 16, 25} and {25, 36, 49, 64, 81}. Since each of these subsets had an odd number of elements (5), we use the middle value. Thus the first quartile value is 9 and the third quartile value is 49. If the data set has an even number of elements, average the middle two values. The quartile values are always either one of the data points, or exactly half way between two data points.

Example: Given the following set of data, find the percentile of the score 104.
70, 72, 82, 83, 84, 87, 100, 104, 108, 109, 110, 115

Find the percentage of scores below 104.

7/12 of the scores are less than 104. This is 58.333%; therefore, the score of 104 is in the 58th percentile.

Example: Find the first, second and third quartile for the data listed.

6, 7, 8, 9, 10, 12, 13, 14, 15, 16, 18, 23, 24, 25, 27, 29, 30, 33, 34, 37

Quartile 1:   The 1st Quartile is the median of the lower half of the data set, which is 11.

Quartile 2:   The median of the data set is the 2nd Quartile, which is 17.

Quartile 3:   The 3rd Quartile is the median of the upper half of the data set, which is 28.

First, find the median value, which is 25. This is the value Q2. Since there is an odd number of values in the data set (nine), include the median in both halves. To find the quartile values, find the medians of the two sets

$$\{1, 4, 9, 16, 25\} \text{ and } \{25, 36, 49, 64, 81\}$$

Since each of these subsets has an odd number of elements (five), use the middle value. Thus, the lower quartile value (Q1) is 9 and the upper quartile value (Q3) is 49.
Another method to find quartile values (if the total data set has an odd number of values) excludes the median from both halves when finding the quartile values. Using this approach on the data set above, exclude the median (25) from each half. To find the quartile values, find the medians of

$$\{1, 4, 9, 16\} \text{ and } \{36, 49, 64, 81\}$$

Since each of these data sets has an even number of elements (four), average the middle two values. Thus the lower quartile value (Q1) is (4+9)/2 = 6.5 and the upper quartile value (Q3) is (49+64)/2 = 56.5. The middle quartile value (Q2) remains 25.

Other methods for calculating quartiles also exist, but these two methods are the most straightforward.

Percentiles and quartiles are typically applied to discrete data distributions, but application to continuous distributions is also possible. In such a case, percentiles and quartiles would be calculated by dividing the area under the curve of the distribution into either 100 (for percentile) or 4 (for quartile) even or approximately even segments. The boundaries of these segments are the percentile or quartile values.

16E. The effects of data transformations on measures of central tendency and variability

A statistical data transformation is the application of a mathematical function to every point in the data set (e.g. squaring every data point or adding 10 to every data point). Data transformations are usually carried out in order to make the data easier to analyze.

Linear data transformations involve linear changes to the data such as adding a constant number or multiplying by a constant number. This is often done to bring the data into a more convenient range for handling.

Linear transformations have the following effect on the mean, median, and standard deviation:

1. If a constant number is added to (or subtracted from) a data set, the mean and median of the data set are shifted by that amount. The standard deviation of the data set remains unchanged.

2. If each data point is multiplied by a certain number, the mean, median, and standard deviation are all increased by the same factor.

Example: If a data set has a mean of 4, a median of 3 and a standard deviation of 1.6, what would happen to these measures if each value in the data set were to be multiplied by 5?

The new mean would be 20: the original mean of 4 multiplied by 5. The new median would be 15, again, the original median multiplied by 5. The new standard deviation would be 8, the original standard deviation of 1.6 multiplied by 5.

<u>Example:</u> If the same data set with a mean of 4, median of 3 and a standard deviation of 1.6 were changed by adding 5 to each value, what would be the effect on the mean, median and standard deviation?

The new mean would be 9: the original mean of 4 plus 5. The new median would be 8: the original median of 3 plus 5. The standard deviation would not change; it would remain 1.6.

Nonlinear data transformations are often performed to get a normal distribution from a skewed or differently shaped distribution. This is because many standard statistical analyses are designed to be performed on normal data. There are many different kinds of nonlinear data transformations. Commonly used ones include the logarithmic, square root, arcsine, reciprocal and squared transformations. The effects of these transformations on central tendency and variability are a lot more complicated that in the linear case and depend on many factors peculiar to each situation.

16F. Evaluating real-world situations to determine appropriate sampling techniques and methods for gathering and organizing data

In cases where the number of events or individuals is too large to collect data on each one, scientists collect information from only a small percentage. This is known as **sampling** or **surveying**. If sampling is done correctly, it should give the investigator nearly the same information he would have obtained by testing the entire population. The survey must be carefully designed, considering both the sampling technique and the size of the sample.

There are a variety of sampling techniques, both **random** and **non-random**. Random sampling is also known as **probability sampling** since the methods of probability theory can be used to ascertain the odds that the sample is representative of the whole population. Statistical methods may be used to determine how large a sample is necessary to give an investigator a specified level of certainty (95% is a typical confidence interval). Conversely, if an investigator has a sample of certain size, those same statistical methods can be used to determine how confident one can be that the sample accurately reflects the whole population.

A truly **random** sample must choose events or individuals without regard to time, place or result. **Simple random sampling** is ideal for populations that are relatively homogeneous with respect to the data being collected.

In some cases an accurate representation of distinct sub-populations requires **stratified random sampling** or **quota sampling**. For instance, if men and women are likely to respond very differently to a particular survey, the total sample population can be separated into these two subgroups and then a random group of respondents selected from each subgroup. This kind of sampling not only provides balanced representation of different subgroups, it also allows comparison of data between subgroups. Stratified sampling is sometimes **proportional**; i.e., the number of samples selected from each subgroup reflects the fraction of the whole population represented by the subgroup.

Sometimes compromises must be made to save time, money or effort. For instance, when conducting a phone survey, calls are typically only made in a certain geographical area and at a certain time of day. This is an example of **cluster random sampling**.

There are three stages to cluster or area sampling: the target population is divided into many regional clusters (groups), a few clusters are randomly selected for study and a few subjects are randomly chosen from within a cluster

Systematic random sampling involves the collection of a sample at defined intervals (for instance, every tenth part to come off a manufacturing line). Here, it is assumed that the population is ordered randomly and there is no hidden pattern that may compromise the randomness of the sampling.

Non-random sampling is also known as **non-probability sampling**. **Convenience sampling** is the method of choosing items arbitrarily and in an unstructured manner from the frame. **Purposive sampling** targets a particular section of the population. **Snowball sampling** (e.g., having survey participants recommend others) and **expert sampling** are other types of non-random sampling.

Obviously, non-random samples are far less representative of the whole population than random ones. They may, however, be the only methods available or may meet the needs of a particular study. The data obtained from sampling may be categorical (e.g., yes or no responses) or numerical. In both cases, results are displayed using a variety of graphical techniques.   See Competency 0017, A for more information on displaying data.

16G. Making appropriate inferences, interpolations and extrapolations from a set of data

The purpose of inferential statistics is to estimate the characteristics of the general population from a sample. It is assumed that the sample we are examining is the result of random sampling or some other method of systematic sampling, so that every person is just as likely to be included in the sample as any other person.

Point estimation, **interval estimation**, **hypothesis testing,** and **prediction** are some of the components of inferential statistics. Point estimation is the evaluation of a single unknown population parameter based on the characteristics of the sample. Interval estimation is the calculation of a range of possible values for an unknown parameter. Prediction involves calculation of the possible values of future observations. The **confidence level** of an estimate or prediction is the proportion of times the estimate is expected to be correct.

Hypothesis testing involves comparing observations with some statement that is expected to be true. This statement or hypothesis is known as the "null hypothesis."

Example: Suppose that the students in your class scored higher than the students in the rest of the country on the SAT, where the mean is 500. The population of students in your class is different from the population of the rest of the country; your class is of the population of high-scoring students. We can test this assumption. If there is no difference between your sample and the population of all students taking the SAT, then we would predict that the population mean would be very similar to your sample mean. The hypothesis that the sample mean is the same as the population mean is the "null hypothesis." If, however, we can reject the null hypothesis, then we can make a statistical statement concerning the null hypothesis. Assume that the mean SAT score for your class is 750. The probability of finding this mean in a random sample drawn from the population of all individuals taking the SAT would be unlikely, but statistically possible.

Interpolation is the estimation of an observation within the sample data range. For instance, if observations of temperature are made every hour on the hour, interpolation may be used to calculate temperature on the half hour. One way of doing this may be to fit a curve to the data points (as discussed in the linear regression section below) so that the points on the curve represent the estimated temperature values at every point in time, including points where no observations were made.

Extrapolation involves prediction of data values outside the range of observation. An example would be prediction of the daily high temperature for next week based on observations for the last few weeks. Particular care must be taken with extrapolation to ensure that the model used to fit the observed data remains valid in the extrapolated domain.

Many errors can be made when interpreting data. The sample size is critical to avoid the probability of accepting the null hypothesis when the alternative hypothesis is true. Errors in variables, or unknown variables not accounted for can distort inference. The type of analysis run on the data is crucial as certain statistical tests are appropriate for some experimental designs and not others and can skew the results. The scope of making appropriate inferences from data is too broad to approach here but there are books on the topic of experimental design and analysis available for those who wish to learn more.

16H.   Interpreting correlation

Correlation is a measure of association between two variables. It varies from -1 to 1, with 0 being a random relationship, 1 being a perfect positive linear relationship, and -1 being a perfect negative linear relationship.

The **correlation coefficient** (r) is used to describe the strength of the association between the variables and the direction of the association.

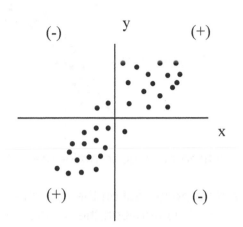

In the above scatter plot, the two variables x and y are plotted on a coordinate plane. Horizontal and vertical lines are drawn through the point of averages of the x and y values. This divides the scatter plot into four quadrants. If a point is in the lower left quadrant, the product of two negatives is positive; in the upper right, the product of two positives is positive. The positive quadrants are depicted with the positive sign (+). In the two remaining quadrants (upper left and lower right), the product of a negative and a positive is negative. The negative quadrants are depicted with the negative sign (-). If r is positive, then there are more points in the positive quadrants and if r is negative, then there are more points in the two negative quadrants.

16I.   Problems involving linear regression models

Regression is a form of statistical analysis used to predict a dependent variable (y) from values of an independent variable (x). A regression equation is derived from a known set of data.

The simplest regression analysis models the relationship between two variables using a linear regression equation: $y = a + bx$, where y is the dependent variable and x is the independent variable. This simple equation denotes a linear relationship between x and y. This form would be appropriate if, when you plotted a graph of x and y, you tended to see the points roughly form along a straight line.

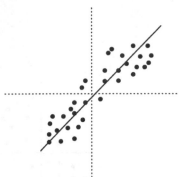

The line can then be used to make predictions.

If all of the data points fell on the line, there would be a perfect correlation ($r = 1.0$) between the x and y data points. These cases represent the best scenarios for prediction. A positive or negative r value represents how y varies with x. When r is positive, y increases as x increases. When r is negative y decreases as x increases.

Example: A teacher wanted to determine how a practice test influenced a student's performance on the actual test. The practice test grade and the subsequent actual test grade for each student are given in the table below:

Practice Test (x)	Actual Test (y)
94	98
95	94
92	95
87	89
82	85
80	78
75	73
65	67
50	45
20	40

We determine the equation for the linear regression line to be $y = 14.650 + 0.834x$.

A new student comes into the class and scores 78 on the practice test. Based on the equation obtained above, what would the teacher predict this student would get on the actual test?

$$y = 14.650 + 0.834(78)$$

$$y = 14.650 + 65.052$$

$$y = 80$$

It is often helpful to use regression to construct a more general trend or distribution based on sample data. To select an appropriate model for the regression, a representative set of data must be examined. It is often helpful, in this case, to plot the data and review it visually on a graph. In this manner, it is relatively simple to select a general class of functions (linear, quadratic, exponential, etc.) that might be used to model the data. There are two basic aspects of regression: **selection of an appropriate curve** that best fits the data and quantification of the "**goodness of fit**" of that curve. For instance, if a line can be constructed that passes through every data point of a distribution, then that line is a perfect fit to the data (and, obviously, linear regression is an appropriate choice for the model). If the distribution of data points seems to bear no particular resemblance to the line, then linear regression is probably not a wise choice, and a quantification of the goodness of fit should reflect this fact.
The following discussion summarizes least squares linear regression analysis. The same principles can be applied to other forms of regression (such as quadratic or exponential).

The Method of Least Squares
Given a set of data, a curve approximation can be fitted to the data by using the **method of least squares**. The best-fit curve, defined by the function $f(x)$, is assumed to approximate a set of data with coordinates (x_i, y_i) by minimizing the sum of squared differences between the curve and the data. Mathematically, the sum of these squared differences (errors) can be written as follows for a data set with n points.

$$S = \sum_{i=1}^{n} \left[f(x_i) - y_i \right]^2$$

Thus, the best-fit curve approximation to a set of data (x_i, y_i) is $f(x)$ such that S is minimized.

Shown below is a set of data and a linear function that approximates it. The vertical distances between the data points and the line are the errors that are squared and summed to find S.

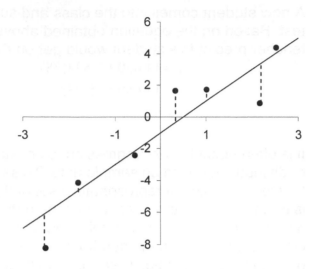

Linear least squares regression

If the curve $f(x)$ is used to approximate a set of data by minimizing the sum of squared errors (or **residuals**), S, then $f(x)$ is called a **least squares regression line**. The process of determining $f(x)$ is called **linear least squares regression**. In this case, $f(x)$ has the following form:

$$f(x) = ax + b$$

Given a set of data $\{(x_1, y_1), (x_2, y_2), (x_3, y_3), \ldots, (x_n, y_n)\}$, the sum S for linear regression is the following.

$$S = \sum_{i=1}^{n} [ax_i + b - y_i]^2$$

To find $f(x)$, it is necessary to find a and b. This can be done by minimizing S. The results are given below.

$$a = \frac{n \sum_{i=1}^{n} x_i y_i - \sum_{i=1}^{n} x_i \sum_{i=1}^{n} y_i}{n \sum_{i=1}^{n} x_i^2 - \left[\sum_{i=1}^{n} x_i \right]^2}$$

Note that the average x value for the data (which is the sum of all x values divided by n) and the average y value for the data (which is the sum of all y values divided by n) can be used to simplify the expression. The average x value is defined as $\bar{x}$ and the average y value is defined as $\bar{y}$.

$$a = \frac{\sum_{i=1}^{n} x_i y_i - n\bar{x}\bar{y}}{\sum_{i=1}^{n} x_i^2 - n\bar{x}^2}$$

Since the expression for b is complicated, it suffices to provide the expression for b in terms of a.

$$b = \frac{1}{n}\left(\sum_{i=1}^{n} y_i - a\sum_{i=1}^{n} x_i\right)$$
$$b = \overline{y} - a\overline{x}$$

Thus, given a set of data, the linear least squares regression line can be found by calculating a and b as shown above.

The **correlation coefficient**, r, can be used as a measure of the quality of $f(x)$ as a fit to the data set. The value of r ranges from zero (for a poor fit) to one (for a good fit). The correlation coefficient formula is given below.

$$r^2 = \frac{\left(\sum_{i=1}^{n} x_i y_i - n\overline{xy}\right)^2}{\left(\sum_{i=1}^{n} x_i^2 - n\overline{x}^2\right)\left(\sum_{i=1}^{n} y_i^2 - n\overline{y}^2\right)}$$

Example: A company has collected data comparing the age of its employees to their respective income (in thousands of dollars). Find the line that best fits the data (using a least squares approach). Also calculate the correlation coefficient for the fit. The data is given below in the form of (age, income).

$$\{(35,42),(27,23),(54,43),(58,64),(39,51),(31,40)\}$$

The data are plotted in the graph below.

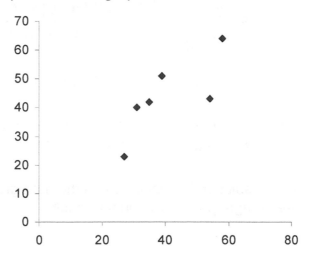

Note that there are six pieces of data. It is helpful to first calculate the following sums:

$$\sum_{i=1}^{6} x_i = 35 + 27 + 54 + 58 + 39 + 31 = 244$$

$$\sum_{i=1}^{6} y_i = 42 + 23 + 43 + 64 + 51 + 40 = 263$$

$$\sum_{i=1}^{6} x_i y_i = 35(42) + 27(23) + 54(43) + 58(64) + 39(51) + 31(40)$$
$$= 11354$$

$$\sum_{i=1}^{6} x_i^2 = 35^2 + 27^2 + 54^2 + 58^2 + 39^2 + 31^2 = 10716$$

$$\sum_{i=1}^{6} y_i^2 = 42^2 + 23^2 + 43^2 + 64^2 + 51^2 + 40^2 = 12439$$

Based on these values, the average x and y values are given below.

$$\overline{x} = \frac{244}{6} \approx 40.67$$

$$\overline{y} = \frac{263}{6} \approx 43.83$$

To find the equation of the least squares regression line, calculate the values of a and b.

$$a = \frac{\sum_{i=1}^{n} x_i y_i - n\overline{x}\overline{y}}{\sum_{i=1}^{n} x_i^2 - n\overline{x}^2} = \frac{11354 - 6(40.67)(43.83)}{10716 - 6(40.67)^2} \approx 0.832$$

$$b = \overline{y} - a\overline{x} = 43.83 - 0.832(40.67) = 9.993$$

Thus, the equation of the least squares regression line is
$$f(x) = 0.832x + 9.993$$

This result can be displayed on the data graph to ensure that there are no egregious errors in the result.

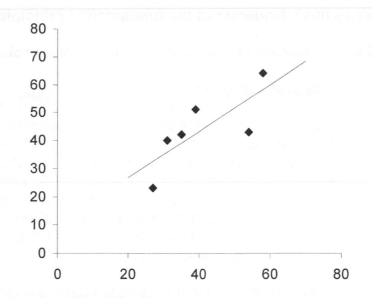

The regression line in the graph above appears to do a good job of approximating the trend of the data. To quantify how well the line fits the data, calculate the correlation coefficient using the formula given above.

$$r^2 = \frac{\left(11354 - 6(40.67)(43.83)\right)^2}{\left(10716 - 6(40.67)^2\right)\left(12439 - 6(43.83)^2\right)}$$

$$r^2 = \frac{(658.603)^2}{(791.707)(912.587)} = 0.600$$

$$r = 0.775$$

Thus, the fit to the data is reasonably good.

Calculators and Regression
Modern handheld calculators, especially graphing calculators, often have built-in tools for handling regression. After entering the data (in the form of lists, for instance), the calculator's regression functions can be employed. It is usually best to test several different functions (if no particular model is obviously appropriate) and to compare the associated residual or correlation coefficient values for each function. For instance, it may be best to test a data set using both linear and exponential models. By comparing the correlation coefficient, the better-fitting curve can be determined. In this case, the closer the value is to unity, the better the fit. Of course, it is necessary to know the features of a particular calculator, as well as its limitations, to accurately employ regression functions.

Competency 0017 Understand the fundamental principles of probability.

17A. Representing possible outcomes for a probabilistic situation

The **probability** of an outcome, given a random experiment (a structured, repeatable experiment where the outcome cannot be predicted—or, alternatively, where the outcome is dependent on "chance"), is the relative frequency of the outcome. The relative frequency of an outcome is the number of times an experiment yields that outcome for a very large (ideally, infinite) number of trials. For instance, if a "fair" coin is tossed a very large number of times, then the relative frequency of a "heads-up" outcome is 0.5, or 50% (that is, one out of every two trials, on average, should be heads up). The probability is this relative frequency.

In probability theory, the **sample space** is a list of all possible outcomes of an experiment. For example, the sample space of tossing two coins is the set {HH, HT, TT, TH}, where H is heads and T is tails, and the sample space of rolling a six-sided die is the set {1, 2, 3, 4, 5, 6}. When conducting experiments with a large number of possible outcomes, it is important to determine the size of the sample space. The size of the sample space can be determined by using the fundamental counting principles and the rules of combinations and permutations.

A **random variable** is a function that corresponds to the outcome of some experiment or event, which is in turn dependent on "chance." For instance, the result of a tossed coin is a random variable: the outcome is either heads or tails, and each outcome has an associated probability. A **discrete variable** is one that can only take on certain specific values. For instance, the number of students in a class can only be a whole number (e.g., 15 or 16, but not 15.5). A **continuous variable**, such as the weight of an object, can take on a continuous range of values.

The probabilities for the possible values of a random variable constitute the **probability distribution** for that random variable. Probability distributions can be discrete, as with the case of the tossing of a coin (there are only two possible distinct outcomes), or they can be continuous, as with, for instance, the outside temperature at a given time of day. In this latter case, the probability is represented as a continuous function over a range of possible temperatures, and finite probabilities can only be measured in terms of ranges of temperatures rather than specific temperatures. This is to say that, for a continuous distribution, it is not meaningful to say "the probability that the outcome is x"; instead, only "the probability that the outcome is between x and Δx" is meaningful. (Note that if each potential outcome in a continuous distribution has a non-zero probability, then the sum of all the probabilities would be greater than one, since there are an infinite number of potential outcomes.) Specific probability distributions are presented later in this discussion.

Example: Find the sample space and construct a probability distribution for a six-sided die (with numbers 1 through 6) where the even numbers are twice as likely as the odd numbers to come up on a given roll (assume the even numbers are equally likely and the odd numbers are equally likely).

The sample space is simply the set of all possible outcomes that can arise in a given trial. For this die, the sample space is {1, 2, 3, 4, 5, 6}. To construct the associated probability distribution, note first that the sum of the probabilities must equal 1. Let the probability of rolling an odd number (1, 3, or 5) be x; the probability of rolling an even number (2, 4, or 6) is then $2x$.

$$1 = p(1) + p(2) + p(3) + p(4) + p(5) + p(6) = 3x + 6x = 9x \qquad x = \frac{1}{9}$$

The probability distribution can be shown as a histogram below.

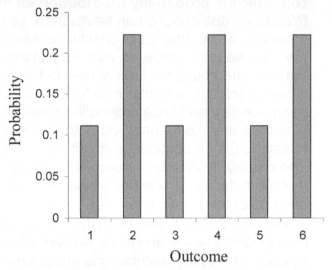

The sum of the probabilities for all the possible outcomes of a discrete distribution (or the integral of the continuous distribution over all possible values) must be equal to unity. The **expected value** of a probability distribution is the same as the **mean value** of a probability distribution. (See below for more discussion of mean values.) The expected value is thus a measure of the central tendency or average value for a random variable with a given probability distribution.

A **Bernoulli trial** is an experiment whose outcome is random and can be either of two possible outcomes, which are called "success" or "failure." Tossing a coin would be an example of a Bernoulli trial. The probability of success is represented by p, with the probability of failure being $q = 1 - p$. Bernoulli trials can be applied to any real-life situation in which there are only two possible outcomes. For example, concerning the birth of a child, the only two possible outcomes for the sex of the child are male or female.

Probability can also be expressed in terms of **odds**. Odds are defined as the ratio of the number of favorable outcomes to the number of unfavorable outcomes. The sum of the favorable outcomes and the unfavorable outcomes should always equal the total possible outcomes.

For example, given a bag of 12 red marbles and 7 green marbles, compute the odds of randomly selecting a red marble.

$$\text{Odds of red} = \frac{12}{19}$$

$$\text{Odds of not getting red} = \frac{7}{19}$$

In the case of flipping a coin, it is equally likely that a head or a tail will be tossed. The odds of tossing a head are 1:1. This is called **even odds**.

17B. Counting strategies (e.g. permutations and combinations)

A **permutation** is the number of possible arrangements of items, without repetition, where order of selection is important.
A **combination** is the number of possible arrangements, without repetition, where order of selection is not important.

Example: If any two numbers are selected from the set {1, 2, 3, 4}, list the possible permutations and combinations.

Combinations	Permutations
12, 13, 14, 23, 24, 34	12, 21, 13, 31, 14, 41,
	23, 32, 24, 42, 34, 43,
six ways	twelve ways

Note that the list of permutations includes 12 and 21 as separate possibilities since the order of selection is important. In the case of combinations, however, the order of selection is not important and, therefore, 12 is the same combination as 21. Hence, 21 is not listed separately as a possibility.
The number of permutations and combinations may also be found by using the formulae given below.

The number of possible permutations in selecting r objects from a set of n is given by

$$_nP_r = \frac{n!}{(n-r)!}$$

The notation $_nP_r$ is read "the number of permutations of n objects taken r at a time."

In our example, two objects are being selected from a set of four.

$$_4P_2 = \frac{4!}{(4-2)!}$$ Substitute known values.

$$_4P_2 = 12$$

The number of possible combinations in selecting r objects from a set of n is given by

$$_nC_r = \frac{n!}{(n-r)!r!}$$

The number of combinations when r objects are selected from n objects.

In our example,

$$_4C_2 = \frac{4!}{(4-2)!2!} \qquad \text{Substitute known values.}$$

$$_4C_2 = 6$$

It can be shown that $_nP_n$, the number of ways n objects can be arranged in a row, is equal to $n!$. We can think of the problem as n positions being filled one at a time. The first position can be filled in n ways using any one of the n objects. Since one of the objects has already been used, the second position can be filled only in $n-1$ ways. Similarly, the third position can be filled in $n-2$ ways and so on. Hence, the total number of possible arrangements of n objects in a row is given by

$$_nP_n = n(n-1)(n-2)........1 = n!$$

Example: Five books are placed in a row on a bookshelf. In how many different ways can they be arranged?
The number of possible ways in which 5 books can be arranged in a row is $5! = 1 \times 2 \times 3 \times 4 \times 5 = 120$.

The formula given above for $_nP_r$, **the number of possible permutations of r objects selected from n objects** can also be proven in a similar manner. If r positions are filled by selecting from n objects, the first position can be filled in n ways, the second position can be filled in $n-1$ ways and so on (as shown before). The rth position can be filled in $n-(r-1) = n-r+1$ ways. Hence,

$$_nP_r = n(n-1)(n-2).....(n-r+1) = \frac{n!}{(n-r)!}$$

The formula for the **number of possible combinations of r objects selected from n**, $_nC_r$, may be derived by using the above two formulae. For the same set of r objects, the number of permutations is $r!$. All of these permutations, however, correspond to the same combination. Hence,

$$_nC_r = \frac{_nP_r}{r!} = \frac{n!}{(n-r)!r!}$$

The number of permutations of n objects in a ring is given by $(n - 1)!$. This can be demonstrated by considering the fact that the number of permutations of n objects in a row is $n!$. When the objects are placed in a ring, moving every object one place to its left will result in the same arrangement. Moving each object two places to its left will also result in the same arrangement. We can continue this kind of movement up to n places to get the same arrangement. Thus the count $n!$ is n times too many when the objects are arranged in a ring. Hence, the number of permutations of n objects in a ring is given by $\frac{n!}{n} = (n-1)!$.

Example: There are 20 people at a meeting. Five of them are selected to lead a discussion. How many different combinations of five people can be selected from the group? If the five people are seated in a row, how many different seating permutations are possible? If the five people are seated around a circular table, how many possible permutations are there?

The number of possible combinations of 5 people selected from the group of 20 is

$$_{20}C_5 = \frac{20!}{15!5!} = \frac{16 \times 17 \times 18 \times 19 \times 20}{1 \times 2 \times 3 \times 4 \times 5} = \frac{1860480}{120} = 15504$$

The number of possible permutations of the five seated in a row is

$$_{20}P_5 = \frac{20!}{15!} = 16 \times 17 \times 18 \times 19 \times 20 = 1860480$$

The number of possible permutations of the five seated in a circle is

$$\frac{_{20}P_5}{5} = \frac{20!}{5 \times 15!} = \frac{16 \times 17 \times 18 \times 19 \times 20}{5} = 372096$$

If the set of n objects contains some objects that are exactly alike, the number of permutations will again be different than $n!$. For instance, if n_1 of the n objects are exactly alike, then switching those objects among themselves will result in the same arrangement. Since we already know that n_1 objects can be arranged in $n_1!$ ways, $n!$ must be reduced by a factor of $n_1!$ to get the correct number of permutations. Thus, the number of permutations of n objects of which n_1 are exactly alike is given by $\frac{n!}{n_1!}$. Generalizing this, we can say that **the number of different permutations of n objects of which n_1 are alike, n_2 are alike,... n_j are alike, is**

$$\frac{n!}{n_1!n_2!...n_j!} \text{ where } n_1 + n_2 ..... + n_j = n$$

Example: A box contains 3 red, 2 blue and 5 green marbles. If all the marbles are taken out of the box and arranged in a row, how many different permutations are possible?

The number of possible permutations is

$$\frac{10!}{3!2!5!} = \frac{6 \times 7 \times 8 \times 9 \times 10}{6 \times 2} = 2520$$

17C. Computing theoretical probabilities for simple and compound events

A **simple event** is one that describes a single outcome, whereas a **compound event** is made-up of two or more simple events. The following discussion uses the symbols $\cap$ to mean "and," $\cup$ to mean "or" and $P(x)$ to mean "the probability of x." Also, $N(x)$ means "the number of ways that x can occur."

Dependent and Independent Events
Dependent events occur when the probability of the second event depends on the outcome of the first event. For example, consider the two events: the home team wins the semifinal round (event A) and the home team wins the final round (event B). The probability of event B is contingent on the probability of event A. If the home team fails to win the semifinal round, it has a zero probability of winning in the final round. On the other hand, if the home team wins the semifinal round, then it may have a finite probability of winning in the final round. Symbolically, the probability of event B given event A is written $P(B|A)$. The conditional probability can be calculated according to the following definition.

$$P(B|A) = \frac{P(A \cap B)}{P(A)}$$

Consider a pair of dice: one red and one green. First the red die is rolled, followed by the green die. It is apparent that these events do not depend on each other, since the outcome of the roll of the green die is not affected by the outcome of the roll of the red die. The total probability of the two independent events can be found by multiplying the separate probabilities.

$$P(A \cap B) = P(A)P(B)$$

$$P(A \cap B) = \left(\frac{1}{6}\right)\left(\frac{1}{6}\right) = \frac{1}{36}$$

In many instances, however, events are not independent. Suppose a jar contains 12 red marbles and 8 blue marbles. If a marble is selected at random and then replaced, the probability of picking a certain color is the same in the second trial as it is in the first trial. If the marble is *not* replaced, then the probability of picking a certain color is *not* the same in the second trial, because the total number of marbles is decreased by one. This is an illustration of conditional probability. If R_n signifies selection of a red marble on the nth trial and B_n signifies selection of a blue marble on the nth trial, then the probability of selecting a red marble in two trials *with replacement* is

$$P(R_1 \cap R_2) = P(R_1)P(R_2) = \left(\frac{12}{20}\right)\left(\frac{12}{20}\right) = \frac{144}{400} = 0.36$$

The probability of selecting a red marble in two trials *without replacement* is

$$P(R_1 \cap R_2) = P(R_1)P(R|R_1) = \left(\frac{12}{20}\right)\left(\frac{11}{19}\right) = \frac{132}{360} \approx 0.367$$

Example: A car has a 75% probability of traveling 20,000 miles without breaking down. It has a 50% probability of traveling 10,000 additional miles without breaking down if it first makes it to 20,000 miles without breaking down. What is the probability that the car reaches 30,000 miles without breaking down?

Let event A be that the car reaches 20,000 miles without breaking down.

$$P(A) = 0.75$$

Event B is that the car travels an additional 10,000 miles without breaking down (assuming it didn't break down for the first 20,000 miles). Since event B is contingent on event A, write the probability as follows:

$$P(B|A) = 0.50$$

Use the conditional probability formula to find the probability that the car travels 30,000 miles $(A \cap B)$ without breaking down.

$$P(B|A) = \frac{P(A \cap B)}{P(A)}$$

$$0.50 = \frac{P(A \cap B)}{0.75}$$

$$P(A \cap B) = (0.50)(0.75) = 0.375$$

Thus, the car has a 37.5% probability of traveling 30,000 consecutive miles without breaking down.

Fundamental Counting Principles
The Addition Principle of Counting states that if A and B are arbitrary events, then the number of ways A and B can occur is given by

$$N(A \cup B) = N(A) + N(B) - N(A \cap B)$$

Furthermore, if A and B are **mutually exclusive** events, then

$$N(A \cup B) = N(A) + N(B)$$

Correspondingly, the probabilities associated with arbitrary events are

$$P(A \cup B) = P(A) + P(B) - P(A \cap B)$$

For mutually exclusive events,

$$P(A \cup B) = P(A) + P(B)$$

Example: In how many ways can you select a black card or a Jack from an ordinary deck of playing cards?

Let B denote selection of a black card and let J denote selection of a jack. Then, since half the cards (26) are black and four are jacks,

$$N(B) = 26$$

$$N(J) = 4$$

Also, since a card can be both black and a jack (the jack of spades and the jack of clubs),

$$N(B \cap J) = 2$$

Thus, the solution is

$$N(B \cup J) = N(B) + N(J) - N(B \cap J) = 26 + 4 - 2 = 28$$

Example: A travel agency offers 40 possible trips: 14 to Asia, 16 to Europe and 10 to South America. In how many ways can you select a trip to Asia or Europe through this agency?

Let A denote selection of a trip to Asia and let E denote selection of a trip to Europe. Since these are mutually exclusive events, then

$$N(A \cup E) = N(A) + N(E) = 14 + 16 = 30$$

Therefore, there are 30 ways you can select a trip to Asia or Europe.

The Multiplication Principle of Counting for Dependent Events states that if A and B are arbitrary events, then the number of ways that A and B can occur in a two-stage experiment is given by

$$N(A \cap B) = N(A)N(B|A)$$

where $N(B|A)$ is the number of ways B can occur given that A has already occurred. If A and B are mutually exclusive events, then

$$N(A \cap B) = N(A)N(B)$$

Also, the probabilities associated with arbitrary events are

$$P(A \cap B) = P(A)P(B|A)$$

For mutually exclusive events,

$$P(A \cap B) = P(A)P(B)$$

Example: How many ways from an ordinary deck of 52 cards can two jacks be drawn in succession if the first card is not replaced into the deck before the second card is drawn (that is, without replacement)?

This is a two-stage experiment. Let A be selection of a jack in the first draw and let B be selection of a jack in the second draw. It is clear that

$$N(A) = 4$$

If the first card drawn is a jack, however, then there are only three remaining jacks remaining for the second draw. Thus, drawing two cards without replacement means the events A and B are dependent, and

$$N(B|A) = 3$$

The solution is then

$$N(A \cap B) = N(A)N(B|A) = (4)(3) = 12$$

<u>Example</u>: How many six-letter code "words" can be formed if repetition of letters is not allowed?

Since these are code words, a word does not have to be in the dictionary; for example, *abcdef* could be a code word. Since the experiment requires choosing each letter without replacing the letters from previous selections, the experiment has six stages. Repetition is not allowed; thus, there are 26 choices for the first letter, 25 for the second, 24 for the third, 23 for the fourth, 22 for the fifth and 21 for the sixth. Therefore, if *A* is the selection of a six-letter code word without repetition, then

$$N(A) = (26)(25)(24)(23)(22)(21) = 165,765,600$$

There are over 165 million ways to choose a six-letter code word with six unique letters.

Finite Probability
Using the fundamental counting principles described above, finite probability problems can be solved. Generally, finding the probability of a particular event or set of events involves dividing the number of ways the particular event can take place by the total number of possible outcomes for the experiment. Thus, by appropriately counting these possible outcomes using the above rules, probabilities can be determined.

<u>Example</u>: Determine the probability of rolling three even numbers on three successive rolls of a six-sided die.

This is a three-stage experiment. First, determine the total number of possible outcomes for three rolls of a die. For each roll,

$$N(\text{roll}) = 6$$

There are three possible even rolls for a die: 2, 4 and 6.

$$N(\text{even}) = 3$$

The probability of rolling an even number on any particular roll is then

$$P(\text{even}) = \frac{N(\text{even})}{N(\text{roll})} = \frac{3}{6} = \frac{1}{2}$$

For three successive rolls, use the multiplication rule for mutually exclusive events.

$$P(3 \text{ even rolls}) = P(\text{even})^3 = \left(\frac{1}{2}\right)^3 = \frac{1}{8} = 0.125$$

Thus, the probability of rolling three successive even numbers using a six-sided die is 0.125.

Example: Find the probability of spinning 6 and then spinning 6 again on a spinner with 8 sections:

Since the compound events are independent, spinning 6 once on the spinner does not affect the probability of spinning 6 again on the spinner.

Using the formula above, P(6 and 6)
$= P(6) \cdot P(6)$
1 of the 8 equal areas is labeled 6, so there is 1 chance in 8 that the spinner will land on 6.

$\dfrac{1}{8}\left(\dfrac{1}{8}\right) = \dfrac{1}{64}$, the probability of spinning 6 two times in a row.

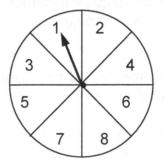

17D. Using simulations to explore real-world situations

Simulations of random events or variables can be helpful in making informal inferences about theoretical probability distributions. Although simulations can involve use of physical situations that bear some similarity to the situation of interest, often times simulations involve computer modeling.

One of the crucial aspects of modeling probability using a computer program is the need for a random number that can be used to "randomize" the aspect of the program that corresponds to the event or variable. Although there is no function on a computer that can provide a truly random number, most programming languages have some function designed to produce a **pseudorandom number**. A pseudorandom number is not truly random, but it is sufficiently unpredictable that it can be used as a random number in many contexts.

Pseudorandom numbers can serve as the basis for simulation of rolling a die, flipping a coin, selecting an object from a collection of different objects, and a range of other situations. If, for instance, the pseudorandom number generator produces a number between zero and 1, simply divide up that range in accordance with the probabilities of each particular outcome. (For instance, assign 0 to 0.5 as heads and 0.5 to 1 as tails for the flip of a fair coin.) By performing a number of simulated trials and tallying the results, empirical probability distributions can be created.

Ideally, as the number of trials goes to infinity, the empirical probability distribution should approach the theoretical distribution. As a result, by performing a sufficiently large number of trials (this number must be at least somewhat justified for the particular situation) should allow informal inferences based on that data. Such inferences, however, must take into account the limitations of the computer, such as the inability to perform an infinite number of trials in finite time and the numerical inaccuracies that are an inherent part of computer programming.

17E. Connections between geometry and probability (e.g. probability as the ratio of 2 areas)

Geometric probability involves studying the probabilities of geometric objects and area, length, volume, etc.

<u>Example:</u> Three semicircles with diameters of 2, 4 and 6 cm are organized as shown. If a point inside the figure is randomly chosen, what is the probability that the point is inside of the shaded area?

Find the ratio of the area of the shaded region to the area of the entire semi-circle. The area of the semi-circle is $\frac{1}{2}\pi r^2$.

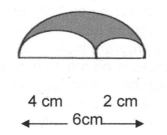

4 cm   2 cm

← ——— 6cm ——— →

The area of the entire semi-circle, A_1 is $A_1 = \frac{1}{2}\pi 3^2 = 4.5\pi$. Find the area of A_u, unshaded area:

$$A_u = \left[\frac{1}{2}\pi 2^2\right] + \left[\frac{1}{2}\pi 1^2\right] = 2\pi + 0.5\pi = 2.5\pi$$

Subtract to find the shaded area, A_S:
$$A_S = 4.5\pi - 2.5\pi = 2\pi$$

The ratio of the shaded area to the total area is:
$$\frac{A_S}{A_1} = \frac{2\pi}{4.5\pi} = \frac{2}{4.5} = \frac{4}{9},$$

$\therefore$ the probability that the point is in the shaded area is $\frac{4}{9}$.

17F. Using probability models to understand real-world phenomena

The following discussion presents three common probability distributions that are used to model different kinds of real life situations. These distributions are the normal distribution, the binomial distribution and the exponential distribution.

The Normal Distribution
A normal distribution is the distribution associated with most sets of real-world data. It is frequently called a **bell curve**. A normal distribution has a **continuous random variable** X with mean μ and variance σ^2. The normal distribution has the following form.

$$f(x) = \frac{1}{\sigma\sqrt{2\pi}}e^{-\frac{1}{2}\left(\frac{x-\mu}{\sigma}\right)^2}$$

The total area under the normal curve is one. Thus,
$$\int_{-\infty}^{\infty} f(x)\,dx = 1$$

Since the area under the curve of this function is one, the distribution can be used to determine probabilities through integration. If a continuous random variable x follows the normal distribution, then the probability that x has a value between a and b is

$$P(a < X \le b) = \int_a^b f(x)\,dx = F(b) - F(a)$$

Since this integral is difficult to evaluate analytically, tables of values are often used. Often, however, the tables use the integral

$$\frac{1}{\sqrt{2\pi}} \int_a^b e^{-\frac{t^2}{2}} dt = F(b) - F(a)$$

To use this form, simply convert x values to t values using

$$t = \frac{x_i - \mu}{\sigma}$$

where x_i is a particular value for the random variable X. This formula is often called the **z-score**.

<u>Example:</u> Albert's Bagel Shop's morning customer load follows a normal distribution, with **mean** (average) 50 and **standard deviation** 10. Determine the probability that the number of customers on a particular morning will be less than 42.

First, convert to a form that allows use of normal distribution tables:

$$t = \frac{x - \mu}{\sigma} = \frac{42 - 50}{10} = -0.8$$

Next, use a table to find the probability corresponding to the z-score. The actual integral in this case is

$$P(X < 42) = \frac{1}{\sqrt{2\pi}} \int_{-\infty}^{-0.8} e^{-\frac{t^2}{2}} dt$$

The table gives a value for $x = 0.8$ of 0.7881. To find the value for $x < -0.8$, subtract this result from one.

$$P(X < 42) = 1 - 0.7881 = 0.2119$$

This means that there is about a 21.2% chance that there will be fewer than 42 customers in a given morning.

Example: The scores on Mr. Rogers' statistics exam follow a normal distribution with mean 85 and standard deviation 5. A student is wondering what is the probability that she will score between a 90 and a 95 on her exam.

To compute $P(90 < x < 95)$, first compute the z-scores for each raw score.

$$z_{90} = \frac{90 - 85}{5} = 1$$

$$z_{95} = \frac{95 - 85}{5} = 2$$

Use the tables to find $P(1 < z < 2)$. To do this, subtract as follows.

$$P(1 < z < 2) = P(z < 2) - P(z < 1)$$

The table yields

$$P(1 < z < 2) = 0.9772 - 0.8413 = 0.1359$$

It can then be concluded that there is a 13.6% chance that the student will score between a 90 and a 95 on her exam.

The Binomial Distribution

The binomial distribution is a probability distribution for discrete random variables and is expressed as follows.

$$f(x) = \binom{n}{x} p^x q^{n-x}$$

where a sequence of n trials of an experiment are performed and where p is the probability of "success" and q is the probability of "failure." The value x is the number of times the experiment yields a successful outcome. Notice that this probability function is the product of p^x (the probability of successful outcomes in x trials) and q^{n-x} (the probability of unsuccessful outcomes in the remainder of the trials). The factor $\binom{n}{x}$ indicates that the x successful trials can be chosen $\binom{n}{x}$ ways (combinations) from the n total trials. (In other words, the successful trials may occur at different points in the sequence.)

<u>Example:</u> A loaded coin has a probability 0.6 of landing heads up. What is the probability of getting three heads in four successive tosses?

Use the binomial distribution. In this case, p is the probability of the coin landing heads up, and $q = 1 - p$ is the probability of the coin landing tails up. Also, the number of "successful" trials (heads up) is 3. Then,

$$f(3) = \binom{4}{3}(0.6)^3(1-0.6)^{4-3}$$

$$f(3) = \frac{4!}{3!(4-3)!}(0.6)^3(0.4)^1$$

$$f(3) = \frac{24}{6(1)}(0.216)(0.4) = 0.3456$$

Thus, there is a 34.56% chance that the loaded coin will land heads up three out of four times.

The Exponential Distribution

The exponential distribution is for continuous random variables and has the following form.

$$f(x) = \lambda e^{-\lambda x}$$

Here, $x \geq 0$. The parameter λ is called the **rate parameter**. For instance, the exponential distribution is often applied to failure rates. If a certain device has a failure rate λ failures per hour, then the probability that a device has failed at time T hours is

$$P(T) = \lambda \int_0^T e^{-\lambda t}dt = -\lambda \frac{1}{\lambda}e^{-\lambda t}\Big|_0^T = -\left[e^{-\lambda T} - e^0\right] = 1 - e^{-\lambda T}$$

Example: Testing has revealed that a newly designed widget has a failure rate of 1 per 5,000 hours of use. What is the probability that a particular part will be operational after a year of continual use?

Use the formula given above for the exponential distribution.

$$P(1\,\text{year}) = 1 - e^{-\lambda(1\,\text{year})}$$

Write λ in terms of failures per year.

$$\lambda = \frac{1\,\text{failure}}{5,000\,\text{hours}}\left(\frac{24\,\text{hours}}{1\,\text{day}}\right)\left(\frac{365\,\text{days}}{1\,\text{year}}\right) = 1.752\,\frac{\text{failures}}{\text{year}}$$

Then

$$P(1\,\text{year}) = 1 - e^{-1.752(1)} = 1 - 0.173 = 0.827$$

Thus, there is an 82.7% probability that the device will be operational after one year of continual use.

Competency 0018 Understand the properties of trigonometric functions and identities.

18A. Degree and radian measure

The argument of a trigonometric function is an angle that is typically expressed in either degrees or radians. A **degree** constitutes an angle corresponding to a sector that is 1/360th of a circle. Therefore, a circle has 360 degrees. A **radian**, on the other hand, is the angle corresponding to a sector of a circle where the arc length of the sector is equal to the radius of the circle. In the case of the unit circle (a circle of radius 1), the circumference is 2π. Thus, there are 2π radians in a circle. Conversion between degrees and radians is a simple matter of using the ratio between the total degrees in a circle and the total radians in a circle.

$$(\text{degrees}) = \frac{180}{\pi} \times (\text{radians})$$

$$(\text{radians}) = \frac{\pi}{180} \times (\text{degrees})$$

Below is a chart showing the relationship between degrees and radians:

DEGREES

0	30	45	60	90	120	135	150	180	210	225	240	270	300	315	330	360
0	$\frac{\pi}{6}$	$\frac{\pi}{4}$	$\frac{\pi}{3}$	$\frac{\pi}{2}$	$\frac{2\pi}{3}$	$\frac{3\pi}{4}$	$\frac{5\pi}{6}$	π	$\frac{7\pi}{6}$	$\frac{5\pi}{4}$	$\frac{4\pi}{3}$	$\frac{3\pi}{2}$	$\frac{5\pi}{3}$	$\frac{7\pi}{4}$	$\frac{11\pi}{6}$	2π

RADIANS

18B. Right Triangle Trigonometry

Trigonometric functions can be related to right triangles: each trigonometric function corresponds to a ratio of certain sides of the triangle with respect to a particular angle. Thus, given the generic right triangle diagram below, the following functions can be specified.

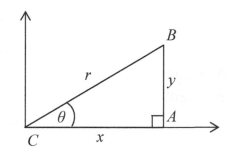

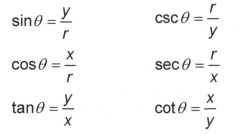

$$\sin\theta = \frac{y}{r} \qquad\qquad \csc\theta = \frac{r}{y}$$

$$\cos\theta = \frac{x}{r} \qquad\qquad \sec\theta = \frac{r}{x}$$

$$\tan\theta = \frac{y}{x} \qquad\qquad \cot\theta = \frac{x}{y}$$

Based on these definitions, the unknown characteristics of a particular right triangle can be calculated based on certain known characteristics. For instance, if the hypotenuse and one of the adjacent angles are both known, the lengths of the other two sides of the triangle can be calculated.

Example: Find the missing side x in the following triangle.

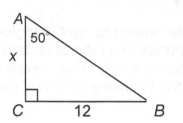

1. Identify the known values. Angle $A = 50$ degrees and the side opposite the given angle is 12. The missing side is the adjacent leg.

2. The information suggests the use of the tangent function

$$\tan A = \frac{\text{opposite}}{\text{adjacent}}$$

3. Write the function.

$$\tan 50 = \frac{12}{x}$$

4. Substitute.

$$1.192 = \frac{12}{x}$$

5. Solve.

$$x(1.192) = 12$$

$$x = 10.069$$

Remember that since angle A and angle B are complementary, angle $B = 90 - 50$ or 40 degrees.

Using this information we could have solved for the same side only this time x is the leg opposite from angle B.

$$\tan B = \frac{\text{opposite}}{\text{adjacent}}$$

1. Write the formula.

$$\tan 40 = \frac{x}{12}$$

2. Substitute.

$$12(.839) = x$$

$$10.069 \approx x$$

3. Solve.

Now that the two sides of the triangle are known, the third side can be found using the Pythagorean Theorem.

Example:

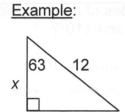

In the triangle ABC, an acute angle is 63 degrees and the length of the hypotenuse is 12. The missing side is the one adjacent to the given angle.

The appropriate trigonometric ratio to use would be cosine since we are looking for the adjacent side and we have the length of the hypotenuse.

$$Cos x = \frac{adjacent}{hypotenuse}$$ 1. Write formula.

$$Cos 63 = \frac{x}{12}$$ 2. Substitute known values.

$$0.454 = \frac{x}{12}$$ 3. Solve.

$$x = 5.448$$

18C. The Laws of Sines and Cosines

Trigonometric functions can also be applied to non-right triangles by way of the law of sines and the law of cosines.

The Law of Sines
Definition: For any triangle ABC, where a, b, and c are the lengths of the sides opposite angles A, B, and C respectively.

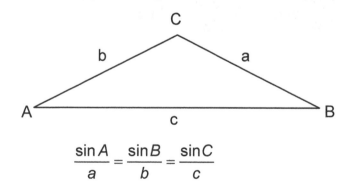

$$\frac{\sin A}{a} = \frac{\sin B}{b} = \frac{\sin C}{c}$$

Example: What is the ratio of the 3 sides of the isosceles triangle below with angles measuring 35^0, 35^0 and 110^0?

Using a calculator or table, find $\sin35^0$ and $\sin110^0$:
$\sin35^0 = .574$ and $\sin110^0 = .939$

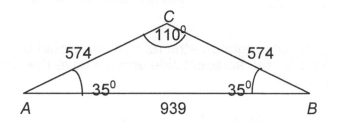

According to the Law of Sines, the ratio of the sides is
$574 : 939 : 574$

If the opposite side of the 110^0 angle is 5" long, how long are the sides opposite the 35^0 angles?

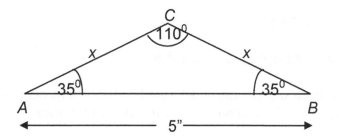

We know that the ratio is $574 : 939 : 574$. Therefore,

$$\frac{x}{5} = \frac{.574}{.939} \text{ and } x = 5\left(\frac{.574}{.939}\right) = 3.06"$$

Example: An inlet is 140 feet wide. The lines of sight from each bank to an approaching ship are 79 degrees and 58 degrees. What are the distances from each bank to the ship?

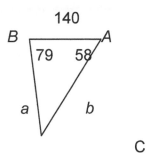

1. Draw and label a sketch.

$$180 - (79 + 58) = 43$$
degrees.

$$\frac{\sin A}{a} = \frac{\sin B}{b} = \frac{\sin C}{c}$$

3. Write formula.

Side opposite 79 degree angle:

$$\frac{\sin 79}{b} = \frac{\sin 43}{140}$$

4. Substitute.

$$b = \frac{140(.9816)}{.6820} = 201.5 \text{ ft}$$

5. Solve.

Side opposite 58 degree angle:

$$\frac{\sin 58}{a} = \frac{\sin 43}{140}$$

6. Substitute.

$$a = \frac{140(.848)}{.6820} = 174.1 \text{ ft}$$

7. Solve.

The Law of Cosines

Definition: For any triangle ABC, when given two sides and the included angle, the other side can be found using one of the formulas below:

$$a^2 = b^2 + c^2 - (2bc)\cos A$$
$$b^2 = a^2 + c^2 - (2ac)\cos B$$
$$c^2 = a^2 + b^2 - (2ab)\cos C$$

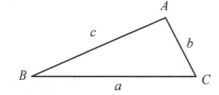

Similarly, when given three sides of a triangle, the included angles can be found using the derivation:

$$\cos A = \frac{b^2 + c^2 - a^2}{2bc}$$
$$\cos B = \frac{a^2 + c^2 - b^2}{2ac}$$
$$\cos C = \frac{a^2 + b^2 - c^2}{2ab}$$

<u>Example</u>: Solve triangle ABC, if angle $B = 87.5°$, $a = 12.3$, and $c = 23.2$. (Compute to the nearest tenth).

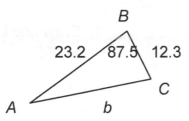

1. Draw and label a sketch.

Find side b.

$b^2 = a^2 + c^2 - (2ac)\cos B$ 2. Write the formula.

$b^2 = (12.3)^2 + (23.2)^2 - 2(12.3)(23.2)(\cos 87.5)$ 3. Substitute.

$b^2 = 664.636$

$b = 25.8$ (rounded)

4. Solve.

Use the law of sines to find angle A.

$\dfrac{\sin A}{a} = \dfrac{\sin B}{b}$ 1. Write formula.

$\dfrac{\sin A}{12.3} = \dfrac{\sin 87.5}{25.8}$ 2. Substitute.

$\sin A = 0.47629$ 3. Solve.

Angle $A = 28.4$

Therefore, angle $C = 180 - (87.5 + 28.4)$
$$= 64.1$$

Example: Solve triangle ABC if $a = 15$, $b = 21$, and $c = 18$. (Round to the nearest tenth).

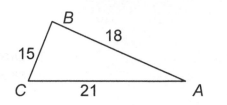

1. Draw and label a sketch.

Find angle A.

$$\cos A = \frac{b^2 + c^2 - a^2}{2bc}$$ 2. Write formula.

$$\cos A = \frac{21^2 + 18^2 - 15^2}{2(21)(18)}$$ 3. Substitute.

$$\cos A = 0.714$$ 4. Solve.
$$\text{Angle } A = 44.4$$

Find angle B.

$$\cos B = \frac{a^2 + c^2 - b^2}{2ac}$$ 5. Write formula.

$$\cos B = \frac{15^2 + 18^2 - 21^2}{2(15)(18)}$$ 6. Substitute.

$$\cos B = 0.2$$ 7. Solve.
$$\text{Angle } B = 78.5$$

Therefore, angle $C = 180 - (44.4 + 78.5)$
$$= 57.1$$

18D. **The relationship between the unit circle and trigonometric functions**

Trigonometry can also be understood in terms of a unit circle on the *x-y* plane. A unit circle has a radius of 1.

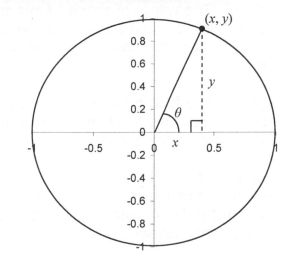

Notice that any given radius forms a right triangle with legs having lengths equal to the position of the point on the circle (*x*, *y*). Since the radius is equal to 1, the values of *x* and *y* are the following:

$$x = \cos\theta$$
$$y = \sin\theta$$

All the properties of trigonometric relationships for right triangles also apply in this case as well.

The equation of the unit circle is $x^2 + y^2 = 1$.

From the unit circle, we can also determine that the trigonometric functions sine and cosine functions are periodic functions.

18E. Graphs and Properties (e.g. amplitude, period, phase shift) of trigonometric functions and their inverses

The trigonometric functions sine, cosine, and tangent are **periodic functions**. The values of periodic functions repeat on regular intervals. Period, amplitude, and phase shift are key properties of periodic functions that can be determined by observation of the graph.

The **period** of a function is the smallest domain containing the complete cycle of the function. For example, the period of a sine or cosine function is the distance between the peaks of the graph.

The **amplitude** of a function is half the distance between the maximum and minimum values of the function.
Phase shift is the amount of horizontal displacement of a function from its original position.

Below is a generic sine/cosine graph with the period and amplitude labeled.

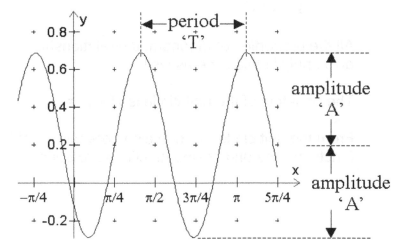

Properties of the graphs of basic trigonometric functions

Function	Period	Amplitude
y = sin x	2π radians	1
y = cos x	2π radians	1
y = tan x	π radians	undefined

Below are the graphs of the basic trigonometric functions,

(a) y = sin x; (b) y = cos x; and (c) y= tan x.

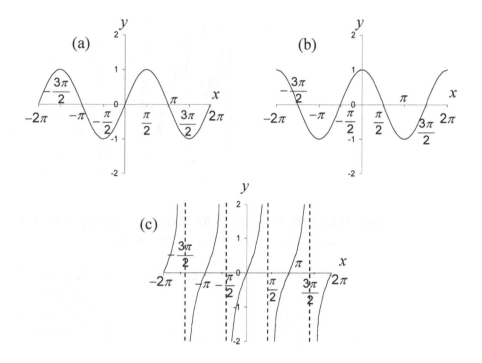

Note that the graph of the tangent function has asymptotes at
$x = \dfrac{2n-1}{2}\pi$, where n = 0, ±1, ±2, ±3,….

The graphs of the reciprocal trigonometric functions are shown below, with (a) $y = \csc x$; (b) $y = \sec x$; and (c) $y = \cot x$.

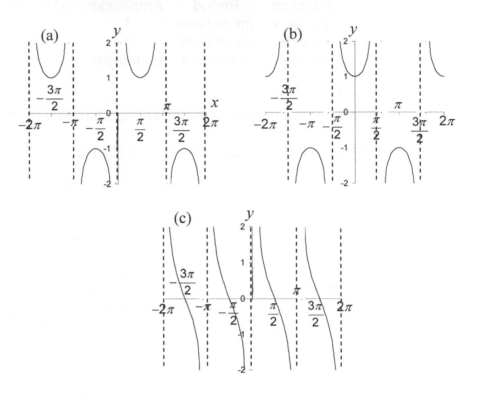

The phase and amplitude for the three reciprocal trigonometric functions are provided in the table below.

Function	Period (radians)	Amplitude
csc θ	2π	Undefined
sec θ	2π	Undefined
cot θ	π	Undefined

Graphing a trigonometric function by hand typically requires a calculator for determining the value of the function for various angles. Nevertheless, simple functions can often be graphed by simply determining the amplitude, period and phase shift. Once these parameters are known, the graph can be sketched approximately. The amplitude of a simple sine or cosine function is simply the multiplicative constant (or function) associated with the trigonometric function. Thus, $2\cos x$, for instance, has an amplitude of 2. The phase shift is typically just a constant added to the argument of the function. For instance, $\sin(x + 1)$ includes a phase shift of 1. A positive phase shift constant indicates that the graph of the function is shifted to the left; a negative phase shift indicates that the graph is shifted to the right.

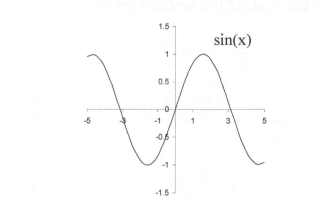

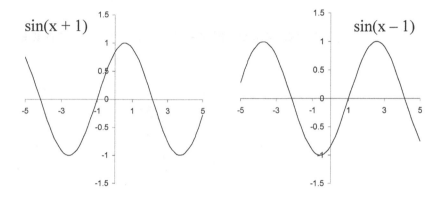

Example: Sketch the graph of the function $f(x) = 4\sin\left(2x + \dfrac{\pi}{2}\right)$.

Notice, first, that the amplitude of the function is 4. Since there is no constant term added to the sine function, the function is centered on the *x*-axis. Find crucial points on the graph by setting *f* equal to zero and solving for *x* to find the roots.

$$f(x) = 0 = 4\sin\left(2x + \dfrac{\pi}{2}\right)$$

$$\sin\left(2x + \dfrac{\pi}{2}\right) = 0$$

$$2x + \dfrac{\pi}{2} = n\pi$$

In the above expression, *n* is an integer.

$$2x = \left(n - \dfrac{1}{2}\right)\pi$$

$$x = \left(n - \dfrac{1}{2}\right)\dfrac{\pi}{2}$$

So, the roots of the function are at

$$x = \pm\frac{\pi}{4}, \pm\frac{3\pi}{4}, \pm\frac{5\pi}{4}, \ldots$$

The maxima and minima of the function are halfway between successive roots. Determine the location of a maximum by testing the function. Try $x = 0$.

$$f(0) = 4\sin\left(2[0] + \frac{\pi}{2}\right) = 4\sin\left(\frac{\pi}{2}\right) = 4$$

Thus, f is maximized at $x = 4$. The function can then be sketched.

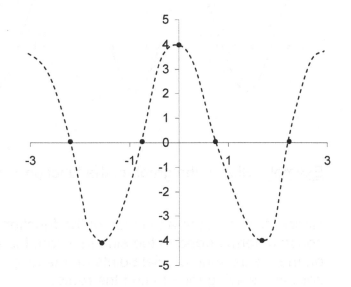

Inverse Trigonometric Functions

The inverse sine function of x is written as arcsin x or $\sin^{-1}x$ and is the angle for which the sine is x; i.e., $\sin(\text{arcsin } x) = x$. Since the sine function is periodic, many values of arcsin x correspond to a particular x. In order to define arcsin as a function, therefore, its range needs to be restricted.

The function **y = arcsin x** has a domain [-1,1] and range $\left[-\frac{\pi}{2}, \frac{\pi}{2}\right]$.

In some books, a restricted inverse function is denoted by a capitalized beginning letter such as in Sin^{-1} or arctan. The arcsin function is shown below.

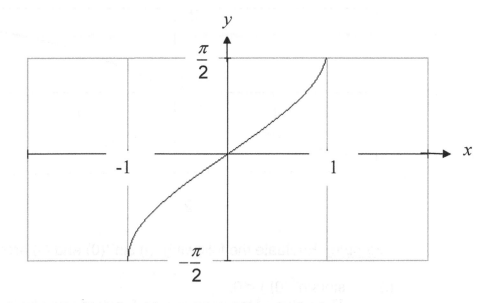

The inverse cosine and tangent functions are defined in the same way: cos(arccos x) = x; tan(arctan x) = x.

The function **y = arccos x** has a domain [-1,1] and range $[0, \pi]$.
The graph of this function is shown below.

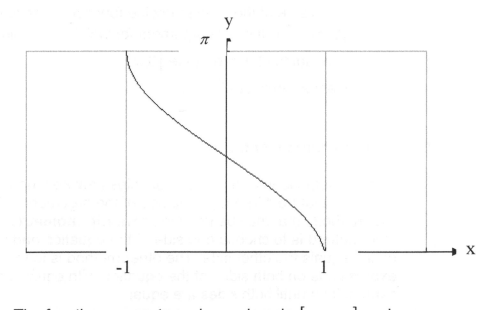

The function **y = arctan x** has a domain $[-\infty, +\infty]$ and range $\left[-\dfrac{\pi}{2}, \dfrac{\pi}{2}\right]$. The plot of the function is shown below.

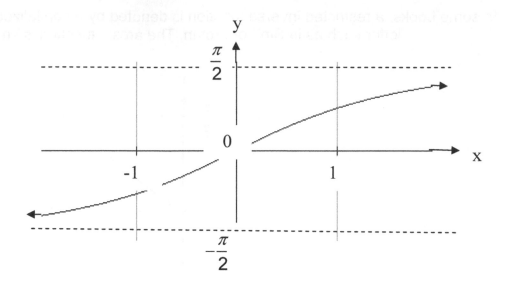

Example: Evaluate the following: (i) sin⁻¹(0) and (ii) arccos(-1)

(i) $\sin(\sin^{-1}(0)) = 0$.
        The value of the inverse sine function must lie in the range
        $\left[-\dfrac{\pi}{2}, \dfrac{\pi}{2}\right]$. Since 0 is the only argument in the range $\left[-\dfrac{\pi}{2}, \dfrac{\pi}{2}\right]$
        for which the sine function is zero, $\sin^{-1}(0) = 0$.

(ii) $\cos\left(\arccos(-1)\right) = -1$
        The value of the inverse cosine function must lie in the range
        $[0, \pi]$. π is the only argument for which the cosine function
        is equal to -1 in the range $[0, \pi]$.
        Hence, $\arccos(-1) = \pi$.

18F.   Trigonometric Identities

Trigonometric identities are relationships between trigonometric functions that hold true for all values of the arguments. There are two methods that may be used to prove **trigonometric identities**. One method is to choose one side of the equation and manipulate it until it equals the other side. The other method is to replace expressions on both sides of the equation with equivalent expressions until both sides are equal.

There are a range of trigonometric identities, including reciprocal and Pythagorean identities, listed below. These basic identities are often used to prove other, more complex ones.

Reciprocal identities:

$$\sin x = \frac{1}{\csc x} \qquad\qquad \sin x \csc x = 1 \qquad\qquad \csc x = \frac{1}{\sin x}$$

$$\cos x = \frac{1}{\sec x} \qquad\qquad \cos x \sec x = 1 \qquad\qquad \sec x = \frac{1}{\cos x}$$

$$\tan x = \frac{1}{\cot x} \qquad\qquad \tan x \cot x = 1 \qquad\qquad \cot x = \frac{1}{\tan x}$$

$$\tan x = \frac{\sin x}{\cos x} \qquad\qquad\qquad\qquad\qquad\qquad \cot x = \frac{\cos x}{\sin x}$$

Pythagorean identities:

$$\sin^2 x + \cos^2 x = 1 \qquad 1 + \tan^2 x = \sec^2 x \qquad 1 + \cot^2 x = \csc^2 x$$

<u>Example:</u> Prove that $\sin^2 \theta + \cos^2 \theta = 1$.

Use definitions of the sine and cosine functions from right triangle trigonometry given in section **18 B.** (x and y are the legs of the triangle and r is the hypotenuse).

$$\left(\frac{y}{r}\right)^2 + \left(\frac{x}{r}\right)^2 = 1$$

$$\frac{x^2 + y^2}{r^2} = 1$$

But the numerator of the above fraction, by the Pythagorean theorem, is simply r^2. Thus

$$\frac{r^2}{r^2} = 1$$

The identity has been proven.

Example: Prove that $\cot x + \tan x = \csc x \sec x$.

Use the reciprocal identities to convert the left side of the equation to sines and cosines. Then combine terms using a common denominator.

$$\frac{\cos x}{\sin x} + \frac{\sin x}{\cos x}$$

$$\frac{\cos^2 x}{\sin x \cos x} + \frac{\sin^2 x}{\sin x \cos x} = \frac{\sin^2 x + \cos^2 x}{\sin x \cos x} = \frac{1}{\sin x \cos x}$$

Finally, convert the expression using the reciprocal identities.

$$\frac{1}{\sin x \cos x} = \csc x \sec x$$

The identity is then proven.

Trigonometric functions involving the sum or difference of two angles can be expressed in terms of functions of each individual angle using the following formulae.

$$\cos(\alpha + \beta) = \cos\alpha\cos\beta - \sin\alpha\sin\beta$$
$$\cos(\alpha - \beta) = \cos\alpha\cos\beta + \sin\alpha\sin\beta$$
$$\sin(\alpha + \beta) = \sin\alpha\cos\beta + \cos\alpha\sin\beta$$
$$\sin(\alpha - \beta) = \sin\alpha\cos\beta - \cos\alpha\sin\beta$$
$$\tan(\alpha + \beta) = \frac{\tan\alpha + \tan\beta}{1 - \tan\alpha\tan\beta}$$
$$\tan(\alpha - \beta) = \frac{\tan\alpha - \tan\beta}{1 + \tan\alpha\tan\beta}$$

Example: Evaluate the following using the appropriate identity:

$$\sin(35°)\cos(55°) + \cos(35°)\sin(55°)$$

Using the sine sum formula,

$$\sin 35° \cos 55° + \cos 35° \sin 55°$$
$$= \sin(35° + 55°) = \sin(90°) = 1$$

Example: Show that $\dfrac{\cos(x+y)}{\cos x \cos y} = 1 - \tan x \tan y$

Applying the cosine sum formula

$$\frac{\cos(x+y)}{\cos x \cos y} = \frac{\cos x \cos y - \sin x \sin y}{\cos x \cos y}$$

$$= 1 - \frac{\sin x \sin y}{\cos x \cos y}$$

$$= 1 - \tan x \tan y$$

The **double angle identities** can be obtained using the sum formulae:

$$\cos 2\alpha = \cos^2 \alpha - \sin^2 \alpha$$

$$\sin 2\alpha = 2 \sin \alpha \cos \alpha$$

$$\tan 2\alpha = \frac{2 \tan \alpha}{1 - \tan^2 \alpha}$$

Example: Show that $\sin(3x) = \sin x \left(3 \cos^2 x - \sin^2 x\right)$

$$\sin(3x) = \sin(2x + x)$$

$$= \sin 2x \cos x + \cos 2x \sin x \qquad \text{Sine Sum Formula}$$

$$= 2 \sin x \cos x \cos x$$

$$+ \left(\cos^2 x - \sin^2 x\right) \sin x \qquad \text{Double Angle Identities}$$

$$= 2 \sin x \cos^2 x + \sin x \cos^2 x - \sin^3 x$$

$$= 3 \sin x \cos^2 x - \sin^3 x$$

$$= \sin x \left(3 \cos^2 x - \sin^2 x\right)$$

The **half angle identities** can be derived by solving the double angle identities for the sine, cosine or tangent of a single angle.

$$\cos\frac{\alpha}{2} = \pm\sqrt{\frac{1+\cos\alpha}{2}}$$

$$\sin\frac{\alpha}{2} = \pm\sqrt{\frac{1-\cos\alpha}{2}}$$

$$\tan\frac{\alpha}{2} = \pm\sqrt{\frac{1-\cos\alpha}{1+\cos\alpha}}$$

The following are some **identities for the inverse trigonometric functions**:

$$\csc^{-1}(x) = \sin^{-1}(1/x) \text{ for } |x| \geq 1$$
$$\sec^{-1}(x) = \cos^{-1}(1/x) \text{ for } |x| \geq 1$$

$$\cot^{-1}(x) = \begin{cases} \tan^{-1}(1/x) & \text{for } x > 0 \\ \tan^{-1}(1/x) + \pi & \text{for } x < 0 \\ \pi/2 & \text{for } x = 0 \end{cases}$$

$$\sin^{-1}x = \cos^{-1}(\sqrt{1-x^2}) \qquad \cos^{-1}x = \sin^{-1}(\sqrt{1-x^2})$$

$$\tan^{-1}x = \cos^{-1}\left(\frac{1}{\sqrt{1+x^2}}\right) \qquad \cos^{-1}x = \tan^{-1}\left(\frac{\sqrt{1-x^2}}{x}\right)$$

$$\tan^{-1}x = \sin^{-1}\left(\frac{x}{\sqrt{1+x^2}}\right) \qquad \sin^{-1}x = \tan^{-1}\left(\frac{x}{\sqrt{1-x^2}}\right)$$

Example: Simplify the expression $\cos(\arcsin x) + \sin(\arccos x)$

$$\arcsin x = \arccos(\sqrt{1-x^2}) \quad \text{identity}$$
$$\Rightarrow \cos(\arcsin x) = \sqrt{1-x^2}$$
$$\arccos x = \arcsin(\sqrt{1-x^2}) \quad \text{identity}$$
$$\Rightarrow \sin(\arccos x) = \sqrt{1-x^2}$$

Hence, $\cos(\arcsin x) + \sin(\arccos x) = \sqrt{1-x^2} + \sqrt{1-x^2} = 2\sqrt{1-x^2}$

Example: Using the identities given above, prove the identity

$$\sin^{-1} x + \cos^{-1} x = \frac{\pi}{2}$$

Since $\sin\left(\dfrac{\pi}{2}\right) = 1$, the identity may be proven by showing that

$$\sin\left(\sin^{-1} x + \cos^{-1} x\right) = 1$$

$$\sin\left(\sin^{-1} x + \cos^{-1} x\right) = \sin(\sin^{-1} x)\cos(\cos^{-1} x)$$

$$+ \cos(\sin^{-1} x)\sin(\cos^{-1} x) \quad \text{sine sum formula}$$

$$= x \cdot x + \sqrt{1-x^2}\sqrt{1-x^2} \qquad \text{inverse identities}$$

$$= x^2 + 1 - x^2 = 1$$

Other similar identities include the following:

$$\tan^{-1} x + \cot^{-1} x = \pi\!/\!{}_2$$

$$\sec^{-1} x + \csc^{-1} x = \pi\!/\!{}_2$$

18G. Solving Trigonometric Equations

Unlike trigonometric identities that are true for all values of the defined variable, trigonometric equations and inequalities are true for some, but not all, of the values of the variable. Most often, trigonometric equations are solved for values between 0 and 360 degrees or 0 and 2π radians. For inequalities, the solution is often a set of intervals, since trigonometric functions are periodic. Solving trigonometric problems is largely the same as solving algebraic equations. Care must be taken, however, due to the periodic nature of trigonometric functions. This often yields multiple (or an infinite number of) solutions.

Trigonometric identities, including sum and difference formulas, are often indispensable in the problem-solving process. These identities allow many complicated functions to be simplified to forms that are more easily managed algebraically.

Some algebraic operation, such as squaring both sides of an equation, will yield extraneous answers. Avoid incorrect solutions by remembering to check all solutions to be sure they satisfy the original equation.

Example: Solve the following equation for x: $\cos x = 1 - \sin x$, where $0° \le x \le 360°$.

Start by squaring both sides of the equation.

$$\cos^2 x = (1 - \sin x)^2 = 1 - 2\sin x + \sin^2 x$$

Substitute using the Pythagorean identity to replace the cosine term.
$$1 - \sin^2 x = 1 - 2\sin x + \sin^2 x$$

Simplify the results.

$$2\sin^2 x - 2\sin x = 0$$
$$\sin x (\sin x - 1) = 0$$

There are two possible solutions to the equation:

$$\sin x = 0 \quad \text{and} \quad \sin x = 1$$
$$x = 0°, 180° \quad\quad\quad x = 90°$$

Thus, the apparent solutions to the problem are $x = 0°$, $90°$ and $180°$. By checking each solution, however, it is found that $x = 180°$ is not a legitimate solution and must be discarded. The actual solutions to the equation are thus $x = 0°$ and $90°$.

Example: Solve the following equation: $\cos^2 x = \sin^2 x$ for $0 \le x \le 2\pi$.

First, use the Pythagorean identity to convert either the cosine or sine term.

$$\cos^2 x = 1 - \cos^2 x$$

Simplify the results.

$$2\cos^2 x = 1$$
$$\cos^2 x = \frac{1}{2}$$
$$\cos x = \pm \frac{1}{\sqrt{2}}$$

Familiarity with the properties of trigonometric functions should lead to the realization that this corresponds to odd integer multiples of $\frac{\pi}{4}$. Alternatively, a calculator can be used to calculate the inverse function. (A detailed review of inverse trigonometric functions is provided earlier in this discussion.)

$$x = \arccos\left(\pm\frac{1}{\sqrt{2}}\right)$$

In either case, the solution is the following:

$$x = \frac{\pi}{4}, \frac{3\pi}{4}, \frac{5\pi}{4}, \frac{7\pi}{4}$$

Example: Solve for x: $\sin x \geq 0$.

Solving a trigonometric inequality involves the same general process as is involved in solving any other inequality. In this case, however, the set of solutions includes an infinite number of intervals, rather than a single interval as is the case for some non-periodic functions. First, replace the inequality symbol with an equal sign. Solve using the inverse function.

$$\sin x = 0$$
$$\arcsin[\sin x] = \arcsin[0]$$
$$x = \arcsin[0]$$

The solutions for x are the following.

$$x = n\pi \qquad n = 0, \pm 1, \pm 2, \pm 3, \ldots$$

These solutions are the points at which the sine function crosses the x-axis. Thus, some set of intervals bounded by these solutions is the set of solutions for the inequality. It is apparent that the sine function is greater than zero for x between 0 and π, and negative for x between π and 2π. This pattern then repeats. Thus, $\sin x$ is greater than zero between $2n\pi$ and $(2n + 1)\pi$ for $n = 0, \pm1, \pm2, \pm3, \ldots$.

$$\sin x \geq 0 \text{ for } 2n\pi \leq x \leq (2n+1)\pi \text{ where } n = 0, \pm1, \pm2, \pm3, \ldots$$

Note that the endpoints of the intervals are included in the solution set. The validity of this solution can be confirmed by looking at a graph of sin x.

18H. Using Trigonometric Functions to Model Periodic Phenomena

Trigonometric functions are commonly used in physics to model different kinds of periodic phenomena. One of the simplest kinds of periodic motion is that observed in pendulums or in masses oscillating at the end of a spring. This is known as simple harmonic motion and involves a cyclical exchange of kinetic energy and potential energy.

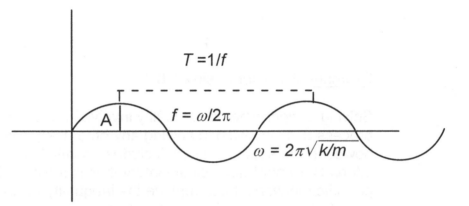

The above diagram depicts the various elements of simple harmonic motion. The displacement of a simple harmonic oscillator varies sinusoidally with time and is given by

$$x = A\cos(\omega t + \delta)$$

where A is the maximum displacement or amplitude, ω is the angular frequency and δ is the phase constant which is zero in the diagram. We can see from the equation that the displacement goes through a full cycle at time intervals given by the period $T = 2\pi / \omega$. The **frequency** f is the number of cycles per second or the number of vibrations made per unit of time. The unit of frequency is the **hertz** (Hz). The **displacement** x is the distance a vibrating object is moved from its normal resting position.

The relationships among the various parameters of a system displaying simple harmonic motion depends on the type of system being examined. Once the displacement is known, the velocity and acceleration of the object undergoing harmonic motion can be calculated by calculating the first derivative with respect to time (for velocity) or the second derivative with respect to time (for acceleration).

Example: The displacement of a mass oscillating at the end of a spring is given by

$$x(t) = x_{max} \cos(2\pi f t + \phi) = x_{max} \cos(\omega t + \phi)$$

Find expressions for the velocity and acceleration of the mass.

If x(t) is differentiated once with respect to time, the velocity of the mass is revealed.

$$v(t) = \frac{\partial x(t)}{\partial t} = -\omega x_{max} \sin(\omega t + \phi)$$

Comparing the expressions for displacement and velocity, we can see that the velocity is maximized when the displacement is zero (all kinetic energy), and the displacement is maximized when the velocity is zero (all potential energy); that is, the displacement and velocity are 90^0 out of phase.

The acceleration can be calculated by differentiating v(t) with respect to time.

$$a(t) = \frac{\partial v(t)}{\partial t} = -\omega^2 x_{max} \cos(\omega t + \phi) = -\omega^2 x(t)$$

The acceleration, as shown above, is in phase with the displacement.

Competency 0019 Understand the conceptual basis of calculus.

19A. The concept of limit

A limit is the value that a function approaches as a variable of the function approaches a certain value. This concept can be understood through graphical illustrations, as with the following example. The graph shows a plot of $y = 2x$. A limit in this case might be the limit of y as x approaches 3. Graphically, this involves tracing the plot of the function to the point at $x = 3$.

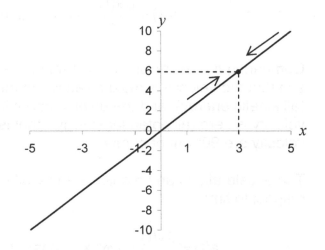

The limit in this case is clearly 6: $2(3) = 6$. The limit can be considered either from the right or left (that is, considering x decreasing toward 3 or x increasing toward 3). In the simple example above, the limit is the same from either direction, but, in some cases, the limit may be different from different directions or the function may not even exist on one side of the limit. Consider the limit of ln x as x approaches zero.

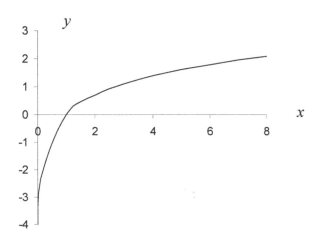

As it turns out, ln x is not defined for $x < 0$. The limit, however, is negative infinity (which could be called "undefined" as well). Nevertheless, it is clear that the graphical concept of a limit only makes sense for x approaching zero from the right, since the function does not exist (for real numbers) to the left of zero.

To find a limit there are two points to remember.
  1. Factor the expression completely and cancel all common factors in fractions.
  2. Substitute the number to which the variable is approaching. In most cases this produces the value of the limit.

If the variable in the limit approaches ∞, factor and simplify first; then examine the result. If the result does not involve a fraction with the variable in the denominator, the limit is usually also equal to ∞. If the variable is in the denominator of the fraction, the denominator is getting larger which makes the entire fraction smaller. In other words, the limit is zero.

<u>Example:</u> Evaluate the following limits.

1. $\lim\limits_{x \to -3} \left(\dfrac{x^2 + 5x + 6}{x + 3} + 4x \right)$

First, factor the numerator. Then cancel the common factors.

$$\lim\limits_{x \to -3} \left(\dfrac{(x + 3)(x + 2)}{x + 3} + 4x \right)$$

$$\lim\limits_{x \to -3} (x + 2 + 4x) = \lim\limits_{x \to -3} (5x + 2)$$

$$5(-3) + 2 = -15 + 2 = -13$$

2. $\lim\limits_{x \to \infty} \dfrac{2x^2}{x^5}$

Cancel the common factors and take the constant outside the limit.

$$2 \lim\limits_{x \to \infty} \dfrac{1}{x^3}$$

Evaluate the limit.

$$2\dfrac{1}{\infty^3} = 0$$

A function f(x) is **continuous** at $x = a$ if $\lim_{x \to a} f(x)$ exists and is equal to $f(a)$. This essentially means that the graph of the function $f(x)$ does not have a break (or discontinuity) at $x = a$.

19B. The relationship between slope and rates of change

The **derivative of a function** has two basic interpretations:
I.   Instantaneous rate of change
II.   Slope of a tangent line at a given point

The slope of a line is simply the change in the vertical (positive y) direction divided by the change in the horizontal (positive x) direction. Since the slope of a line is constant over the entire domain of the function, any two points can be used to calculate the slope.

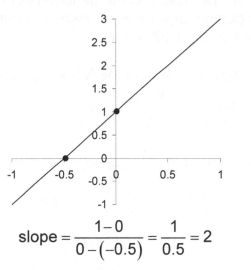

$$\text{slope} = \frac{1-0}{0-(-0.5)} = \frac{1}{0.5} = 2$$

Although the specific approach used for lines cannot be used for curves, it can be used in the general sense if the distance between the points (along the x-axis) becomes zero.

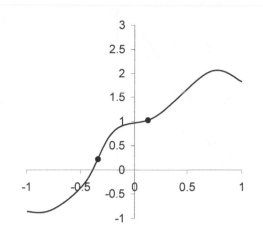

The equation for slope can be written as follows.

$$\text{slope} = \frac{f(x + \Delta x) - f(x)}{\Delta x}$$

This is also known as the difference quotient. For a curve defined by the function f, the difference quotient computes the slope of the secant line through the two points with x-coordinates x and x + h. If the two points on the line are chosen sufficiently close together so that the function does not vary significantly from the line between those points, then the difference quotient can serve as a good approximation for the slope (and, therefore, to the derivative as well). The difference quotient is used in the definition of the derivative.

Take the limit as Δx goes to zero. This is the definition of the derivative, which is written as either f '(x) or as $\frac{df(x)}{dx}$.

$$f'(x) = \lim_{\Delta x \to 0} \frac{f(x + \Delta x) - f(x)}{\Delta x}$$

This fundamental definition of the derivative can be used to derive formulas for derivatives of specific types of functions. For instance, consider $f(x) = x^2$. Based on this formula, which defines the slope over an infinitesimal width Δx, the derivative can be seen as the **instantaneous rate of change** of the function.

The derivative of a function at a point can likewise be interpreted as the **slope of a line tangent to the function** at that same point. Pick a point (for instance, at x = −3) on the graph of a function and draw a tangent line at that point. Find the derivative of the function and substitute the value x = −3. This result will be the slope of the tangent line.

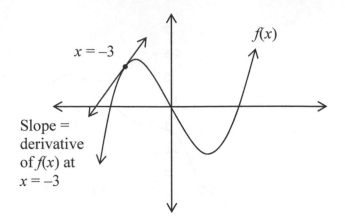

19C. How the derivative relates to maxima, minima, points of inflection, and concavity of curves

Differential calculus can be a helpful tool in analyzing functions and the graphs of functions. Derivatives deal with the slope (or rate of change) of a function, and this information can be used to calculate the locations and values of extrema (maxima and minima) and inflection points, as well as to determine information concerning concavity.

The concept of extrema (maxima and minima) can be differentiated into local (or relative) and global (or absolute) extrema. For instance, consider the following function:

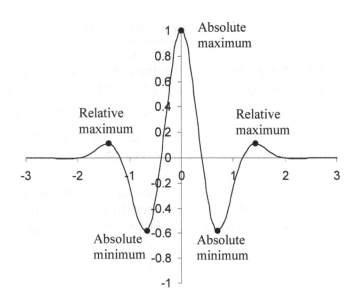

It is apparent that there are a number of peaks and valleys, each of which could, in some sense, be called a maximum or minimum. To allow greater clarity, local and global extrema can be specified. For instance, the peak at $x = 0$ is the maximum for the entire function. Additionally, the valleys at about $x = \pm 0.7$ both correspond to an (equivalent) minimum for the entire function. These are absolute extrema. On the other hand, the peaks at about $x = \pm 1.4$ are each a maximum for the function within a specific area; thus, they are relative maxima. Relative extrema are extreme values of the function over some limited interval. The points at which the derivative of a function is equal to zero are called **critical points** (the x values are called **critical numbers**).

By inspection of any graph, it is apparent that all extrema (where the function is continuous on either side of the maximum or minimum point) are located at points where the slope of the function is zero. This is to say that the derivative of the function at an extremum is zero. It is not necessarily the case, however, that all points where the derivative of the function is zero correspond to extrema. Consider the function $y = x^3$, whose graph is shown below.

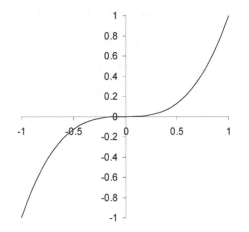

The derivative of y is $3x^2$, and the function is equal to zero only at $x = 0$. Nevertheless, the function y does not have an extremum at $x = 0$. The only cases where critical points correspond to extrema are when the derivative of the function actually crosses the x-axis. These cases correspond to the function having a positive slope on one side of the critical point and a negative slope on the other. This is a requirement for an extremum. (Notice that, for the plot of $y = x^3$, the function has a positive slope on both sides of the critical point.)

A positive slope on the left side of a critical point and a negative slope on the right side indicate that the critical point is a maximum.

If the slope is negative on the left and positive on the right, then the critical point corresponds to a minimum. If the slopes on either side are both positive or both negative, then there is no extremum at the critical point.

Whether a critical point is an extremum can be determined using the second derivative f''. A critical point corresponds to the function f having zero slope. Thus, f' is zero at these points. As noted above, f has a maximum at the critical point only if f' crosses the x-axis. If f' is zero at a point but does not cross the x-axis, however, then that point is either a maximum or minimum of the function f', i.e. a critical number of f' ($f''=0$),. As a result, if the critical number of f is also a critical number of f' (i.e. $f''=0$), the critical point does not correspond to an extremum of f. The procedure for finding extrema for $f(x)$ is thus the following.

    1. Calculate $f'(x)$.

    2. Solve $f'(x) = 0$; the solutions of this equation are the critical numbers.

    3. Calculate $f''(x)$.

    4. Evaluate $f''(x)$ for each critical number c. If:

        a. $f''(c) = 0$, the critical point is not an extremum of f.

        b. $f''(c) > 0$, the critical point is a minimum of f.

        c. $f''(c) < 0$, the critical point is a maximum of f.

Example: Find the maxima and minima of $f(x) = 2x^4 - 4x^2$ on the closed interval [–2, 1].

First, differentiate the function and set the result equal to zero.
$$\frac{df}{dx} = 8x^3 - 8x = 0$$

Next, solve by factoring to find the critical numbers.
$$8x(x^2 - 1) = 0$$
$$x(x - 1)(x + 1) = 0$$

The solutions for this equation, which are also the critical numbers, are $x = -1$, 0 and 1. For each critical number, it is necessary to determine whether the point corresponds to a maximum, minimum or neither.
$$\frac{d^2f}{dx^2} = 24x^2 - 8$$

Test each critical point by substituting into the result above.
$$f''(-1) = 24(-1)^2 - 8 = 24 - 8 = 16 \rightarrow \text{minimum}$$
$$f''(0) = 24(0)^2 - 8 = -8 \rightarrow \text{maximum}$$
$$f''(1) = 24(1)^2 - 8 = 24 - 8 = 16 \rightarrow \text{minimum}$$

The critical numbers correspond to the minima (–1, –2) and (1, –2) and to the maximum (0, 0). The endpoint of the closed interval at x = –2 should also be tested to determine if it constitutes an extremum, as such may not be detectable using derivatives (the minimum at the endpoint x = 1 was detected, however). This endpoint corresponds to (–2, 16), which is the absolute maximum. Absolute minima exist at (–1, –2) and (1, –2), and a relative maximum exists at (0, 0).
The second derivative of a function can also be viewed in terms of concavity. The first derivative reveals whether a curve is increasing or decreasing (increasing or decreasing) from the left to the right. In much the same way, the second derivative relates whether the curve is concave up (slope increasing) or concave down (slope decreasing). Curves that are concave can be viewed as "collecting water"; curves that are concave down can be viewed as "dumping water."

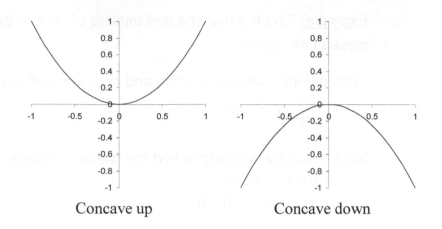

Concave up   Concave down

A **point of inflection** is a point where a curve changes from being concave up to concave down (or vice versa). To find these points, find the critical numbers of the first derivative of the function (that is, solve the equation for which the second derivative of the function is set equal to zero). A critical number coincides with an inflection point if the curve is concave up on one side of the value and concave down on the other. The critical number is the x coordinate of the inflection point. To get the y coordinate, plug the critical number into the **original** function.

Example: Find the inflection points of $f(x) = 2x - \tan x$ over the interval $-\dfrac{\pi}{2} < x < \dfrac{\pi}{2}$.

First, calculate the second derivative of f.

$$f''(x) = \frac{d^2 f(x)}{dx^2} = \frac{d}{dx}\left[\frac{d}{dx}(2x - \tan x)\right]$$

$$f''(x) = \frac{d}{dx}\left[2 - \sec^2 x\right] = -2\sec x \frac{d}{dx}\sec x$$

$$f''(x) = -2\sec x\left(\sec x \tan x\right) = -2\sec^2 x \tan x$$

Set the second derivative equal to zero and solve.

$$f''(x) = -2\sec^2 x \tan x = 0$$

The function is zero for either sec x = 0 or tan x = 0. Only tan x = 0, however, has real solutions. This means that the inflection points are at $x = n\pi$, where n = 0, 1, 2, etc. Within the given interval, however, the only solution is x = 0. Substituting this value into the original equation yields the following:

$$f(0) = 2(0) - \tan 0 = 0 - 0 = 0$$

Thus, the inflection point for this function on the interval $-\dfrac{\pi}{2} < x < \dfrac{\pi}{2}$ is (0, 0). The plot of the function is shown below, along with the associated inflection point. As hinted earlier, the inflection point can be seen graphically as the point at which the slope changes from an increasing value to a decreasing value (or vice versa).

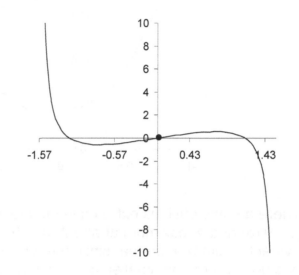

Example: Identify approximately the locations of the extrema (excluding the endpoints) and inflection points for the following graph.

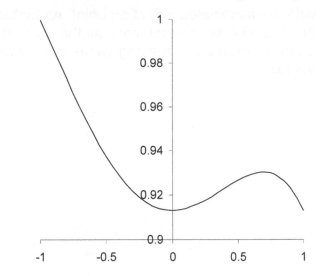

There are two obvious extrema in the graph: a minimum at about (0, .915) and a maximum at about (0.7, 0.93). These extrema are evidently relative extrema, since the function (at least apparently) has both larger and smaller values elsewhere. There is also an obvious concavity shift between the maximum and minimum. The inflection point is at about (0.35, 0.92). The extrema and inflection points are shown marked below.

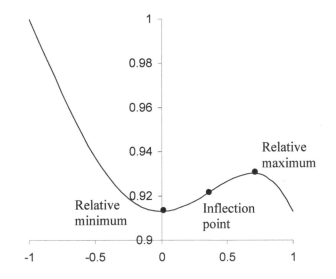

Extreme value problems, also known as **max-min problems** or **optimization problems**, entail using the first derivative to find values that either maximize or minimize some quantity, such as area, profit or volume.

Example: A manufacturer wishes to construct an open box from a square piece of metal by cutting squares from each corner and folding up the sides. The metal is 12 feet on each side. What are the dimensions of the squares to be cut out such that the volume of the box is maximized?

First, draw a figure that represents the situation. Assume that the squares to be cut from the metal have sides of length x. Noting that the metal has sides of length 12 feet, this leaves 12 – 2x feet remaining on each side after the squares are cut out.

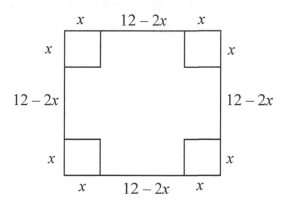

The volume V(x) of the box formed when the sides are folded up is the following:

$$V(x) = x(12 - 2x)^2$$

Simplify and take the first derivative of the result.

$$V(x) = x(144 - 48x + 4x^2) = 4x^3 - 48x^2 + 144x$$
$$V'(x) = 12x^2 - 96x + 144$$

Set the first derivative to zero and solve by factoring.

$$V'(x) = 12x^2 - 96x + 144 = 0$$
$$(x - 6)(x - 2) = 0$$

The solutions are then x = 2 feet and x = 6 feet. Note that, if x = 6 feet, the sides of the box become zero in width. This, therefore, is not a legitimate solution. Choose x = 2 feet as the solution that leads to the largest volume of the box.

19D. The relationship between integration and the area under a curve

Riemann Sums

The formal definition of an integral is based on the **Riemann sum**. A Riemann sum is the sum of the areas of a set of rectangles that is used to approximate the area under the curve of a function. Given a function f defined over some closed interval $[a, b]$, the interval can be divided into a set of n arbitrary partitions, each of length Δx_i.

Within the limits of each partition, some value $x = c_i$ can be chosen such that Δx_i and $f(c_i)$ define the width and height (respectively) of a rectangle. The sum of the aggregate of all the rectangles defined in this manner over the interval $[a, b]$ is the Riemann sum. Consider, for example, the function $f(x) = x^2 + 1$ over the interval $[0,1]$. The plot of the function is shown below.

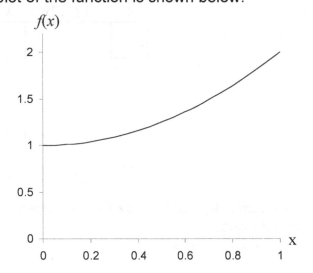

Partition the interval into segments of width 0.2 along the x-axis, and choose the function value $f(c_i)$ at the center of each interval. This function value is the height of the respective rectangle.

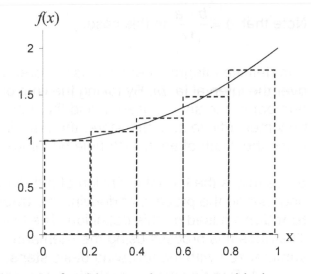

The Riemann sum for this case is expressed below.

$$\sum_{i=1}^{5} 0.2f(0.2i - 0.1) = 1.33$$

This expression is the sum of the areas of all the rectangles shown above. This is an approximation of the area under the curve of the function (and a reasonably accurate one, as well—the actual area is $\frac{4}{3}$).

Generally, the Riemann sum for arbitrary partitioning and selection of the values c_i is the following:

$$\sum_{i=1}^{n} f(c_i) \Delta x_i$$

where c_i is within the closed interval defined by the partition Δx_i.

Definite Integrals
The **definite integral** is defined as the limit of the Riemann sum as the widths of the partitions Δx_i go to zero (and, consequently, n goes to infinity). Thus, the definite integral can be expressed mathematically as follows:

$$\int_a^b f(x)\,dx = \lim_{\Delta x_m \to 0} \sum_{i=1}^{n} f(c_i)\Delta x_i$$

where Δx_m is the width of the largest partition. If the partitioning of the interval is such that each partition has the same width, then the definition can be written as follows:

$$\int_a^b f(x)\,dx = \lim_{\Delta x \to 0} \sum_{i=1}^{n} f(c_i)\Delta x$$

Note that $n = \dfrac{b-a}{\Delta x}$ in this case.

The definite integral, therefore, is the area under the curve of $f(x)$ over the interval $[a, b]$. By taking the limit of the Riemann sum, the number of rectangles used to find the area under the curve becomes infinite and, therefore, the error in the result goes to zero since the width of each rectangle becomes infinitesimal.

Since this is the formal definition of a definite integral, it is helpful to understand the process of deriving the **integrals of algebraic functions** based on this definition. The following example illustrates this process using the Riemann sum. The process can be summarized with the following basic steps.

    1. Partition the interval into n segments of equal width.
    2. Substitute the value of the function into the Riemann sum using the x value at the center of each subinterval.
    3. Write the sum in closed form.
    4. Take the limit of the result as n approaches infinity.

<u>Example:</u> For $f(x) = x^2$, find the values of the Riemann sum over the interval $[0, 1]$ using n subintervals of equal width, each evaluated at the right endpoint of each subinterval. Find the limit of the Riemann sum.

Take the interval $[0, 1]$ and subdivide it into n subintervals each of length $\dfrac{1}{n}$.

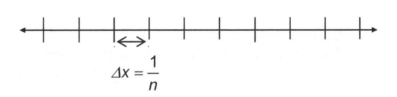

The endpoints of the ith subinterval are

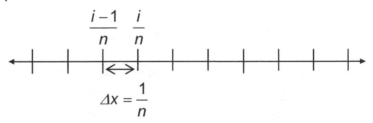

Let $x_i = \dfrac{i}{n}$ be the right endpoint. Draw a line of length $f(x_i) = \left(\dfrac{i}{n}\right)^2$ at the right-hand endpoint.

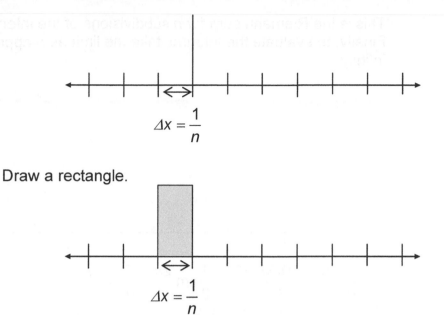

$$\Delta x = \frac{1}{n}$$

Draw a rectangle.

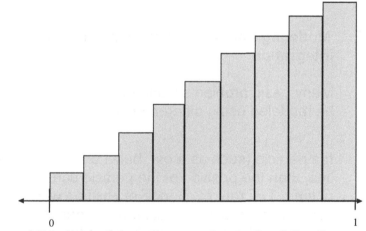

$$\Delta x = \frac{1}{n}$$

The area of this rectangle is $f(x)\Delta x$.

$$f(x)\Delta x = \left(\frac{i}{n}\right)^2 \frac{1}{n} = \frac{i^2}{n^3}$$

Now draw all n rectangles (drawing below not to scale).

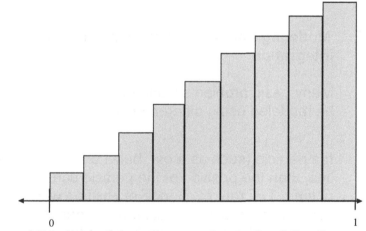

The sum of the area of these rectangles is the following.

$$\sum_{i=1}^{n} \frac{i^2}{n^3} = \frac{1}{n^3} \sum_{i=1}^{n} i^2$$

The sum can be evaluated as follows.

$$\frac{1}{n^3} \sum_{i=1}^{n} i^2 = \frac{1}{n^3} \frac{n(n+1)(2n+1)}{6}$$

This is the Riemann sum for *n* subdivisions of the interval [0, 1]. Finally, to evaluate the integral, take the limit as *n* approaches infinity.

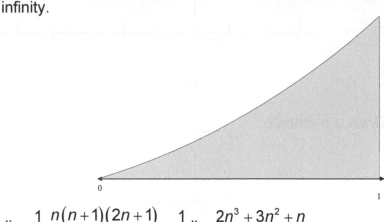

$$\lim_{n \to \infty} \frac{1}{n^3} \frac{n(n+1)(2n+1)}{6} = \frac{1}{6} \lim_{n \to \infty} \frac{2n^3 + 3n^2 + n}{n^3}$$

$$= \frac{1}{6} \lim_{n \to \infty} \left(2 + \frac{3}{n} + \frac{1}{n^2} \right) = \frac{1}{3}$$

This is the correct answer. Thus,

$$\int_0^1 x^2 dx = \frac{1}{3}$$

19E. Modeling and solving basic problems using differentiation and integration

Many basic problems using rate of change of a certain quantity may be modeled using differentiation.

If a particle (such as a car, bullet or other object) is moving along a line, then the position of the particle can be expressed as a function of time. The rate of change of position with respect to time is the velocity of the object; thus, the first derivative of the distance function yields the velocity function for the particle. Substituting a value for time into this expression provides the instantaneous velocity of the particle at that time. The absolute value of the derivative is the speed (magnitude of the velocity) of the particle. A positive value for the velocity indicates that the particle is moving forward (that is, in the positive *x* direction); a negative value indicates the particle is moving backward (that is, in the negative *x* direction).

The acceleration of the particle is the rate of change of the velocity. The second derivative of the position function (which is also the first derivative of the velocity function) yields the acceleration function. If a value for time produces a positive acceleration, the particle's velocity is increasing; if it produces a negative value, the particle's velocity is decreasing. If the acceleration is zero, the particle is moving at a constant speed.

Example: The motion of a particle moving along a line is according to the equation $s(t) = 20 + 3t - 5t^2$, where s is in meters and t is in seconds. Find the position, velocity and acceleration of the particle at $t = 2$ seconds.

To find the position, simply use $t = 2$ in the given position function. Note that the initial position of the particle is $s(0) = 20$ meters.

$$s(2) = 20 + 3(2) - 5(2)^2$$
$$s(2) = 20 + 6 - 20 = 6\,\text{m}$$

To find the velocity of the particle, calculate the first derivative of $s(t)$ and then evaluate the result for $t = 2$ seconds.

$$s'(t) = v(t) = 3 - 10t$$
$$v(2) = 3 - 10(2) = 3 - 20 = -17\,\text{m/s}$$

Finally, for the acceleration of the particle, calculate the second derivative of $s(t)$ (also equal to the first derivative of $v(t)$) and evaluate for $t = 2$ seconds.

$$s''(t) = v'(t) = a(t) = -10\,\text{m/s}^2$$

Since the acceleration function $a(t)$ is a constant, the acceleration is always -10 m/s^2 (the velocity of the particle decreases every second by 10 meters per second).

Some rate problems may involve functions with different parameters that are each dependent on time. In such a case, implicit differentiation may be required. Often times, related rate problems give certain rates in the description, thus eliminating the need to have specific functions of time for every parameter. Related rate problems are otherwise solved in the same manner as other similar problems.

Example: A spherical balloon is inflated such that its radius is increasing at a constant rate of 1 inch per second. What is the rate of increase of the volume of the balloon when the radius is 10 inches?

First, write the equation for the volume of a sphere in terms of the radius, r.

$$V(r) = \frac{4}{3}\pi r^3$$

Differentiate the function implicitly with respect to time, t, by using the chain rule.

$$\frac{dV(r)}{dt} = \frac{4}{3}\pi \frac{d}{dt}(r^3)$$

$$\frac{dV(r)}{dt} = \frac{4}{3}\pi(3r^2)\frac{dr}{dt} = 4\pi r^2 \frac{dr}{dt}$$

To find the solution to the problem, use the radius value $r = 10$ inches and the rate of increase of the radius $\frac{dr}{dt} = 1$ in/sec. Calculate the resulting rate of increase of the volume, $\frac{dV(r)}{dt}$.

$$\frac{dV(10)}{dt} = 4\pi(10\,\text{in})^2\,1\,\text{in/sec} = 400\pi\,\text{in}^3/\text{sec} \approx 1257\,\text{in}^3/\text{sec}$$

Taking the integral of a function and evaluating it over some interval on x provides the total **area under the curve** (or, more formally, the **area bounded by the curve and the x-axis**). Thus, the area of geometric figures can be determined when the figure can be cast as a function or set of functions in the coordinate plane. Remember, though, that regions above the x-axis have "positive" area and regions below the x-axis have "negative" area. It is necessary to account for these positive and negative values when finding the area under curves. The boundaries between positive and negative regions are delineated by the roots of the function.

Example: Find the area under the following function on the given interval: $f(x) = \sin x$; $[0, 2\pi]$.

First, find the roots of the function on the interval.

$$f(x) = \sin x = 0$$
$$x = 0, \pi$$

The function $\sin x$ is positive over $[0, \pi]$ (since $\sin\frac{\pi}{2} = 1$) and negative over $[\pi, 2\pi]$ (since $\sin\frac{3\pi}{2} = -1$). Use these intervals for the integration to find the area A under the curve.

$$A = \int_0^{2\pi} |\sin x|\, dx = \left|\int_0^{\pi} \sin x\, dx\right| + \left|\int_{\pi}^{2\pi} \sin x\, dx\right|$$

$$A = \left|-\cos x\Big|_0^{\pi}\right| + \left|-\cos x\Big|_{\pi}^{2\pi}\right| = \left|-\cos\pi + \cos 0\right| + \left|-\cos 2\pi + \cos\pi\right|$$

$$A = |1+1| + |-1-1| = 2 + 2 = 4$$

Thus, the total area under the curve of $f(x) = \sin x$ on the interval $[0, 2\pi]$ is 4 square units.

Integral calculus, in addition to differential calculus, is a powerful tool for analysis of problems involving linear motion. The derivative of the position (or displacement) function is the velocity function, and the derivative of a velocity function is the acceleration function. As a result, the antiderivative of an acceleration function is a velocity function, and the antiderivative of the velocity function is a position (or displacement) function. Solving word problems of this type involve converting the information given into an appropriate integral expression. To find the constant of integration, use the conditions provided in the problem (such as an initial displacement, velocity or acceleration).

Example: A particle moves along the x-axis with acceleration $a(t) = 3t - 1\dfrac{cm}{sec^2}$. At time $t = 4$ seconds, the particle is moving to the left at 3 cm per second. Find the velocity of the particle at time $t = 2$ seconds.

Evaluate the antiderivative of the acceleration function $a(t)$ to get the velocity function $v(t)$ along with the unknown constant of integration C.

$$v(t) = \int a(t)\, dt = \int (3t - 1)\, dt$$

$$v(t) = \frac{3t^2}{2} - t + C$$

Use the condition that at time $t = 4$ seconds, the particle has a velocity of -3 cm/sec.

$$v(4) = \frac{3(4)^2}{2} - 4 + C = -3$$

$$\frac{48}{2} - 4 + C = -3$$

$$C = -3 + 4 - 24 = -23 \frac{cm}{sec}$$

Now evaluate $v(t)$ at time $t = 2$ seconds to get the solution to the problem.

$$v(t) = \frac{3t^2}{2} - t - 23 \frac{cm}{sec}$$

$$v(2) = \frac{3(2)^2}{2} - 2 - 23 \frac{cm}{sec} = 6 - 25 \frac{cm}{sec} = -19 \frac{cm}{sec}$$

19F. The development of calculus

Credit for the development of calculus in the West is typically assigned to Isaac Newton and Gottfried Leibniz, who essentially developed calculus simultaneously. Differential calculus was developed as a method for dealing with problems such as tangent lines, velocity and acceleration of particles, and problems dealing with extrema. Other mathematicians, although not credited with having fully developed calculus in the manner of Newton or Leibniz, contributed with partial solutions to the problems mentioned above. These mathematicians included such figures as Pierre de Fermat, René Descartes, Christian Huygens and Isaac Barrow.
Since its development, calculus (both differential and integral) has been a crucial tool in both the further development of abstract mathematical theory and in the development of modern physics. Newtonian mechanics, for instance, which deals with the motion of objects, is founded upon calculus as a basis for discussion of the relationship between position, velocity and acceleration.

Competency 0020 Understand the principles of discrete/finite mathematics.

20A. Properties of sets

A set is a collection of objects or elements that are not ordered. Elements of a set are not repeated. Some examples of sets are {a, b, c, d, e}, {10, 20, 30, 40....100} and {All animals found in Africa}. The **cardinality** of a set is the number of elements contained within the set. If L is defined as the set $\{10,11,12,13,14,15\}$, then the cardinality of L is 6.

A **subset** of a set consists of some of the elements in the set. If B is a subset of A, then every element of B is included in A. This is written as $B \subseteq A$. A **proper subset** of a set consists of some of the elements in a set, never all of them. If C is a proper subset of A then every element of C is included in A and A has at least one element that is not in C. The proper subset relationship is written as $C \subset A$. An improper subset of A is the set A itself. For instance, the set {All mammals found in Africa} is a proper subset of the set {All animals found in Africa}. If two sets are equal, then they are subsets of each other.

An **empty set** has no elements and is denoted by ø. It is a subset of all sets. The universal set U is a set containing all conceivable elements.

The **complement** A' of a set A consists of all elements of the **universal** set U (all possible elements under consideration) that do not belong to A. For instance, if U = {All letters of the alphabet} and A = {All consonants} then A' = {All vowels}. The universal and the null sets are complements of each other.

A **union** of two sets, written as $A \cup B$, is a set that contains all the elements of both sets. An **intersection** of two sets, written as $A \cap B$, is a set that contains the elements common to both sets.

Example: If A = {2,4,6,8,10} and B = {1,2,3,4,5}, find the union and intersection of the two sets.
  $A \cup B$ = {1,2,3,4,5,6,8,10} and $A \cap B$ = {2,4}.

Example: Ann, Marie, Tom, Hanna, Mike, Sam and Mitchell are children in a class. Ann, Tom and Mike take music. Hanna, Mike, Mitchell and Tom take drama. *A* is the set of children who take music. *B* is the set of children who take drama.
(i) List set *A* and set *B*. (ii) What is the union of *A* and *B*? (iii) What is the intersection of *A* and *B*? (iv) What is the complement of *A*? (v) What is the complement of the intersection of *A* and *B*?

A = {Ann, Tom, Mike};
B = {Hanna, Mike, Mitchell, Tom}
$A \cup B$ = {Ann, Tom, Mike, Hanna, Mitchell}
$A \cap B$ = {Tom, Mike}
A' = {Marie, Hanna, Sam, Mitchell}
$(A \cap B)$' = {Ann, Marie, Hanna, Sam, Mitchell}

Example: Find the union and intersection of the sets of real and complex numbers.

The set of real numbers is expressed as $\mathbb{R}$ and the set of complex numbers is expressed as $\mathbb{C}$. Since the set of real numbers is contained in the set of complex numbers,
$$\mathbb{R} \cup \mathbb{C} = \mathbb{C}$$
Only the real numbers are common to both sets. Thus
$$\mathbb{R} \cap \mathbb{C} = \mathbb{R}$$

20B. Recursive patterns and relations; Problems involving iteration

Sequences can be **finite** or **infinite**. An example of a finite sequence is a sequence whose domain consists of the set {1, 2, 3, ... n} or the first *n* positive integers. An example of an infinite sequence is a sequence whose domain consists of the set {1, 2, 3, ...}; which is, in other words, all positive integers.

A **recurrence relation** is an equation that defines a sequence recursively; in other words, each term of the sequence is defined as a function of the preceding terms. For instance, the formula for the balance of a mortgage principal after *i* payments can be expressed recursively as follows.

$$A_i = A_{i-1}\left(1 + \frac{r}{n}\right) - M \quad \text{where} \quad A_0 = P$$

Here, A_i is the remaining principal on the mortgage after the ith payment, r is the annual interest rate, which is compounded n times annually, and M is the monthly payment. The initial value P is the original loan amount for the mortgage.

Although this formula is not helpful as it stands for directly calculating parameters of a mortgage, it can be helpful for calculating balances (for example) given a specific set of circumstances somewhere within a mortgage term. Compound interest and annuities can also be expressed in recursive form.

<u>Example</u>: You deposit $5,000 in your savings account. Your bank pays 5% interest compounded annually. How much will your account be worth at the end of 10 years?

Let V represent the amount of money in the account and V_n represent the amount of money after n years.

The amount in the account after n years equals the amount in the account after $n - 1$ years plus the interest for the nth year. This can be expressed as the recurrence relation V_0 where your initial

$$V_0 = V_0$$
$$V_1 = 1.05V_0$$
$$V_2 = 1.05V_1 = (1.05)^2 V_0$$
$$V_3 = 1.05V_2 = (1.05)^3 V_0$$
$$......$$

deposit is represented by. $V_n = (1.05)V_{n-1} = (1.05)^n V_0$

Inserting the given values into the equation, you get
$$V_{10} = (1.05)^{10}(5,000) = 8,144 .$$

You determine that after investing $5,000 in an account earning 5% interest, compounded annually for 10 years, you would have $8,144.

Calculation of a past or future term by applying the recursive formula multiple times is called **iteration**.

Sequences of numbers can be defined by iteratively applying a recursive pattern. For instance, the Fibonacci sequence is defined as follows.
$$F_i = F_{i-1} + F_{i-2} \quad \text{where} \quad F_0 = 0 \text{ and } F_1 = 1$$

Applying this recursive formula gives the sequence {0, 1, 1, 2, 3, 5, 8, 13, 21, …}.

t is sometimes difficult or impossible to write recursive relations in explicit or closed form. In such cases, especially where computer programming is involved, the recursive form can still be helpful. When the elements of a sequence of numbers or values depend on one or more previous values, then it is possible that a recursive formula could be used to summarize the sequence.

If a value or number from a later point in the sequence (that is, other than the beginning) is known and it is necessary to find previous terms, then the indices of the recursive relation can be adjusted to find previous values instead of later ones. Consider, for instance, the Fibonacci sequence.

$$F_i = F_{i-1} + F_{i-2}$$
$$F_{i+2} = F_{i+1} + F_i$$
$$F_i = F_{i+2} - F_{i+1}$$

Thus, if any two consecutive numbers in the Fibonacci sequence are known, then the previous numbers of the sequence can be found (in addition to the later numbers).

Example: Write a recursive formula for the following sequence: {2, 3, 5, 9, 17, 33, 65, …}.
By inspection, it can be seen that each number in the sequence is equal to twice the previous number, less one. If the numbers in the sequence are indexed such that for the first number $i = 1$ and so on, then the recursion relation is the following.

$$N_i = 2N_{i-1} - 1$$

Example: If a recursive relation is defined by $N_i = N_{i-1}^2$ and the fourth term is 65,536, what is the first term?
Adjust the indices of the recursion and then solve for N_i.

$$N_{i+1} = N_i^2$$
$$N_i = \sqrt{N_{i+1}}$$

Use this relationship to backtrack to the first term.

$$N_3 = \sqrt{N_4} = \sqrt{65,536} = 256$$
$$N_2 = \sqrt{N_3} = \sqrt{256} = 16$$
$$N_1 = \sqrt{N_2} = \sqrt{16} = 4$$

The first term of the sequence is thus 4.

20C. Properties of algorithms

An **algorithm** is a prescribed series of tasks for performing a calculation or other process. An algorithm can involve multiplication, subtraction, integration or some combination of these or other operations. Computer programs typically rely on algorithms, which, in the digital context, is a series of (sometimes complex) sequential and often repetitive set of binary operations. A simple example is an algorithm that generates the Fibonacci numbers mentioned in the previous section. The following "pseudocode" illustrates such an algorithm for generating the first N Fibonacci numbers.

$$F_i \leftarrow 0$$
$$F_{i+1} \leftarrow 1$$
If $N \geq 0$, Output F_i
If $N \geq 1$, Output F_{i+1}
$$i \leftarrow 2$$
While $i \leq N$:
$$\quad F_{i+2} \leftarrow F_i + F_{i+1}$$
$$\quad \text{Output } F_{i+2}$$
$$\quad F_i \leftarrow F_{i+1}$$
$$\quad F_{i+1} \leftarrow F_{i+2}$$
$$\quad i \leftarrow i+1$$
End

This algorithm "outputs" the first N Fibonacci numbers regardless of the value chosen for N (assuming N is an integer greater than or equal to zero).

Algorithms typically require some set of conditions such that there is an end point at which the procedure is considered complete. Algorithms that do not employ such considerations, or algorithms that are poorly implemented, may end up as infinite loops that may not produce any meaningful result. For instance, the While loop in the above pseudocode terminates when i exceeds N. If this condition was replaced by a tautology (such as $i = i$), then the loop would never terminate and the algorithm would (if continually followed) simply keep outputting Fibonacci numbers.

Some algorithms can be hand traced, as with the above simple example, thus allowing the programmer or creator to examine the performance of the algorithm on a step-by-step basis. Some algorithms, however, are so complex as to not permit any practical use of hand tracing.

When working with computers and calculators we employ **algorithmic thinking**, which means performing mathematical tasks by creating a sequential and often repetitive set of steps. Again, consider generating the Fibonacci numbers utilizing the MR and M+ keys found on most calculators. The table below shows Entry made in the calculator, the value x seen in the display, and the value M contained in the memory.

Entry	ON/AC		1	M+	+	M+	MR	+	M+	MR	+	...
x	0	1	1		1	1	2	3	3	5	8	...
M	0	0	1		1	2	2	2	5	5	5	...

This eliminates the need to repeatedly enter required numbers. Computers have to be programmed, and many advanced calculators are programmable. A **program** is a series of steps of an algorithm that are entered into a computer or calculator. The main advantage of using a program is that once the algorithm is entered, a result may be obtained by merely hitting a single keystroke to select the program, thereby eliminating the need to continually enter a large number of steps. Teachers find that programmable calculators are excellent for investigating "what if?" situations.

20D. Finite differences

Finite differences can serve in some contexts as the discrete version of a differential. In differential and integral calculus, the differential dx (for instance) represents an infinitesimal difference along the x-axis, where

$$dx = \lim_{h \to 0} (x + h) - x$$

In a discrete or finite context, the finite difference can be written as Δx, which would simply be the same as h above.

Finite differences are important to, for instance, computer modeling of physical phenomena. In such cases, where analytical modeling is not possible, finite differences have an important role in numerical techniques like finite element finite difference methods.

A derivative in the context of discrete mathematics uses finite differences (actually, finite difference quotients). Given a set of data or a discrete function f, the derivative is expressed below.

$$\frac{\Delta f}{\Delta x} = \frac{f(x+h)-f(x)}{h}$$

The variable h could be a time or distance increment for the range of f, which in turn could be some form of numerical physical data or other set of numerical information.

Example: Find the derivative of the following set of measurement data, where each measurement is taken at an interval of 1 second: {0, 3, 5, 6, 2, -7, -10}.

Use the expression for the derivative in a discrete context. The variable h (or Δx) is 1 second.

$$\frac{\Delta f}{\Delta x} = \frac{f(x+1)-f(x)}{1} = f(x+1)-f(x)$$

The derivative in this case is found between each two adjacent data points, so the number of elements in the set of derivatives is one less than that of the data, for a total of six elements. Each element is the difference between adjacent elements, as indicated by the expression above. The solution is then the following:
{3, 2, 1, −4, −9, −3}

20E. Linear programming

Linear programming is the optimization of a linear quantity that is subject to constraints expressed as linear equations or inequalities. It is often used in various industries, ecological sciences and governmental organizations to determine or project production costs, the amount of pollutants dispersed into the air, etc. The key to most linear programming problems is to organize the information in the word problem into a chart or graph of some type.

Example: The YMCA wants to sell raffle tickets to raise at least $32,000. If they must pay $7,250 in expenses and prizes out of the money collected from the tickets, how many tickets worth $25 each must they sell?

Since they want to raise at least $32,000, that means they would be happy to get $32,000 or more. This requires an inequality.
        Let x = number of tickets sold
        Then $25x$ = total money collected for x tickets
Total money minus expenses is greater than $32,000.

$25x - 7250 \geq 32000$

$25x \geq 39250$

$x \geq 1570$
If they sell 1,570 tickets or more, they will raise AT LEAST $32,000.

Example: A printing manufacturer makes two types of printers: a Printmaster and a Speedmaster printer. The Printmaster requires 10 cubic feet of space, weighs 5,000 pounds and the Speedmaster takes up 5 cubic feet of space and weighs 600 pounds. The total available space for storage before shipping is 2,000 cubic feet and the weight limit for the space is 300,000 pounds. The profit on the Printmaster is $125,000 and the profit on the Speedmaster is $30,000. How many of each machine should be stored to maximize profitability and what is the maximum possible profit?

First, let x represent the number of Printmaster units sold and let y represent the number of Speedmaster units sold. Then, the equation for the space required to store the units is the following.
        $10x + 5y \leq 2000$
        $2x + y \leq 400$

Since the number of units for both models must be no less than zero, also impose the restrictions that $x \geq 0$ and $y \geq 0$. The restriction on the total weight can be expressed as follows.
        $5000x + 600y \leq 300000$
        $25x + 3y \leq 1500$

The expression for the profit P from sales of the printer units is the following.
        $P = \$125{,}000x + \$30{,}000y$

The solution to this problem, then, is found by maximizing P subject to the constraints given in the preceding inequalities, along with the constraints that $x \geq 0$ and $y \geq 0$. The equations are grouped below for clarity.

$$x \geq 0$$
$$y \geq 0$$
$$2x + y \leq 400$$
$$25x + 3y \leq 1500$$
$$P = \$125,000x + \$30,000y$$

The two inequalities in two variables are plotted in the graph below. The shaded region represents the set of solutions that obey both inequalities. (Note that the shaded region in fact only includes points where both x and y are whole numbers.)

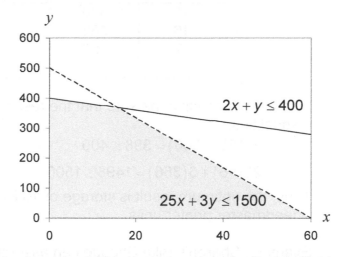

Note that the border of the shaded region that is formed by the two inequalities includes the solutions that constitute the maximum value of y for a given value of x. Note also that x cannot exceed 60 (since it would violate the second inequality). The solution to the problem, then, must lie on the border of the shaded region, since the border spans all the possible solutions that maximize the use of space and weight for a given number x.

To visualize the solution, plot the profit as a function of the solutions to the inequalities that lie along the border of the shaded area.

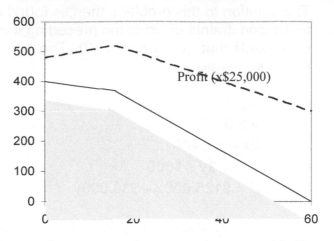

The profit curve shows a maximum at about $x = 16$. Test several values using a table to verify this result.

x	y	P (x$25,000)
15	370	519
16	366	519.2
17	358	514.6

Also double check to be sure that the result obeys the two inequalities.

$$2(16) + (366) = 398 \leq 400$$

$$25(16) + 3(366) = 1498 \leq 1500$$

Thus, the optimum result is storage of 16 Printmaster and 366 Speedmaster printer units.

Example: Sharon's Bike Shoppe can assemble a 3-speed bike in 30 minutes and a 10-speed bike in 60 minutes. The profit on each bike sold is $60 for a 3 speed or $75 for a 10-speed bike. How many of each type of bike should it assemble during an 8-hour day (480 minutes) to maximize the possible profit? Total daily profit must be at least $300.

Let x be the number of 3-speed bikes and y be the number of 10-speed bikes. Since there are only 480 minutes to use each day, the first inequality is the following.

$$30x + 60y \leq 480$$

$$x + 2y \leq 16$$

Since the total daily profit must be at least \$300, then the second inequality can be written as follows, where P is the profit for the day.

$$P = \$60x + \$75y \geq \$300$$
$$4x + 5y \geq 20$$

To visualize the problem, plot the two inequalities and show the potential solutions as a shaded region.

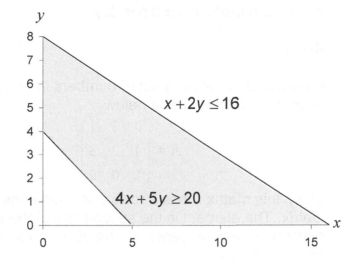

The solution to the problem is the ordered pair of whole numbers in the shaded area that maximizes the daily profit. The profit curve is added as shown below.

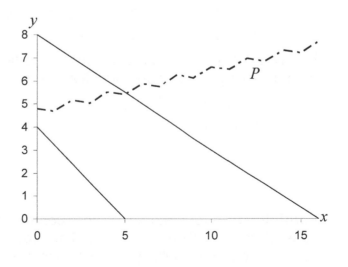

Based on the above plot, it is clear that the profit is maximized for the case where only 3-speed bikes (corresponding to x) are manufactured. Thus, the correct solution can be found by solving the first inequality for $y = 0$.

$$x + 2(0) \le 16$$
$$x \le 16$$

The manufacture of 16 3-speed bikes (and no 10-speed bikes) maximizes profit to \$960 per day.

20F. Matrices

A **matrix** is an ordered set of numbers in rectangular form. An example matrix is shown below.

$$A = \begin{pmatrix} 0 & 3 & 1 \\ 4 & 2 & 3 \\ 1 & 0 & 2 \end{pmatrix}$$

Since this matrix A has 3 rows and 3 columns, it is called a 3×3 matrix. The element in the second row of the third column would be denoted as $A_{2,3}$. In general, a matrix with r rows and c columns is an $r \times c$ matrix.

Matrices can be **added or subtracted** only if their dimensions are the same. To add (subtract) compatible matrices, simply add (subtract) the corresponding elements, as with the example below for 2×2 matrices.

$$\begin{pmatrix} a_{11} & a_{12} \\ a_{21} & a_{22} \end{pmatrix} + \begin{pmatrix} a_{11} & a_{12} \\ a_{21} & a_{22} \end{pmatrix} = \begin{pmatrix} a_{11} + b_{11} & a_{12} + b_{12} \\ a_{21} + b_{21} & a_{22} + b_{22} \end{pmatrix}$$

Matrix addition and subtraction obey the rules of associativity, commutativity, identity and additive inverse.

$$\bar{A} + (\bar{B} + \bar{C}) = (\bar{A} + \bar{B}) + \bar{C}$$
$$\bar{A} + \bar{B} = \bar{B} + \bar{A}$$
$$\bar{A} + 0 = \bar{A}$$
$$\bar{A} + (-\bar{A}) = 0$$

Multiplication for matrices is more complicated, except for the case of multiplication by a scalar. The product of a matrix and a scalar is found by multiplying each element of the matrix by the scalar.

$$c\begin{pmatrix} a_{11} & a_{12} \\ a_{21} & a_{22} \end{pmatrix} = \begin{pmatrix} ca_{11} & ca_{12} \\ ca_{21} & ca_{22} \end{pmatrix}$$

Multiplication of two matrices is only defined if the number of columns in the first matrix is equal to the number of rows in the second matrix. Matrix multiplication is not necessarily commutative. Given an $n \times m$ matrix ($\bar{A}$) multiplied by an $m \times p$ matrix ($\bar{B}$) (multiplied in that order), the product is an $n \times p$ matrix. Each element C_{ij} in the product matrix is equal to the sum of each element in the ith row of the $n \times m$ matrix multiplied by each corresponding element in the jth column of the $m \times p$ matrix. Thus, each element C_{ij} of the product matrix $\bar{A}\bar{B}$ is equal to the following, where

$\bar{A}\bar{B} = \bar{C}$:

$$C_{ij} = \sum_{k=1}^{m} A_{ik} B_{kj}$$

Consider the following example.

$$\begin{pmatrix} 1 & 2 & 3 \\ 4 & 5 & 6 \end{pmatrix} \begin{pmatrix} 7 \\ 8 \\ 9 \end{pmatrix}$$

The solution is found as follows.

$$\begin{pmatrix} 1 & 2 & 3 \\ 4 & 5 & 6 \end{pmatrix} \begin{pmatrix} 7 \\ 8 \\ 9 \end{pmatrix} = \begin{pmatrix} (1)(7)+(2)(8)+(3)(9) \\ (4)(7)+(5)(8)+(6)(9) \end{pmatrix} = \begin{pmatrix} 50 \\ 122 \end{pmatrix}$$

Matrix multiplication obeys the rules of associativity and distributivity, but not commutativity.

$$\bar{A}(\bar{B}\bar{C}) = (\bar{A}\bar{B})\bar{C}$$

$$\bar{A}(\bar{B}+\bar{C}) = \bar{A}\bar{B} + \bar{A}\bar{C}$$

$$(\bar{B}+\bar{C})\bar{A} = \bar{B}\bar{A} + \bar{C}\bar{A}$$

Example: Determine the product $\bar{A}\bar{B}$ of the following matrices.

$$\bar{A} = \begin{pmatrix} -1 & 2 & 8 \\ 4 & -3 & 7 \\ 0 & 1 & 4 \end{pmatrix}, \quad \bar{B} = \begin{pmatrix} 0 & 5 & 0 \\ 7 & -2 & -1 \\ -8 & 0 & 3 \end{pmatrix}$$

The product AB is a 3 × 3 matrix. The first column of AB is the dot product of the first column in B with each row of A.

$$\overline{AB} = \begin{pmatrix} -1 & 2 & 8 \\ 4 & -3 & 7 \\ 0 & 1 & 4 \end{pmatrix} \begin{pmatrix} 0 & 5 & 0 \\ 7 & -2 & -1 \\ -8 & 0 & 3 \end{pmatrix} = \begin{pmatrix} 0+14-64 & \bullet & \bullet \\ -21-56 & \bullet & \bullet \\ 7-32 & \bullet & \bullet \end{pmatrix}$$

The other columns of AB are found using the same approach for the other columns of B.

$$\overline{AB} = \begin{pmatrix} -50 & -9 & 22 \\ -77 & 26 & 24 \\ -25 & -2 & 11 \end{pmatrix}$$

Matrices are often used to solve systems of equations. They are also used by physicists, mathematicians and biologists to organize and study data such as population growth, and they are used in finance for such purposes as investment growth and portfolio analysis. Matrices are easily translated into computer code in high-level programming languages and can be easily expressed in electronic spreadsheets.

The following is a simple financial example of using a matrix to solve a problem. A company has two stores. The income and expenses (in dollars) for the two stores, for three months, are shown in the matrices.

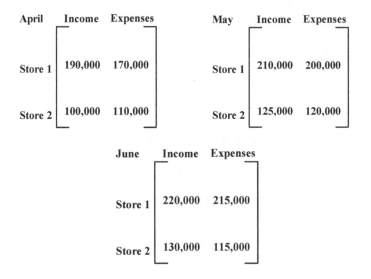

April	Income	Expenses
Store 1	190,000	170,000
Store 2	100,000	110,000

May	Income	Expenses
Store 1	210,000	200,000
Store 2	125,000	120,000

June	Income	Expenses
Store 1	220,000	215,000
Store 2	130,000	115,000

The owner wants to know what his first-quarter income and expenses were, so he adds the three matrices.

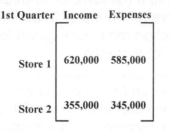

Then, to find the profit for each store:
Profit for Store 1 = $620,000 - $585,000 = $35,000
Profit for Store 2 = $355,000 - $345,000 = $10,000

20G. Characteristics and applications of graphs and trees

A **graph** is a set of points (or nodes) and lines (or edges) that connect some subset of these points. A **finite graph** has a limited number of both nodes and edges. An example graph is shown below. Note that not all of the nodes in a graph need be connected to other nodes.

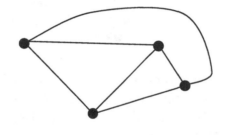

The edges of a graph may or may not have a specified direction or orientation; also, the edges (and nodes) may or may not have some assigned label or value. For instance, a graph representing airline flight paths might include nodes that represent cities and edges the represent the direction and distance of the paths between the cities. A **tree** is a graph that does not include any closed loops. In addition, a tree has no unconnected nodes (separate nodes or groups of connected nodes constitute a separate tree—groups of several trees are called a forest). In addition, the edges that connect the nodes of a tree do not have a direction or orientation. A **finite tree**, like a finite graph, has a limited number of edges and nodes. The graph shown above is not a tree, but it takes the form of a tree with a few alterations.

A **network** is a graph (directed or undirected) where each edge is assigned a positive real number in accordance with a specific function. The function may correspond to the distance between two points on a map, for instance.

Trees and graphs can be used to represent a wide variety of types of information. They can also be useful tools for solving problems that involve maps, hierarchies, directories, structures, communications networks and a range of other objects.

Example: Find the shortest path between points A and B on the following directed graph.

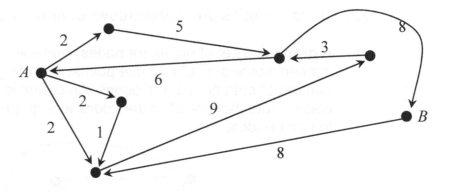

Taking careful note of the direction of the edges, find the possible routes through the graph from A to B. Only two paths are possible; choose the path with the smallest sum of the values along the associated edges.

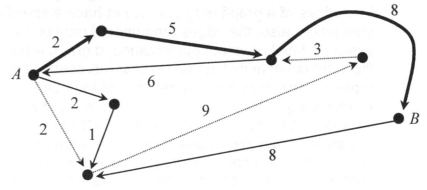

The total distance for the shortest path is $2 + 5 + 8 = 15$.

SUBAREA VI.   INTEGRATION OF KNOWLEDGE AND UNDERSTANDING

Competency 0021   Prepare an organized, developed analysis on a topic related to one or more of the following: number sense and operations; patterns, relations, and algebra; geometry and measurement; data analysis, statistics, and probability; and trigonometry, calculus, and discrete mathematics.

Open response questions are designed to probe the depth of a student's understanding of mathematical concepts. These questions, therefore, go beyond the straightforward application of a formula. They require a higher level of reasoning and also the ability to make connections between different areas of mathematics. Open response questions also test communication skills by requiring clear and concise answers often accompanied by diagrams and graphs.

The goal in a multiple choice question is simply to come up with the correct answer. Sometimes all you need to do is eliminate the wrong answers without necessarily understanding exactly how the right answer is arrived at. For an open response question, on the other hand, you are required to explain every step in your thinking and, in some cases, even identify the underlying concepts needed to solve the problem.

Characteristics of open response questions (a typical question may have one or more of the following features):

1.   The problem is very similar to a standard problem but deviates slightly in some respect.
2.   Multiple representations of a problem are involved; for instance, a diagram as well as a data table may be used.
3.   Data or description of a situation is given and you are asked to create a data table, diagram, equation, or graph.
4.   Alternatively, a diagram or graph of an equation is given and you have to provide a detailed analysis of the information it presents.
5.   There are multiple steps, sometimes of increasing complexity, with each step building on the previous one.
6.   Explanations are required for each step in the problem.
7.   Description of underlying concepts is required.
8.   There is often a real world orientation.

When you are faced with a question of this type, the answer may sometimes jump out at you and the approach or formula to be used may be obvious. There are times, however, when you have no idea how to get started on a solution. In a situation like this you need to rely on some pre-determined strategy. Here are some suggestions for approaching an open response question:

1. Make sure to read and re-read the problem several times so you understand exactly what is asked for. If necessary underline or highlight salient points, significant words, and numbers. It may be helpful to write them in the form of a table.

    Example: A business makes a profit of $29440 in April which is 15% greater than the profit made in March. The profit made in March was 8% below the February profit. How much more profit was made in February than in March?

April	$29440	15% more than March
March	?	8% less than February
February	?	

2. Put some time into thinking through the problem before you put pen to paper. This will help you avoid common pitfalls such as
    (a)   Answering a different question about the same problem and not the one that was asked; e.g. finding the perimeter of a geometric figure instead of area.
    (b)   Missing the exact wording; e.g. In the above example you may be tempted to assume that the March profit is 15% less than the April number and erroneously take the 15% on the April value instead of the March value.
    (c)   Mistaking the problem for a more typical one that has a standard formula; e.g. finding the volume of a sphere instead of a hemisphere.

3. Don't be discouraged if you proceed with a certain approach and hit a wall. Even if you have to start over, you have learned something about the problem.

4. If you have no idea how to approach the problem, try the guess and check approach at first. That will give you a sense of the kind of problem you are dealing with. You may be able to identify a pattern or at least eliminate some possibilities.

Example: Mary is 5 years older than Jennifer who is 8 years younger than Sarah. Their ages add up to 43. How old is Jennifer?

Start with any age and look for a pattern:

Jennifer	Mary	Sarah	Total
5	10	13	28
6	11	14	31
7	12	15	34

Adding 1 year to Jennifer's age increases the total by 3. Since the total must be 9 years more than 34, Jennifer's age must be 3 years more than 7 = 10.

Example: In the addition problem $\begin{array}{r} BB \\ +BB \\ \hline ABC \end{array}$, A, B, C represent

different digits. Find A, B & C.

Try a random number B=3. Since 33+33 = 66, you realize immediately that in order to have a digit in the hundreds place, B must be 5 or greater. Thus you have narrowed down the possible range of answers.

5. Even if you are not asked to draw a diagram you may want to create one anyway as an aid to your own understanding of the problem. Draw the important events or variables with numbers and show the connections between them. Label the parts of the diagram appropriately. For instance, in the age problem above, you may draw a simple line diagram as follows:

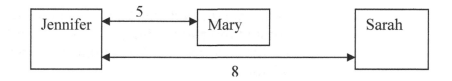

6.   Keep open response questions in mind while studying:
    (a)   Make sure you understand the reasoning behind rules and how rules are connected to one another. One is often tempted to skip these explanations since they are not needed to solve standard problems.
    (b)   Limit use of calculators. Keep your number sense alive.

The following sections contain some example problems. Even though they are categorized by area, you will find that there is a lot of overlap such as the use of algebra in number problems or the use of geometry in calculus.

21A.   Number Sense And Operations

1.   Three added to one-fourth of a number results in one-third of that number. Find the number.
(a)   Demonstrate at least two ways of solving this problem.
(b)   For each method, explain the steps.
(c)   For each method, identify the underlying concepts.

First method: Three is the difference between one-third and one-fourth of the number.

Since $\dfrac{1}{3} - \dfrac{1}{4} = \dfrac{4-3}{12} = \dfrac{1}{12}$, $\dfrac{1}{12}$ of the number is 3.

Hence, the number is 3x12=36.

In order to solve the problem using this method, a student must be familiar with fractions and the standard method for addition and subtraction of fractions. The combination of fractions also requires the understanding of LCM.

Second method: This problem may be also solved using a diagrammatic representation of the two fractions involved.

A rectangle divided into 12 parts (the LCM of 3 and 4) is used to represent the two fractions of the number. From the diagram it is clear that one part in 12 is equal to 3. Hence the number is 12x3=36.

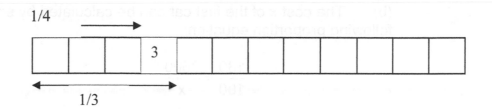

In order to use this method to solve the problem, a student must understand fractions as well s the concept of LCM.

<u>Third method</u>: This problem may also be solved using algebraic methods.

Let the unknown number be x. Then we can represent the given statement using the following equation:
$$\frac{1}{4}x + 3 = \frac{1}{3}x$$

Rearranging the terms and solving for x:
$$\frac{1}{3}x - \frac{1}{4}x = 3$$
$$\Rightarrow \frac{4x - 3x}{12} = 3$$
$$\Rightarrow \frac{x}{12} = 3$$
$$\Rightarrow x = 36$$

This method requires knowledge of basic algebra including the solution of equations using fractions.

2.   A man sold two cars for $6,500 each. On the first car he made a profit of 30% and on the second car he lost 30%.
(a)   Did he make a profit overall or did he lose money?
(b)   What was the percentage of his net gain or loss?

(a)   Since both cars were sold for the same price, the first car was cheaper than the second. Since the percentage is the same in both cases, the profit on the first car was smaller than the loss on the second car. Hence, even without calculating the actual amounts, one can conclude that the man lost money overall.

(b)   The cost x of the first car can be calculated by setting up the following proportion equation:

$$\frac{130}{100} = \frac{3500}{x}$$

Cross-multiplying and solving for x,

$$130x = 350000$$

$$\Rightarrow x = \frac{350000}{130} = 2692.31$$

The cost y of the second car can be calculated by setting up the following proportion equation:

$$\frac{70}{100} = \frac{3500}{y}$$

Cross-multiplying and solving for y,

$$70y = 350000$$

$$\Rightarrow y = \frac{350000}{70} = 5000$$

Net cost of the two cars = $7692.31
Net sale price for the cars= $7000

Hence, net percentage loss=
$$\frac{7692.31 - 7000}{7692.31} \times 100 = \frac{692.31}{7692.31} \times 100 = 9\%$$

21B.   Patterns, Relations, And Algebra

1.   An open swimming pool 50 ft long and 20 ft wide has a wide walkway of uniform breadth running all around it. If the area of the walkway is four times that of the pool, what is the outer perimeter of the walkway? Round your answer to the tenth of a foot.
(a)   Draw and label a diagram to represent the problem described above.
(b)   Write an equation expressing the relationships between the different dimensions.
(c)   Explain the steps in your solution.

How does the total area of the large rectangle including the pool and walkway change as the width of the walkway changes? Describe the pattern.

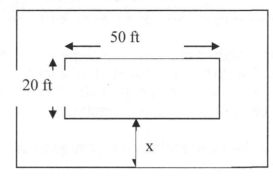

Let the width of the walkway be x ft.
Then, the length of the large rectangle = 50 + 2x ft
The width of the large rectangle = 20 + 2x ft

The area of the swimming pool = 20 x 50 = 1000 sq. ft
The area of the large rectangle including the walkway and swimming pool = (20 + 2x)(50 + 2x) sq. ft

Since the area of the walkway is 4 times that of the swimming pool, the area of the large rectangle including both the walkway and swimming pool is 5 times that of the swimming pool.

This relationship maybe expressed using the following quadratic equation:

$$(20 + 2x)(50 + 2x) = 5000$$

Multiplying out the terms and rearranging them in the standard form we get:

$$1000 + 100x + 40x + 4x^2 = 5000$$

$$\Rightarrow 4x^2 + 140x + 1000 = 5000$$

$$\Rightarrow 4x^2 + 140x - 4000 = 0$$

$$\Rightarrow x^2 + 35x - 1000 = 0$$

The quadratic formula can be used to solve the equation:

$$x = \frac{-35 \pm \sqrt{35^2 - 4 \cdot 1 \cdot (-1000)}}{2} = \frac{-35 \pm \sqrt{1225 + 4000}}{2} = \frac{-35 \pm 72.28}{2}$$

Since the width of the walkway cannot be a negative number, we choose the positive solution:

$$x = \frac{-35 + 72.28}{2} = \frac{37.28}{2} = 18.64$$

Hence, the length of the large rectangle = 50+18.64 x 2 = 50 + 37.28 = 87.3 ft (to the nearest tenth of a foot).
The width of the large rectangle = 20 + 37.28 = 57.3 ft
Thus, the perimeter of the large rectangle = 2(87.3+57.3)= 289.2 ft

The area of the large rectangle is related to the width of the walkway as follows:
$$\text{Area} = (20 + 2x)(50 + 2x) = 4x^2 + 140x + 1000$$

This is a quadratic function and hence we expect to see the area increase in a non-linear fashion as x increases.

To observe the relation between the area of the large triangle and the value of x, we tabulate a set of values with a fixed increment:

X	Length of rectangle	Width of rectangle	Area
0	50	20	1000
5	60	30	1800
10	70	40	2800
15	80	50	4000
20	90	60	5400
25	100	70	7000

The table shows that every time the width of the walkway is increased by 5 ft, the area of the large rectangle increases by 200 sq.ft. more than it did the previous time.

2.   Two friends live on an east-west street and agree to meet at a park on the same street due east from both of their houses. Nancy leaves home at 8:00 a.m. and drives at 30 mph to the park which is 25 miles from her house. Susan lives 15 miles away from the park and leaves home at a later time driving at 50 mph. If both of them reach the park at the same time, what time did Susan leave home? Include the following in your solution:

(a)   A diagram showing the locations and known distances in the problem.

(b)   Equations to represent the relationship between distance driven and time for both Nancy and Susan.

(c)   A graph of the above equations. Explain what each element of the graph represents.

Nancy's house   Susan's house   15 miles   Park

25 miles

Let d be the distance in miles from Nancy's house and t the time elapsed in hours after Nancy leaves home. Then $d = 0$ at Nancy's house and $t = 0$ at 8 a.m. Since Nancy drives at a constant speed, the distance traveled by Nancy can be represented by the following linear equation

$$d = 30t$$

where the slope of the line is the speed 30 mph.

If Susan leaves home at time t_0 and distance d_0 from Nancy's house, the distance traveled by Susan is given by

$$d = 50(t - t_0) + d_0$$

Since we know that $d_0 = 10$ miles (distance from Nancy's house to Susan's house), we can write the equation as

$$d = 50(t - t_0) + 10$$

If both Nancy and Susan reach the park at time t_1, then using equation $d = 30t$, we can find t_1:

$$25 = 30t_1; \; t_1 = \frac{25}{30} = \frac{5}{6} \text{hr}$$

Substituting d = 25 and t = $\frac{5}{6}$ in equation $d = 50(t - t_0) + 10$ we get

$$25 = 50(\frac{5}{6} - t_0) + 10$$

$$\Rightarrow 50(\frac{5}{6} - t_0) = 15$$

$$\Rightarrow \frac{5}{6} - t_0 = \frac{3}{10}$$

$$\Rightarrow t_0 = \frac{5}{6} - \frac{3}{10} = \frac{25 - 9}{30} = \frac{16}{30} = \frac{8}{15} hr$$

Thus, Susan left home $\frac{8}{15}$ hr after Nancy at 8:32 a.m.

The above equations are represented graphically as follows:

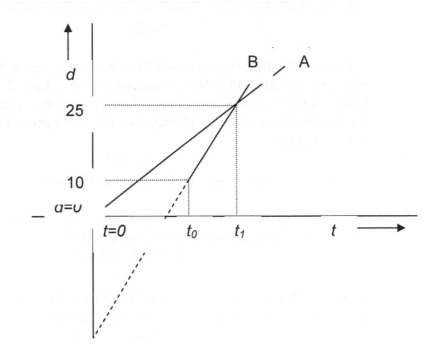

Line A represents the distance driven by Nancy as a function of time. Line B represents the distance driven by Susan. Since both of them drive at constant speeds, the two lines are straight lines. The slopes of the lines represent the speeds at which Nancy and Susan drive. Since Susan drove faster than Nancy, line B has a larger slope. The intersection point of the two lines represents their meeting point at the park and the time at which they reached the park. Note that line B has a negative y-intercept if extended before time t_0. This simply indicates that if Susan had been traveling at the same speed and in the same direction at time t=0 (the time Nancy left home), then she would have started out at a location to the west of Nancy's house.

21C. Geometry And Measurement

1.   Find the area of the figure bounded by lines joining the points (0,0), (0,5),(5,10),(10,5),(5,0),(0,0) in the order given.
(a)   Draw and label the figure on a coordinate plane.
(b)   Explain every step of your reasoning.

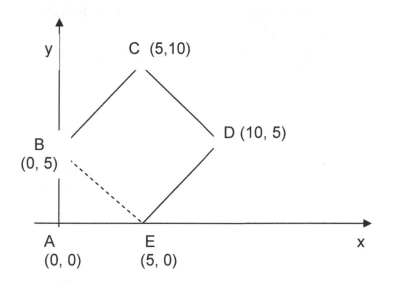

The figure ABCDE is the combination of a right triangle ABE and a square BCDE.

We can demonstrate that BCDE is a square as follows:

Length of line BC = $\sqrt{(0-5)^2 + (5-10)^2} = \sqrt{25+25} = \sqrt{50} = 5\sqrt{2}$

Slope of line BC = $\dfrac{10-5}{5-0} = \dfrac{5}{5} = 1$

Length of line ED = $\sqrt{(5-10)^2 + (0-5)^2} = \sqrt{25+25} = \sqrt{50} = 5\sqrt{2}$

Slope of line ED = $\dfrac{5-0}{10-5} = \dfrac{5}{5} = 1$

Since BC and ED are equal in length and have the same slope, BCDE is a parallelogram. Hence BE is equal to and parallel to CD.

Length of line BE (and CD) =
$\sqrt{(0-5)^2 + (5-0)^2} = \sqrt{25+25} = \sqrt{50} = 5\sqrt{2}$

Slope of line BE (and CD) = $\dfrac{5-0}{0-5} = \dfrac{5}{-5} = -1$

BE and CD are equal in length to BC and ED.
Since slope of ED x slope of BE = -1, the two lines are perpendicular to each other. Thus, BCDE is a square with side of length $5\sqrt{2}$.
Therefore, the area of the figure ABCDE = area of ABE + area of BCDE

$$= \frac{1}{2}5 \times 5 + (5\sqrt{2})^2 = 12.5 + 50 = 62.5 \text{ sq. units}$$

2.   Three tennis balls are stacked one on top of the other in a cylindrical container. The balls touch the sides and top of the container.
(a)   Draw a diagram to illustrate the problem.
(b)   How is the volume of the container related to the radius of a tennis ball? Write an equation to demonstrate the relationship.
(c)   What is the volume of the container if the radius of a tennis ball is 5 cm?

r

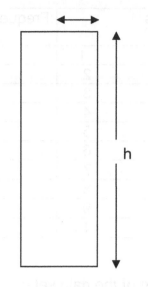

Since the tennis balls touch the sides of the container, the radius *r* of the cylinder is the same as the radius of a ball. The height h of the cylinder is equal to 3 times the diameter of a tennis ball, i.e. *h =6r*.

Hence, the volume of the container is given by the equation
$$V = \pi r^2 h = \pi r^2 (6r)$$
$$\Rightarrow V = 6\pi r^3$$

If r = 5 cm, $V = 6\pi(5)^3 = 750\pi\,cm^3$.

21D. Data Analysis, Statistics, And Probability

1.   The frequency distribution below shows the summary of some test results where people scored points ranging from 0 to 10. One person scored 1 point, 4 people scored 2 points and so on.
(a)   Find the mean, median, mode and standard deviation of the data set.
(b)   Draw a histogram of the distribution.
(c)   How does the data compare to a normal distribution?

Points	Frequency	Cumulative Frequency
1	1	1
2	4	5
3	30	35
4	25	60
5	12	72
6	7	79
7	6	85
8	6	91
9	2	93
10	1	94

The mean of the data set =
(1x1+2x4+3x30+4x25+5x12+6x7+7x6+8x6+9x2+10x1)=
(1+8+90+100+60+42+42+48+18+10)=419/94=4.5

The median score (the point at which the cumulative frequency reaches or surpasses the value 47) = 4

The mode or value with the highest frequency = 3

The standard deviation of the data set =

$$\sqrt{\frac{(-3.5)^2 + 4(-2.5)^2 + 30(-1.5)^2 + 25(-0.5)^2 + 12(0.5)^2 + 7(1.5)^2 + 6(2.5)^2 + 6(3.5)^2 + 2(4.5)^2 + (5.5}{94}}$$

$$\sqrt{\frac{12.25 + 25 + 67.5 + 62.5 + 3 + 15.75 + 37.5 + 73.5 + 40.5 + 30.25}{94}} = \sqrt{\frac{367.75}{94}} = 2.0$$

The frequency distribution from the above example is displayed below as a histogram.

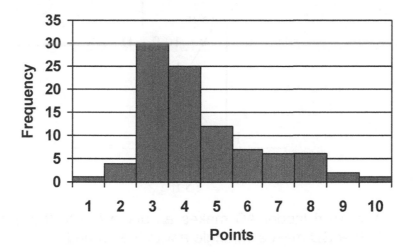

This distribution is not normal. A normal distribution is symmetric with one peak exactly in the middle. Also, the mean, median, and mode are identical for a normal distribution. In this case, the peak value or mode is on the left with a long tail on the right. The mean and median are not very far apart (4, and 4.5) but the mode is much smaller with a value of 3.

21E. Trigonometry, Calculus, And Discrete Mathematics

1.   Two ladders of length 10 ft and 15 ft are leaning against two parallel walls as shown below. If the distance between the walls is 5 ft, find, using trigonometric ratios, the height above the ground where the two ladders cross each other to the nearest tenth of a foot.

(a)   Label the relevant positions and angles in the diagram.

(b)   Show all the steps in your work.

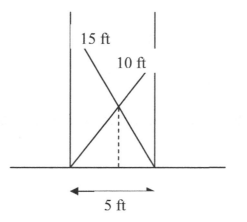

The diagram with the position and angle labels added:

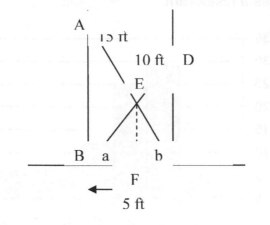

The 15 ft ladder AC makes an angle b with the ground. The 10ft ladder BD makes an angle a with the ground.

First, we find the angles a and b using trigonometric ratios:

$$\cos a = \frac{BC}{BD} = \frac{5}{10} = \frac{1}{2}; \Rightarrow a = \cos^{-1}(\frac{1}{2}) = 60^0$$

$$\cos b = \frac{BC}{AC} = \frac{5}{15} = \frac{1}{3}; \Rightarrow b = \cos^{-1}(\frac{1}{3}) = 70.5^0$$

Considering triangle EBF, $\tan a = \frac{EF}{BF}; \Rightarrow BF = \frac{EF}{\tan a}$

Considering triangle ECF, $\tan b = \frac{EF}{FC}; \Rightarrow FC = \frac{EF}{\tan b}$

Since BF+FC=5,

$$\frac{EF}{\tan a} + \frac{EF}{\tan b} = 5$$

$$\Rightarrow EF(\frac{1}{\tan a} + \frac{1}{\tan b}) = 5$$

$$\Rightarrow EF(0.58 + 0.35) = 5$$

$$\Rightarrow EF = \frac{5}{0.93} = 5.38$$

Hence, the two ladders cross each other 5.4 ft above the ground.

2.   A cone must be constructed for a science experiment with a slant height of 20 cm. Find the radius and height needed to maximize the volume of the cone.

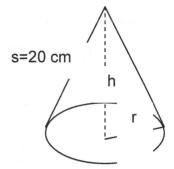

For a cone of height h and radius r, the slant height and volume are given by

$$s = \sqrt{r^2 + h^2}; \quad V = \frac{1}{3}\pi r^2 h$$

If s= 20 cm, then

$$\sqrt{r^2 + h^2} = 20$$
$$\Rightarrow r^2 + h^2 = 400$$
$$\Rightarrow h = \sqrt{400 - r^2}$$

and the volume $V = \frac{1}{3}\pi r^2 h = \frac{1}{3}\pi r^2 \sqrt{400 - r^2}$

To find the maximum value of the volume, we set the derivate of the volume with respect to r equal to zero:

$$\frac{d}{dr}(\frac{1}{3}\pi r^2 \sqrt{400 - r^2}) = 0$$
$$\Rightarrow \frac{1}{3}\pi(r^2 \frac{d}{dr}(\sqrt{400 - r^2}) + \sqrt{400 - r^2}\frac{d}{dr}(r^2)) = 0$$
$$\Rightarrow r^2 \frac{(-2r)}{2\sqrt{400 - r^2}} + 2r\sqrt{400 - r^2} = 0$$
$$\Rightarrow -r^3 + 2r(400 - r^2) = 0$$
$$\Rightarrow -3r^3 + 800r = 0$$
$$\Rightarrow 3r^2 = 800; \quad \Rightarrow r = \sqrt{\frac{800}{3}} = 16.3$$
$$h = \sqrt{400 - r^2} = \sqrt{400 - \frac{800}{3}} = \sqrt{\frac{400}{3}} = 11.5$$

Thus the radius of the cone must be 16.3 cm and the height of the cone must be 11.5 cm.

Answer Key to Practice Problems

Competency 0007

page 87

Question #1   Question #2

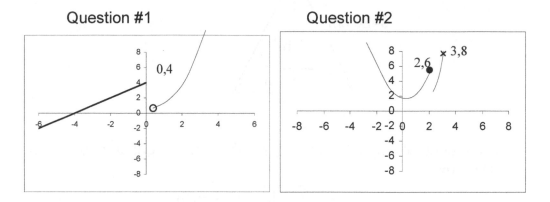

Competency 0008

page 104

Question #1 $y = \dfrac{3}{4}x + \dfrac{17}{4}$

Question #2 $x = 11$

Question #3 $y = \dfrac{3}{5}x + \dfrac{42}{5}$

Question #4 $y = 5$

page 112

Question #1   x > 3

Question #2   x = 2

Question #3   x ≤ 6

Question #4   x = -4

Competency 0010

page 132

Question #1   It takes Curly 15 minutes to paint the elephant alone

Question #2   The original fraction is $\dfrac{5}{15}$.

Question #3   The car was traveling at 68mph and the truck was traveling at 62mph

page 137

Question #1

Question #2

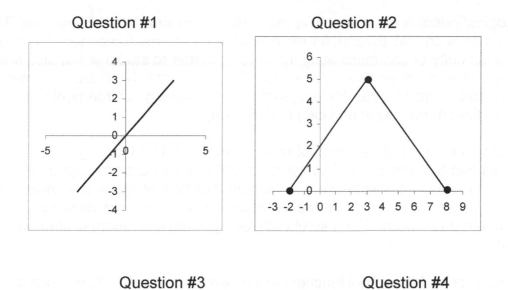

Question #3

Question #4

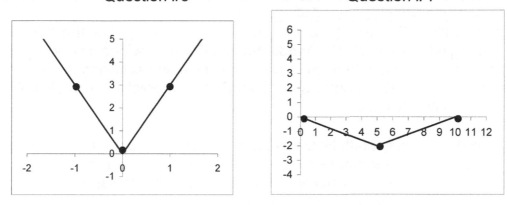

Essential Tips for Every Math Teacher

Pedagogical principles and teaching methods are important for all teachers. They are particularly critical, though, for math teaching since math teachers not only face the difficulty of communicating the subject matter to students but also that of surmounting an all-pervasive cultural fear of mathematics. Math teachers need to take particular care to foster learning in a non-threatening environment that is at the same time genuinely stimulating and challenging.

The National Council of Teachers of Mathematics (NCTM) (http://www.nctm.org/) Principles and Standards emphasizes the teacher's obligation to support all students not only in developing basic mathematics knowledge and skills but also in their ability to understand and reason mathematically to solve problems relevant to today's world. The use of technology in the classroom is strongly advocated.

Resources for middle school teachers are available on the NCTM website at http://www.nctm.org/resources/middle.aspx.
The Mathematics Pathway (http://msteacher.org/math.aspx) on the National Science Digital Library (NSDL) Middle School Portal provides a very comprehensive and rich treasure trove of helpful material linking to various resources on the web including articles as well as interactive instructional modules on various topics.

The Drexel University Math Forum website provides the opportunity to interact with mentors and other math educators online. Some of the material on this website requires paid subscription but there are openly available archives as well. An overview of what the site provides is available at http://mathforum.org/about.forum.html. You may find the "Teacher2Teacher" service particularly useful; you can ask questions or browse the archives for a wealth of nitty-gritty everyday teaching information, suggestions and links to teaching tools.

This website for sixth grade contains animated lessons, discussions of strategies and a glossary of terms using few words and plenty of illustrations.
http://students.resa.net/stoutcomputerclass/1math.htm

Other instructional and professional development resources:

http://archives.math.utk.edu/k12.html
http://www.learnalberta.ca/Launch.aspx?content=/content/mesg/html/math6web/math6shell.html
http://mmap.wested.org/webmath/

Pedagogical Principles

Maintain a supportive, non-threatening environment

Many students unfortunately perceive mathematics as a threat. This becomes a particular critical issue at the middle school level where they learn algebra for the first time and are required to think in new ways. Since fear "freezes" the brain and makes thinking really difficult, a student's belief that he is no good at math becomes a self-fulfilling prophecy. A teacher's primary task in this situation is to foster a learning environment where every student feels that he or she can learn to think mathematically. Here are some ways to go about this:

Accept all comments and questions: Acknowledge all questions and comments that students make. If what the student says is inaccurate or irrelevant to the topic in hand, point that out gently but also show your understanding of the thought process that led to the comment. This will encourage students to speak up in class and enhance their learning.

Set aside time for group work: Assign activities to groups of students comprised of mixed ability levels. It is often easier for students to put forward their own thoughts as part of a friendly group discussion than when they are sitting alone at their desks with a worksheet. The more proficient students can help the less able ones and at the same time clarify their own thinking. You will essentially be using the advanced students in the class as a resource in a manner that also contributes to their own development. The struggling students will feel supported by their peers and not isolated from them.

Encourage classroom discussion of math topics: For instance, let the whole class share different ways in which they approach a certain problem. It will give you insight into your students' ways of thinking and make it easier to help them. It will allow even those who just listen to understand and correct errors in their thinking without being put on the spot.

Engage and challenge students

Maintaining a non-threatening environment should not mean dumbing down the math content in the classroom. The right level of challenge and relevance to their daily lives can help to keep students interested and learning. Here are some ideas:

Show connections to the real world: Use real life examples of math problems in your teaching. Some suggestions are given in the next section. Explain the importance of math literacy in society and the pitfalls of not being mathematically aware. An excellent reference is "The 10 Things All Future Mathematicians and Scientists Must Know" by Edward Zaccaro. The title of the book is misleading since it deals with things that every educated person, not just mathematicians and scientists, should know.

<u>Use technology:</u> Make use of calculators and computers including various online, interactive resources in your teaching. The natural affinity today's children have for these devices will definitely help them to engage more deeply in their math learning.

<u>Demonstrate "messy" math:</u> Children often have the mistaken belief that every math problem can be solved by following a particular set of rules; they either know the rules or they don't. In real life, however, math problems can be approached in different ways and often one has to negotiate several blind alleys before getting to the real solution. Children instinctively realize this while doing puzzles or playing games. They just don't associate this kind of thinking with classroom math. The most important insight any math teacher can convey to students is the realization that even if they don't know how to do a problem at first, they can think about it and figure it out as long as they are willing to stay with the problem and make mistakes in the process. An obvious way to do this, of course, is to introduce mathematical puzzles and games in the classroom. The best way, however, is for teachers themselves to take risks occasionally with unfamiliar problems and demonstrate to the class how one can work one's way out of a clueless state.

<u>Show the reasoning behind rules:</u> Even when it is not a required part of the curriculum, explain, whenever possible, how a mathematical rule is derived or how it is connected to other rules. For instance, in explaining the rule for finding the area of a trapezoid, show how one can get to it by thinking of the trapezoid as two triangles. This will reinforce the students' sense of mathematics as something that can be logically arrived at and not something for which they have to remember innumerable rules. Another way to reinforce this idea is to do the same problem using different approaches.

<u>Be willing to take occasional side trips:</u> Be flexible at times and go off topic in order to explore more deeply any questions or comments from the students. Grab a teaching opportunity even if it is irrelevant to the topic under discussion.

Help every student gain a firm grasp of fundamentals
While discussion, reasoning and divergent thinking is to be encouraged, it can only be done on a firm scaffolding of basic math knowledge. A firm grasp of math principles, for most people, does require rote exercises and doing more and more of the same problems. Just as practicing scales is essential for musical creativity, math creativity can only be built on a foundation strengthened by drilling and repetition. Many educators see independent reasoning and traditional rule-based drilling as opposing approaches. An effective teacher, however, must maintain a balance between the two and ensure that students have the basic tools they need to think independently.

<u>Make sure all students actually know basic math rules and concepts</u>: Test students regularly for basic math knowledge and provide reinforcement with additional practice wherever necessary.

<u>Keep reviewing old material</u>: Don't underestimate your students' ability to forget what they haven't seen in a while. Link new topics whenever possible with things your students have learned before and take the opportunity to review previous learning. Most math textbooks nowadays have a spiral review section created with this end in mind.

<u>Keep mental math muscles strong:</u> The calculator, without question, is a very valuable learning tool. Many students, unfortunately, use it as a crutch to the point that they lose the natural feel for numbers and ability to estimate that people develop through mental calculations. As a result, they are often unable to tell when they punch a wrong button and get a totally unreasonable answer. Take your students through frequent mental calculation exercises; you can easily integrate it into class discussions. Teach them useful strategies for making mental estimates.

Specific Teaching Methods

Some commonly used teaching techniques and tools are described below along with links to further information. The links provided in the first part of this chapter also provide a wealth of instructional ideas and material.

A very useful resource is the book "Family Math: The Middle School Years" from the Lawrence Hall of Science, University of California at Berkeley. Although this book was developed for use by families, teachers in school can choose from the many simple activities and games used to reinforce two significant middle school skills, algebraic reasoning and number sense. A further advantage is that all the activities are based on NCTM standards and each activity lists the specific math concepts that are covered.

Here are some tools you can use to make your teaching more effective:

Classroom openers
To start off your class with stimulated, interested and focused students, provide a short opening activity every day. You can make use of thought-provoking questions, puzzles or tricks. Also use relevant puzzles or tricks to illustrate specific topics at any point in your class. The following website provides some ideas:

http://mathforum.org/k12/k12puzzles/

Real life examples

Connect math to other aspects of your students' lives by using examples and data from the real world whenever possible. It will not only keep them engaged, it will also help answer the perennial question "Why do we have to learn math?" Online resources to get you started:

1. Using weather concepts to teach math:
   http://www.nssl.noaa.gov/edu/ideas/

2. Election math in the classroom:
   http://mathforum.org/t2t/faq/election.html

3. Math worksheets related to the Iditarod, an annual Alaskan sled dog race:
   http://www.educationworld.com/a_lesson/lesson/lesson302.shtml

4. Personal finance examples:
   http://www.publicdebt.treas.gov/mar/marmoneymath.htm

5. Graphing with real data:
   http://www.middleweb.com/Graphing.html

Manipulatives

Manipulatives can help all students learn; particularly those oriented more towards visual and kinesthetic learning. Here are some ideas for the use of manipulatives in the classroom:

1. Use tiles, pattern blocks or geoboards to demonstrate geometry concepts such as shapes, area and perimeter. In the example shown below, 12 tiles are used to form different rectangles.

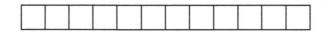

12 x 1

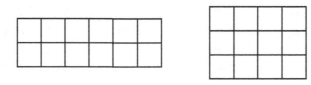

6 x 2

3 x 4

2. Stacks of blocks representing numbers are useful for teaching basic statistics concepts such as mean, median and mode. Rearranging the blocks to make each stack the same height would demonstrate the mean or average value of the data set. The example below shows a data set represented by stacks of blocks. Rearranging the blocks to make the height of each stack equal to three shows that this is the mean value.

2 1 3 5 4 1 3 3 5

3. Tiles, blocks, or other countable manipulatives such as beans can also be used to demonstrate numbers in different bases. Each stack will represent a place with the number of blocks in the stack showing the place value.

4. Playing cards can be used for a discussion of probability.

5. Addition and subtraction of integers, positive and negative, is a major stumbling block for many middle school students. Two sets of tiles, marked with pluses and minuses respectively, can be used to demonstrate these concepts visually with each "plus" tile canceling a "minus" tile.

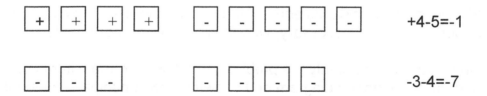

6. Percentages may be visualized using two parallel number lines, one showing the actual numbers, the other showing the percentages.

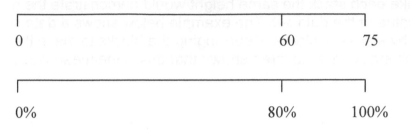

A practical demonstration of percent changes can be made by photocopying a figure using different copier magnifications.

7. Algeblocks are blocks designed specifically for the teaching of algebra with manipulatives:
http://www.etacuisenaire.com/algeblocks/algeblocks.jsp

Software
Many of the online references in this section link to software for learning. A good site that provides easy to use virtual manipulatives as well as accompanying worksheets in some cases is the following:
http://boston.k12.ma.us/teach/technology/select/index.html

Spreadsheets can be very effective math learning tools. Here are some ideas for using spreadsheets in the classroom:
http://www.angelfire.com/wi2/spreadsheet/necc.html

Word problem strategies
Word problems, a challenge for many students even in elementary school, become more complicated and sometimes intimidating in the middle grades. Here are some ideas students can use to tackle them:

1. Identify significant words and numbers in the problem. Highlight or underline them. If necessary, write them in the form of a table.

2. Draw diagrams to clarify the problem. Put down the main items or events and numbers on the diagram and show the relationships between them.

3. Rewrite the problem using fewer and simpler words. One way is to have a standard format for this as shown in the example below.
   Problem: Calculate the cost of 3 pencils given that 5 pencils cost 25 cents.
   Rewrite as:
   Cost of 5 pencils = 25 cents
   Cost of 1 pencil = 25/5 = 5 cents
   Cost of 3 pencils = 5 X 3 = 15 cents

4. If you have no idea how to approach the problem, try the guess and check approach at first. That will give you a sense of the kind of problem you are dealing with.

5. Create similar word problems of your own.

Equation rule
Solving algebraic equations is a challenge for many learners particularly when they think they need to remember many different rules. Emphasize the fact that they only need to keep only one rule in mind whether they are adding, subtracting, multiplying or dividing numbers or variables:

"Do the same thing to both sides"

A balance or teeter-totter metaphor can help to clarify their understanding of equations. You can also use manipulatives to demonstrate.

Mental math practice
Give students regular practice in doing mental math. The following website offers many mental calculation tips and strategies:
http://mathforum.org/k12/mathtips/mathtips.html

Because frequent calculator use tends to deprive students of a sense of numbers, they will often approach a sequence of multiplications and divisions the hard way. For instance, asked to calculate 770 x 36/ 55, they will first multiply 770 and 36 and then do a long division with the 55. They fail to recognize that both 770 and 55 can be divided by 11 and then by 5 to considerably simplify the problem. Give students plenty of practice in multiplying and dividing a sequence of integers and fractions so they are comfortable with canceling top and bottom terms.

Math language
There is an explosion of new math words as students enter the middle grades and start learning algebra and geometry.

This website provides an animated, colorfully illustrated dictionary of math terms:
http://www.amathsdictionaryforkids.com/

The following site is not colorful and animated but contains brief and clear definitions and many more advanced math terms:
http://www.amathsdictionaryforkids.com/

WEB LINKS

ALGEBRA
Algebra
Algebra in bite-size pieces with quiz at the end
http://library.thinkquest.org/20991/alg/index.html
Algebra II: http://library.thinkquest.org/20991/alg2/index.html

Different levels plus quiz
http://www.math.com/homeworkhelp/Algebra.html

Clicking on the number leads to solution
http://www.math.armstrong.edu/MathTutorial/index.html

Algebraic Structures
Symbols and sets of numbers:
http://www.wtamu.edu/academic/anns/mps/math/mathlab/beg_algebra/beg_alg_tut2_sets.htm

Integers: http://amby.com/educate/math/integer.html
Card game to add and subtract integers: http://www.education-world.com/a_tsl/archives/03-1/lesson001.shtml
Multiplying integers: http://www.aaastudy.com/mul65_x2.htm

Rational/irrational numbers: http://regentsprep.org/regents/math/math-topic.cfm?TopicCode=rational

Several complex number exercise pages:
http://math.about.com/od/complexnumbers/Complex_Numbers.htm

Polynomial Equations and Inequalities
Systems of equations lessons and practice:
http://regentsprep.org/regents/math/math-topic.cfm?TopicCode=syslin
More practice:
http://www.sparknotes.com/math/algebra1/systemsofequations/problems3.rhtml
Word problems system of equations:
http://regentsprep.org/REgents/math/ALGEBRA/AE3/PracWord.htm
Inequalities: http://regentsprep.org/regents/Math/solvin/PSolvIn.htm
Inequality tutorial, examples, problems
http://www.wtamu.edu/academic/anns/mps/math/mathlab/beg_algebra/beg_alg_tut18_ineq.htm
Graphing linear inequalities tutorial
http://www.wtamu.edu/academic/anns/mps/math/mathlab/beg_algebra/beg_alg_tut24_ineq.htm

Quadratic equations tutorial, examples, problems
✓http://www.wtamu.edu/academic/anns/mps/math/mathlab/col_algebra/col_alg_tut
17_quad.htm
Practice factoring: http://regentsprep.org/Regents/math/math-
topic.cfm?TopicCode=factor
Synthetic division tutorial:
http://www.wtamu.edu/academic/anns/mps/math/mathlab/col_algebra/col_alg_tut
37_syndiv.htm
Synthetic division Examples and problems: http://www.tpub.com/math1/10h.htm

Functions
Function, domain, range intro and practice
http://www.mathwarehouse.com/algebra/relation/math-function.php
Equations with rational expressions tutorial
http://www.wtamu.edu/academic/anns/mps/math/mathlab/col_algebra/col_alg_tut
15_rateq.htm
Practice with rational expressions
http://education.yahoo.com/homework_help/math_help/problem_list?id=minialg1
gt_7_1
Practice simplifying radicals
http://www.bhs87.org/math/practice/radicals/radicalpractice.htm
Radical equations – lesson and practice
http://regentsprep.org/REgents/mathb/mathb-topic.cfm?TopicCode=7D3
Logarithmic functions tutorial
http://www.wtamu.edu/academic/anns/mps/math/mathlab/col_algebra/col_alg_tut
43_logfun.htm

Linear Algebra
Practice operations with matrices
http://www.castleton.edu/Math/finite/operation_practice.htm
Matrices, introduction and practice
http://www.math.csusb.edu/math110/src/matrices/basics.html
Vector practice tip: http://www.phy.mtu.edu/~suits/PH2100/vecdot.html

GEOMETRY
Geometry
http://library.thinkquest.org/20991/geo/index.html
http://www.math.com/students/homeworkhelp.html#geometry
http://regentsprep.org/Regents/math/geometry/math-GEOMETRY.htm

Parallelism
Parallel lines practice
http://www.algebralab.org/lessons/lesson.aspx?file=Geometry_AnglesParallelLin
esTransversals.xml

Plane Euclidean Geometry
Geometry facts and practice http://www.aaaknow.com/geo.htm
Triangles intro and practice
http://www.staff.vu.edu.au/mcaonline/units/geometry/triangles.html
Polygons exterior and interior angles practice
http://regentsprep.org/Regents/Math/math-topic.cfm?TopicCode=poly
Angles in circles practice
http://regentsprep.org/Regents/math/geometry/GP15/PcirclesN2.htm
Congruence of triangles – lessons, practice
http://regentsprep.org/Regents/math/geometry/GP4/indexGP4.htm
Pythagorean theorem and converse
http://regentsprep.org/Regents/math/geometry/GP13/indexGP13.htm
Circle equation practice
http://www.regentsprep.org/Regents/math/algtrig/ATC1/circlepractice.htm
Interactive parabola http://www.mathwarehouse.com/geometry/parabola/
Ellipse practice problems http://www.mathwarehouse.com/ellipse/equation-of-ellipse.php#equationOfEllipse

Three-Dimensional Geometry
3D figures intro and examples
http://www.mathleague.com/help/geometry/3space.htm

Transformational Geometry
Interactive transformational geometry practice on coordinate plane
http://www.shodor.org/interactivate/activities/Transmographer/
Similar triangles practice
http://regentsprep.org/Regents/math/similar/PracSim.htm
http://www.algebralab.org/practice/practice.aspx?file=Geometry_UsingSimilarTriangles.xml

NUMBER THEORY
Natural Numbers
http://online.math.uh.edu/MiddleSchool/Vocabulary/NumberTheoryVocab.pdf
GCF and LCM practice
http://teachers.henrico.k12.va.us/math/ms/C1Files/01NumberSense/1_5/6035prac.htm

PROBABILITY AND STATISTICS
Probability
Probability intro and practice
http://www.mathgoodies.com/lessons/vol6/intro_probability.html
Permutation and combination practice
http://www.regentsprep.org/Regents/math/algtrig/ATS5/PCPrac.htm
Conditional probability problems
http://homepages.ius.edu/MEHRINGE/T102/Supplements/HandoutConditionalProbability.htm

Statistics

Statistics lessons and interactive practice

http://www.aaaknow.com/sta.htm

Range, mean, median, mode exercises

http://www.mathgoodies.com/lessons/vol8/practice_vol8.html

http://regentsprep.org/regents/Math/mean/Pmeasure.htm

Sample Test

1. Which of the following is a prime number?
   (Easy)(Competency 1)

   A) 13

   B) 4

   C) 15

   D) 21

2. Given that n is a positive even integer, 5n + 4 will always be divisible by:
   (Average Rigor)(Competencies 1 and 6)

   A) 4

   B) 5

   C) 5n

   D) 2

3. Which of the following is always composite if *x* is odd, *y* is even, and both *x* and *y* are greater than or equal to 2?
   (Rigorous)(Competency 1)

   A) $x+y$ $3+2=5$

   B) $3x+2y$ — $9+4=12$

   C) $5xy$ $15\frac{1}{2}$ $15y$ ...

   D) $5x+3y$
      $15+6=11P$

4. Given that x, y, and z are prime numbers, which of the following is true?
   (Average Rigor)(Competency 1)

   A) x + y is always prime

   B) xyz is always prime

   C) xy is sometimes prime

   D) x + y is sometimes prime

5. Find the GCF of $2^2 \cdot 3^2 \cdot 5$ and $2^2 \cdot 3 \cdot 7$.
   (Average Rigor)(Competency 1)

   A) $2^5 \cdot 3^3 \cdot 5 \cdot 7$

   B) $2 \cdot 3 \cdot 5 \cdot 7$

   C) $2^2 \cdot 3$

   D) $2^3 \cdot 3^2 \cdot 5 \cdot 7$

6. Given even numbers x and y, which could be the LCM of x and y?
   (Average Rigor)(Competency 1)

   A) $\frac{xy}{2}$

   B) 2xy

   C) 4xy

   D) xy

7. Jason has five baseball cards. His friend Marcus gives him six more baseball cards. How many baseball cards does Jason have in all?
(Competency 1; Easy)

   A)   5

   B)   11

   C)   30

   D)   1

8. What is the answer to this problem?
(Competency 1; Easy)

   $$25 \div 5 =$$

   A)   5

   B)   30

   C)   125

   D)   20

9. Which words in a test problem would indicate that an addition operation is needed?
(Competency 1; Average rigor)

   A)   Each

   B)   How many

   C)   In each group

   D)   How many more than

10. A teacher is introducing the concept of multiplication to \ her third grade students. What is another way she might write 4 x 5?
(Competency 1; Average rigor)

   A)   4 + 5

   B)   5 + 4

   C)   4 + 4 + 4 + 4 + 4

   D)   5 + 5 + 5 + 5 + 5

11. A teacher plans an activity that involves students calculating how many chair legs are in the classroom, given that there are 30 chairs and each chair has 4 legs. This activity is introducing the ideas of:
(Competency 1; Average rigor)

   A)   Probability

   B)   Statistics

   C)   Geometry

   D)   Algebra

12. **What math principle is reinforced by matching numerals with number words?** (*Competency 1; Rigorous*)

A) Sequencing

B) Greater than and less than

C) Number representations

D) Rote counting

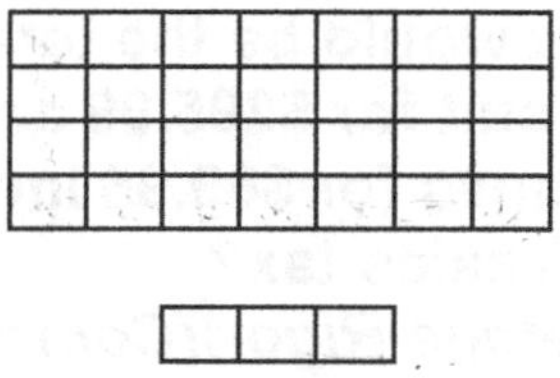

13. **The above diagram would be least appropriate for illustrating which of the following?** (*Average Rigor)(Competency 2)*

A) $7 \times 4 + 3$

B) $31 \div 8$

C) 28×3

D) $31 - 3$

14. $24 - 3 \times 7 + 2 =$
(*Average Rigor)(Competency 2)*

A) 5

B) 149

C) −3

D) 189

15. $7t - 4 \cdot 2t + 3t \cdot 4 \div 2 =$
(*Average Rigor)(Competency 2)*

A) 5t

B) 0

C) 31t

D) 18t

16. **Which of the following does not correctly relate an inverse operation?**
(*Average Rigor)(Competency 2)*

A) $a - b = a + -b$

B) $a \times b = b \div a$

C) $\sqrt{a^2} = a$

D) $a \times \frac{1}{a} = 1$

17. Given a,b,y, and z are real numbers and ay + b = z, Prove
$$y = \frac{z + -b}{a}$$

Statement	Reason
1) ay + b = z	1) Given
2) −b is a real number	2) Closure
3) (ay +b) + −b = z + −b	3) Addition property of Identity
4) ay + (b + −b) = z + −b	4) Associative
5) ay + 0 = z + −b	5) Additive inverse
6) ay = z + −b	6) Addition property of identity
7) $a = \frac{z + -b}{y}$	7) Division

Which reason is incorrect for the corresponding statement?
(Easy)(Competency 2)

   A) step 3

   B) step 4

   C) step 5

   D) step 6

18. Which of the following illustrates an inverse property?
(Easy)(Competency 2)

   A) a + b = a – b

   B) a + b = b + a

   C) a + 0 = a

   D) a + (−a) =0

19. Convert 0.75 into a fraction in lowest terms.
(Easy) (Competency 3)

   A) $\frac{6}{8}$

   B) $\frac{5}{8}$

   C) $\frac{4}{3}$

   D) $\frac{3}{4}$

20. What would be the total cost of a suit for $295.99 and a pair of shoes for $69.95 including 6.5% sales tax?
(Average Rigor)(Competency 3)

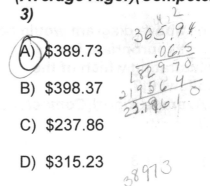

   A) $389.73

   B) $398.37

   C) $237.86

   D) $315.23

21. A student had 60 days to appeal the results of an exam. If the results were received on March 23, what was the last day that the student could appeal?
(Average Rigor)(Competency 3)

   A) May 21

   B) May 22

   C) May 23

   D) May 24

22. Sandra has $34.00, Carl has $42.00. How much more does Carl have than Sandra?

    Which would be the best method for finding the answer?
    (Easy)(Competency 3)

    A) addition

    B) subtraction

    C) division

    D) both A and B are equally correct

23. If three cups of concentrate are needed to make 2 gallons of fruit punch, how many cups are needed to make 5 gallons?
    (Easy)(Competency 3)

    A) 6 cups

    B) 7 cups

    C) 7.5 cups

    D) 10 cups

24. A sofa sells for $520. If the retailer makes a 30% profit, what was the wholesale price?
    (Average Rigor)(Competency 3)

    A) $400

    B) $676

    C) $490

    D) $364

25. Which statement is an example of the identity axiom of addition?
    (Easy)(Competency 4)

    A) $3 + -3 = 0$

    B) $3x = 3x + 0$

    C) $3 \cdot \frac{1}{3} = 1$

    D) $3 + 2x = 2x + 3$

26. Which axiom is incorrectly applied?
    (Average Rigor)(Competency 4)

    $$3x + 4 = 7$$

    Step a. $3x + 4 - 4 = 7 - 4$

       additive equality

    Step b. $3x + 4 - 4 = 3$

       commutative axiom of addition

    Step c. $3x + 0 = 3$

       additive inverse

    Step d. $3x = 3$

       additive identity

    A) step a

    B) step b

    C) step c

    D) step d

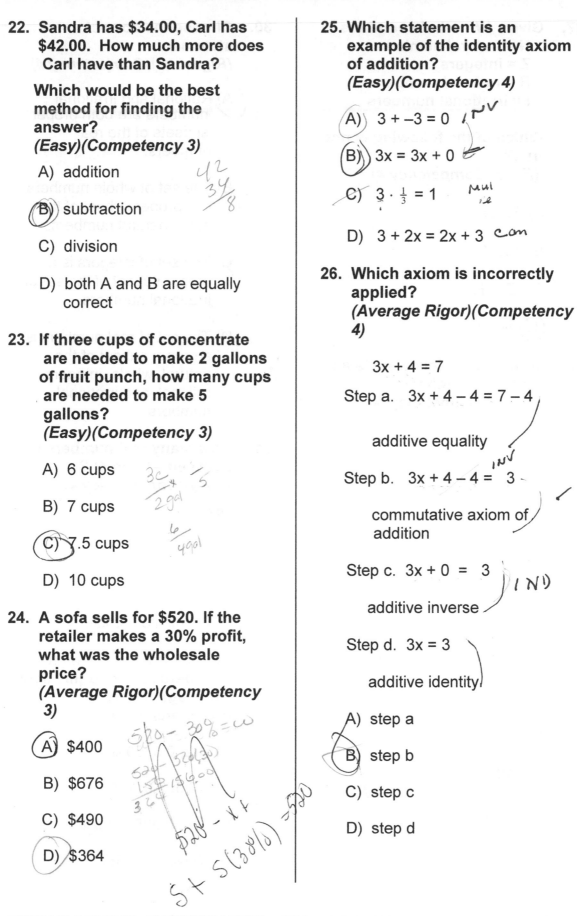

27. Given W = whole numbers
    N = natural numbers
    Z = integers
    R = rational numbers
    I = irrational numbers

    Which of the following is not true?
    (Easy)(Competency 4)

    A) $R \subset I$

    B) $W \subset Z$

    C) $Z \subset R$

    (D) $N \subseteq W$

28. Which of the following is an irrational number?
    (Easy)(Competency 4)

    A) .362626262...

    B) $4\frac{1}{3}$

    (C) $\sqrt{5}$

    D) $-\sqrt{16}$

29. Which denotes a complex number?
    (Rigorous)(Competency 4)

    A) 3.678678678...

    B) $-\sqrt{27}$

    C) $123^{1/2}$

    D) $(-100)^{1/2}$

30. Choose the correct statement:
    (Rigorous)(Competency 4)

    A) Rational and irrational numbers are both proper subsets of the real numbers.

    B) The set of whole numbers is a proper subset of the set of natural numbers.

    C) The set of integers is a proper subset of the set of irrational numbers.

    D) The set of real numbers is a proper subset of the natural, whole, integers, rational, and irrational numbers.

31. How many real numbers lie between −1 and +I ?
    (Easy)(Competency 4)

    A) 0

    B) 1

    C) 17

    D) an infinite number

32. Choose the set in which the members are **not** equivalent.
    (Average Rigor)
    (Competency 4)

    A) 1/2, 0.5, 50%

    B) 10/5, 2.0, 200%

    C) 3/8, 0.385, 38.5%

    D) 7/10, 0.7, 70%

33. $.\overline{63}$ into a fraction in simplest form.
    (Average Rigor)
    (Competency 4)

    A) 63/100

    B) 7/11

    C) 6 3/10

    D) 2/3

34. Express .0000456 in scientific notation.
    (Average)(Competency 4)

    A) $4.56 x 10^{-4}$

    B) $45.6 x 10^{-6}$

    C) $4.56 x 10^{-6}$

    D) $4.56 x 10^{-5}$

35. $(3.8 \times 10^{17}) \times (.5 \times 10^{-12})$
    (Average Rigor)
    (Competency 4)

    A) 19×10^5

    B) 1.9×10^5

    C) 1.9×10^6

    D) 1.9×10^7

36. $$\frac{3.5 \times 10^{-10}}{0.7 \times 10^4}$$
    (Rigorous)(Competency 4)

    A) 0.5×10^6

    B) 5.0×10^{-6}

    C) 5.0×10^{-14}

    D) 0.5×10^{-14}

37. {1,4,7,10, . . .}

    What is the 40th term in this sequence?
    (Average Rigor)(Competency 5)

    A) 43

    B) 121

    C) 118

    D) 120

38. {6,11,16,21, . .}

    Find the sum of the first 20 terms in the sequence.
    (Average Rigor) (Competency 5)

    A) 1070

    B) 1176

    C) 969

    D) 1069

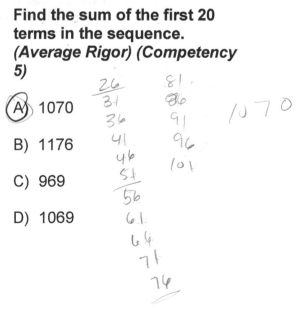

39. Find the sum of the first one hundred terms in the progression.
(–6, –2, 2 . . .)
(Rigorous)(Competency 5)

A) 19,200

B) 19,400

C) –604

D) 604

40. If y varies inversely as x and x is 4 when y is 6, what is the constant of variation?
(Rigorous)(Competency 6)

A) 2

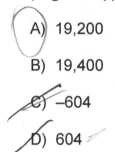

B) 12

C) 3/2

D) 24

41. The constant of variation for an inverse proportion is xy. If y varies directly as x and x is 2 when y is 6, what is x when y is 18?
(Rigorous)(Competency 6)

A) 3

B) 6

C) 26

D) 36

42. The volume of water flowing through a pipe varies directly with the square of the radius of the pipe. If the water flows at a rate of 80 liters per minute through a pipe with a radius of 4 cm, at what rate would water flow through a pipe with a radius of 3 cm?
(Average Rigor)(Competency 6)

A) 45 liters per minute

B) 6.67 liters per minute

C) 60 liters per minute

D) 4.5 liters per minute

43. Three less than four times a number is five times the sum of that number and 6. Which equation could be used to solve this problem?
(Average Rigor)(Competency 6)

A) $3 - 4n = 5(n + 6)$

B) $3 - 4n + 5n = 6$

C) $4n - 3 = 5n + 6$

D) $4n - 3 = 5(n + 6)$

44. Mr. Brown feeds his cat premium cat food which costs $40 per month. Approximately how much will it cost to feed her for one year?
(Easy)(Competency 6)

A) $500

B) $400

C) $80

D) $4800

45. Joe reads 20 words/min., and Jan reads 80 words/min. How many minutes will it take Joe to read the same number of words that it takes Jan 40 minutes to read?
(Rigorous)(Competencies 3 and 6)

(A) 10

(B) 20

(C) 80

(D) 160

46. Which set illustrates a function?
(Easy)(Competency 7)

A) { (0,1) (0,2) (0,3) (0,4) }

B) { (3,9) (−3,9) (4,16) (−4,16)}

C) {(1,2) (2,3) (3,4) (1,4) }

D) { (2,4) (3,6) (4,8) (4,16) }

47. Give the domain for the function over the set of real numbers:
$$y = \frac{3x+2}{2x^2-3}$$
(Rigorous)(Competency 7)

A) all real numbers

B) all real numbers, $x \neq 0$

C) all real numbers, $x \neq -2$ or 3

D) all real numbers, $x \neq \dfrac{\pm\sqrt{6}}{2}$

48. State the domain of the function $f(x) = \dfrac{3x-6}{x^2-25}$
(Rigorous)(Competency 7)

A) $x \neq 2$

B) $x \neq 5, -5$

C) $x \neq 2, -2$

D) $x \neq 5$

49. Solve for x: $3x + 5 \geq 8 + 7x$
(Average Rigor)(Competency 8)

A) $x \geq -\frac{3}{4}$

B) $x \leq -\frac{3}{4}$

C) $x \geq \frac{3}{4}$

D) $x \leq \frac{3}{4}$

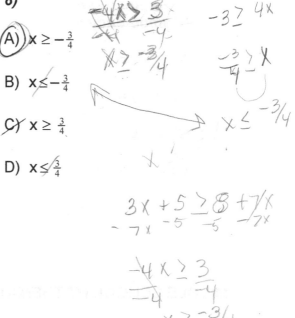

50. Which graph represents the solution set for $x^2 - 5x > -6$?
    (Rigorous)(Competency 8)

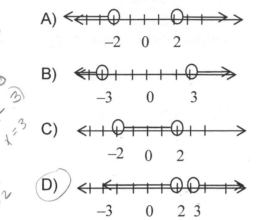

A) <image: number line with open circles at 1 and 2, marked −2, 0, 2>

B) <image: number line with open circles, marked −3, 0, 3>

C) <image: number line with open circles, marked −2, 0, 2>

D) <image: number line with open circles at 2 and 3, marked −3, 0, 2 3>

(handwritten:) $x^2 - 5x > -6$
$x^2 - 5x + 6 = 0$
$(x - 2)(x - 3)$
$x = 3$
$x - 2 = 0$
$x = 2$

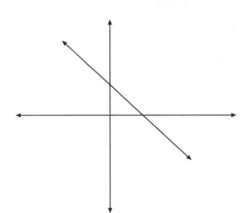

51. Which equation is represented by the above graph?
    (Average Rigor)
    (Competency 8)

A) $x - y = 3$

B) $x - y = -3$

C) $x + y = 3$

D) $x + y = -3$

(handwritten:) $-y = -x + 3$
$-y = -x - 3$
$-y = -x + 3$
$-y = -x - 3$
$y = -x + 3$
$y = -x - 3$

52. Identify the proper sequencing of subskills when teaching graphing inequalities in two dimensions
    (Easy)(Competency 8)

A) shading regions, graphing lines, graphing points, determining whether a line is solid or broken

B) graphing points, graphing lines, determining whether a line is solid or broken, shading regions

C) graphing points, shading regions, determining whether a line is solid or broken, graphing lines

D) graphing lines, determining whether a line is solid or broken, graphing points, shading regions

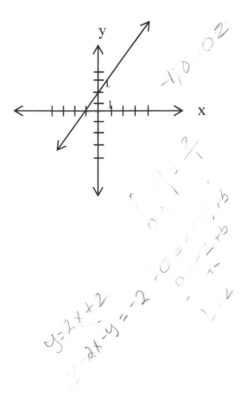

53. **What is the equation of the above graph?**
(Rigorous)(Competency 8)

A) $2x + y = 2$

B) $2x - y = -2$

C) $2x - y = 2$

D) $2x + y = -2$

54. **What is the solution set for the following equations?**
(Rigorous)(Competency 8)

$3x + 2y = 12$
$12x + 8y = 15$

A) all real numbers

B) $x = 4, y = 4$

C) $x = 2, y = -1$

D) $\varnothing$

55. **Solve for x and y:**
$x = 3y + 7$
$7x + 5y = 23$
(Rigorous)(Competency 8)

A) $(-1, 4)$

B) $(4, -1)$

C) $(\frac{-29}{7}, \frac{-26}{7})$

D) $(10, 1)$

56. **Solve the system of equations for x, y and z.**
(Rigorous)(Competency 8)

$3x + 2y - z = 0$
$2x + 5y = 8z$
$x + 3y + 2z = 7$

A) $(-1, 2, 1)$

B) $(1, 2, -1)$

C) $(-3, 4, -1)$

D) $(0, 1, 2)$

57. **How is the following read?**
(Competency 8; Easy)

$3 < 5$

A) Three is less than five

B) Five is greater than three

C) Three is greater than five

D) Five is less than three

58. **The discriminant of a quadratic equation is evaluated and determined to be –3. The equation has...**
(Rigorous)(Competency 9)

A) one real root

B) one complex root

C) two roots, both real

D) two roots, both complex

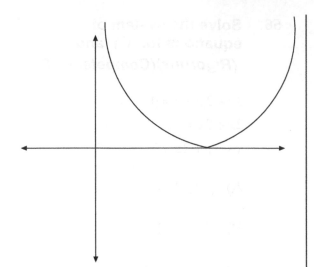

59. Which equation is graphed above?
(Rigorous)(Competency 9)

A) $y = 4(x + 3)^2$

B) $y = 4(x - 3)^2$

C) $y = 3(x - 4)^2$

D) $y = 3(x + 4)^2$

60. Which graph represents the equation of $y = x^2 + 3x$?
(Rigorous)(Competency 9)

A)   B)

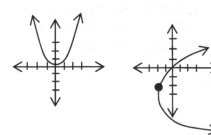

C)   D)

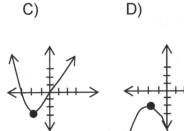

61. Solve for x.

$3x^2 - 2 + 4(x^2 - 3) = 0$
(Rigorous)(Competency 9)

A) $\{-\sqrt{2}, \sqrt{2}\}$

B) $\{2, -2\}$

C) $\{0, \sqrt{3}, -\sqrt{3}\}$

D) $\{7, -7\}$

62. Which of the following is a factor of $6 + 48m^3$
(Average Rigor)(Competency 9)

A) $(1 + 2m)$

B) $(1 - 8m)$

C) $(1 + m - 2m)$

D) $(1 - m + 2m)$

63. Factor completely:
$8(x - y) + a(y - x)$
(Average Rigor)(Competency 9)

A) $(8 + a)(y - x)$

B) $(8 - a)(y - x)$

C) $(a - 8)(y - x)$

D) $(a - 8)(y + x)$

64. The formula for solving a quadratic equation is...
(Competency 9, Average)

A) $x = \dfrac{-b \pm \sqrt{b^2 - 4ac}}{2a}$

B) $x = \dfrac{-b \pm \sqrt{b^2 - 4a}}{2a}$

C) $x = \dfrac{b \pm \sqrt{b^2 - 4ac}}{2a}$

D) $x = \dfrac{b \pm \sqrt{b^3 - 4ac}}{2a}$

65. Which of the following is a factor of $k^3 - m^3$?
(Average Rigor)
(Competency 10)

A) $k^2 + m^2$

B) $k + m$

C) $k^2 - m^2$

D) $k - m$

66. Find the zeroes of
$f(x) = x^3 + x^2 - 14x - 24$
(Rigorous)(Competency 10)

A) 4, 3, 2

B) 3, −8

C) 7, −2, −1

D) 4, −3, −2

67. Solve for x:
$|\,2x + 3\,| > 4$
(Rigorous)(Competency 10)

A) $-\frac{7}{2} > x > \frac{1}{2}$

B) $-\frac{1}{2} > x > \frac{7}{2}$

C) $x < \frac{7}{2}$ or $x < -\frac{1}{2}$

D) $x < -\frac{7}{2}$ or $x > \frac{1}{2}$

68. Graph the solution:
$|x| + 7 < 13$
(Rigorous)(Competency 10)

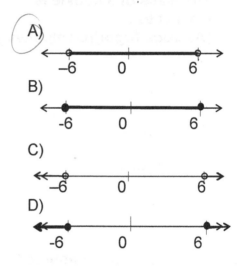

69. Solve for x: $18 = 4 + |2x|$
(Average Rigor)(Competency 10)

A) $\{-11, 7\}$

B) $\{-7, 0, 7\}$

C) $\{-7, 7\}$

D) $\{-11, 11\}$

70. Seventh grade students are working on a project using non-standard measurement. Which would not be an appropriate instrument for measuring the length of the classroom?
(Easy)(Competency 11)

A) a student's foot

B) a student's arm span

C) a student's jump

D) all are appropriate

71. The mass of a cookie is closest to…
(Average Rigor)(Competency 11)

A) 0.5 kg

B) 0.5 grams

C) 15 grams

D) 1.5 grams

72. A man's waist measures 90 cm. What is the greatest possible error for the measurement?
(Average)(Competency 11)

A) ± 1 m

B) ±8 cm

C) ±1 cm

D) ±5 mm

73. 4 square yards is equivalent to…
(Average)(Competency 11)

A) 12 square feet

B) 48 square feet

C) 36 square feet

D) 108 square feet

74. If a circle has an area of 25 cm^2, what is its circumference to the nearest tenth of a centimeter?
(Rigorous)(Competency 11)

A) 78.5 cm

B) 17.7 cm

C) 8.9 cm

D) 15.7 cm

75. Find the area of the figure below.
(Rigorous)(Competency 11)

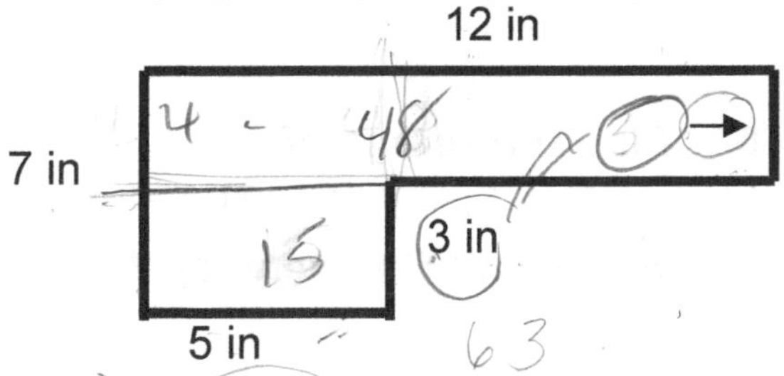

A) 56 in^2

B) 27 in^2

C) 71 in^2

D) 170 in^2

76. Find the area of the Shaded region given square ABCD with side AB=10m and circle E. *(Rigorous)(Competency 11)*

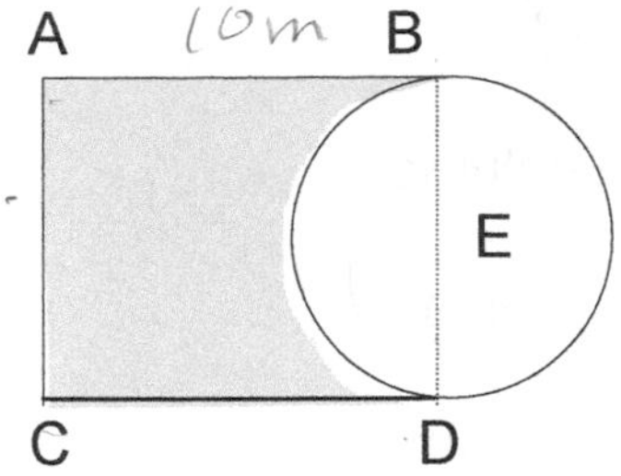

A) 178.5 m²

B) 139.25 m²

C) 71 m²

D) 60.75 m²

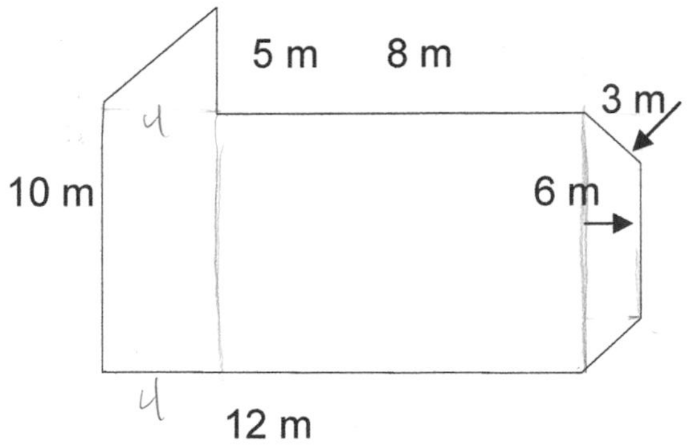

77. Compute the area of the polygon shown above. *(Rigorous)(Competency 11)*

A) 178 m²

B) 154 m²

C) 43 m²

D) 188 m²

78. Find the area of the figure pictured below. *(Rigorous)(Competency 11)*

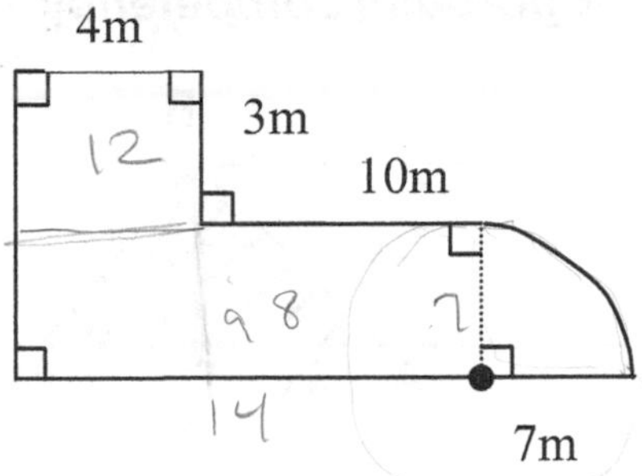

A) 136.47 m²

B) 148.48 m²

C) 293.86 m²

D) 178.47 m²

79. Given a 30 meter x 60 meter garden with a circular fountain with a 5 meter radius, calculate the area of the portion of the garden not occupied by the fountain. *(Rigorous)(Competency 11)*

A) 1721 m²

B) 1879 m²

C) 2585 m²

D) 1015 m²

80. Determine the area of the shaded region of the trapezoid in terms of *x* and *y*. *(Rigorous)(Competency 11)*

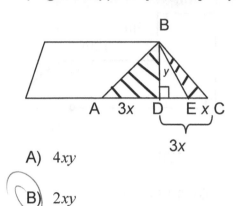

A) $4xy$

B) $2xy$

C) $3x^2y$

D) There is not enough information given.

81. If the radius of a right circular cylinder is doubled, how does its volume change? *(Rigorous)(Competency 11)*

A) no change

B) also is doubled

C) four times the original

D) pi times the original

82. Students are working with a set of rulers and various small objects from the classroom. Which concept are these students exploring? *(Competency 11; Average rigor)*

A) Volume

B) Weight

C) Length

D) Temperature

83. The term "cubic feet" indicates which kind of measurement? *(Competency 11; Average rigor)*

A) Volume

B) Mass

C) Length

D) Distance

84. Given XY ≅ YZ and ∠AYX ≅ ∠AYZ. Prove △AYZ ≅ △AYX.

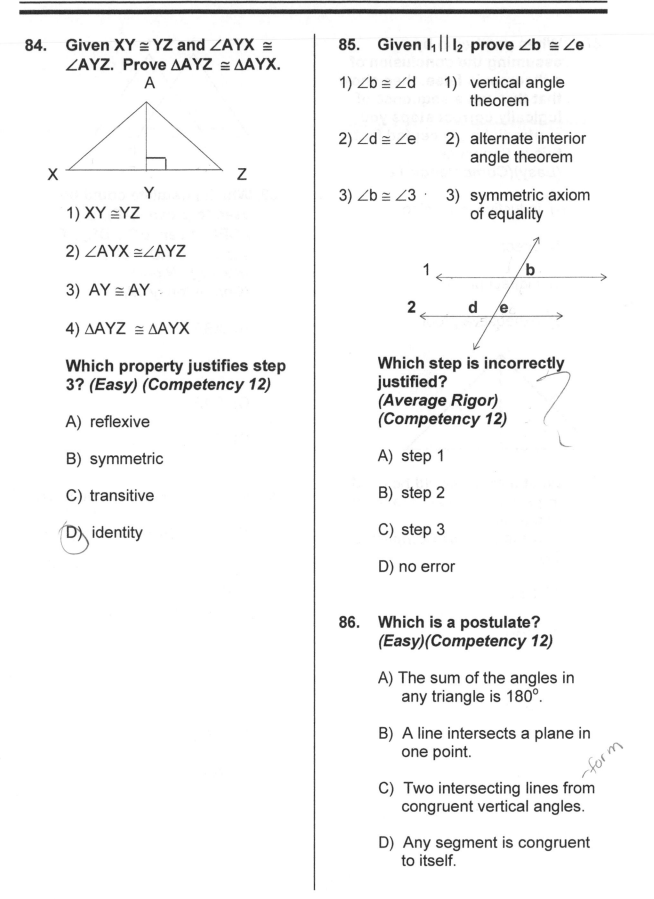

1) XY ≅ YZ

2) ∠AYX ≅ ∠AYZ

3) AY ≅ AY

4) △AYZ ≅ △AYX

Which property justifies step 3? *(Easy) (Competency 12)*

A) reflexive

B) symmetric

C) transitive

D) identity

85. Given l₁ ∥ l₂ prove ∠b ≅ ∠e

1) ∠b ≅ ∠d   1) vertical angle theorem

2) ∠d ≅ ∠e   2) alternate interior angle theorem

3) ∠b ≅ ∠3   3) symmetric axiom of equality

Which step is incorrectly justified?
(Average Rigor)
(Competency 12)

A) step 1

B) step 2

C) step 3

D) no error

86. **Which is a postulate?**
(Easy)(Competency 12)

A) The sum of the angles in any triangle is 180°.

B) A line intersects a plane in one point.

C) Two intersecting lines from congruent vertical angles.

D) Any segment is congruent to itself.

87. When you begin by assuming the conclusion of a theorem is false, then show that through a sequence of logically correct steps you contradict an accepted fact, this is known as *(Easy)(Competency 12)*

A) inductive reasoning

B) direct proof

C) indirect proof

D) exhaustive proof

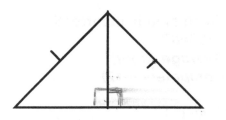

88. What method could be used to prove the above triangles congruent? *(Average Rigor)(Competency 12)*

A) SSS

B) SAS

C) AAS

D) SSA

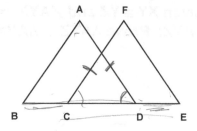

89. Which postulate could be used to prove △ABD ≅ △CEF, given BC ≅ DE, ∠C ≅ ∠D, and AD ≅ CF? *(Average Rigor) (Competency 12)*

A) ASA

B) SAS

C) SAA

D) SSS

90. Which theorem can be used to prove $\triangle BAK \cong \triangle MKA$? *(Rigorous)(Competency 12)*

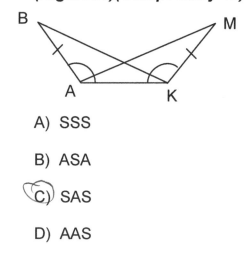

A) SSS

B) ASA

C) SAS

D) AAS

91. Given that QO⊥NP and QO=NP, quadrilateral NOPQ can most accurately be described as a...
(Easy)(Competency 12)

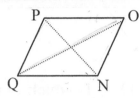

(A) parallelogram

B) rectangle ✗

C) square ✗

D) rhombus

92. Choose the correct statement concerning the median and altitude in a triangle.
(Average Rigor)(Competency 12)

A) The median and altitude of a triangle may be the same segment.

B) The median and altitude of a triangle are always different segments.

(C) The median and altitude of a right triangle are always the same segment.

D) The median and altitude of an isosceles triangle are always the same segment.

93. Which of the following can be defined?
(Easy)(Competency 12)

(A) point

B) ray

C) line

D) plane

94. Choose the diagram which illustrates the construction of a perpendicular to the line at a given point on the line.
(Average Rigor)(Competency 12)

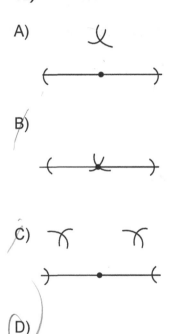

95. How many equal angles does an equilateral triangle have?
(Easy)(Competency 13)

A) 0

B) 1

C) 2

D) 3

96. Given similar polygons with corresponding sides of lengths 9 and 15, find the perimeter of the smaller polygon if the perimeter of the larger polygon is 150 units.
(Rigorous)(Competency 13)

A) 54

B) 135

C) 90

D) 126

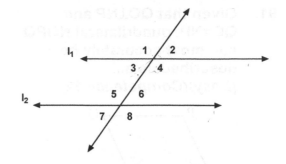

97. Given $l_1 \parallel l_2$ which of the following is true?
(Average Rigor)(Competency 13)

A) ∠1 and ∠8 are congruent and alternate interior angles

B) ∠2 and ∠3 are congruent and corresponding angles

C) ∠3 and ∠4 are adjacent and supplementary angles

D) ∠3 and ∠5 are adjacent and supplementary angles

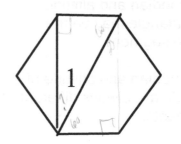

98. Given the regular hexagon above, determine the measure of angle 1.
(Rigorous)(Competency 13)

A) 30°

B) 60°

C) 120°

D) 45°

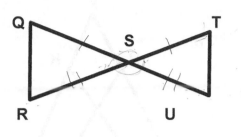

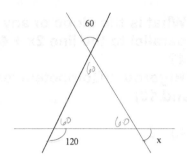

Note: Figure not drawn to scale.

99. Given QS ≅ TS and RS ≅US, prove △QRS ≅ △TUS.

I) QS ≅ TS	1) Given
2) RS ≅ US	2) Given
3) ∠TSU ≅ ∠QSR	3) ?
4) △TSU ≅ △QSR	4) SAS

Give the reason which justifies step 3.
(Average Rigor)(Competency 13)

A) Congruent parts of congruent triangles are congruent

B) Reflexive axiom of equality

C) Alternate interior angle Theorem

D) Vertical angle theorem

100. In the figure above, what is the value of *x*?
(Rigorous)(Competency 13)

A) 50

B) 60

C) 75

D) 80

101. Line p has a negative slope and passes through the point (0, 0). If line q is perpendicular to line p, which of the following must be true?
(Rigorous)(Competency 13)

A) Line q has a negative y-intercept.

B) Line q passes through the point (0,0)

C) Line q has a positive slope.

D) Line q has a positive y-intercept.

102. What is the slope of any line parallel to the line $2x + 4y = 4$?
(Rigorous)(Competencies 8 and 13)

   A) -2

   B) -1

   C) - ½

   D) 2

$2x + 4y = 4$

$4y = \dfrac{-2x + 4}{4}$

$\dfrac{4}{4} = \dfrac{-2}{4}x + 1$

$y = \dfrac{-2}{4}x$

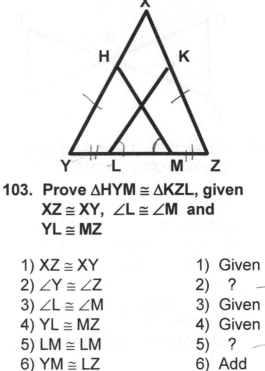

103. Prove $\triangle HYM \cong \triangle KZL$, given $XZ \cong XY$, $\angle L \cong \angle M$ and $YL \cong MZ$

1) $XZ \cong XY$	1) Given
2) $\angle Y \cong \angle Z$	2) ?
3) $\angle L \cong \angle M$	3) Given
4) $YL \cong MZ$	4) Given
5) $LM \cong LM$	5) ?
6) $YM \cong LZ$	6) Add
7) $\triangle HYM \cong \triangle KZL$	7) ASA

Which could be used to justify steps 2 and 5?
(Average Rigor)(Competency 13)

   A) CPCTC, Identity

   B) Isosceles Triangle Theorem, Identity

   C) SAS, Reflexive

   D) Isosceles Triangle Theorem, Reflexive

104. What is the degree measure of an interior angle of a regular 10-sided polygon?
(Rigorous)(Competency 13)

A) 18°

B) 36°

C) 144°

D) 54°

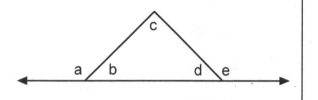

105. Which of the following statements is true about the number of degrees in each angle?
(Rigorous)(Competency 13)

A) $a + b + c = 180°$

B) $a = e$

C) $b + c = e$

D) $c + d = e$

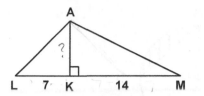

106. Given altitude AK with measurements as indicated, determine the length of AK.
(Rigorous)(Competency 13)

A) 98

B) $7\sqrt{2}$

C) $\sqrt{21}$

D) $7\sqrt{3}$

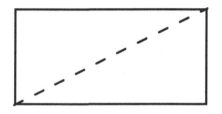

107. The above diagram is most likely used in deriving a formula for which of the following?
(Easy)(Competency 13)

A) the area of a rectangle

B) the area of a triangle

C) the perimeter of a triangle

D) the surface area of a prism

MIDDLE SCHOOL MATHEMATICS 409

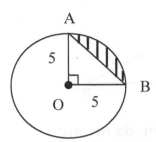

108. Compute the area of the shaded region, given a radius of 5 meters. O is the center.
(Rigorous)(Competency 13)

A) 7.13 cm²

B) 7.13 m²

C) 78.5 m²

D) 19.63 m²

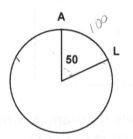

109. What is the measure of major arc AL?
(Average Rigor)(Competency 13)

A) 50°

B) 25°

C) 100°

D) 310°

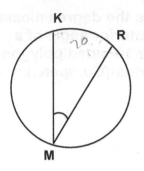

110. If arc KR = 70° what is the measure of ∠M?
(Rigorous)(Competency 13)

A) 290°

B) 35°

C) 140°

D) 110°

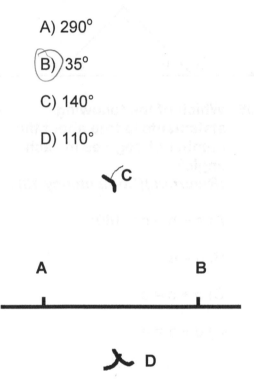

111. The above construction can be completed to make...
(Easy)(Competency 13)

A) an angle bisector

B) parallel lines

C) a perpendicular bisector

D) skew lines

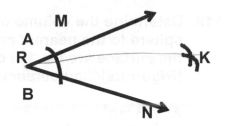

112. A line from R to K will form...
(Easy)(Competency 13)

A) an altitude of RMN

B) a perpendicular bisector of MN

C) a bisector of MRN

D) a vertical angle

113. What is the measure of minor arc AD, given measure of arc PS is 40° and $m < K = 10°$ **?**
(Rigorous)(Competency 13)

A) 50°

B) 20°

C) 30°

D) 25°

114. Compute the surface area of the prism.
(Rigorous)(Competency 14)

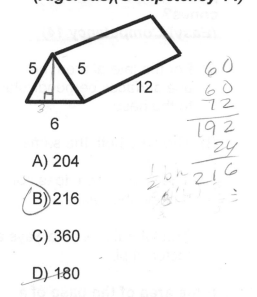

A) 204

B) 216

C) 360

D) 180

115. If the base of a regular square pyramid is tripled, how does its volume change?
(Rigorous)(Competency 14)

A) double the original

B) triple the original

C) nine times the original

D) no change

116. How does lateral area differ from total surface area in prisms, pyramids, and cones?
(Easy)(Competency 14)

A) For the lateral area, only use surfaces perpendicular to the base.

B) They are both the same.

C) The lateral area does not include the base.

D) The lateral area is always a factor of pi.

117. If the area of the base of a cone is tripled, the volume will be...
(Average Rigor)(Competency 14)

A) the same as the original

B) 9 times the original

C) 3 times the original

D) 3 π times the original

118. Find the height of a box with surface area of 94 sq. ft. with a width of 3 feet and a depth of 4 feet.
(Rigorous)(Competency 14)

A) 3 ft.

B) 4 ft.

C) 5 ft

D) 6 ft.

119. Determine the volume of a sphere to the nearest cm if the surface area is 113 cm^2.
(Rigorous)(Competency 14)

A) 113 cm^3

B) 339 cm^3

C) 37.7 cm^3

D) 226 cm^3

120. Ginny and Nick head back to their respective colleges after being home for the weekend. They leave their house at the same time and drive for 4 hours. Ginny drives due south at the average rate of 60 miles per hour and Nick drives due east at the average rate of 60 miles per hour. What is the straight-line distance between them, in miles, at the end of the 4 hours?
(Rigorous)(Competency 15)

A) $120\sqrt{2}$

B) 240

C) $240\sqrt{2}$

D) 288

121. Find the distance between (3,7) and (–3,4).
(Average Rigor)
(Competency 15)

A) 9

B) 45

C) $3\sqrt{5}$

D) $5\sqrt{3}$

122. Find the midpoint of (2,5) and (7,–4).
(Average Rigor)(Competency 15)

A) (9,–1)

B) (5, 9)

C) (9/2, –1/2)

D) (9/2, 1/2)

123. Given segment AC with B as its midpoint find the coordinates of C if A = (5,7) and B = (3, 6.5).
(Rigorous)(Competency 15)

A) (4, 6.5)

B) (1, 6)

C) (2, 0.5)

D) (16, 1)

124. Find the median of the following set of data:

14   3   7   6   11   20

(Average Rigor)(Competency 16)

A) 9

B) 8.5

C) 7

D) 11

125. Compute the median for the following data set:

{12, 19, 13, 16, 17, 14}

(Average Rigor)(Competency 16)

A) 14.5

B) 15.17

C) 15

D) 16

126. Corporate salaries are listed for several employees. Which would be the best measure of central tendency?
(Average Rigor)(Competency 16)

$24,000 $24,000 $26,000
$28,000 $30,000 $120,000

A) mean

B.) median

C) mode

D) no difference

127. A student scored in the 87th percentile on a standardized test. Which would be the best interpretation of his score?
(Average Rigor)(Competency 16)

A) Only 13% of the students who took the test scored higher.

B) This student should be getting mostly Bs on his report card.

C) This student performed below average on the test.

D) This is the equivalent of missing 13 questions on a 100 question exam.

128. Which type of graph uses symbols to represent quantities?
(Competency 16; Easy)

A) Bar graph

B) Line graph

C) Pictograph

D) Circle graph

129. Which of the following types of graphs would be best to use to record the eye color of the students in the class?
(Skill 5.13; Average rigor)

A) Bar graph or circle graph

B) Pictograph or bar graph

C) Line graph or pictograph

D) Line graph or bar graph

130. Which statement is true about George's budget? *(Easy)(Competency 16)*

A) George spends the greatest portion of his income on food.

B) George spends twice as much on utilities as he does on his mortgage.

C) George spends twice as much on utilities as he does on food.

D) George spends the same amount on food and utilities as he does on mortgage.

131. What conclusion can be drawn from the graph below?

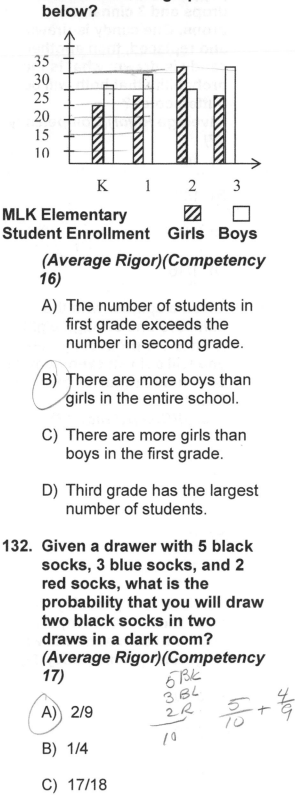

MLK Elementary Student Enrollment Girls ▨ Boys ☐

(Average Rigor)(Competency 16)

A) The number of students in first grade exceeds the number in second grade.

B) There are more boys than girls in the entire school.

C) There are more girls than boys in the first grade.

D) Third grade has the largest number of students.

132. Given a drawer with 5 black socks, 3 blue socks, and 2 red socks, what is the probability that you will draw two black socks in two draws in a dark room? *(Average Rigor)(Competency 17)*

A) 2/9

B) 1/4

C) 17/18

D) 1/18

133. A sack of candy has 3 peppermints, 2 butterscotch drops and 3 cinnamon drops. One candy is drawn and replaced, then another candy is drawn; what is the probability that both will be butterscotch?
(Average Rigor)(Competency 17)

A) 1/2

B) 1/28

C) 1/4

D) 1/16

134. Given a spinner with the numbers one through eight, what is the probability that you will spin an even number or a number greater than four?
(Easy)(Competency 17)

A) 1/4

B) 1/2

C) ¾

D) 1

135. If a horse will probably win three races out of ten, what are the odds that he will win?
(Rigorous)(Competency 17)

A) 3:10

B) 7:10

C) 3:7

D) 7:3

136. A jar contains 3 red marbles, 5 white marbles, 1 green marble and 15 blue marbles. If one marble is picked at random from the jar, what is the probability that it will be red?
(Competency 17, Average)

A) 1/3

B) 1/8

C) 3/8

D) 1/24

137. If there are three people in a room, what is the probability that at least two of them will share a birthday? (Assume a year has 365 days)
(Competency 17; Rigorous)

A) 0.67

B) 0.05

C) 0.008

D) 0.33

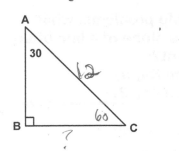

138. If AC = 12, determine BC.

(Average Rigor)(Competency 18)

A) 6

B) 4

C) $6\sqrt{3}$

D) $3\sqrt{6}$

139. Which expression is not equal to sinx?
(Competency 18; Rigorous)

A) $\sqrt{1-\cos^2 x}$

B) $\tan x \cos x$

C) $1/\csc x$

D) $1/\sec x$

140. For an acute angle x, sinx = 3/5. What is cotx?
(Competency 18; Rigorous)

A) 5/3

B) ¾

C) 1.33

D) 1

141. Solve for v_0: $d = at(v_t - v_0)$
(Rigorous)(Competency 19)

A) $v_0 = atd - v_t$

B) $v_0 = d - atv_t$

C) $v_0 = atv_t - d$

D) $v_0 = (atv_t - d)/at$

142. L'Hospital's rule provides a method to evaluate which of the following?
(Competency 19; Rigorous)

A) Limit of a function

B) Derivative of a function

C) Sum of an arithmetic series

D) Sum of a geometric series

143. Find the following limit: $\lim\limits_{x \to 2} \dfrac{x^2 - 4}{x - 2}$

(Competency 19; Rigorous)

A) 0

B) Infinity

C) 2

D) 4

144. Find the following limit.

$$\lim_{x \to 0} \frac{\sin 2x}{5x}$$

(Competency 19; Rigorous)

A) Infinity

B) 0

C) 1.4

D) 1

145. What is the sum of the first 20 terms of the geometric sequence (2,4,8,16,32,…)
(Competency 20; Rigorous)

A) 2097150

B) 1048575

C) 524288

D) 1048576

146. In real-life problems, what does the slope of a line often represent?
(Average Rigor)
(Competency 21)

A) Total Growth

B) Average Rate of Change

C) Time

D) Profit

Answer Key

1. A	38. A	75. A	112. C
2. D	39. A	76. D	113. B
3. C	40. D	77. B	114. B
4. D	41. B	78. B	115. B
5. C	42. A	79. A	116. C
6. A	43. D	80. B	117. C
7. B	44. A	81. C	118. C
8. A	45. D	82. C	119. A
9. B	46. B	83. A	120. C
10. C	47. D	84. A	121. C
11. D	48. B	85. A	122. D
12. C	49. B	86. D	123. B
13. C	50. D	87. C	124. A
14. A	51. C	88. B	125. C
15. A	52. B	89. B	126. B
16. B	53. B	90. C	127. A
17. A	54. D	91. C	128. C
18. D	55. B	92. A	129. B
19. D	56. A	93. B	130. C
20. A	57. A	94. D	131. B
21. B	58. D	95. D	132. A
22. B	59. B	96. C	133. D
23. C	60. C	97. C	134. C
24. A	61. A	98. A	135. C
25. B	62. A	99. D	136. B
26. B	63. C	100. B	137. C
27. A	64. A	101. C	138. A
28. C	65. D	102. C	139. D
29. D	66. D	103. D	140. B
30. A	67. D	104. C	141. D
31. D	68. A	105. C	142. A
32. C	69. C	106. B	143. D
33. B	70. D	107. B	144. C
34. D	71. C	108. B	145. A
35. B	72. D	109. D	146. B
36. C	73. C	110. B	
37. C	74. B	111. C	

Rigor Table

Question	Easy	Average	Rigorous		Question	Easy	Average	Rigorous
1	1				38		1	
2		1			39			1
3			1		40			1
4		1			41			1
5		1			42		1	
6		1			43		1	
7	1				44	1		
8	1				45			1
9		1			46	1		
10		1			47			1
11		1			48			1
12			1		49		1	
13		1			50			1
14		1			51		1	
15		1			52	1		
16		1			53			1
17	1				54			1
18	1				55			1
19	1				56			1
20		1			57	1		
21		1			58			1
22	1				59			1
23	1				60			1
24		1			61			1
25	1				62		1	
26		1			63		1	
27	1				64		1	
28	1				65		1	
29			1		66			1
30			1		67			1
31	1				68			1
32		1			69		1	
33		1			70	1		
34		1			71		1	
35		1			72		1	
36			1		73		1	
37		1			74			1
					75			1

Number					Number			
76			1		116	1		
77			1		117		1	
78			1		118			1
79			1		119			1
80			1		120			1
81			1		121		1	
82		1			122		1	
83		1			123			1
84	1				124		1	
85		1			125		1	
86	1				126		1	
87	1				127		1	
88		1			128	1		
89		1			129		1	
90			1		130	1		
91	1				131		1	
92		1			132		1	
93	1				133		1	
94		1			134	1		
95	1				135			1
96			1		136		1	
97		1			137			1
98			1		138		1	
99		1			139			1
100			1		140			1
101			1		141			1
102			1		142			1
103		1			143			1
104			1		144			1
105			1		145			1
106			1		146		1	
107	1							
108			1		Total	30	58	58
109		1				20%	40%	40%
110			1					
111	1							
112	1							
113			1					
114			1					
115			1					

Rationales with Sample Questions

1. Which of the following is a prime number? *(Easy)(Competency 1)*

   A) 13
   B) 4
   C) 15
   D) 21

Answer: A

A prime number is divisible by only one and itself. In other words, it only has two factors. Answer B, 4, has is divisible by 2. Answer C, 15, is divisible by 5 and 3. Answer D, 21, is 7 and 3. Only answer A, 13, is prime because it has no factors other than 13 and 1.

2. Given that n is a positive even integer, 5n + 4 will always be divisible by: *(Competencies 1 and 6)*

   A) 4

   B) 5

   C) 5n

   D) 2

Answer: D

5n is always even and even number added to an even number is always an even number, thus divisible by 2.

3. Which of the following is always composite if x is odd, y is even, and both x and y are greater than or equal to 2? *(Rigorous)(Competency 1)*

A) $x+y$

B) $3x+2y$

C) $5xy$

D) $5x+3y$

Answer: C

A composite number is a number which is not prime. The prime number sequence begins 2,3,5,7,11,13,17,.... To determine which of the expressions is <u>always</u> composite, experiment with different values of x and y, such as x=3 and y=2, or x=5 and y=2. It turns out that 5xy will always be an even number, and therefore, composite, if y=2.

4. Given that x, y, and z are prime numbers, which of the following is true? *(Average Rigor)(Competency 1)*

A) x + y is always prime

B) xyz is always prime

C) xy is sometimes prime

D) x + y is sometimes prime

Answer: D

x + y is sometimes prime. B and C show the products of two numbers which are always composite. x + y may be true, but not always, A.

5. Find the GCF of $2^2 \cdot 3^2 \cdot 5$ and $2^2 \cdot 3 \cdot 7$. *(Average Rigor)(Competency 1)*

> A) $2^5 \cdot 3^3 \cdot 5 \cdot 7$
>
> B) $2 \cdot 3 \cdot 5 \cdot 7$
>
> C) $2^2 \cdot 3$
>
> D) $2^3 \cdot 3^2 \cdot 5 \cdot 7$

Answer: C

Choose the number of each prime factor that is in common.

6. Given even numbers x and y, which could be the LCM of x and y? *(Average Rigor)(Competency 1)*

> A) $\frac{xy}{2}$
>
> B) $2xy$
>
> C) $4xy$
>
> D) xy

Answer: A

Although choices B, C and D are common multiples, when both numbers are even, the product can be divided by two to obtain the least common multiple.

7. Jason has five baseball cards. His friend Marcus gives him six more baseball cards. How many baseball cards does Jason have in all? *(Competency 1; Easy)*

> A.   5
> B.   11
> C.   30
> D.   1

Answer B: 11

The words *in all* indicate that this is an addition problem: 5 + 6 = 11. The correct answer is 11.

8. **What is the answer to this problem?** *(Competency 1; Easy)*

    25 ÷ 5 =

    A. 5
    B. 30
    C. 125
    D. 20

Answer A: 5

Twenty-five can be divided into five equal groups of five.

9. **Which words in a test problem would indicate that an addition operation is needed?** *(Competency 1; Average rigor)*

    A. Each
    B. How many
    C. In each group
    D. How many more than

Answer B: How many

Addition operations are indicated by the following words: total, sum, in all, join, how many. Subtraction operations are indicated by the following words: difference, how many more than, how many less than, left. Multiplication operations are indicated by the following words: in all, each, of. Division operations are indicated by the following words: in each group, per, divide.

10. **A teacher is introducing the concept of multiplication to her third grade students. What is another way she might write 4 x 5?** *(Competency 1; Average rigor)*

    A. 4 + 5
    B. 5 + 4
    C. 4 + 4 + 4 + 4 + 4
    D. 5 + 5 + 5 + 5 + 5

Answer C: 4 + 4 + 4 + 4 + 4

The multiplication concept can translate to an addition problem. 4 x 5 is the same as the number 4 added 5 times.

11. **A teacher plans an activity that involves students calculating how many chair legs are in the classroom, given that there are 30 chairs and each chair has 4 legs. This activity is introducing the ideas of:** *(Competency 1; Average rigor)*

 A. Probability
 B. Statistics
 C. Geometry
 D. Algebra

30 × 4 =

Answer D: Algebra

This activity involves recognizing patterns. It could also involve problem-solving by developing an expression that represents the problem. Activities such as this do not introduce the terms of algebra, but they introduce some of the ideas of algebra.

12. **What math principle is reinforced by matching numerals with number words?** *(Competency 1; Rigorous)*

 A. Sequencing
 B. Greater than and less than
 C. Number representations
 D. Rote counting

Answer C: Number representations

The students are practicing recognition that a numeral (such as 5) has a corresponding number word (five) that represents the same math concept. They are not putting numbers in order (sequencing), and they are not comparing two numbers for value (greater than or less than). In this activity, students are also not counting in order just for the sake of counting (rote counting).

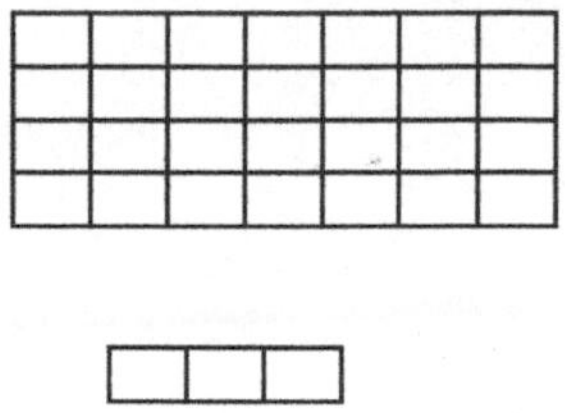

13. The above diagram would be least appropriate for illustrating which of the following? (*Average Rigor*)(*Competency 2*)

A) $7 \times 4 + 3$

B) $31 \div 8$

C) 28×3

D) $31 - 3$

Answer: C

C is inappropriate. A shows a 7x4 rectangle with 3 additional units. B is the division based on A . D shows how mental subtraction might be visualized leaving a composite difference.

14. $24 - 3 \times 7 + 2 =$ (*Average Rigor*)(*Competency 2*)

A) 5

B) 149

C) –3

D) 189

Answer: A

According to the order of operations, multiplication is performed first, then addition and subtraction from left to right.

15. $7t - 4 \cdot 2t + 3t \cdot 4 \div 2 =$ *(Average Rigor)(Competency 2)*

 A) 5t

 B) 0

 C) 31t

 D) 18t

Answer: A

First perform multiplication and division from left to right; 7t −8t + 6t, then add and subtract from left to right.

16. Which of the following does not correctly relate an inverse operation? *(Average Rigor)(Competency 2)*

 A) $a - b = a + -b$

 B) $a \times b = b \div a$

 C) $\sqrt{a^2} = a$

 D) $a \times \frac{1}{a} = 1$

Answer: B

B is always false. A, C, and D illustrate various properties of inverse relations.

17. **Given a, b, y, and z are real numbers and ay + b = z, Prove**

$$y = \frac{z + -b}{a}$$

Statement	Reason
1) ay + b = z	1) Given
2) −b is a real number	2) Closure
3) (ay +b) + −b = z + −b	3) Addition property of Identity
4) ay + (b + −b) = z + −b	4) Associative
5) ay + 0 = z + −b	5) Additive inverse
6) ay = z + −b	6) Addition property of identity
7) $a = \dfrac{z + -b}{y}$	7) Division

Which reason is incorrect for the corresponding statement? *(Easy)(Skill 6.25)*

A) step 3

B) step 4

C) step 5

D) step 6

Answer: A

The operation used in step 3 is that of additive inverse, rather than additive identity (addition property of identity), since:

b + −b = 0

Therefore, −b added to both sides of the equation is a legitimate operation justified by additive inverse.

18. **Which of the following illustrates an inverse property?** *(Easy)(Competency 2)*

    A) $a + b = a - b$

    B) $a + b = b + a$

    C) $a + 0 = a$

    D) $a + (-a) = 0$

Answer: D

Answer is D because $a + (-a) = 0$ is a statement of the Additive Inverse Property of Algebra.

19. **Convert 0.75 into a fraction in lowest terms.** *(Easy) (Competency 3)*

    A) $\dfrac{6}{8}$

    B) $\dfrac{5}{8}$

    C) $\dfrac{4}{3}$

    D) $\dfrac{3}{4}$

Answer: D

While $\dfrac{6}{8}$, answer A, also equals 0.75, the question asks for a fraction in lowest terms. Thus, the correct answer is answer D, $\dfrac{3}{4}$.

20. What would be the total cost of a suit for $295.99 and a pair of shoes   for $69.95 including 6.5% sales tax? *(Average Rigor)(Competency 3)*

  A) $389.73

  B) $398.37

  C) $237.86

  D) $315.23

Answer: A

Before the tax, the total comes to $365.94. Then .065(365.94) = 23.79. With the tax added on, the total bill is 365.94 + 23.79 = $389.73. (Quicker way: 1.065(365.94) = 389.73.)

21. A student had 60 days to appeal the results of an exam. If the results were received on March 23, what was the last day that the student could appeal? *(Average Rigor)(Competency 3)*

  A) May 21

  B) May 22

  C) May 23

  D) May 24

Answer: B

Recall: 30 days in April and 31 in March. 8 days in March + 30 days in April + 22 days in May brings him to a total of 60 days on May 22. **Answer is B.**

22. **Sandra has $34.00, Carl has $42.00. How much more does Carl have than Sandra? Which would be the best method for finding the answer?** *(Easy)(Competency 3)*

    A) addition

    B) subtraction

    C) division

    D) both A and B are equally correct

Answer: B

To find how much more money Carl has than Sandra, it is necessary to subtract Sandra's amount from Carl's amount. This gives $42.00 - $34.00 = $8.00, which is indeed the difference. Answer B is then the correct response.

23. **If three cups of concentrate are needed to make 2 gallons of fruit punch, how many cups are needed to make 5 gallons?** *(Easy)(Competency 3)*

    A) 6 cups

    B) 7 cups

    C) 7.5 cups

    D) 10 cups

Answer: C

Set up the proportion $3/2 = x/5$, cross multiply to obtain $15=2x$, then divide both sides by 2.

24. A sofa sells for $520. If the retailer makes a 30% profit, what was the wholesale price? *(Average Rigor)(Competency 3)*

   A) $400

   B) $676

   C) $490

   D) $364

Answer: A

Let x be the wholesale price, then x + .30x = 520, 1.30x = 520. divide both sides by 1.30.

25. Which statement is an example of the identity axiom of addition? *(Easy)(Competency 4)*

   A) $3 + -3 = 0$

   B) $3x = 3x + 0$

   C) $3 \cdot \frac{1}{3} = 1$

   D) $3 + 2x = 2x + 3$

Answer: B

Illustrates the identity axiom of addition. A illustrates additive inverse, C illustrates the multiplicative inverse, and D illustrates the commutative axiom of addition.

26. Which axiom is incorrectly applied? (*Average Rigor*)(*Competency 4*)

$3x + 4 = 7$

Step a. $3x + 4 - 4 = 7 - 4$
additive equality

Subtraction

Step b. $3x + 4 - 4 = 3$
commutative axiom of addition

Step c. $3x + 0 = 3$
additive inverse

Step d. $3x = 3$
additive identity

A) step a

B) step b

C) step c

D) step d

Answer: B

In simplifying from step a to step b, 3 replaced $7 - 4$, therefore the correct justification would be subtraction or substitution.

27. Given W = whole numbers
    N = natural numbers
    Z = integers
    R = rational numbers
     I = irrational numbers

    Which of the following is not true? (*Easy*)(*Competency 4*)

    A) $R \subset I$

    B) $W \subset Z$

    C) $Z \subset R$

    D) $N \subset W$

Answer: A

The rational numbers are not a subset of the irrational numbers. All of the other statements are true.

28. Which of the following is an irrational number? (*Easy*)(*Competency 4*)

    A) .362626262...

    B) $4\frac{1}{3}$

    C) $\sqrt{5}$

    D) $-\sqrt{16}$

Answer: C

5 is an irrational number A and B can both be expressed as fractions. D can be simplified to –4, an integer and rational number.

29. Which denotes a complex number? *(Rigorous)(Competency 4)*

    A) 3.678678678...

    B) $-\sqrt{27}$

    C) $123^{1/2}$

    D) $(-100)^{1/2}$

Answer: D

A complex number is the square root of a negative number. The complex number is defined as the square root of -1. The exponent ½ represents a square root.

30. Choose the correct statement: *(Rigorous)(Competency 4*

    A) Rational and irrational numbers are both proper subsets of the real numbers.

    B) The set of whole numbers is a proper subset of the set of natural numbers.

    C) The set of integers is a proper subset of the set of irrational numbers.

    D) The set of real numbers is a proper subset of the natural, whole, integers, rational, and irrational numbers.

Answer: A

A proper subset is completely contained in but not equal to the original set.

31. How many real numbers lie between −1 and +1 ? *(Easy)(Competency 4)*

    A) 0

    B) 1

    C) 17

    D) an infinite number

Answer: D

There are an infinite number of real numbers between any two real numbers.

32. **Choose the set in which the members are <u>not</u> equivalent.** *(Average Rigor)(Competency 4)*

    A) 1/2, 0.5, 50%

    B) 10/5, 2.0, 200%

    C) 3/8, 0.385, 38.5%

    D) 7/10, 0.7, 70%

Answer: C

3/8 is equivalent to .375 and 37.5%.

33. **Change $.\overline{63}$ into a fraction in simplest form.** *(Average Rigor)(Competency 4)*

    A) 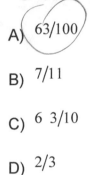 63/100

    B) 7/11

    C) 6 3/10

    D) 2/3

Answer: B

Let N = .636363…. Then multiplying both sides of the equation by 100 or 10^2 (because there are 2 repeated numbers), we get 100N = 63.636363). Then subtracting the two equations gives 99N = 63 or N = $\frac{63}{99} = \frac{7}{11}$.

34. Express .0000456 in scientific notation. *(Average)(Competency 4)*

A) $4.56x10^{-4}$

B) $45.6x10^{-6}$

C) $4.56x10^{-6}$

D) $4.56x10^{-5}$

Answer: D

In scientific notation, the decimal point belongs to the right of the 4, the first significant digit. To get from 4.56×10^{-5} back to 0.0000456, we would move the decimal point 5 places to the left. **Answer is D.**

35. $(3.8 \times 10^{17}) \times (.5 \times 10^{-12})$ *(Average Rigor)(Competency 4)*

A) 19×105

B) 1.9×105

C) 1.9×106

D) 1.9×107

Answer: B

Multiply the decimals and add the exponents.

36. $3.5 \times 10{-10}$
0.7×104 *(Rigorous)(Competency 4)*

A) 0.5×10^6

B) 5.0×10^{-6}

C) 5.0×10^{-14}

D) 0.5×10^{-14}

Answer: C

Divide the decimals and subtract the exponents.

MIDDLE SCHOOL MATHEMATICS 438

37. {1,4,7,10, . . .} **What is the 40th term in this sequence?** *(Average Rigor)(Competency 5)*

A) 43

B) 121

C) 118

D) 120

Answer: C

The simplest way to determine the correct answer is to write out the entire sequence up to the 40th term. However, a much simpler method is more advisable. Consider that the 1st term is 1+0(3), the 2nd term is 1+1(3), the 3rd term is 1+2(3) and so on. Thus, following this pattern, the nth term of the sequence is 1+(n-1)3. Using this formula, it is sufficient to simply replace n with the number 40. This yields 1+(40-1)3 = 1+(39)3 = 1+117 = 118. Answer C is therefore correct.

38. $\{6,11,16,21, . .\}$ Find the sum of the first 20 terms in the sequence. *(Average Rigor)(Competency 5)*

   A) 1070

   B) 1176

   C) 969

   D) 1069

Answer: A

The above sequence is arithmetic with a constant difference of 5. The last term of the sequence, l, which is the 20th term, can be found as follows:

$$l = a_1 + (n-1)d$$

Here, d is the constant difference between terms, which is 5. Using this formula, the 20th term is found to be $l = 101$. The sum of the first n terms can be found using the following formula:

$$sum = \frac{1}{2}n(a_1 + l)$$
$$sum = \frac{1}{2} \cdot 20(6 + 101) = 1070$$

Thus, the correct answer is A.

39. **Find the sum of the first one hundred terms in the progression. $(-6, -2, 2 \dots)$** *(Rigorous)(Competency 5)*

   A) 19,200

   B) 19,400

   C) –604

   D) 604

Answer: A

To find the 100th term: $t_{100} = -6 + 99(4) = 390$. To find the sum of the first 100 terms: $S = \frac{100}{2}(-6 + 390) = 19200$.

40. If y varies inversely as x and x is 4 when y is 6, what is the constant of variation? *(Rigorous)(Competency 6)*

A) 2

B) 12

C) 3/2

D) 24

Answer: D

The constant of variation for an inverse proportion is xy.

41. The constant of variation for an inverse proportion is xy. If y varies directly as x and x is 2 when y is 6, what is x when y is 18? *(Rigorous)(Competency 6)*

A) 3

B) 6

C) 26

D) 36

Answer: B

y/x–216=x/18, Solve 36=6x.

42. The volume of water flowing through a pipe varies directly with the square of the radius of the pipe. If the water flows at a rate of 80 liters per minute through a pipe with a radius of 4 cm, at what rate would water flow through a pipe with a radius of 3 cm? *(Average Rigor)(Competency 6)*

A) 45 liters per minute

B) 6.67 liters per minute

C) 60 liters per minute

D) 4.5 liters per minute

Answer: A

Set up the direct variation: $\dfrac{V}{r^2} = \dfrac{V}{r^2}$. Substituting gives $\dfrac{80}{16} = \dfrac{V}{9}$. Solving for V gives 45 liters per minute.

43. Three less than four times a number is five times the sum of that number and 6. Which equation could be used to solve this problem?   *(Average Rigor)(Competency 6)*

A) $3 - 4n = 5(n + 6)$

B) $3 - 4n + 5n = 6$

C) $4n - 3 = 5n + 6$

D) $4n - 3 = 5(n + 6)$

Answer: D

Be sure to enclose the sum of the number and 6 in parentheses.

44. **Mr. Brown feeds his cat premium cat food which costs $40 per month. Approximately how much will it cost to feed her for one year? *(Easy)(Competency 6)***

  A) $500

  B) $400

  C) $80

  D) $4800

Answer: A

12(40) = 480 which is closest to $500.

45. **Joe reads 20 words/min., and Jan reads 80 words/min. How many minutes will it take Joe to read the same number of words that it takes Jan 40 minutes to read?** *(Rigorous)(Competencies 3 and 6)*

  A) 10

  B) 20

  C) 80

  D) 160

Answer: D

If Jan reads 80 words/minute, she will read 3200 words in 40 minutes.

$$\frac{3200}{20} = 160$$

At 20 words per minute, it will take Joe 160 minutes to read 3200 words.

46. **Which set illustrates a function?** *(Easy)(Competency 7)*

A) $\{ (0,1) \ (0,2) \ (0,3) \ (0,4) \}$

B) $\{ (3,9) \ (-3,9) \ (4,16) \ (-4,16)\}$

C) $\{(1,2) \ (2,3) \ (3,4) \ (1,4) \}$

D) $\{ (2,4) \ (3,6) \ (4,8) \ (4,16) \}$

Answer: B

Each number in the domain can only be matched with one number in the range. A is not a function because 0 is mapped to 4 different numbers in the range. In C, 1 is mapped to two different numbers. In D, 4 is also mapped to two different numbers.

47. **Give the domain for the function over the set of real numbers:** $y=\dfrac{3x+2}{2x^2-3}$
   (Rigorous)(Competency 7)

A) all real numbers

B) all real numbers, $x \neq 0$

C) all real numbers, $x \neq -2$ or 3

D) all real numbers, $x \neq \dfrac{\pm\sqrt{6}}{2}$

Answer: D

Solve the denominator for 0. These values will be excluded from the domain.
$$2x^2 - 3 = 0$$
$$2x^2 = 3$$
$$x^2 = 3/2$$
$$x = \sqrt{\tfrac{3}{2}} = \sqrt{\tfrac{3}{2}} \bullet \sqrt{\tfrac{2}{2}} = \tfrac{\pm\sqrt{6}}{2}$$

48. **State the domain of the function** $f(x) = \dfrac{3x-6}{x^2-25}$

   (Rigorous)(Competency 7)

   A) $x \neq 2$

   B) $x \neq 5, -5$

   C) $x \neq 2, -2$

   D) $x \neq 5$

Answer: B

The values of 5 and −5 must be omitted from the domain of all real numbers because if x took on either of those values, the denominator of the fraction would have a value of 0, and therefore the fraction would be undefined.

49. **Solve for x: 3x + 5 ≥ 8 + 7x** *(Average Rigor)(Competency 8)*

   A) $x \geq -\frac{3}{4}$

   B) $x \leq -\frac{3}{4}$

   C) $x \geq \frac{3}{4}$

   D) $x \leq \frac{3}{4}$

Answer: B

Using additive equality, −3 ≥ 4x. Divide both sides by 4 to obtain −3/4 ≥ x. Carefully determine which answer choice is equivalent.

50. **Which graph represents the solution set for** $x^2 - 5x > -6$ **?**
(Rigorous)(Competency 8)

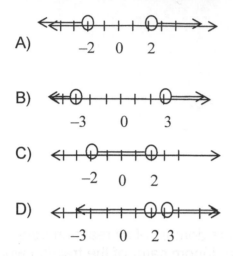

A)
     −2   0   2

B)
     −3   0   3

C)
     −2   0   2

D)
     −3   0   2 3

Answer: D

Rewriting the inequality gives $x^2 - 5x + 6 > 0$. Factoring gives $(x - 2)(x - 3) > 0$. The two cut-off points on the number line are now at $x = 2$ and $x = 3$. Choosing a random number in each of the three parts of the number line, we test them to see if they produce a true statement. If $x = 0$ or $x = 4$, $(x-2)(x-3)>0$ is true. If $x = 2.5$, $(x-2)(x-3)>0$ is false. Therefore the solution set is all numbers smaller than 2 or greater than 3.

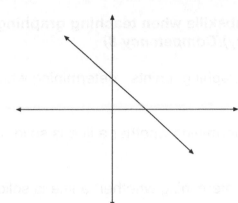

51. **Which equation is represented by the above graph?** (*Average Rigor*)*(Competency 8)*

   A) $x - y = 3$

   B) $x - y = -3$

   C) $x + y = 3$

   D) $x + y = -3$

Answer: C

By looking at the graph, we can determine the slope to be –1 and the y-intercept to be 3. Write the slope intercept form of the line as $y = -1x + 3$. Add x to both sides to obtain $x + y = 3$, the equation in standard form.

52. Identify the proper sequencing of subskills when teaching graphing inequalities in two dimensions *(Easy)(Competency 8)*

   A) shading regions, graphing lines, graphing points, determining whether a line is solid or broken

   B) graphing points, graphing lines, determining whether a line is solid or broken, shading regions

   C) graphing points, shading regions, determining whether a line is solid or broken, graphing lines

   D) graphing lines, determining whether a line is solid or broken, graphing points, shading regions

Answer: B

Graphing points is the most fundamental subskill for graphing inequalities in two dimensions. Next follows the graphing of lines, and then determining whether the line is solid or broken. The graphing of lines requires, at a minimum, the graphing of two points (such as the x- and y-intercepts). Once the line has been graphed (perhaps with a light marking), it can next be determined whether the line is solid or broken, depending on the inequality being graphed. Finally, the shading of appropriate regions on the graph may be undertaken.

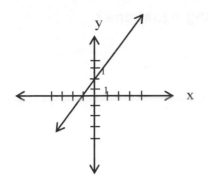

53. What is the equation of the above graph? *(Rigorous)(Competency 8)*

A) $2x + y = 2$

B) $2x - y = -2$

C) $2x - y = 2$

D) $2x + y = -2$

Answer: B

By observation, we see that the graph has a y-intercept of 2 and a slope of 2/1 = 2. Therefore its equation is y = mx + b = 2x + 2. Rearranging the terms gives 2x – y = –2.

54. **What is the solution set for the following equations?**
(Rigorous)(Competency 8)

$$3x + 2y = 12$$
$$12x + 8y = 15$$

A) all real numbers

B) x = 4, y = 4

C) x = 2, y = –1

D) ∅

Answer: D

Multiplying the top equation by –4 and adding results in the equation 0 = –33. Since this is a false statement, the correct choice is the null set.

55. **Solve for x and y: x= 3y + 7, 7x + 5y = 23** *(Rigorous)(Competency 8)*

A) (–1,4)

B) (4, –1)

C) $(\frac{-29}{7}, \frac{-26}{7})$

D) (10, 1)

Answer: B

Substituting x in the second equation results in 7(3y + 7) + 5y = 23. Solve by distributing and grouping like terms: 26y+49 = 23, 26y = –26, y = –1.
Substitute y into the first equation to obtain x.

56. Solve the system of equations for x, y and z. *(Rigorous)(Competency 8)*

$$3x + 2y - z = 0$$
$$2x + 5y = 8z$$
$$x + 3y + 2z = 7$$

A) $(-1,\ 2,\ 1)$

B) $(1,\ 2,\ -1)$

C) $(-3,\ 4,\ -1)$

D) $(0,\ 1,\ 2)$

Answer: A

Multiplying equation 1 by 2, and equation 2 by –3, and then adding together the two resulting equations gives $-11y + 22z = 0$. Solving for y gives y = 2z. In the meantime, multiplying equation 3 by –2 and adding it to equation 2 gives $-y - 12z = -14$. Then substituting 2z for y, yields the result z = 1. Subsequently, one can easily find that y = 2, and x = –1.

57. How is the following read? *(Competency 8; Easy)*

    3 < 5

A)   Three is less than five
B)   Five is greater than three
C)   Three is greater than five
D)   Five is less than three

Answer A: Three is less than five

Reading left to right: *three is less than five.*

58. The discriminant of a quadratic equation is evaluated and determined to be –3. The equation has... *(Rigorous)(Competency 9)*

A) one real root

B) one complex root

C) two roots, both real

D) two roots, both complex

Answer: D

The discriminant is the number under the radical sign. Since it is negative, the two roots of the equation are complex.

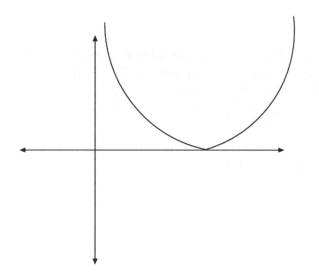

59. Which equation is graphed above? *(Rigorous)(Competency 9)*

A) $y = 4(x + 3)^2$

B) $y = 4(x - 3)^2$

C) $y = 3(x - 4)^2$

D) $y = 3(x + 4)^2$

Answer: B

Since the vertex of the parabola is three units to the left, we choose the solution where 3 is subtracted from x, then the quantity is squared.

60. **Which graph represents the equation of** $y = x^2 + 3x$ **?**
    (Rigorous)(Competency 9)

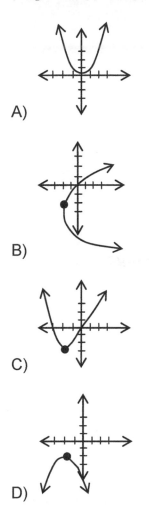

A)

B)

C)

D)

Answer: C

B is not the graph of a function. D is the graph of a parabola where the coefficient of x^2 is negative. A appears to be the graph of $y = x^2$. To find the x-intercepts of $y = x^2 + 3x$, set $y = 0$ and solve for x: $0 = x^2 + 3x = x(x + 3)$ to get $x = 0$ or $x = -3$. Therefore, the graph of the function intersects the x-axis at x=0 and x=−3.

61. Solve for x. $3x^2 - 2 + 4(x^2 - 3) = 0$ *(Rigorous)(Competency 9)*

A) $\{-\sqrt{2}, \sqrt{2}\}$

B) $\{2, -2\}$

C) $\{0, \sqrt{3}, -\sqrt{3}\}$

D) $\{7, -7\}$

Answer: A

Distribute and combine like terms to obtain $7x^2 - 14 = 0$.
Add 14 to both sides, then divide by 7. Since $x^2 = 2$, $x = \sqrt{2}$

62. Which of the following is a factor of $6 + 48m^3$ *(Average Rigor)(Competency 9)*

A) $(1 + 2m)$

B) $(1 - 8m)$

C) $(1 + m - 2m)$

D) $(1 - m + 2m)$

Answer: A

Removing the common factor of 6 and then factoring the sum of two cubes gives $6 + 48m^3 = 6(1 + 8m^3) = 6(1 + 2m)(1^2 - 2m + (2m)^2)$.

63. Factor completely: $8(x - y) + a(y - x)$ *(Average Rigor)(Competency 9)*

A) $(8 + A)(y - x)$

B) $(8 - A)(y - x)$

C) $(a - 8)(y - x)$

D) $(a - 8)(y + x)$

Answer: C

Glancing first at the solution choices, factor $(y - x)$ from each term. This leaves -8 from the first reran and a from the send term: $(a - 8)(y - x)$.

MIDDLE SCHOOL MATHEMATICS 454

64. **The formula for solving a quadratic equation is...**

A) $x = \dfrac{-b \pm \sqrt{b^2 - 4ac}}{2a}$

B) $x = \dfrac{-b \pm \sqrt{b^2 - 4a}}{2a}$

C) $x = \dfrac{b \pm \sqrt{b^2 - 4ac}}{2a}$

D) $x = \dfrac{b \pm \sqrt{b^3 - 4ac}}{2a}$

Answer: A

65. **Which of the following is a factor of k3 – m3 ?** *(Average Rigor)(Competency 10)*

A) $k^2 + m^2$

B) $k + m$

C) $k^2 - m^2$

D) $k - m$

Answer: D

The complete factorization for a difference of cubes is $(k - m)(k^2 + mk + m2)$.

66. Find the zeroes of $f(x) = x^3 + x^2 - 14x - 24$ *(Rigorous)(Competency 10)*

    A) 4, 3, 2

    B) 3, –8

    C) 7, –2, –1

    D) 4, –3, –2

Answer: D

Possible rational roots of the equation $0 = x^3 + x^2 - 14x - 24$ are all the positive and negative factors of 24. By substituting into the equation, we find that –2 is a root, and therefore that x+2 is a factor. By performing the long division $(x^3 + x^2 - 14x - 24)/(x+2)$, we can find that another factor of the original equation is $x^2 - x - 12$ or (x–4)(x+3). Therefore the zeros of the original function are –2, –3, and 4.

67. Solve for x: $|2x +3| > 4$ *(Rigorous)(Competency 10)*

    A) $-\frac{7}{2} > x > \frac{1}{2}$

    B) $-\frac{1}{2} > x > \frac{7}{2}$

    C) $x < \frac{7}{2}$ or $x < -\frac{1}{2}$

    D) $x < -\frac{7}{2}$ or $x > \frac{1}{2}$

Answer: D

The quantity within the absolute value symbols must be either > 4 or < –4.
Solve the two inequalities 2x + 3 > 4 or 2x + 3 < –4

68. Graph the solution: $|x| + 7 < 13$ *(Rigorous)(Competency 10)*

A)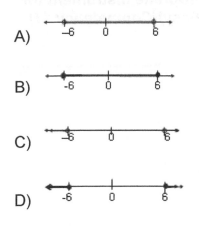

B)

C)

D)

Answer: A

Solve by adding –7 to each side of the inequality. Since the absolute value of x is less than 6, x must be between –6 and 6. The end points are not included so the circles on the graph are hollow.

69. Solve for x: $18 = 4 + |2x|$ *(Average Rigor)(Competency 10)*

A) $\{-11, 7\}$

B) $\{-7, 0, 7\}$

C) $\{-7, 7\}$

D) $\{-11, 11\}$

Answer: C

Using the definition of absolute value, two equations are possible: $18 = 4 + 2x$ or $18 = 4 - 2x$. Solving for x gives x = 7 or x = –7.

70. **Seventh grade students are working on a project using non-standard measurement. Which would not be an appropriate instrument for measuring the length of the classroom?** *(Easy)(Competency 11)*

A) a student's foot

B) a student's arm span

C) a student's jump

D) all are appropriate

Answer: D

Although measurements usually involve such typical units as feet, meters and inches, measurements can be made using any defined non-standard unit. As long as the unit is applied consistently (that is, as long as it does not change), it can be used as legitimately as such standard units as feet or meters. Since the length of a student's foot, arm span and jump can all be defined and used consistently, they all constitute appropriate instruments or units for measurement, despite the fact that they do not involve traditional units.

71. **The mass of a cookie is closest to** *(Average Rigor)(Competency 11)*

A) 0.5 kg

B) 0.5 grams

C) 15 grams

D) 1.5 grams

Answer: C

A cookie is measured in grams.

72. **A man's waist measures 90 cm. What is the greatest possible error for the measurement?** *(Average)(Competency 11)*

A) ± 1 m

B) ±8 cm

C) ±1 cm

D) ±5 mm

Answer: D

The greatest possible error of measurement is ± 1/2 unit, in this case 0.5 cm or 5 mm.

73. **4 square yards is equivalent to** *(Average)(Competency 11)*

A) 12 square feet

B) 48 square feet

C) 36 square feet

D) 108 square feet

Answer: C

There are 9 square feet in a square yard.

74. **If a circle has an area of 25 cm^2, what is its circumference to the nearest tenth of a centimeter?** *(Rigorous)(Competency 11)*

A) 78.5 cm

B) 17.7 cm

C) 8.9 cm

D) 15.7 cm

Answer: B

Find the radius by solving $\Pi r^2 = 25$. Then substitute r=2.82 into $C = 2\Pi r$ to obtain the circumference.

75. Find the area of the figure below. *(Rigorous)(Competency 11)*

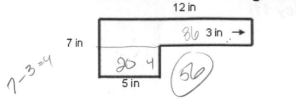

Answer: A

Divide the figure into two rectangles with a horizontal line. The area of the top rectangle is 36 in, and the bottom is 20 in.

76. Find the area of the shaded region given square ABCD with side AB=10m and circle E. *(Rigorous)(Competency 11)*

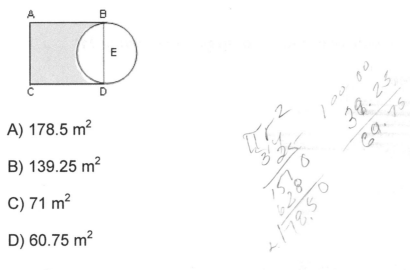

A) 178.5 m²

B) 139.25 m²

C) 71 m²

D) 60.75 m²

Answer: D

Find the area of the square $10^2 = 100$, then subtract 1/2 the area of the circle. The area of the circle is $\Pi r^2 = (3.14)(5)(5)=78.5$. Therefore the area of the shaded region is $100 - 39.25 - 60.75$.

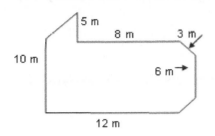

77. Compute the area of the polygon shown above.
(Rigorous)(Competency 11)

A) 178 m²

B) 154 m²

C) 43 m²

D) 188 m²

Answer: B

Divide the figure into a triangle, a rectangle and a trapezoid. The area of the triangle is 1/2 bh = 1/2 (4)(5) = 10. The area of the rectangle is bh = 12(10) = 120. The area of the trapezoid is 1/2(b + B)h = 1/2(6 + 10)(3) = 1/2 (16)(3) = S4. Thus, the area of the figure is 10 + 120 + 24 =154.

78. Find the area of the figure pictured below. *(Rigorous)(Competency 11)*

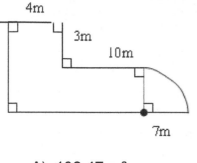

A) 136.47 m²

B) 148.48 m²

C) 293.86 m²

D) 178.47   m²

Answer: B

Divide the figure into 2 rectangles and one quarter circle. The tall rectangle on the left will have dimensions 10 by 4 and area 40. The rectangle in the center will have dimensions 7 by 10 and area 70. The quarter circle will have area $.25(\pi)7^2 = 38.48$. The total area is therefore approximately 148.48.

79. Given a 30 meter x 60 meter garden with a circular fountain with a 5 meter radius, calculate the area of the portion of the garden not occupied by the fountain. *(Rigorous)(Competency 11)*

A) 1721 m²

B) 1879 m²

C) 2585 m²

D) 1015 m²

Answer: A

Find the area of the garden and then subtract the area of the fountain: $30(60) - \pi(5)^2$ or approximately 1721 square meters. **Answer is A.**

80. **Determine the area of the shaded region of the trapezoid in terms of x and y.** *(Rigorous)(Competency 11)*

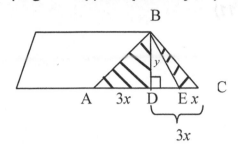

A) $4xy$

B) $2xy$

C) $3x^2y$

D) There is not enough information given.

Answer: B

To find the area of the shaded region, find the area of triangle ABC and then subtract the area of triangle DBE. The area of triangle ABC is .5(6x)(y) = 3xy. The area of triangle DBE is .5(2x)(y) = xy. The difference is 2xy.

81. **If the radius of a right circular cylinder is doubled, how does its volume change?** *(Rigorous)(Competency 11)*

A) no change

B) also is doubled

C) four times the original

D) pi times the original

Answer: C

If the radius of a right circular cylinder is doubled, the volume is multiplied by four because in he formula, the radius is squared, therefore the new volume is 2 x 2 or four times the original.

82. **Students are working with a set of rulers and various small objects from the classroom. Which concept are these students exploring?** (*Average rigor*)(*Competency 11*)

   A) Volume
   B) Weight
   C) Length
   D) Temperature

Answer C: Length

The use of a ruler indicates that the activity is based on exploring length.

83. **The term "cubic feet" indicates which kind of measurement?** (*Average rigor*)(*Competency 11*)

   A) Volume
   B) Mass
   C) Length
   D) Distance

Answer A: Volume

The word *cubic* indicates that this is a term describing volume.

84. Given XY ≅ YZ and ∠AYX ≅ ∠AYZ. Prove △AYZ ≅ △AYX.

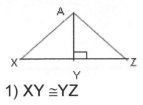

1) XY ≅ YZ

2) ∠AYX ≅ ∠AYZ

3) AY ≅ AY

4) △AYZ ≅ △AYX

Which property justifies step 3? *(Easy) (Competency 12)*

    A) reflexive

    B) symmetric

    C) transitive

    D) identity

Answer: A

The reflexive property states that every number or variable is equal to itself and every segment is congruent to itself.

85. Given $l_1 \| l_2$ prove $\angle b \cong \angle e$

1) $\angle b \cong \angle d$	1) vertical angle theorem
2) $\angle d \cong \angle e$	2) alternate interior angle theorem
3) $\angle b \cong \angle 3$	3) symmetric axiom of equality

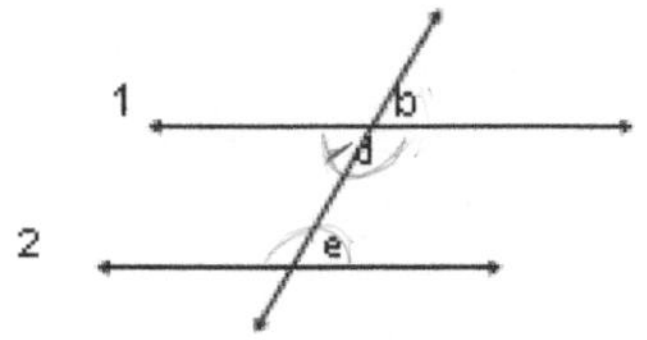

Which step is incorrectly justified? (*Average Rigor*) (*Competency 12*)

A) step 1

B) step 2

C) step 3

D) no error

Answer: A

Step 3 can be justified by the transitive property.

86. **Which is a postulate?** *(Easy)(Competency 12)*

A) The sum of the angles in any triangle is 180°.

B) A line intersects a plane in one point.

C) Two intersecting lines from congruent vertical angles.

D) Any segment is congruent to itself.

Answer: D

A postulate is an accepted property of real numbers or geometric figures which cannot be proven, A, B. and C are theorems which can be proven.

87. When you begin by assuming the conclusion of a theorem is false, then show that through a sequence of logically correct steps you contradict an accepted fact, this is known as *(Easy)(Competency 12)*

    A) inductive reasoning

    B) direct proof

    C) indirect proof

    D) exhaustive proof

Answer: C

By definition this describes the procedure of an indirect proof.

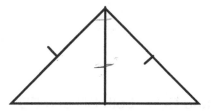

88. What method could be used to prove the above triangles congruent? *(Average Rigor)(Competency 12)*

    A) SSS

    B) SAS

    C) AAS

    D) SSA

Answer: B

Use SAS with the last side being the vertical line common to both triangles.

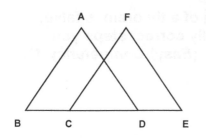

89. **Which postulate could be used to prove ΔABD ≅ ΔCEF, given BC ≅ DE, ∠C ≅ ∠D, and AD ≅ CF?** *(Average Rigor)(Competency 12)*

   A) ASA

   B) SAS

   C) SAA

   D) SSS

Answer: B

To obtain the final side, add CD to both BC and ED.

90. **Which theorem can be used to prove $\triangle BAK \cong \triangle MKA$?** *(Rigorous)(Competency 12)*

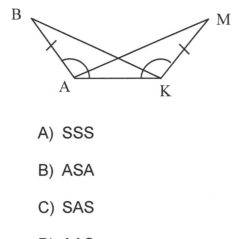

   A) SSS

   B) ASA

   C) SAS

   D) AAS

Answer: C

Since side AK is common to both triangles, the triangles can be proved congruent by using the Side-Angle-Side Postulate.

91. **Given that QO⊥NP and QO=NP, quadrilateral NOPQ can most accurately be described as a** *(Easy)(Competency 12)*

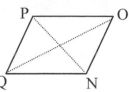

A) parallelogram

B) rectangle

C) square

D) rhombus

Answer: C

In an ordinary parallelogram, the diagonals are not perpendicular or equal in length. In a rectangle, the diagonals are not necessarily perpendicular. In a rhombus, the diagonals are not equal in length. In a square, the diagonals are both perpendicular and congruent.

92. **Choose the correct statement concerning the median and altitude in a triangle.** *(Average Rigor)(Competency 12)*

A) The median and altitude of a triangle may be the same segment.

B) The median and altitude of a triangle are always different segments.

C) The median and altitude of a right triangle are always the same segment.

D) The median and altitude of an isosceles triangle are always the same segment.

Answer: A

The most one can say with certainty is that the median (segment drawn to the midpoint of the opposite side) and the altitude (segment drawn perpendicular to the opposite side) of a triangle <u>may</u> coincide, but they more often do not. In an isosceles triangle, the median and the altitude to the <u>base</u> are the same segment.

93. **Which of the following can be defined?** *(Easy)(Competency 12)*

   A) point

   B) ray

   C) line

   D) plane

Answer: B

The point, line, and plane are the three undefined concepts on which plane geometry is based.

94. **Choose the diagram which illustrates the construction of a perpendicular to the line at a given point on the line.** *(Average Rigor)(Competency 12)*

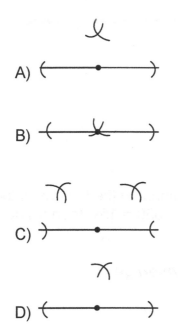

A)

B)

C)

D)

Answer: D

Given a point on a line, place the compass point there and draw two arcs intersecting the line in two points, one on either side of the given point. Then using any radius larger than half the new segment produced, and with the pointer at each end of the new segment, draw arcs which intersect above the line. Connect this new point with the given point.

95. **How many equal angles does an equilateral triangle have?** *(Easy)(Competency 13)*

A)   0

B)   1

C)   2

D)   3

Answer: D

All angles (3) of an equilateral triangle are equal. Each angle measures 60 degrees.

96. Given similar polygons with corresponding sides of lengths 9 and 15, find the perimeter of the smaller polygon if the perimeter of the larger polygon is 150 units. *(Rigorous)(Competency 13)*

   A) 54

   B) 135

   C) 90

   D) 126

Answer: C

The perimeters of similar polygons are directly proportional to the lengths of their sides, therefore 9/15 = x/150. Cross multiply to obtain 1350 = 15x, then divide by 15 to obtain the perimeter of the smaller polygon.

97. Given $l_1 \parallel l_2$ which of the following is true? *(Average Rigor)(Competency 13)*

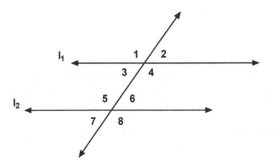

   A) $\angle 1$ and $\angle 8$ are congruent and alternate interior angles

   B) $\angle 2$ and $\angle 3$ are congruent and corresponding angles

   C) $\angle 3$ and $\angle 4$ are adjacent and supplementary angles

   D) $\angle 3$ and $\angle 5$ are adjacent and supplementary angles

Answer: C

The angles in A are exterior. In B, the angles are vertical. The angles in D are consecutive, not adjacent.

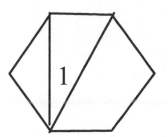

98. **Given the regular hexagon above, determine the measure of angle 1.**
    (Rigorous)(Competency 13)

    A) 30°

    B) 60°

    C) 120°

    D) 45°

Answer: A

Each interior angle of the hexagon measures 120°. The isosceles triangle on the left has angles which measure 120, 30, and 30. By alternate interior angle theorem, ∠1 is also 30.

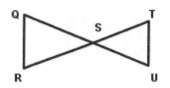

99. **Given QS $\cong$ TS and RS $\cong$ US, prove $\triangle$QRS $\cong$ $\triangle$TUS.**
(Average Rigor)(Competency 13)

I) QS $\cong$ TS	1) Given
2) RS $\cong$ US	2) Given
3) $\angle$TSU $\cong$ $\angle$QSR 3) ?	
4) $\triangle$TSU $\cong$ $\triangle$QSR	4) SAS

A) Congruent parts of congruent triangles are congruent

B) Reflexive axiom of equality

C) Alternate interior angle Theorem

D) Vertical angle theorem

Answer: D

Angles formed by intersecting lines are called vertical angles and are congruent.

100. **Angles formed by intersecting lines are called vertical angles and are congruent.**

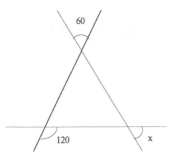

Note: Figure not drawn to scale.

In the figure above, what is the value of x? *(Rigorous)(Competency 13)*

A) 50

B) 60

C) 75

D0 80

Answer: B

The angles within the triangle make up 180°. Opposite angles are equal, therefore, the angle opposite the 60° angle is also 60°. Adjacent angles add to 180° (straight line). Therefore, the angle inside the triangle adjacent to the 120° angle is 60°. The third angle in the triangle would then be 60° (180 – 60 – 60). Since x is opposite this third angle, it would also be 60°.

101. **Line *p* has a negative slope and passes through the point (0, 0). If line *q* is perpendicular to line *p*, which of the following must be true?** *(Rigorous)(Competency 13)*

A) Line *q* has a negative *y*-intercept.

B) Line *q* passes through the point (0,0)

C) Line *q* has a positive slope.

D) Line *q* has a positive *y*-intercept.

Answer: C

Draw a picture to help you visualize the problem.

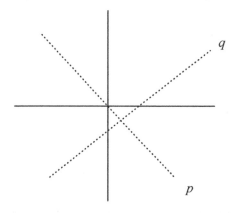

Choices (A) and (D) are not correct because line *q* could have a positive or a negative *y*-intercept. Choice (B) is incorrect because line *q* does not necessarily pass through (0, 0). Since line *q* is perpendicular to line *p*. which has a negative slope, it must have a positive slope.

102. What is the slope of any line parallel to the line 2x + 4y = 4?
(Rigorous)(Competencies 8 and 13)

A) -2

B) -1

C) – ½

D) 2

Answer: C

The formula for slope is y = mx + b, where m is the slope. Lines that are parallel have the same slope.

$$2x + 4y = 4$$
$$4y = -2x + 4$$
$$y = \frac{-2x}{4} + 1$$
$$y = \frac{-1}{2}x + 1$$

103. Prove △HYM ≅ △KZL, given XZ ≅ XY, ∠L ≅ ∠M and YL ≅ MZ

1) XZ ≅ XY   1) Given
2) ∠Y ≅ ∠Z   2) ?
3) ∠L ≅ ∠M   3) Given
4) YL ≅ MZ   4) Given
5) LM ≅ LM   5) ?
6) YM ≅ LZ   6) Add
7) △HYM ≅ △KZL   7) ASA

Which could be used to justify steps 2 and 5? *(Average Rigor)(Competency 13)*

A) CPCTC, Identity

B) Isosceles Triangle Theorem, Identity

C) SAS, Reflexive

D) Isosceles Triangle Theorem, Reflexive

Answer: D

The isosceles triangle theorem states that the base angles are congruent, and the reflexive property states that every segment is congruent to itself.

104.   **What is the degree measure of an interior angle of a regular 10-sided polygon?** *(Rigorous)(Competency 13)*

A) 18°

B) 36°

C) 144°

D) 54°

Answer: C

Formula for finding the measure of each interior angle of a regular polygon with n sides is $\frac{(n-2)180}{n}$. For n=10, we get $\frac{8(180)}{10} = 144$.

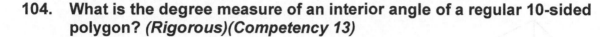

105.   **Which of the following statements is true about the number of degrees in each angle?** *(Rigorous)(Competency 13)*

A) a + b + c = 180°

B) a = e

C) b + c = e

D) c + d = e

Answer: C

In any triangle, an exterior angle is equal to the sum of the remote interior angles.

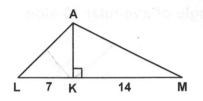

106. **Given altitude AK with measurements as indicated, determine the length of AK.** *(Rigorous)(Competency 13)*

    A) 98

    B) $7\sqrt{2}$

    C) $\sqrt{21}$

    D) $7\sqrt{3}$

Answer: B

The attitude from the right angle to the hypotenuse of any right triangle is the geometric mean of the two segments which are formed. Multiply 7 x 14 and take the square root.

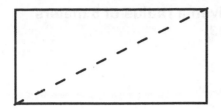

107. **The above diagram is most likely used in deriving a formula for which of the following?** *(Easy)(Competency 13)*

    A) the area of a rectangle

    B) the area of a triangle

    C) the perimeter of a triangle

    D) the surface area of a prism

Answer: B

The rectangle in the diagram is divided by a diagonal line segment into two congruent triangles. Since the triangles are congruent, the area of each triangle is equal to half the area of the rectangle. As a result, using the rectangle (or, more generally, the parallelogram) formed by the two congruent triangles, a formula for the area of a triangle can be derived. Thus, answer B is most likely to be the correct answer.

108. **Compute the area of the shaded region, given a radius of 5 meters. O is the center.** *(Rigorous)(Competency 13)*

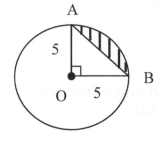

A) 7.13 cm²

B) 7.13 m²

C) 78.5 m²

D) 19.63 m²

Answer: B

Area of triangle AOB is .5(5)(5) = 12.5 square meters. Since $\dfrac{90}{360} = .25$, the area of sector AOB (pie-shaped piece) is approximately .25(π)5² = 19.63. Subtracting the triangle area from the sector area to get the area of segment AB, we get approximately 19.63–12.5 = 7.13 square meters.

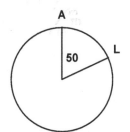

109. **What is the measure of major arc AL ?** *(Average Rigor)(Competency 13)*

A) 50°

B) 25°

C) 100°

D) 310°

Answer: D

Minor arc AC measures 50°, the same as the central angle. To determine the measure of the major arc, subtract from 360.

MIDDLE SCHOOL MATHEMATICS 482

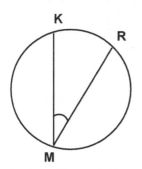

110. If arc KR = 70° what is the measure of ∠M? *(Rigorous)(Competency 13)*

    A) 290°

    B) 35°

    C) 140°

    D) 110°

Answer: B

An inscribed angle is equal to one half the measure of the intercepted arc.

111. The above construction can be completed to make *(Easy)(Competency 13)*

    A) an angle bisector

    B) parallel lines

    C) a perpendicular bisector

    D) skew lines

Answer: C

The points marked C and D are the intersection of the circles with centers A and B.

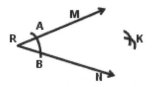

112. A line from R to K will form *(Easy)(Competency 13)*

    A) an altitude of RMN

    B) a perpendicular bisector of MN

    C) a bisector of MRN

    D) a vertical angle

Answer: C

Using a compass, point K is found to be equidistant from A and B.

**113. What is the measure of minor arc AD, given measure of arc PS is 40°
and $m < K = 10°$?** *(Rigorous)(Competency 13)*

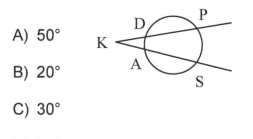

    A) 50°

    B) 20°

    C) 30°

    D) 25°

Answer: B

The formula relating the measure of angle K and the two arcs it intercepts is
$m\angle K = \frac{1}{2}(mPS - mAD)$. Substituting the known values, we get $10 = \frac{1}{2}(40 - mAD)$.
Solving for mAD gives an answer of 20 degrees.

114. Compute the surface area of the prism. (*Rigorous*)(*Competency 14*)

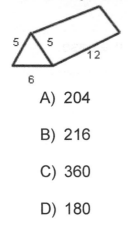

    A) 204

    B) 216

    C) 360

    D) 180

Answer: B

There are five surfaces which make up the prism. The bottom rectangle has area 6 x 12 = 72. The sloping sides are two rectangles each with an area of 5 x 12 = 60. The height of the and triangles is determined to be 4 using the Pythagorean theorem. Therefore each triangle has area 1/2bh = 1/2(6)(4) –12. Thus, the surface area is 72 + 60 + 60 + 12 + 12 = 216.

115. If the base of a regular square pyramid is tripled, how does its volume change? (*Rigorous*)(*Competency 14*)

    A) double the original

    B) triple the original

    C) nine times the original

    D) no change

Answer: B

Using the general formula for a pyramid V = 1/3 bh, since the base is tripled and is not squared or cubed in the formula, the volume is also tripled.

116. **How does lateral area differ from total surface area in prisms, pyramids, and cones?** *(Easy)(Competency 14)*

   A) For the lateral area, only use surfaces perpendicular to the base.

   B) They are both the same.

   C) The lateral area does not include the base.

   D) The lateral area is always a factor of pi.

Answer: C

The lateral area does not include the base.

117. **If the area of the base of a cone is tripled, the volume will be** *(Easy)(Competency 14)*

   A) the same as the original

   B) 9 times the original

   C) 3 times the original

   D) 3π times the original

Answer: C

The formula for the volume of a cone is $V = \dfrac{1}{3}Bh$, where B is the area of the circular base and h is the height. If the area of the base is tripled, the volume becomes $V = \dfrac{1}{3}(3B)h = Bh$, or three times the original area.

118. Find the height of a box with surface area of 94 sq. ft. with a width of 3 feet and a depth of 4 feet. *(Rigorous)(Competency 14)*

 A) 3 ft.

 B) 4 ft.

 C) 5 ft

 D) 6 ft.

Answer: C

$94 = 2(3h) + 2(4h) + 2(12)$
$94 = 6h + 8h + 24$
$94 = 14h + 24$
$70 = 14h$
$5 = h$

119. Determine the volume of a sphere to the nearest cm if the surface area is 113 cm^2. *(Rigorous)(Competency 14)*

 A) 113 cm^3

 B) 339 cm^3

 C) 37.7 cm^3

 D) 226 cm^3

Answer: A

Solve for the radius of the sphere using $A = 4\Pi r^2$. The radius is 3. Then, find the volume using $4/3\ \Pi r^3$. Only when the radius is 3 are the volume and surface area equivalent.

120. Ginny and Nick head back to their respective colleges after being home for the weekend. They leave their house at the same time and drive for 4 hours. Ginny drives due south at the average rate of 60 miles per hour and Nick drives due east at the average rate of 60 miles per hour. What is the straight-line distance between them, in miles, at the end of the 4 hours? *(Rigorous)(Competency 15)*

A) $120\sqrt{2}$

B) 240

C) $240\sqrt{2}$

D) 288

Answer: C

Draw a picture.

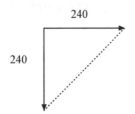

We have a right triangle, so we can use the Pythagorean Theorem to find the distance between the two points.

$$240^2 + 240^2 = c^2$$
$$2(240)^2 = c^2$$
$$240\sqrt{2} = c$$

121. **Find the distance between (3,7) and (–3,4). *(Average Rigor)(Competency 15)***

    A) 9

    B) 45

    C) $3\sqrt{5}$

    D) $5\sqrt{3}$

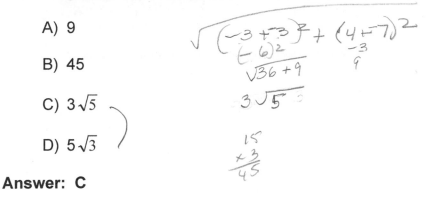

Answer: C

Using the distance formula

$$\sqrt{[3-(-3)]^2 + (7-4)^2}$$
$$=\sqrt{36+9}$$
$$=3\sqrt{5}$$

122. **Find the midpoint of (2,5) and (7,–4). *(Average Rigor)(Competency 15)***

    A) (9,–1)

    B) (5, 9)

    C) (9/2, –1/2)

    D) (9/2, 1/2)

Answer: D

Using the midpoint formula

x = (2 + 7)/2   y = (5 + –4)/2

123. Given segment AC with B as its midpoint find the coordinates of C if A = (5,7) and B = (3, 6.5). *(Rigorous)(Competency 15)*

A) (4, 6.5)

B) (1, 6)

C) (2, 0.5)

D) (16, 1)

Answer: B

The formula for the midpoint of a segment with endpoints (x_1, y_1) and (x_2, y_2) is:

$$\left(x_{mid}, y_{mid}\right) = \left(\frac{x_1 + x_2}{2}, \frac{y_1 + y_2}{2}\right)$$

Expressing this formula in terms of the given information (coordinates of points A and B) yields:

$$(3, 6.5) = \left(\frac{5 + x_C}{2}, \frac{7 + y_C}{2}\right)$$

Each coordinate may be found by algebraically solving the two resulting equations:

$$3 = \frac{5 + x_C}{2} \qquad\qquad 6.5 = \frac{7 + y_C}{2}$$
$$6 = 5 + x_C \qquad\qquad 13 = 7 + y_C$$
$$x_C = 1 \qquad\qquad y_C = 6$$

Thus, the correct answer is (1, 6).

124. Find the median of the following set of data:

    14 3 7 6 11 20

(Average Rigor)(Competency 16)

A) 9

B) 8.5

C) 7

D) 11

Answer: A

Place the numbers is ascending order: 3 6 7 11 14 20. Find the average of the middle two numbers (7+11)12 =9.

125. Compute the median for the following data set: {12, 19, 13, 16, 17, 14}
**   *(Average Rigor)(Competency 16)***

A) 14.5

B) 15.17

C) 15

D) 16

Answer: C

Arrange the data in ascending order: 12,13,14,16,17,19. The median is the middle value in a list with an odd number of entries. When there is an even number of entries, the median is the mean of the two center entries. Here the average of 14 and 16 is 15.

126. Corporate salaries are listed for several employees. Which would be   the best measure of central tendency? *(Average Rigor)(Competency   16)*

$24,000 $24,000 $26,000 $28,000 $30,000 $120,000

A) mean

B.) median

C) mode

D) no difference

Answer: B

The median provides the best measure of central tendency in this case where the mode is the lowest number and the mean would be disproportionately skewed by the outlier $120,000.

127. A student scored in the 87th percentile on a standardized test. Which would be the best interpretation of his score? *(Average Rigor)(Competency 16)*

A) Only 13% of the students who took the test scored higher.

B) This student should be getting mostly Bs on his report card.

C) This student performed below average on the test.

D) This is the equivalent of missing 13 questions on a 100 question exam.

Answer: A

Percentile ranking tells how the student compared to the norm or the other students taking the test. It does not correspond to the percentage answered correctly, but can indicate how the student compared to the average student tested.

128. **Which type of graph uses symbols to represent quantities?**
     (Easy) (Competency 16)

     A.   Bar graph
     B.   Line graph
     C.   Pictograph
     D.   Circle graph

Answer C: Pictograph

A pictograph shows comparison of quantities using symbols. Each symbol represents a number of items.

129. **Which of the following types of graphs would be best to use to record the eye color of the students in the class?** *(Average rigor)* *(Competency 16)*

     A.   Bar graph or circle graph
     B.   Pictograph or bar graph
     C.   Line graph or pictograph
     D.   Line graph or bar graph

Answer B: Pictograph or bar graph

A pictograph or a line graph could be used. In this activity, a line graph would not be used because it shows change over time. Although a circle graph could be used to show a percentage of students with brown eyes, blue eyes, etc. that representation would be too advanced for early childhood students.

130. Which statement is true about George's budget? *(Easy)(Competency 16)*

A) George spends the greatest portion of his income on food.

B) George spends twice as much on utilities as he does on his mortgage.

C) George spends twice as much on utilities as he does on food.

D) George spends the same amount on food and utilities as he does on mortgage.

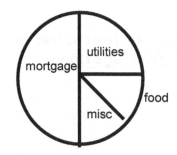

Answer: C

George spends twice as much on utilities than on food.

131. **What conclusion can be drawn from the graph below?** *(Average Rigor)(Competency 16)*

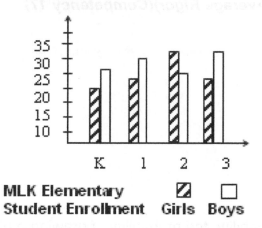

A) The number of students in first grade exceeds the number in second grade.

B) There are more boys than girls in the entire school.

C) There are more girls than boys in the first grade.

D) Third grade has the largest number of students.

Answer: B

In Kindergarten, first grade, and third grade, there are more boys than girls. The number of extra girls in grade two is more than made up for by the extra boys in all the other grades put together.

132. **Given a drawer with 5 black socks, 3 blue socks, and 2 red socks, what is the probability that you will draw two black socks in two draws in a dark room?** (*Average Rigor*)(*Competency 17*)

    A) 2/9

    B) 1/4

    C) 17/18

    D) 1/18

Answer: A

In this example of conditional probability, the probability of drawing a black sock on the first draw is 5/10. It is implied in the problem that there is no replacement, therefore the probability of obtaining a black sock in the second draw is 4/9. Multiply the two probabilities and reduce to lowest terms.

133. **A sack of candy has 3 peppermints, 2 butterscotch drops and 3 cinnamon drops. One candy is drawn and replaced, then another candy is drawn; what is the probability that both will be butterscotch?** (*Average Rigor*)(*Competency 17*)

    A) 1/2

    B) 1/28

    C) 1/4

    D) 1/16

Answer: D

With replacement, the probability of obtaining a butterscotch on the first draw is 2/8 and the probability of drawing a butterscotch on the second draw is also 2/8. Multiply and reduce to lowest terms.

134. Given a spinner with the numbers one through eight, what is the probability that you will spin an even number or a number greater than four? (Easy)(Competency 17)

    A) 1/4

    B) 1/2

    C) ¾

    D) 1

Answer: C

There are 8 favorable outcomes: 2,4,5,6,7,8 and 8 possibilities. Reduce 6/8 to 3/4.

135. If a horse will probably win three races out of ten, what are the odds that he will win? *(Rigorous)(Competency 17)*

    A) 3:10

    B) 7:10

    C) 3:7

    D) 7:3

Answer: C

The odds are that he will win 3 and lose 7.

136. A jar contains 3 red marbles, 5 white marbles, 1 green marble and 15 blue marbles. If one marble is picked at random from the jar, what is the probability that it will be red? *(Average)(Competency 17)*

    A) 1/3
    B) 1/8
    C) 3/8
    D) 1/24

Answer: B

The total number of marbles is 24 and the number of red marbles is 3. Thus the probability of picking a red marble from the jar is 3/24=1/8.

137. **If there are three people in a room, what is the probability that at least two of them will share a birthday? (Assume a year has 365 days)** *(Rigorous)(Competency 17)*

   A) 0.67
   B) 0.05
   C) 0.008
   D) 0.33

Answer: C

The best way to approach this problem is to use the fact that
the probability of an event + the probability of the event not happening = 1.
First find the probability that no two people will share a birthday and then subtract that from one.
The probability that two of the people will not share a birthday = 364/365 (since the second person's birthday can be one of the 364 days other than the birthday of the first person).
The probability that the third person will also not share either of the first two birthdays = (364/365) * (363/365) = 0.992.
Therefore, the probability that at least two people will share a birthday = 1 – 0.992 = 0.008.

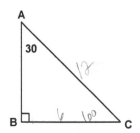

138. **If AC = 12, determine BC.** *(Average Rigor)(Competency 18)*

   A) 6

   B) 4

   C) $6\sqrt{3}$

   D) $3\sqrt{6}$

Answer: A

In a 30-60- 90 right triangle, the leg opposite the 30° angle is half the length of the hypotenuse.

139. Which expression is not equal to sinx?
(*Rigorous*)(*Competency 18*)

A) $\sqrt{1 - \cos^2 x}$
B) $\tan x \cos x$
C) $1 / \csc x$
D) $1 / \sec x$

Answer: D
Using the basic definitions of the trigonometric functions and the Pythagorean identity, we see that the first three options are all identical to sinx.
secx= 1/cosx is not the same as sinx.

140. For an acute angle x, sinx = 3/5. What is cotx?
(*Rigorous*)(*Competency 18*)

A) 5/3
B) 3/4
C) 1.33
D) 1

Answer: B

Using the Pythagorean Identity, we know sin²x + cos²x = 1. Thus

$$\cos x = \sqrt{1 - \frac{9}{25}} = \frac{4}{5}; \cot x = \frac{\cos x}{\sin x} = \frac{4}{3}.$$

141. Solve for v_0 : $d = at(v_t - v_0)$ (*Rigorous*)(*Competency 19*)

A) $v_0 = atd - v_t$

B) $v_0 = d - atv_t$

C) $v_0 = atv_t - d$

D) $v_0 = (atv_t - d)/at$

Answer: D

Using the Distributive Property and other properties of equality to isolate v_0 gives d = atv$_t$ – atv$_0$,   atv$_0$ = atv$_t$ – d,   v$_0$ = $\dfrac{atv_t - d}{at}$.

142. L'Hospital's rule provides a method to evaluate which of the following?
   (Rigorous) (Competency 19)

   A)   Limit of a function
   B)   Derivative of a function
   C)   Sum of an arithmetic series
   D)   Sum of a geometric series

Answer: A

L'Hospital's rule is used to find the limit of a function by taking the derivatives of the numerator and denominator. Since the primary purpose of the rule is to find the limit, A is the correct answer.

143. Find the following limit: $\lim\limits_{x \to 2} \dfrac{x^2 - 4}{x - 2}$ (Rigorous)(Competency 19)

   A)   0
   B)   Infinity
   C)   2
   D)   4

Answer: D

First factor the numerator and cancel the common factor to get the limit.

$$\lim\limits_{x \to 2} \dfrac{x^2 - 4}{x - 2} = \lim\limits_{x \to 2} \dfrac{(x - 2)(x + 2)}{(x - 2)} = \lim\limits_{x \to 2}(x + 2) = 4$$

144. Find the following limit: $\lim\limits_{x \to 0} \dfrac{\sin 2x}{5x}$ (Rigorous) (Competency 19)

   A)   Infinity
   B)   0
   C)   1.4
   D)   1

Answer: C

Since substituting x=0 will give an undefined answer, we can use L'Hospital's rule and take derivatives of both the numerator and denominator to find the limit.

$$\lim\limits_{x \to 0} \dfrac{\sin 2x}{5x} = \lim\limits_{x \to 0} \dfrac{2\cos 2x}{5} = \dfrac{2}{5} = 1.4$$

145. **What is the sum of the first 20 terms of the geometric sequence (2,4,8,16,32,…)?** *(Rigorous)* *(Competency 20)*

    A) 2097150
    B) 1048575
    C) 524288
    D) 1048576

Answer: A

For a geometric sequence $a, ar, ar^2, …, ar^n$, the sum of the first n terms is given by $\dfrac{a(r^n - 1)}{r - 1}$. In this case a=2 and r=2. Thus the sum of the first 20 terms of the sequence is given by $\dfrac{2(2^{20} - 1)}{2 - 1} = 2097150$.

146. **In real-life problems, what does the slope of a line often represent?** *(Average Rigor)* *(Competency 21)*

    A)   Total Growth
    B)   Average Rate of Change
    C)   Time
    D)   Profit

Answer: B

The slope of a line is often used to model and represent average rate of change.

XAMonline, INC. 21 Orient Ave. Melrose, MA 02176

Toll Free number 800-509-4128

TO ORDER Fax 781-662-9268 OR www.XAMonline.com

MASSACHUSETTS TEST FOR EDUCATOR LICENTURE
- MTEL - 2008

PO#   Store/School:

Address 1:

Address 2 (Ship to other):

City, State Zip

Credit card number_____-_____-_____-_____   expiration_____

EMAIL _____

PHONE   **FAX**

ISBN	TITLE	Qty	Retail	Total
978-1-58197-287-0	MTEL Communication and Literacy Skills 01		$27.95	
978-1-58197-592-5	MTEL General Curriculum (formerly Elementary) 03		$28.95	
978-1-58197-607-6	MTEL History 06 (Social Science)		$59.95	
978-1-58197-283-2	MTEL English 07		$59.95	
978-1-58197-349-5	MTEL Mathematics 09		$32.95	
978-1-58197-593-2	MTEL General Science 10		$59.95	
978-1-58197-041-8	MTEL Physics 11		$59.95	
978-1-58197-883-4	MTEL Chemistry 12		$59.95	
978-1-58197-687-8	MTEL Biology 13		$59.95	
978-1-58197-683-0	MTEL Earth Science 14		$59.95	
978-1-58197-676-2	MTEL Early Childhood 02		$73.50	
978-1-58197-893-3	MTEL Visual Art Sample Test 17		$15.00	
978-1-58197-8988	MTEL Political Science/ Political Philosophy 48		$59.95	
978-1-58197-886-5	MTEL Physical Education 22		$59.95	
978-1-58197-887-2	MTEL French Sample Test 26		$15.00	
978-1-58197-888-9	MTEL Spanish 28		$59.95	
978-1-58197-889-6	MTEL Middle School Mathematics 47		$59.95	
978-1-58197-890-2	MTEL Middle School Humanities 50		$59.95	
978-1-58197-891-9	MTEL Middle School Mathematics-Science 51		$59.95	
978-1-58197-266-5	MTEL Foundations of Reading 90 (requirement all El. Ed)		$59.95	
			SUBTOTAL	
			Ship	$8.25
			TOTAL	

CPSIA information can be obtained at www.ICGtesting.com
Printed in the USA
LVOW022003020713

341223LV00003B/258/P